D0092745

FUTURE SHOCK

Future Shock is the classic that changed our view of tomorrow. Published in over fifty countries, its startling insights into accelerating change led a president to ask his advisers for a special report, inspired composers to write symphonies and rock music, gave a powerful new concept to social science, and added a phrase to our language. *Future Shock* is the most important study of change and adaptation in our time.

THE WALL STREET JOURNAL: "Explosive . . . brilliantly formulated."

LONDON DAILY EXPRESS: "Alvin Toffler has sent something of a shock-wave through Western society."

LE FIGARO: "The best study of our times that I know. . . . Of all the books that I have read in the last 20 years, it is by far the one that has taught me the most."

THE TIMES OF INDIA: "To the elite . . . who often get committed to age-old institutions or material goals alone, let Toffler's *FUTURE SHOCK* be a lesson and a warning."

MANCHESTER GUARDIAN: "An American book that will . . . reshape our thinking. . . . The book is more than a book, and it will do more than send reviewers raving. . . . It is a spectacular outcrop of a formidable, organized intellectual effort. . . . For the first time in history scientists are marrying the insights of artists, poets, dramatists, and novelists to statistical analysis and operational research. The two cultures have met and are being merged. Alvin Toffler is one of the first exhilarating, liberating results."

THE CHRISTIAN SCIENCE MONITOR: "Packed with ideas, explanations, constructive suggestions. . . . Revealing, exciting, encouraging, brilliant."

NEWSWEEK: "In the risky business of social and cultural criticism, there appears an occasional book that manages—through some happy combination of accident and insight—to shape our perceptions of its times. Alvin Toffler's immensely readable yet disquieting study may serve the same purpose for our own increasingly volatile world: even before reading the book, one is ready to acknowledge the point of the title—that we suffer from 'future shock.'"

Bantam Books by Alvin Toffler
Ask your bookseller for books you have missed

FUTURE SHOCK
THE THIRD WAVE
POWERSHIFT

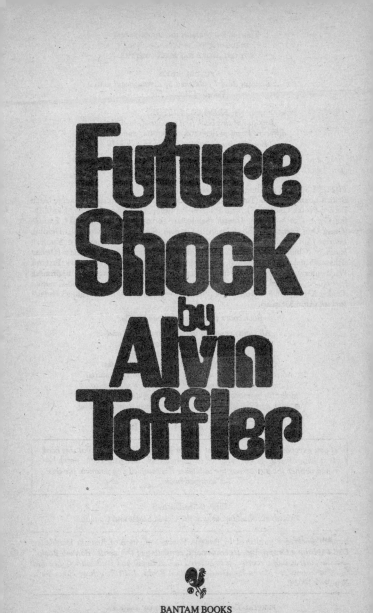

Future Shock

by Alvin Toffler

BANTAM BOOKS
NEW YORK · TORONTO · LONDON · SYDNEY · AUCKLAND

This edition contains the complete text
of the original hardcover edition.
NOT ONE WORD HAS BEEN OMITTED.

FUTURE SHOCK
*A Bantam Book / published by arrangement with
Random House, Inc.*

PRINTING HISTORY
*Portions of this book first appeared, in slightly
different form, in* HORIZON, REDBOOK, *and* PLAYBOY
Random House edition published July 1970
Literary Guild edition published 1970
Psychology Today edition published 1970
Bantam edition / August 1971

FUTURE SHOCK also appears in translation:
British Commonwealth (The Bodley Head [hard] / Pan Books [paper]); *Arabic* (Arab
Record Press); *Chinese* (Sichuan People's Publisher, China Translation and Publish-
ing Cor.); *Czech* (Prace); *Danish* (Samlerens Forlag); *Dutch* (Unieboek); *Finnish*
(Otava Oy); *French* (Editions Denoel); *German* (Scherz) *Greek* (Iniochus-Delphi);
Hebrew (Am Oved); *Indonesian* (P. T. Pantja Simpati); *Italian* (Sperling & Kupfer);
Japanese (Chuo Koron-Sha); *Korean* (Korea Economic Daily); *Malaysian* (Dewan
Bahasa Pustaka); *Norwegian* (J. S. Cappelens Forlag); *Polish* (Pantwowy Instytut
Wydawniczy); *Portuguese, Brazil* (Distribuidora Record de Serviços de Imprensa);
Portuguese, Portugal (Livros do Brasil); *Romanian* (Editura Politica); *Serbo-Croatian*
(Otokar Kersovani); *Spanish, World* (Plaza y Janes); *Swedish* (Albert Bonniers Forlag);
Turkish (Altin Kitaplar).

Back cover photo by Adrienne Helitzer.

*All rights reserved under International and
Pan-American Copyright Conventions.
Copyright © 1970 by Alvin Toffler.
Cover art copyright © 1990 by Bantam Books.
No part of this book may be reproduced or transmitted
in any form or by any means, electronic or mechanical,
including photocopying, recording, or by any information
storage and retrieval system, without permission in writing
from the publisher.
For information address: Bantam Books.*

*If you purchased this book without a cover you should be aware that this book
is stolen property. It was reported as "unsold and destroyed" to the publisher
and neither the author nor the publisher has received any payment for this
"stripped book."*

ISBN 0-553-20626-5
Published simultaneously in the United States and Canada

*Bantam Books are published by Bantam Books, a division of Bantam Doubleday
Dell Publishing Group, Inc. Its trademark, consisting of the words "Bantam Books"
and the portrayal of a rooster, is Registered in U.S. Patent and Trademark Office and
in other countries. Marca Registrada. Bantam Books, 1540 Broadway, New York,
New York 10036.*

PRINTED IN THE UNITED STATES OF AMERICA

RAD   53   52   51   50   49   48   47

For Sam, Rose, Heidi and Karen,
My closest links with time . . .

CONTENTS

INTRODUCTION

This is a book about what happens to people when they are overwhelmed by change. It is about the ways in which we adapt—or fail to adapt—to the future.

Much has been written about the future. Yet, for the most part, books about the world to come sound a harsh metallic note. These pages, by contrast, concern themselves with the "soft" or human side of tomorrow. Moreover, they concern themselves with the steps by which we are likely to reach tomorrow. They deal with common, everyday matters—the products we buy and discard, the places we leave behind, the corporations we inhabit, the people who pass at an ever faster clip through our lives. The future of friendship and family life is probed. Strange new subcultures and life styles are investigated, along with an array of other subjects from politics and playgrounds to skydiving and sex.

What joins all these—in the book as in life—is the roaring current of change, a current so powerful today that it overturns institutions, shifts our values and shrivels our roots. Change is the process by which the future invades our lives, and it is important to look at it closely, not merely from the grand perspectives of history, but also from the vantage point of the living, breathing individuals who experience it.

1

The acceleration of change in our time is, itself, an elemental force. This accelerative thrust has personal and psychological, as well as sociological, consequences. In the pages ahead, these effects of acceleration are, for the first time, systematically explored. The book argues forcefully, I hope, that, unless man quickly learns to control the rate of change in his personal affairs as well as in society at large, we are doomed to a massive adaptational breakdown.

In 1965, in an article in *Horizon*, I coined the term "future shock" to describe the shattering stress and disorientation that we induce in individuals by subjecting them to too much change in too short a time. Fascinated by this concept, I spent the next five years visiting scores of universities, research centers, laboratories, and government agencies, reading countless articles and scientific papers and interviewing literally hundreds of experts on different aspects of change, coping behavior, and the future. Nobel prizewinners, hippies, psychiatrists, physicians, businessmen, professional futurists, philosophers, and educators gave voice to their concern over change, their anxieties about adaptation, their fears about the future. I came away from this experience with two disturbing convictions.

First, it became clear that future shock is no longer a distantly potential danger, but a real sickness from which increasingly large numbers already suffer. This psycho-biological condition can be described in medical and psychiatric terms. It is the disease of change.

Second, I gradually came to be appalled by how little is actually known about adaptivity, either by those who call for and create vast changes in our society, or by those who supposedly prepare us to cope with those changes. Earnest intellectuals talk bravely about "educating for change" or "preparing people for the future." But we know virtually nothing about how to do it. In the most rapidly changing environment to which man has ever been exposed, we remain pitifully ignorant of how the human animal copes.

Our psychologists and politicians alike are puzzled by the seemingly irrational resistance to change exhibited by certain individuals and groups. The corporation head who wants to reorganize a department, the educator who wants to introduce a new teaching method, the mayor who wants to achieve peaceful integration of the races in his city—all, at one time or another, face this blind resistance. Yet we know little about its sources. By the same token, why do some men hunger, even rage for change, doing all in their power to create it, while others flee from it? I not only found no ready answers to such questions, but discovered that we lack even an adequate theory of adaptation, without which it is extremely unlikely that we will ever find the answers.

The purpose of this book, therefore, is to help us come to terms with the future—to help us cope more effectively with both personal and social change by deepening our understanding of how men respond to it. Toward this end, it puts forward a broad new theory of adaptation.

It also calls attention to an important, though often overlooked, distinction. Almost invariably, research into the effects of change concentrate on the destinations toward which change carries us, rather than the speed of the journey. In this book, I try to show that the *rate* of change has implications quite apart from, and sometimes more important than, the *directions* of change. No attempt to understand adaptivity can succeed until this fact is grasped. Any attempt to define the "content" of change must include the consequences of pace itself as part of that content.

William Ogburn, with his celebrated theory of cultural lag, pointed out how social stresses arise out of the uneven rates of change in different sectors of society. The concept of future shock—and the theory of adaptation that derives from it—strongly suggests that there must be balance, not merely between rates of change in different sectors, but between the pace of environmental change and the limited pace of human response. For future shock grows out of the increasing lag between the two.

The book is intended to do more than present a theory, however. It is also intended to demonstrate a method. Previously, men studied the past to shed light on the present. I have turned the time-mirror around, convinced that a coherent image of the future can also shower us with valuable insights into today. We shall find it increasingly difficult to understand our personal and public problems without making use of the future as an intellectual tool. In the pages ahead, I deliberately exploit this tool to show what it can do.

Finally, and by no means least important, the book sets out to change the reader in a subtle yet significant sense. For reasons that will become clear in the pages that follow, successful coping with rapid change will require most of us to adopt a new stance toward the future, a new sensitive awareness of the role it plays in the present. This book is designed to increase the future-consciousness of its reader. The degree to which the reader, after finishing the book, finds himself thinking about, speculating about, or trying to anticipate future events, will provide one measure of its effectiveness.

With these ends stated, several reservations are in order. One has to do with the perishability of fact. Every seasoned reporter has had the experience of working on a fast-breaking story that changes its shape and meaning even before his words are put down on paper. Today the whole world is a fast-breaking story. It is inevitable, therefore, in a book written over the course of several years, that some of its facts will have been superseded between the time of research and writing and the time of publication. Professors identified with University A move, in the interim, to University B. Politicians identified with Position X shift, in the meantime, to Position Y.

While a conscientious effort has been made during

› writing to update *Future Shock*, some of the facts presented are no doubt already obsolete. (This, of course, is true of many books, although authors don't like to talk about it.) The obsolescence of data has a special significance here, however, serving as it does to verify the book's own thesis about the rapidity of change. Writers have a harder and harder time keeping up with reality. We have not yet learned to conceive, research, write and publish in "real time." Readers, therefore, must concern themselves more and more with general theme, rather than detail.

Another reservation has to do with the verb "will." No serious futurist deals in "predictions." These are left for television oracles and newspaper astrologers. No one even faintly familiar with the complexities of forecasting lays claim to absolute knowledge of tomorrow. In those deliciously ironic words purported to be a Chinese proverb: "To prophesy is extremely difficult—especially with respect to the future."

This means that every statement about the future ought, by rights, be accompanied by a string of qualifiers—ifs, ands, buts, and on the other hands. Yet to enter every appropriate qualification in a book of this kind would be to bury the reader under an avalanche of maybes. Rather than do this, I have taken the liberty of speaking firmly, without hesitation, trusting that the intelligent reader will understand the stylistic problem. The word "will" should always be read as though it were preceded by "probably" or "in my opinion." Similarly, all dates applied to future events need to be taken with a grain of judgment.

The inability to speak with precision and certainty about the future, however, is no excuse for silence. Where "hard data" are available, of course, they ought to be taken into account. But where they are lacking, the responsible writer—even the scientist—has both a right and an obligation to rely on other kinds of evidence, including impressionistic or anecdotal data and the opinions of well-informed people. I have done so throughout and offer no apology for it.

In dealing with the future, at least for the purpose
at hand, it is more important to be imaginative and
insightful than to be one hundred percent "right."
Theories do not have to be "right" to be enormously
useful. Even error has its uses. The maps of the world
drawn by the medieval cartographers were so hopelessly inaccurate, so filled with factual error, that they
elicit condescending smiles today when almost the
entire surface of the earth has been charted. Yet the
great explorers could never have discovered the New
World without them. Nor could the better, more accurate maps of today been drawn until men, working
with the limited evidence available to them, set down
on paper their bold conceptions of worlds they had
never seen.

We who explore the future are like those ancient
mapmakers, and it is in this spirit that the concept of
future shock and the theory of the adaptive range are
presented here—not as final word, but as a first approximation of the new realities, filled with danger
and promise, created by the accelerative thrust.

Part One:

THE DEATH OF PERMANENCE

Chapter 1

THE 800TH LIFETIME

In the three short decades between now and the twenty-first century, millions of ordinary, psychologically normal people will face an abrupt collision with the future. Citizens of the world's richest and most technologically advanced nations, many of them will find it increasingly painful to keep up with the incessant demand for change that characterizes our time. For them, the future will have arrived too soon.

This book is about change and how we adapt to it. It is about those who seem to thrive on change, who crest its waves joyfully, as well as those multitudes of others who resist it or seek flight from it. It is about our capacity to adapt. It is about the future and the shock that its arrival brings.

Western society for the past 300 years has been caught up in a fire storm of change. This storm, far from abating, now appears to be gathering force. Change sweeps through the highly industrialized countries with waves of ever accelerating speed and unprecedented impact. It spawns in its wake all sorts of curious social flora—from psychedelic churches and "free universities" to science cities in the Arctic and wife-swap clubs in California.

It breeds odd personalities, too: children who at twelve are no longer childlike; adults who at fifty are children of twelve. There are rich men who playact poverty, computer programmers who turn on with LSD. There are anarchists who, beneath their dirty denim shirts, are outrageous conformists, and conformists who, beneath their button-down collars, are outrageous anarchists. There are married priests and atheist ministers and Jewish Zen Buddhists. We have pop . . . and op . . . and *art cinétique* . . . There are Playboy Clubs and homosexual movie theaters . . . amphetamines and tranquilizers . . . anger, affluence, and oblivion. Much oblivion.

Is there some way to explain so strange a scene without recourse to the jargon of psychoanalysis or the murky clichés of existentialism? A strange new society is apparently erupting in our midst. Is there a way to understand it, to shape its development? How can we come to terms with it?

Much that now strikes us as incomprehensible would be far less so if we took a fresh look at the racing rate of change that makes reality seem, sometimes, like a kaleidoscope run wild. For the acceleration of change does not merely buffet industries or nations. It is a concrete force that reaches deep into our personal lives, compels us to act out new roles, and confronts us with the danger of a new and powerfully upsetting psychological disease. This new disease can be called "future shock," and a knowledge of its sources and symptoms helps explain many things that otherwise defy rational analysis.

THE UNPREPARED VISITOR

The parallel term "culture shock" has already begun to creep into the popular vocabulary. Culture shock is the effect that immersion in a strange culture has on the unprepared visitor. Peace Corps volunteers suffer from it in Borneo or Brazil. Marco Polo probably suffered from it in Cathay. Culture shock is what happens when a traveler suddenly finds himself in a place where yes may mean no, where a "fixed price" is negotiable, where to be kept waiting in an outer office is no cause for insult, where laughter may signify anger. It is what happens when the familiar psychological cues that help an individual to function in society are suddenly withdrawn and replaced by new ones that are strange or incomprehensible.

The culture shock phenomenon accounts for much of the bewilderment, frustration, and disorientation that plagues Americans in their dealings with other societies. It causes a breakdown in communication, a misreading of reality, an inability to cope. Yet culture shock is relatively mild in comparison with the much more serious malady, future shock. Future shock is the dizzying disorientation brought on by the premature arrival of the future. It may well be the most important disease of tomorrow.

Future shock will not be found in *Index Medicus* or in any listing of psychological abnormalities. Yet, unless intelligent steps are taken to combat it, millions of human beings will find themselves increasingly disoriented, progressively incompetent to deal rationally with their environments. The malaise, mass neurosis, irrationality, and free-floating violence already apparent in contemporary life are merely a foretaste of what may lie ahead unless we come to understand and treat this disease.

Future shock is a time phenomenon, a product of the greatly accelerated rate of change in society. It arises from the superimposition of a new culture on an old one. It is culture shock in one's own society. But its impact is far worse. For most Peace Corps men, in fact most travelers, have the comforting knowledge that the culture they left behind will be there to return to. The victim of future shock does not.

Take an individual out of his own culture and set him down suddenly in an environment sharply different from his own, with a different set of cues to react to—different conceptions of time, space, work, love, religion, sex, and everything else—then cut him off from any hope of retreat to a more familiar social landscape, and the dislocation he suffers is doubly severe. Moreover, if this new culture is itself in constant turmoil, and if—worse yet—its values are incessantly changing, the sense of disorientation will be still further intensified. Given few clues as to what kind of behavior is rational under the radically new circumstances, the victim may well become a hazard to himself and others.

Now imagine not merely an individual but an entire society, an entire generation—including its weakest, least intelligent, and most irrational members —suddenly transported into this new world. The result is mass disorientation, future shock on a grand scale.

This is the prospect that man now faces. Change is avalanching upon our heads and most people are grotesquely unprepared to cope with it.

BREAK WITH THE PAST

Is all this exaggerated? I think not. It has become a cliché to say that what we are now living through is a "second industrial revolution." This phrase is supposed to impress us with the speed and profundity of the change around us. But in addition to being platitudinous, it is misleading. For what is occurring now is, in all likelihood, bigger, deeper, and more important than the industrial revolution. Indeed, a growing body of reputable opinion asserts that the present movement represents nothing less than the second great divide in human history, comparable in magnitude only with that first great break in historic continuity, the shift from barbarism to civilization.

This idea crops up with increasing frequency in the writings of scientists and technologists. Sir George Thomson, the British physicist and Nobel prizewinner, suggests in *The Foreseeable Future* that the nearest historic parallel with today is not the industrial revolution but rather the "invention of agriculture in the neolithic age." John Diebold, the American automation expert, warns that "the effects of the technological revolution we are now living through will be deeper than any social change we have experienced before." Sir Leon Bagrit, the British computer manufacturer, insists that automation by itself represents "the greatest change in the whole history of mankind."

Nor are the men of science and technology alone in these views. Sir Herbert Read, the philosopher of art, tells us that we are living through "a revolution so fundamental that we must search many past centuries for a parallel. Possibly the only comparable change is the one that took place between the Old and the New Stone Age . . ." And Kurt W. Marek, who under the name C. W. Ceram is best-known as the author of *Gods, Graves and Scholars*, observes that "we, in the twentieth century, are concluding an era of mankind five thousand years in length . . . We are not, as Spengler supposed, in the situation of Rome at the beginning of the Christian West, but in that of the year 3000 B.C. We open our eyes like prehistoric man, we see a world totally new."

One of the most striking statements of this theme has come from Kenneth Boulding, an eminent economist and imaginative social thinker. In justifying his view that the present moment represents a crucial turning point in human history, Boulding observes that "as far as many statistical series related to activities of mankind are concerned, the date that divides human history into two equal parts is well within living memory." In effect, our century represents The Great Median Strip running down the center of human history. Thus he asserts, "The world of today . . . is as different from the world in which I was born as that world was from Julius Caesar's. I was born in the middle of human history, to date, roughly. Almost as much has happened since I was born as happened before."

This startling statement can be illustrated in a number of ways. It has been observed, for example, that if the last 50,000 years of man's existence were divided into lifetimes of approximately sixty-two years each, there have been about 800 such lifetimes. Of these 800, fully 650 were spent in caves.

Only during the last seventy lifetimes has it been possible to communicate effectively from one lifetime to another—as writing made it possible to do. Only during the last six lifetimes did masses of men ever see a printed word. Only during the last four has it been possible to measure time with any precision. Only in the last two has anyone anywhere used an electric motor. And the overwhelming majority of all the material goods we use in daily life today have been developed within the present, the 800th, lifetime.

This 800th lifetime marks a sharp break with all past human experience because during this lifetime man's relationship to resources has reversed itself. This is most evident in the field of economic development. Within a single lifetime, agriculture, the original basis of civilization, has lost its dominance in nation after nation. Today in a dozen major countries agriculture employs fewer than 15 percent of the economically active population. In the United States, whose farms feed 200,000,000 Americans plus the equivalent of another 160,000,000 people around the world, this figure is already below 6 percent and it is still shrinking rapidly.

Moreover, if agriculture is the first stage of economic development and industrialism the second, we can now see that still another stage—the third—has suddenly been reached. In about 1956 the United States became the first major power in which more than 50 percent of the non-farm labor force ceased to wear the blue collar of factory or manual labor. Blue collar workers were outnumbered by those in the so-called white-collar occupations—in retail trade, administration, communications, research, education, and other service categories. Within the same lifetime a society for the first time in human history not only threw off the yoke of agriculture, but managed within a few brief decades to throw off the yoke of manual labor as well. The world's first service economy had been born.

Since then, one after another of the technologically advanced countries have moved in the same direction. Today, in those nations in which agriculture is down to the 15 percent level or below, white collars already outnumber blue in Sweden, Britain, Belgium, Canada, and the Netherlands. Ten thousand years for agriculture. A century or two for industrialism. And now, opening before us—super-industrialism.

Jean Fourastié, the French planner and social philosopher, has declared that "Nothing will be less industrial than the civilization born of the industrial revolution." The significance of this staggering fact has yet to be digested. Perhaps U Thant, Secretary General of the United Nations, came closest to summarizing the meaning of the shift to super-industrialism when he declared that "The central stupendous truth about developed economies today is that they can have—in anything but the shortest run—the kind and scale of resources they decide to have. . . . It is no longer resources that limit decisions. It is the decision that makes the resources. This is the fundamental revolutionary change—perhaps the most revolutionary man has ever known." This monumental reversal has taken place in the 800th lifetime.

This lifetime is also different from all others because of the astonishing expansion of the scale and scope of change. Clearly, there have been other lifetimes in which epochal upheavals occurred. Wars, plagues, earthquakes, and famine rocked many an earlier social order. But these shocks and upheavals were contained within the borders of one or a group of adjacent societies. It took generations, even centuries, for their impact to spread beyond these borders.

In our lifetime the boundaries have burst. Today the network of social ties is so tightly woven that the consequences of contemporary events radiate instantaneously around the world. A war in Vietnam alters basic political alignments in Peking, Moscow, and Washington, touches off protests in Stockholm, affects financial transactions in Zurich, triggers secret diplomatic moves in Algiers.

Indeed, not only do *contemporary* events radiate instantaneously—now we can be said to be feeling the impact of all *past* events in a new way. For the past is doubling back on us. We are caught in what might be called a "time skip."

An event that affected only a handful of people at the time of its occurrence in the past can have large-scale consequences today. The Peloponnesian War, for example, was little more than a skirmish by modern standards. While Athens, Sparta and several nearby city-states battled, the population of the rest of the globe remained largely unaware of and undisturbed by the war. The Zapotec Indians living in Mexico at the time were wholly untouched by it. The ancient Japanese felt none of its impact.

Yet the Peloponnesian War deeply altered the future course of Greek history. By changing the movement of men, the geographical distribution of genes, values, and ideas, it affected later events in Rome, and, through Rome, all Europe. Today's Europeans are to some small degree different people because that conflict occurred.

In turn, in the tightly wired world of today, these Europeans influence Mexicans and Japanese alike. Whatever trace of impact the Peloponnesian War left on the genetic structure, the ideas, and the values of today's Europeans is now exported by them to all parts of the world. Thus today's Mexicans and Japanese feel the distant, twice-removed impact of that war even though their ancestors, alive during its occurrence, did not. In this way, the events of the past, skipping as it were over generations and centuries, rise up to haunt and change us today.

When we think not merely of the Peloponnesian War but of the building of the Great Wall of China, the Black Plague, the battle of the Bantu against the

Hamites—indeed, of all the events of the past—the cumulative implications of the time-skip principle take on weight. Whatever happened to some men in the past affects virtually all men today. This was not always true. In short, all history is catching up with us, and this very difference, paradoxically, underscores our break with the past. Thus the scope of change is fundamentally altered. Across space and through time, change has a power and reach in this, the 800th lifetime, that it never did before.

But the final, qualitative difference between this and all previous lifetimes is the one most easily overlooked. For we have not merely extended the scope and scale of change, we have radically altered its pace. We have in our time released a totally new social force—a stream of change so accelerated that it influences our sense of time, revolutionizes the tempo of daily life, and affects the very way we "feel" the world around us. We no longer "feel" life as men did in the past. And this is the ultimate difference, the distinction that separates the truly contemporary man from all others. For this acceleration lies behind the impermanence—the transience—that penetrates and tinctures our consciousness, radically affecting the way we relate to other people, to things, to the entire universe of ideas, art and values.

To understand what is happening to us as we move into the age of super-industrialism, we must analyze the processes of acceleration and confront the concept of transience. If acceleration is a new social force, transience is its psychological counterpart, and without an understanding of the role it plays in contemporary human behavior, all our theories of personality, all our psychology, must remain pre-modern. Psychology without the concept of transience cannot take account of precisely those phenomena that are peculiarly contemporary.

By changing our relationship to the resources that surround us, by violently expanding the scope of change, and, most crucially, by accelerating its pace, we have broken irretrievably with the past. We have cut ourselves off from the old ways of thinking, of feeling, of adapting. We have set the stage for a completely new society and we are now racing toward it. This is the crux of the 800th lifetime. And it is this that calls into question man's capacity for adaptation—how will he fare in this new society? Can he adapt to its imperatives? And if not, can he alter these imperatives?

Before even attempting to answer such questions, we must focus on the twin forces of acceleration and transience. We must learn how they alter the texture of existence, hammering our lives and psyches into new and unfamiliar shapes. We must understand how —and why—they confront us, for the first time, with the explosive potential of future shock.

Chapter 2

THE ACCELERATIVE THRUST

Early in March, 1967, in eastern Canada, an eleven-year-old child died of old age.

Ricky Gallant was only eleven years old chronologically, but he suffered from an odd disease called progeria—advanced aging—and he exhibited many of the characteristics of a ninety-year-old person. The symptoms of progeria are senility, hardened arteries, baldness, slack, and wrinkled skin. In effect, Ricky was an old man when he died, a long lifetime of biological change having been packed into his eleven short years.

Cases of progeria are extremely rare. Yet in a metaphorical sense the high technology societies all suffer from this peculiar ailment. They are not growing old or senile. But they *are* experiencing super-normal rates of change.

Many of us have a vague "feeling" that things are moving faster. Doctors and executives alike complain that they cannot keep up with the latest developments in their fields. Hardly a meeting or conference takes place today without some ritualistic oratory about "the challenge of change." Among many there is an uneasy mood—a suspicion that change is out of control.

Not everyone, however, shares this anxiety. Millions

sleepwalk their way through their lives as if nothing had changed since the 1930's, and as if nothing ever will. Living in what is certainly one of the most exciting periods in human history, they attempt to withdraw from it, to block it out, as if it were possible to make it go away by ignoring it. They seek a "separate peace," a diplomatic immunity from change.

One sees them everywhere: Old people, resigned to living out their years, attempting to avoid, at any cost, the intrusions of the new. Already-old people of thirty-five and forty-five, nervous about student riots, sex, LSD, or miniskirts, feverishly attempting to persuade themselves that, after all, youth was always rebellious, and that what is happening today is no different from the past. Even among the young we find an incomprehension of change: students so ignorant of the past that they see nothing unusal about the present.

The disturbing fact is that the vast majority of people, including educated and otherwise sophisticated people, find the idea of change so threatening that they attempt to deny its existence. Even many people who understand intellectually that change is accelerating, have not internalized that knowledge, do not take this critical social fact into account in planning their own personal lives.

TIME AND CHANGE

How do we *know* that change is accelerating? There is, after all, no absolute way to measure change. In the awesome complexity of the universe, even within any given society, a virtually infinite number of streams of change occur simultaneously. All "things" —from the tiniest virus to the greatest galaxy—are, in reality, not things at all, but processes. There is no static point, no nirvana-like un-change, against which to measure change. Change is, therefore, necessarily relative.

It is also uneven. If all processes occurred at the

same speed, or even if they accelerated or decelerated in unison, it would be impossible to observe change. The future, however, invades the present at differing speeds. Thus it becomes possible to compare the speed of different processes as they unfold. We know, for example, that compared with the biological evolution of the species, cultural and social evolution is extremely rapid. We know that some societies transform themselves technologically or economically more rapidly than others. We also know that different sectors within the same society exhibit different rates of change—the disparity that William Ogburn labeled "cultural lag." It is precisely the unevenness of change that makes it measurable.

We need, however, a yardstick that makes it possible to compare highly diverse processes, and this yardstick is time. Without time, change has no meaning. And without change, time would stop. Time can be conceived as the intervals during which events occur. Just as money permits us to place a value on both apples and oranges, time permits us to compare unlike processes. When we say that it takes three years to build a dam, we are really saying it takes three times as long as it takes the earth to circle the sun or 31,000,000 times as long as it takes to sharpen a pencil. Time is the currency of exchange that makes it possible to compare the rates at which very different processes play themselves out.

Given the unevenness of change and armed with this yardstick, we still face exhausting difficulties in measuring change. When we speak of the rate of change, we refer to the number of events crowded into an arbitrarily fixed interval of time. Thus we need to define the "events." We need to select our intervals with precision. We need to be careful about the conclusions we draw from the differences we observe. Moreover, in the measurement of change, we are today far more advanced with respect to physical processes than social processes. We know far better, for example, how to measure the rate at which blood flows through the body than the rate at which a rumor flows through society.

Even with all these qualifications, however, there is widespread agreement, reaching from historians and archaeologists all across the spectrum to scientists, sociologists, economists and psychologists, that, many social processes are speeding up—strikingly, even spectacularly.

SUBTERRANEAN CITIES

Painting with the broadest of brush strokes, biologist Julian Huxley informs us that "The tempo of human evolution during recorded history is at least 100,000 times as rapid as that of pre-human evolution." Inventions or improvements of a magnitude that took perhaps 50,000 years to accomplish during the early Paleolithic era were, he says, "run through in a mere millennium toward its close; and with the advent of settled civilization, the unit of change soon became reduced to the century." The rate of change, accelerating throughout the past 5000 years, has become, in his words, "particularly noticeable during the past 300 years."

C. P. Snow, the novelist and scientist, also comments on the new visibility of change. "Until this century . . ." he writes, social change was "so slow, that it would pass unnoticed in one person's lifetime. That is no longer so. The rate of change has increased so much that our imagination can't keep up." Indeed, says social psychologist Warren Bennis, the throttle has been pushed so far forward in recent years that "No exaggeration, no hyperbole, no outrage can realistically describe the extent and pace of change. . . . In fact, only the exaggerations appear to be true."

What changes justify such super-charged language? Let us look at a few—change in the process by which man forms cities, for example. We are now undergoing the most extensive and rapid urbanization the world has ever seen. In 1850 only four cities on the face of the earth had a population of 1,000,000 or more. By 1900 the number had increased to nineteen. But by 1960, there were 141, and today world urban population is rocketing upward at a rate of 6.5 percent per year, according to Edgar de Vries and J. P. Thysse of the Institute of Social Science in The Hague. This single stark statistic means a doubling of the earth's urban population within eleven years.

One way to grasp the meaning of change on so phenomenal a scale is to imagine what would happen if all existing cities, instead of expanding, retained their present size. If this were so, in order to accommodate the new urban millions we would have to build a duplicate city for each of the hundreds that already dot the globe. A new Tokyo, a new Hamburg, a new Rome and Rangoon—and all within eleven years. (This explains why French urban planners are sketching subterranean cities—stores, museums, warehouses and factories to be built under the earth, and why a Japanese architect has blueprinted a city to be built on stilts out over the ocean.)

The same accelerative tendency is instantly apparent in man's consumption of energy. Dr. Homi Bhabha, the late Indian atomic scientist who chaired the first International Conference on the Peaceful Uses of Atomic Energy, once analyzed this trend. "To illustrate," he said, "let us use the letter 'Q' to stand for the energy derived from burning some 33,000 million tons of coal. In the eighteen and one half centuries after Christ, the total energy consumed averaged less than one half Q per century. But by 1850, the rate had risen to one Q per century. Today, the rate is about ten Q per century." This means, roughly speaking, that half of all the energy consumed by man in the past 2,000 years has been consumed in the last one hundred.

Also dramatically evident is the acceleration of economic growth in the nations now racing toward super-industrialism. Despite the fact that they start from a large industrial base, the annual percentage increases in production in these countries are formidable. And the rate of increase is itself increasing.

In France, for example, in the twenty-nine years between 1910 and the outbreak of the second world war, industrial production rose only 5 percent. Yet between 1948 and 1965, in only seventeen years, it increased by roughly 220 percent. Today growth rates of from 5 to 10 percent per year are not uncommon among the most industrialized nations. There are ups and downs, of course. But the direction of change has been unmistakable.

Thus for the twenty-one countries belonging to the Organization for Economic Cooperation and Development—by and large, the "have" nations—the average annual rate of increase in gross national product in the years 1960–1968 ran between 4.5 and 5.0 percent. The United States grew at a rate of 4.5 percent, and Japan led the rest with annual increases averaging 9.8 percent.

What such numbers imply is nothing less revolutionary than a doubling of the total output of goods and services in the advanced societies about every fifteen years—and the doubling times are shrinking. This means, generally speaking, that the child reaching teen age in any of these societies is literally surrounded by twice as much of everything newly man-made as his parents were at the time he was an infant. It means that by the time today's teen-ager reaches age thirty, perhaps earlier, a second doubling will have occurred. Within a seventy-year lifetime, perhaps five such doublings will take place—meaning, since the increases are compounded, that by the time the individual reaches old age the society around him will be producing thirty-two times as much as when he was born.

Such changes in the ratio between old and new have, as we shall show, an electric impact on the habits, beliefs, and self-image of millions. Never in previous history has this ratio been transformed so radically in so brief a flick of time.

THE TECHNOLOGICAL ENGINE

Behind such prodigious economic facts lies that great, growling engine of change—technology. This is not to say that technology is the only source of change in society. Social upheavals can be touched off by a change in the chemical composition of the atmosphere, by alterations in climate, by changes in fertility, and many other factors. Yet technology is indisputably a major force behind the accelerative thrust.

To most people, the term technology conjures up images of smoky steel mills or clanking machines. Perhaps the classic symbol of technology is still the assembly line created by Henry Ford half a century ago and made into a potent social icon by Charlie Chaplin in *Modern Times.* This symbol, however, has always been inadequate, indeed, misleading, for technology has always been more than factories and machines. The invention of the horse collar in the middle ages led to major changes in agricultural methods and was as much a technological advance as the invention of the Bessemer furnace centuries later. Moreover, technology includes techniques, as well as the machines that may or may not be necessary to apply them. It includes ways to make chemical reactions occur, ways to breed fish, plant forests, light theaters, count votes or teach history.

The old symbols of technology are even more misleading today, when the most advanced technological processes are carried out far from assembly lines or open hearths. Indeed, in electronics, in space technology, in most of the new industries, relative silence and clean surroundings are characteristic—even sometimes essential. And the assembly line—the organization of armies of men to carry out simple repetitive functions—is an anachronism. It is time for our symbols of technology to change—to catch up with the quickening changes in technology, itself.

This acceleration is frequently dramatized by a thumbnail account of the progress in transportation. It has been pointed out, for example, that in 6000 B.C. the fastest transportation available to man over long distances was the camel caravan, averaging eight miles per hour. It was not until about 1600 B.C. when the chariot was invented that the maximum speed was raised to roughly twenty miles per hour.

So impressive was this invention, so difficult was it to exceed this speed limit, that nearly 3,500 years later, when the first mail coach began operating in England in 1784, it averaged a mere ten mph. The first steam locomotive, introduced in 1825, could muster a top speed of only thirteen mph, and the great sailing ships of the time labored along at less than half that speed. It was probably not until the 1880's that man, with the help of a more advanced steam locomotive, managed to reach a speed of one hundred mph. It took the human race millions of years to attain that record.

It took only fifty-eight years, however, to quadruple the limit, so that by 1938 airborne man was cracking the 400-mph line. It took a mere twenty-year flick of time to double the limit again. And by the 1960's rocket planes approached speeds of 4000 mph, and men in space capsules were circling the earth at 18,000 mph. Plotted on a graph, the line representing progress in the past generation would leap vertically off the page.

Whether we examine distances traveled, altitudes reached, minerals mined, or explosive power harnessed, the same accelerative trend is obvious. The pattern, here and in a thousand other statistical series, is absolutely clear and unmistakable. Millennia or centuries go by, and then, in our own times, a sudden bursting of the limits, a fantastic spurt forward.

The reason for this is that technology feeds on itself. Technology makes more technology possible, as we can see if we look for a moment at the process of innovation. Technological innovation consists of three stages, linked together into a self-reinforcing cycle. First, there is the creative, feasible idea. Second, its practical application. Third, its diffusion through society.

The process is completed, the loop closed, when the diffusion of technology embodying the new idea, in turn, helps generate new creative ideas. Today there is evidence that the time between each of the steps in this cycle has been shortened.

Thus it is not merely true, as frequently noted, that 90 percent of all the scientists who ever lived are now alive, and that new scientific discoveries are being made every day. These new ideas are put to work much more quickly than ever before. The time between original concept and practical use has been radically reduced. This is a striking difference between ourselves and our ancestors. Appollonius of Perga discovered conic sections, but it was 2000 years before they were applied to engineering problems. It was literally centuries between the time Paracelsus discovered that ether could be used as an anaesthetic and the time it began to be used for that purpose.

Even in more recent times the same pattern of delay was present. In 1836 a machine was invented that mowed, threshed, tied straw into sheaves and poured grain into sacks. This machine was itself based on technology at least twenty years old at the time. Yet it was not until a century later, in the 1930's, that such a combine was actually marketed. The first English patent for a typewriter was issued in 1714. But a century and a half elapsed before typewriters became commercially available. A full century passed between the time Nicholas Appert discovered how to can food and the time canning became important in the food industry.

Today such delays between idea and application are almost unthinkable. It is not that we are more eager or less lazy than our ancestors, but we have, with the passage of time, invented all sorts of social devices to hasten the process. Thus we find that the time between the first and second stages of the innovative cycle—between idea and application—has been cut radically. Frank Lynn, for example, in studying twenty major innovations, such as frozen food, antibiotics, integrated circuits and synthetic leather, found that since the beginning of this century more than sixty percent has been slashed from the average time needed for a major scientific discovery to be translated into a useful technological form. Today a vast and growing research and development industry is consciously working to reduce the lag still further.

But if it takes less time to bring a new idea to the marketplace, it also takes less time for it to sweep through the society. Thus the interval between the second and third stages of the cycle—between application and diffusion—has likewise been sliced, and the pace of diffusion is rising with astonishing speed. This is borne out by the history of several familiar household appliances. Robert B. Young at the Stanford Research Institute has studied the span of time between the first commercial appearance of a new electrical appliance and the time the industry manufacturing it reaches peak production of the item.

Young found that for a group of appliances introduced in the United States before 1920—including the vacuum cleaner, the electric range, and the refrigerator —the average span between introduction and peak production was thirty-four years. But for a group that appeared in the 1939–1959 period—including the electric frying pan, television, and washer-dryer combination—the span was only eight years. The lag had shrunk by more than 76 percent. "The post-war group," Young declared, "demonstrated vividly the rapidly accelerating nature of the modern cycle."

The stepped-up pace of invention, exploitation, and diffusion, in turn, accelerates the whole cycle still further. For new machines or techniques are not merely a product, but a source, of fresh creative ideas.

Each new machine or technique, in a sense, changes

all existing machines and techniques, by permitting us to put them together into new combinations. The number of possible combinations rises exponentially as the number of new machines or techniques rises arithmetically. Indeed, each new combination may, itself, be regarded as a new super-machine.

The computer, for example, made possible a sophisticated space effort. Linked with sensing devices, communications equipment, and power sources, the computer became part of a configuration that in aggregate forms a single new super-machine—a machine for reaching into and probing outer space. But for machines or techniques to be combined in new ways, they have to be altered, adapted, refined or otherwise changed. So that the very effort to integrate machines into super-machines compels us to make still further technological innovations.

It is vital to understand, moreover, that technological innovation does not merely combine and recombine machines and techniques. Important new machines do more than suggest or compel changes in other machines—they suggest novel solutions to social, philosophical, even personal problems. They alter man's total intellectual environment—the way he thinks and looks at the world.

We all learn from our environment, scanning it constantly—though perhaps unconsciously—for models to emulate. These models are not only other people. They are, increasingly, machines. By their presence, we are subtly conditioned to think along certain lines. It has been observed, for example, that the clock came along before the Newtonian image of the world as a great clock-like mechanism, a philosophical notion that has had the utmost impact on man's intellectual development. Implied in this image of the cosmos as a great clock were ideas about cause and effect and about the importance of external, as against internal, stimuli, that shape the everyday behavior of all of us today. The clock also affected our conception of time so that the idea that a day is divided into twenty-four equal segments of sixty minutes each has become almost literally a part of us.

Recently, the computer has touched off a storm of fresh ideas about man as an interacting part of larger systems, about his physiology, the way he learns, the way he remembers, the way he makes decisions. Virtually every intellectual discipline from political science to family psychology has been hit by a wave of imaginative hypotheses triggered by the invention and diffusion of the computer—and its full impact has not yet struck. And so the innovative cycle, feeding on itself, speeds up.

If technology, however, is to be regarded as a great engine, a mighty accelerator, then knowledge must be regarded as its fuel. And we thus come to the crux of the accelerative process in society, for the engine is being fed a richer and richer fuel every day.

KNOWLEDGE AS FUEL

The rate at which man has been storing up useful knowledge about himself and the universe has been spiraling upward for 10,000 years. The rate took a sharp upward leap with the invention of writing, but even so it remained painfully slow over centuries of time. The next great leap forward in knowledge-acquisition did not occur until the invention of movable type in the fifteenth century by Gutenberg and others. Prior to 1500, by the most optimistic estimates, Europe was producing books at a rate of 1000 titles per year. This means, give or take a bit, that it would take a full century to produce a library of 100,000 titles. By 1950, four and a half centuries later, the rate had accelerated so sharply that Europe was producing 120,000 titles a year. What once took a century now took only ten months. By 1960, a single decade later, the rate had made another significant jump, so that a century's work could be completed in seven and a half months. And, by the mid-sixties, the output of books on a world scale, Europe included, approached the prodigious figure of 1000 titles per *day*.

One can hardly argue that every book is a net gain for the advancement of knowledge. Nevertheless, we find that the accelerative curve in book publication does, in fact, crudely parallel the rate at which man discovered new knowledge. For example, prior to Gutenberg only 11 chemical elements were known. Antimony, the 12th, was discovered at about the time he was working on his invention. It was fully 200 years since the 11th, arsenic, had been discovered. Had the same rate of discovery continued, we would by now have added only two or three additional elements to the periodic table since Gutenberg. Instead, in the 450 years after his time, some seventy additional elements were discovered. And since 1900 we have been isolating the remaining elements not at a rate of one every two centuries, but of one every three years.

Furthermore, there is reason to believe that the rate is still rising sharply. Today, for example, the number of scientific journals and articles is doubling, like industrial production in the advanced countries, about every fifteen years, and according to biochemist Philip Siekevitz, "what has been learned in the last three decades about the nature of living beings dwarfs in extent of knowledge any comparable period of scientific discovery in the history of mankind." Today the United States government alone generates 100,000 reports each year, plus 450,000 articles, books and papers. On a worldwide basis, scientific and technical literature mounts at a rate of some 60,000,000 pages a year.

The computer burst upon the scene around 1950. With its unprecedented power for analysis and dissemination of extremely varied kinds of data in unbelievable quantities and at mind-staggering speeds, it has become a major force behind the latest acceleration in knowledge-acquisition. Combined with other increasingly powerful analytical tools for observing the invisible universe around us, it has raised the rate of knowledge-acquisition to dumbfounding speeds.

Francis Bacon told us that "Knowledge . . . is power." This can now be translated into contemporary terms. In our social setting, "Knowledge is change"— and accelerating knowledge-acquisition, fueling the great engine of technology, means accelerating change.

THE FLOW OF SITUATIONS

Discovery. Application. Impact. Discovery. We see here a chain reaction of change; a long, sharply rising curve of acceleration in human social development. This accelerative thrust has now reached a level at which it can no longer, by any stretch of the imagination, be regarded as "normal." The normal institutions of industrial society can no longer contain it, and its impact is shaking up all our social institutions. Acceleration is one of the most important and least understood of all social forces.

This, however, is only half the story. For the speed-up of change is a psychological force as well. Although it has been almost totally ignored by psychology, the rising rate of change in the world around us disturbs our inner equilibrium, altering the very way in which we experience life. Acceleration without translates into acceleration within.

This can be illustrated, though in a highly over-simplified fashion, if we think of an individual life as a great channel through which experience flows. This flow of experience consists—or is conceived of consisting—of innumerable "situations." Acceleration of change in the surrounding society drastically alters the flow of situations through this channel.

There is no neat definition of a situation, yet we would find it impossible to cope with experience if we did not mentally cut it up into these manageable units. Moreover, while the boundary lines between situations may be indistinct, every situation has a certain "wholeness" about it, a certain integration.

Every situation also has certain identifiable components. These include "things"—a physical setting of natural or man-made objects. Every situation occurs in a "place"—a location or arena within which the action occurs. (It is not accidental that the Latin root *"situ"* means place.) Every social situation also has, by definition, a cast of characters—people. Situations also involve a location in the organizational network of society and a context of ideas or information. Any situation can be analyzed in terms of these five components.

But situations also involve a separate dimension which, because it cuts across all the others, is frequently overlooked. This is duration—the span of time over which the situation occurs. Two situations alike in all other respects are not the same at all if one lasts longer than another. For time enters into the mix in a crucial way, changing the meaning or content of situations. Just as the funeral march played at too high a speed becomes a merry tinkle of sounds, so a situation that is dragged out has a distinctly different flavor or meaning than one that strikes us in staccato fashion, erupting suddenly and subsiding as quickly.

Here, then, is the first delicate point at which the accelerative thrust in the larger society crashes up against the ordinary daily experience of the contemporary individual. For the acceleration of change, as we shall show, shortens the duration of many situations. This not only drastically alters their "flavor," but hastens their passage through the experiential channel. Compared with life in a less rapidly changing society, more situations now flow through the channel in any given interval of time—and this implies profound changes in human psychology.

For while we tend to focus on only one situation at a time, the increased rate at which situations flow past us vastly complicates the entire structure of life, multiplying the number of roles we must play and the number of choices we are forced to make. This, in turn, accounts for the choking sense of complexity about contemporary life.

Moreover, the speeded-up flow-through of situations demands much more work from the complex focusing mechanisms by which we shift our attention from one situation to another. There is more switching back and forth, less time for extended, peaceful attention to one problem or situation at a time. This is what lies behind the vague feeling noted earlier that "Things are moving faster." They are. Around us. And through us.

There is, however, still another, even more powerfully significant way in which the acceleration of change in society increases the difficulty of coping with life. This stems from the fantastic intrusion of novelty, newness into our existence. Each situation is unique. But situations often resemble one another. This, in fact, is what makes it possible to learn from experience. If each situation were wholly novel, without some resemblance to previously experienced situations, our ability to cope would be hopelessly crippled.

The acceleration of change, however, radically alters the balance between novel and familiar situations. Rising rates of change thus compel us not merely to cope with a faster flow, but with more and more situations to which previous personal experience does not apply. And the psychological implications of this simple fact, which we shall explore later in this book, are nothing short of explosive.

"When things start changing outside, you are going to have a parallel change taking place inside," says Christopher Wright of the Institute for the Study of Science in Human Affairs. The nature of these inner changes is so profound, however, that, as the accelerative thrust picks up speed, it will test our ability to live within the parameters that have until now defined man and society. In the words of psychoanalyst Erik Erikson, "In our society at present, the 'natural course of events' is precisely that the rate of change should continue to accelerate up to the as-yet-unreached limits of human and institutional adaptability."

To survive, to avert what we have termed future shock, the individual must become infinitely more adaptable and capable than ever before. He must search out totally new ways to anchor himself, for all the old roots—religion, nation, community, family, or profession—are now shaking under the hurricane impact of the accelerative thrust. Before he can do so, however, he must understand in greater detail how the effects of acceleration penetrate his personal life, creep into his behavior and alter the quality of existence. He must, in other words, understand transience.

Chapter 3

THE PACE OF LIFE

His picture was, until recently, everywhere: on television, on posters that stared out at one in airports and railroad stations, on leaflets, matchbooks and magazines. He was an inspired creation of Madison Avenue—a fictional character with whom millions could subconsciously identify. Young and clean-cut, he carried an attaché case, glanced at his watch, and looked like an ordinary businessman scurrying to his next appointment. He had, however, an enormous protuberance on his back. For sticking out from between his shoulder blades was a great, butterfly-shaped key of the type used to wind up mechanical toys. The text that accompanied his picture urged keyed-up executives to "unwind"—to slow down—at the Sheraton Hotels. This wound-up man-on-the-go was, and still is, a potent symbol of the people of the future, millions of whom feel just as driven and hurried as if they, too, had a huge key in the back.

The average individual knows little and cares less about the cycle of technological innovation or the relationship between knowledge-acquisition and the rate of change. He is, on the other hand, keenly aware of the pace of his own life—whatever that pace may be.

The pace of life is frequently commented on by

ordinary people. Yet, oddly enough, it has received almost no attention from either psychologists or sociologists. This is a gaping inadequacy in the behavioral sciences, for the pace of life profoundly influences behavior, evoking strong and contrasting reactions from different people.

It is, in fact, not too much to say that the pace of life draws a line through humanity, dividing us into camps, triggering bitter misunderstanding between parent and child, between Madison Avenue and Main Street, between men and women, between American and European, between East and West.

PEOPLE OF THE FUTURE

The inhabitants of the earth are divided not only by race, nation, religion or ideology, but also, in a sense, by their position in time. Examining the present populations of the globe, we find a tiny group who still live, hunting and food-foraging, as men did millennia ago. Others, the vast majority of mankind, depend not on bear-hunting or berry-picking, but on agriculture. They live, in many respects, as their ancestors did centuries ago. These two groups taken together compose perhaps 70 percent of all living human beings. They are the people of the past.

By contrast, somewhat more than 25 percent of the earth's population can be found in the industrialized societies. They lead modern lives. They are products of the first half of the twentieth century, molded by mechanization and mass education, brought up with lingering memories of their own country's agricultural past. They are, in effect, the people of the present.

The remaining two or three percent of the world's population, however, are no longer people of either the past or present. For within the main centers of technological and cultural change, in Santa Monica, California and Cambridge, Massachusetts, in New

York and London and Tokyo, are millions of men and
women who can already be said to be living the way
of life of the future. Trendmakers often without being aware of it, they live today as millions more will
live tomorrow. And while they account for only a few
percent of the global population today, they already
form an international nation of the future in our
midst. They are the advance agents of man, the earliest citizens of the world-wide super-industrial society
now in the throes of birth.

What makes them different from the rest of mankind? Certainly, they are richer, better educated,
more mobile than the majority of the human race.
They also live longer. But what specifically marks
the people of the future is the fact that they are
already caught up in a new, stepped-up pace of life.
They "live faster" than the people around them.

Some people are deeply attracted to this highly
accelerated pace of life—going far out of their way
to bring it about and feeling anxious, tense or uncomfortable when the pace slows. They want desperately to be "where the action is." (Indeed, some
hardly care what the action is, so long as it occurs at
a suitably rapid clip.) James A. Wilson has found,
for example, that the attraction for a fast pace of
life is one of the hidden motivating forces behind
the much publicized "brain-drain"—the mass migration of European scientists to the United States
and Canada. After studying 517 English scientists and
engineers who migrated, Wilson concluded that it
was not higher salaries or better research facilities
alone, but also the quicker tempo that lured them.
The migrants, he writes, "are not put off by what
they indicate as the 'faster pace' of North America;
if anything, they appear to *prefer* this pace to others."
Similarly, a white veteran of the civil rights movement in Mississippi reports: "People who are used to
a speeded-up urban life . . . can't take it for long in
the rural South. That's why people are always driving
somewhere for no particular reason. Traveling is the

drug of The Movement." Seemingly aimless, this driving about is a compensation mechanism. Understanding the powerful attraction that a certain pace of life can exert on the individual helps explain much otherwise inexplicable or "aimless" behavior.

But if some people thrive on the new, rapid pace, others are fiercely repelled by it and go to extreme lengths to "get off the merry-go-round," as they put it. To engage at all with the emergent super-industrial society means to engage with a faster moving world than ever before. They prefer to disengage, to idle at their own speed. It is not by chance that a musical entitled *Stop the World—I Want to Get Off* was a smash hit in London and New York a few seasons ago.

The quietism and search for new ways to "opt out" or "cop out" that characterizes certain (though not all) hippies may be less motivated by their loudly expressed aversion for the values of a technological civilization than by an unconscious effort to escape from a pace of life that many find intolerable. It is no coincidence that they describe society as a "rat-race"—a term that refers quite specifically to pacing.

Older people are even more likely to react strongly against any further acceleration of change. There is a solid mathematical basis for the observation that age often correlates with conservatism: time passes more swiftly for the old.

When a fifty-year-old father tells his fifteen-year-old son that he will have to wait two years before he can have a car of his own, that interval of 730 days represents a mere 4 percent of the father's lifetime to date. It represents over 13 percent of the boy's lifetime. It is hardly strange that to the boy the delay seems three or four times longer than to the father. Similarly, two hours in the life of a four-year-old may be the felt equivalent of twelve hours in the life of her twenty-four-year-old mother. Asking the child to wait two hours for a piece of candy may be the equivalent of asking the mother to wait fourteen hours for a cup of coffee.

There may be a biological basis as well, for such differences in subjective response to time. "With advancing age," writes psychologist John Cohen of the University of Manchester, "the calendar years seem progressively to shrink. In restrospect every year seems shorter than the year just completed, possibly as a result of the gradual slowing down of metabolic processes." In relation to the slowdown of their own biological rhythms, the world would appear to be moving faster to older people, even if it were not.

Whatever the reasons, any acceleration of change that has the effect of crowding more situations into the experiential channel in a given interval is magnified in the perception of the older person. As the rate of change in society speeds up, more and more older people feel the difference keenly. They, too, become dropouts, withdrawing into a private environment, cutting off as many contacts as possible with the fast-moving outside world, and, finally, vegetating until death. We may never solve the psychological problems of the aged until we find the means —through biochemistry or re-education—to alter their time sense, or to provide structured enclaves for them in which the pace of life is controlled, and even, perhaps, regulated according to a "sliding scale" calendar that reflects their own subjective perception of time.

Much otherwise incomprehensible conflict—between generations, between parents and children, between husbands and wives—can be traced to differential responses to the acceleration of the pace of life. The same is true of clashes between cultures.

Each culture has its own characteristic pace. F. M. Esfandiary, the Iranian novelist and essayist, tells of a collision between two different pacing systems when German engineers in the pre-World War II period were helping to construct a railroad in his country. Iranians and Middle Easterners generally take a far more relaxed attitude toward time than Americans or Western Europeans. When Iranian work crews consistently showed up for work ten minutes late, the Germans, themselves super-punctual and always in a hurry, fired them in droves. Iranian engineers had a difficult time persuading them that by Middle Eastern standards the workers were being heroically punctual, and that if the firings continued there would soon be no one left to do the work but women and children.

This indifference to time can be maddening to those who are fast-paced and clock-conscious. Thus Italians from Milan or Turin, the industrial cities of the North, look down upon the relatively slow-paced Sicilians, whose lives are still geared to the slower rhythms of agriculture. Swedes from Stockholm or Göteborg feel the same way about Laplanders. Americans speak with derision of Mexicans for whom *mañana* is soon enough. In the United States itself, Northerners regard Southerners as slow-moving, and middle-class Negroes condemn working-class Negroes just up from the South for operating on "C.P.T."— Colored People's Time. In contrast, by comparison with almost anyone else, white Americans and Canadians are regarded as hustling, fast-moving gogetters.

Populations sometimes actively resist a change of pace. This explains the pathological antagonism toward what many regard as the "Americanization" of Europe. The new technology on which superindustrialism is based, much of it blue-printed in American research laboratories, brings with it an inevitable acceleration of change in society and a concomitant speed-up of the pace of individual life as well. While anti-American orators single out computers or Coca-Cola for their barbs, their real objection may well be to the invasion of Europe by an alien time sense. America, as the spearhead of superindustrialism, represents a new, quicker, and very much unwanted tempo.

Precisely this issue is symbolized by the angry outcry that has greeted the recent introduction of Amer-
ican-style drugstores in Paris. To many Frenchmen,
their existence is infuriating evidence of a sinister
"cultural imperialism" on the part of the United
States. It is hard for Americans to understand so
passionate a response to a perfectly innocent soda
fountain. What explains it is the fact that at Le Drug-
store the thirsty Frenchman gulps a hasty milkshake
instead of lingering for an hour or two over an aper-
itif at an outdoor bistro. It is worth noticing that, as
the new technology has spread in recent years, some
30,000 bistros have padlocked their doors for good,
victims, in the words of *Time* magazine, of a "short-
order culture." (Indeed, it may well be that the
widespread European dislike for *Time*, itself, is not
entirely political, but stems unconsciously from the
connotation of its title. *Time*, with its brevity and
breathless style, exports more than the American
Way of Life. It embodies and exports the American
Pace of Life.)

DURATIONAL EXPECTANCY

To understand why acceleration in the pace of life
may prove disruptive and uncomfortable, it is important to grasp the idea of "durational expectancies."

Man's perception of time is closely linked with his
internal rhythms. But his responses to time are culturally conditioned. Part of this conditioning consists of building up within the child a series of
expectations about the duration of events, processes
or relationships. Indeed, one of the most important
forms of knowledge that we impart to a child is a
knowledge of how long things last. This knowledge is
taught in subtle, informal and often unconscious ways.
Yet without a rich set of socially appropriate du-

rational expectancies, no individual could function successfully.

From infancy on the child learns, for example, that when Daddy leaves for work in the morning, it means that he will not return for many hours. (If he does, something is wrong; the schedule is askew. The child senses this. Even the family dog—having also learned a set of durational expectancies—is aware of the break in routine.) The child soon learns that "mealtime" is neither a one-minute nor a five-hour affair, but that it ordinarily lasts from fifteen minutes to an hour. He learns that going to a movie lasts two to four hours, but that a visit with the pediatrician seldom lasts more than one. He learns that the school day ordinarily lasts six hours. He learns that a relationship with a teacher ordinarily extends over a school year, but that his relationship with his grandparents is supposed to be of much longer duration. Indeed, some relationships are supposed to last a lifetime. In adult behavior, virtually all we do, from mailing an envelope to making love, is premised upon certain spoken or unspoken assumptions about duration.

It is these durational expectancies, different in each society but learned early and deeply ingrained, that are shaken up when the pace of life is altered.

This explains a crucial difference between those who suffer acutely from the accelerated pace of life and those who seem rather to thrive on it. Unless an individual has adjusted his durational expectancies to take account of continuing acceleration, he is likely to suppose that two situations, similar in other respects, will also be similar in duration. Yet the accelerative thrust implies that at least certain kinds of situations will be compressed in time.

The individual who has internalized the principle of acceleration—who understands in his bones as well as his brain that things are moving faster in the world around him—makes an automatic, unconscious compensation for the compression of time. Anticipating that situations will endure less long, he is less frequently caught off guard and jolted than the person whose durational expectancies are frozen, the person who does not routinely anticipate a frequent shortening in the duration of situations.

In short, the pace of life must be regarded as something more than a colloquial phrase, a source of jokes, sighs, complaints or ethnic put-downs. It is a crucially important psychological variable that has been all but ignored. During past eras, when change in the outer society was slow, men could, and did, remain unaware of this variable. Throughout one's entire lifetime the pace might vary little. The accelerative thrust, however, alters this drastically. For it is precisely through a step-up in the pace of life that the increased speed of broad scientific, technological and social change makes itself felt in the life of the individual. A great deal of human behavior is motivated by attraction or antagonism toward the pace of life enforced on the individual by the society or group within which he is embedded. Failure to grasp this principle lies behind the dangerous incapacity of education and psychology to prepare people for fruitful roles in a super-industrial society.

THE CONCEPT OF TRANSIENCE

Much of our theorizing about social and psychological change presents a valid picture of man in relatively static societies—but a distorted and incomplete picture of the truly contemporary man. It misses a critical difference between the men of the past or present and the men of the future. This difference is summed up in the word "transience."

The concept of transience provides a long-missing link between sociological theories of change and the psychology of individual human beings. Integrating both, it permits us to analyze the problems of high-speed change in a new way. And, as we shall see, it gives us a method—crude but powerful—to measure inferentially the rate of situation flow.

Transience is the new "temporariness" in everyday life. It results in a mood, a feeling of impermanence. Philosophers and theologians, of course, have always been aware that man is ephemeral. In this grand sense, transience has always been a part of life. But today the feeling of impermanence is more acute and intimate. Thus Edward Albee's character, Jerry, in *The Zoo Story*, characterizes himself as a "permanent transient." And critic Harold Clurman, commenting on Albee, writes: "None of us occupy abodes of safety —true homes. We are all the same 'people in all the rooming houses everywhere,' desperately and savagely trying to effect soul-satisfying connections with our neighbors." We are, in fact, all citizens of the Age of Transience.

It is, however, not only our relationships with people that seem increasingly fragile or impermanent. If we divide up man's experience of the world outside himself, we can identify certain classes of relationships. Thus, in addition to his links with other people, we may speak of the individual's relationship with things. We can single out for examination his relationships with places. We can analyze his ties to the institutional or organizational environment around him. We can even study his relationship to certain ideas or to the information flow in society.

These five relationships—plus time—form the fabric of social experience. This is why, as suggested earlier, things, places, people, organizations and ideas are the basic components of all situations. It is the individual's distinctive relationship to each of these components that structures the situation.

And it is precisely these relationships that, as acceleration occurs in society, become foreshortened, telescoped in time. Relationships that once endured for long spans of time now have shorter life expectancies. It is this abbreviation, this compression, that gives rise to the almost tangible feeling that we live, rootless and uncertain, among shifting dunes.

Transience, indeed, can be defined quite specifically in terms of the rate at which our relationships turn over. While it may be difficult to prove that situations, as such, take less time to pass through our experience than before, it is possible to break them down into their components, and to measure the rate at which these components move into and out of our lives—to measure, in other words, the duration of relationships.

It will help us understand the concept of transience if we think in terms of the idea of "turnover." In a grocery store, for example, milk turns over more rapidly than, say, canned asparagus. It is sold and replaced more rapidly. The "through-put" is faster. The alert businessman knows the turnover rate for each of the items he sells, and the general rate for the entire store. He knows, in fact, that his turnover rate is a key indicator of the health of the enterprise.

We can, by analogy, think of transience as the rate of turnover of the different kinds of relationships in an individual's life. Moreover, each of us can be characterized in terms of this rate. For some, life is marked by a much slower rate of turnover than for others. The people of the past and present lead lives of relatively "low transience"—their relationships tend to be long-lasting. But the people of the future live in a condition of "high transience"—a condition in which the duration of relationships is cut short, the through-put of relationships extremely rapid. In their lives, things, places, people, ideas, and organizational structures all get "used up" more quickly.

This affects immensely the way they experience reality, their sense of commitment, and their ability—or inability—to cope. It is this fast through-put, combined with increasing newness and complexity in the environment, that strains the capacity to adapt and creates the danger of future shock.

If we can show that our relationships with the outer world are, in fact, growing more and more transient, we have powerful evidence for the assumption that the flow of situations is speeding up. And we have an incisive new way of looking at ourselves and others. Let us, therefore, explore life in a high transience society.

Part Two:

TRANSIENCE

Chapter 4

THINGS:
THE THROW-AWAY SOCIETY

"Barbie," a twelve-inch plastic teen-ager, is the best-known and best-selling doll in history. Since its introduction in 1959, the Barbie doll population of the world has grown to 12,000,000—more than the human population of Los Angeles or London or Paris. Little girls adore Barbie because she is highly realistic and eminently dress-upable. Mattel, Inc., makers of Barbie, also sells a complete wardrobe for her, including clothes for ordinary daytime wear, clothes for formal party wear, clothes for swimming and skiing.

Recently Mattel announced a new improved Barbie doll. The new version has a slimmer figure, "real" eyelashes, and a twist-and-turn waist that makes her more humanoid than ever. Moreover, Mattel announced that, for the first time, any young lady wishing to purchase a new Barbie would receive a trade-in allowance for her old one.

What Mattel did not announce was that by trading in her old doll for a technologically improved model, the little girl of today, citizen of tomorrow's super-industrial world, would learn a fundamental lesson about the new society: that man's relationships with *things* are increasingly temporary.

The ocean of man-made physical objects that surrounds us is set within a larger ocean of natural

objects. But increasingly, it is the technologically produced environment that matters for the individual.
The texture of plastic or concrete, the iridescent
glisten of an automobile under a streetlight, the staggering vision of a cityscape seen from the window of
a jet—these are the intimate realities of his existence.
Man-made things enter into and color his consciousness. Their number is expanding with explosive force,
both absolutely and relative to the natural environment. This will be even more true in super-industrial
society than it is today.

Anti-materialists tend to deride the importance of
"things." Yet things are highly significant, not merely
because of their functional utility, but also because of
their psychological impact. We develop relationships
with things. Things affect our sense of continuity or
discontinuity. They play a role in the structure of
situations and the foreshortening of our relationships
with things accelerates the pace of life.

Moreover, our attitudes toward things reflect basic
value judgments. Nothing could be more dramatic
than the difference between the new breed of little
girls who cheerfully turn in their Barbies for the new
improved model and those who, like their mothers and
grandmothers before them, clutch lingeringly and
lovingly to the same doll until it disintegrates from
sheer age. In this difference lies the contrast between
past and future, between societies based on permanence, and the new, fast-forming society based on
transience.

THE PAPER WEDDING GOWN

That man-thing relationships are growing more and
more temporary may be illustrated by examining the
culture surrounding the little girl who trades in her
doll. This child soon learns that Barbie dolls are by no
means the only physical objects that pass into and
out of her young life at a rapid clip. Diapers, bibs,

paper napkins, Kleenex, towels, non-returnable soda
bottles—all are used up quickly in her home and
ruthlessly eliminated. Corn muffins come in baking
tins that are thrown away after one use. Spinach is
encased in plastic sacks that can be dropped into a
pan of boiling water for heating, and then thrown
away. TV dinners are cooked and often served on
throw-away trays. Her home is a large processing
machine through which objects flow, entering and
leaving, at a faster and faster rate of speed. From birth
on, she is inextricably embedded in a throw-away
culture.

The idea of using a product once or for a brief
period and then replacing it, runs counter to the grain
of societies or individuals steeped in a heritage of
poverty. Not long ago Uriel Rone, a market researcher
for the French advertising agency Publicis, told me:
"The French housewife is not used to disposable
products. She likes to keep things, even old things,
rather than throw them away. We represented one
company that wanted to introduce a kind of plastic
throw-away curtain. We did a marketing study for
them and found the resistance too strong." This resistance, however, is dying all over the developed
world.

Thus a writer, Edward Maze, has pointed out that
many Americans visiting Sweden in the early 1950's
were astounded by its cleanliness. "We were almost
awed by the fact that there were no beer and soft
drink bottles by the roadsides, as, much to our shame,
there were in America. But by the 1960's, lo and be-
hold, bottles were suddenly blooming along Swedish
highways . . . What happened? Sweden had become
a buy, use and throw-away society, following the
American pattern." In Japan today throw-away tissues
are so universal that cloth handkerchiefs are regarded
as old fashioned, not to say unsanitary. In England
for sixpence one may buy a "Dentamatic throw-away
toothbrush" which comes already coated with tooth-
paste for its one-time use. And even in France, dis-

posable cigarette lighters are commonplace. From cardboard milk containers to the rockets that power space vehicles, products created for short-term or one-time use are becoming more numerous and crucial to our way of life.

The recent introduction of paper and quasi-paper clothing carried the trend toward disposability a step further. Fashionable boutiques and working-class clothing stores have sprouted whole departments devoted to gaily colored and imaginatively designed paper apparel. Fashion magazines display breathtakingly sumptuous gowns, coats, pajamas, even wedding dresses made of paper. The bride pictured in one of these wears a long white train of lace-like paper that, the caption writer notes, will make "great kitchen curtains" after the ceremony.

Paper clothes are particularly suitable for children. Writes one fashion expert: "Little girls will soon be able to spill ice cream, draw pictures and make cutouts on their clothes while their mothers smile benignly at their creativity." And for adults who want to express their own creativity, there is even a "paint-yourself-dress" complete with brushes. Price: $2.00.

Price, of course, is a critical factor behind the paper explosion. Thus a department store features simple A-line dresses made of what it calls "devil-may-care cellulose fiber and nylon." At $1.29 each, it is almost cheaper for the consumer to buy and discard a new one than to send an ordinary dress to the cleaners. Soon it will be. But more than economics is involved, for the extension of the throw-away culture has important psychological consequences.

We develop a throw-away mentality to match our throw-away products. This mentality produces, among other things, a set of radically altered values with respect to property. But the spread of disposability through the society also implies decreased durations in man-thing relationships. Instead of being linked with a single object over a relatively long span of time,

we are linked for brief periods with the succession of
objects that supplant it.

THE MISSING SUPERMARKET

The shift toward transience is even manifest in architecture—precisely that part of the physical environment that in the past contributed mostly heavily to
man's sense of permanence. The child who trades in
her Barbie doll cannot but also recognize the transience of buildings and other large structures that
surround her. We raze landmarks. We tear down
whole streets and cities and put new ones up at a
mind-numbing rate.

"The average age of dwellings has steadily declined," writes E. F. Carter of the Stanford Research
Institute, "from being virtually infinite in the days of
caves to . . . approximately a hundred years for houses
built in United States colonial days, to about forty
years at present." And Michael Wood, an English
writer comments: The American ". . . made his world
yesterday, and he knows exactly how fragile, how
shifting it is. Buildings in New York literally disappear
overnight, and the face of a city can change completely in a year."

Novelist Louis Auchincloss complains angrily that
"The horror of living in New York is living in a city
without a history . . . All eight of my great-grand-
parents lived in the city . . . and only one of the
houses they lived in . . . is still standing. That's what
I mean by the vanishing past." Less patrician New
Yorkers, whose ancestors landed in America more
recently, arriving there from the barrios of Puerto
Rico, the villages of Eastern Europe or the plantations
of the South, might voice their feelings quite differently. Yet the "vanishing past" is a real phenomenon,
and it is likely to become far more widespread, en-
gulfing even many of the history-drenched cities of
Europe.

Buckminster Fuller, the designer-philosopher, once described New York as a "continual evolutionary process of evacuations, demolitions, removals, temporarily vacant lots, new installations and repeat. This process is identical in principle to the annual rotation of crops in farm acreage—plowing, planting the new seed, harvesting, plowing under, and putting in another type of crop . . . Most people look upon the building operations blocking New York's streets . . . as temporary annoyances, soon to disappear in a static peace. They still think of permanence as normal, a hangover from the Newtonian view of the universe. But those who have lived in and with New York since the beginning of the century have literally experienced living with Einsteinian relativity."

That children, in fact, internalize this "Einsteinian relativity" was brought home to me forcibly by a personal experience. Some time ago my wife sent my daughter, then twelve, to a supermarket a few blocks from our Manhattan apartment. Our little girl had been there only once or twice before. Half an hour later she returned perplexed. "It must have been torn down," she said, "I couldn't find it." It hadn't been. New to the neighborhood, Karen had merely looked on the wrong block. But she is a child of the Age of Transience, and her immediate assumption—that the building had been razed and replaced—was a natural one for a twelve-year-old growing up in the United States at this time. Such an idea would probably never have occurred to a child faced with a similar predicament even half a century ago. The physical environment was far more durable, our links with it less transient.

THE ECONOMICS OF IMPERMANENCE

In the past, permanence was the ideal. Whether engaged in handcrafting a pair of boots or in constructing a cathedral, all man's creative and productive energies went toward maximizing the durability of the product. Man built to last. He had to. As long as the society around him was relatively unchanging each object had clearly defined functions, and economic logic dictated the policy of permanence. Even if they had to be repaired now and then, the boots that cost fifty dollars and lasted ten years were less expensive than those that cost ten dollars and lasted only a year.

As the general rate of change in society accelerates, however, the economics of permanence are—and must be—replaced by the economics of transience.

First, advancing technology tends to lower the costs of manufacture much more rapidly than the costs of repair work. The one is automated, the other remains largely a handcraft operation. This means that it often becomes cheaper to replace than to repair. It is economically sensible to build cheap, unrepairable, throwaway objects, even though they may not last as long as repairable objects.

Second, advancing technology makes it possible to improve the object as time goes by. The second-generation computer is better than the first, and the third is better than the second. Since we can anticipate further technological advance, more improvements coming at ever shorter intervals, it often makes hard economic sense to build for the short term rather than the long. David Lewis, an architect and city planner with Urban Design Associates in Pittsburgh, tells of certain apartment houses in Miami that are torn down after only ten years of existence. Improved air conditioning systems in newer buildings hurt the rentability of these "old" buildings. All things considered, it becomes cheaper to tear down the ten-year-old buildings than to modify them.

Third, as change accelerates and reaches into more and more remote corners of the society, uncertainty about future needs increases. Recognizing the inevitability of change, but unsure as to the demands it will impose on us, we hesitate to commit large resources for rigidly fixed objects intended to serve unchanging purposes. Avoiding commitment to fixed forms and functions, we build for short-term use or, alternatively, attempt to make the product itself adaptable. We "play it cool" technologically.

The rise of disposability—the spread of the throw-away culture—is a response to these powerful pressures. As change accelerates and complexities multiply, we can expect to see further extensions of the principle of disposability, further curtailment of man's relationships with things.

THE PORTABLE PLAYGROUND

There are other responses besides disposability that also lead to the same psychological effect. For example, we are now witnessing the wholesale creation of objects designed to serve a series of short-term purposes instead of a single one. These are not throw-away items. They are usually too big and expensive to discard. But they are so constructed that they may be dismantled, if necessary, and relocated after each use.

Thus the board of education of Los Angeles has decided that fully 25 percent of that city's classrooms will, in the future, be temporary structures that can be moved around as needed. Every major United States school district today uses some temporary classrooms. More are on the way. Indeed, temporary classrooms are to the school construction industry what paper dresses are to the clothing industry—a foretaste of the future.

The purpose of temporary classrooms is to help school systems cope with rapidly shifting population densities. But temporary classrooms, like disposable clothes, imply man-thing relationships of shorter duration than in the past. Thus the temporary classroom teaches something even in the absence of a teacher. Like the Barbie doll, it provides the child with a vivid lesson in the impermanence of her surroundings. No sooner does the child internalize a thorough knowledge of the classroom—the way it fits into the surrounding architecture, the way the desks feel on a hot day, the way sound reverberates in it, all the subtle smells and textures that individualize any structure and lend it reality—than the structure itself may be physically removed from her environment to serve other children in another place.

Nor are mobile classrooms a purely American phenomenon. In England, architect Cedric Price has designed what he calls a "thinkbelt"—an entirely mobile university intended to serve 20,000 students in North Staffordshire. "It will," he says, "rely on temporary buildings rather than permanent ones." It will make "great use of mobile and variable physical enclosures" —classrooms, for example, built inside railroad cars so that they may be shunted anywhere along the four-mile campus.

Geodesic domes to house expositions, air-inflated plastic bubbles for use as command posts or construction headquarters, a whole array of pick-up-and-move temporary structures are flowing from the drawing boards of engineers and architects. In New York City, the Department of Parks has decided to build twelve "portable playgrounds"—small, temporary playgrounds to be installed on vacant city lots until other uses are found for the land, at which time the playgrounds can be dismounted and moved elsewhere. There was a time when a playground was a reasonably permanent fixture in a neighborhood, when one's children and even, perhaps, one's children's children might, each in their turn, experience it in roughly the same way. Super-industrial playgrounds, however, refuse to stay put. They are temporary by design.

THE MODULAR "FUN PALACE"

The reduction in the duration of man-thing relationships brought about by the proliferation of throw-away items and temporary structures is further intensified by the rapid spread of "modularism." Modularism may be defined as the attempt to lend whole structures greater permanence at the cost of making their sub-structures less permanent. Thus Cedric Price's "thinkbelt" plan proposes that faculty and student apartments consist of pressed-steel modules that can be hoisted by crane and plugged into building frames. The frames become the only relatively permanent parts of the structure. The apartment modules can be shifted around as needed, or even, in theory, completely discarded and replaced.

It needs to be emphasized here that the distinction between disposability and mobility is, from the point of view of the duration of relationships, a thin one. Even when modules are not discarded, but merely rearranged, the result is a new configuration, a new entity. It is as if one physical structure had, in reality, been discarded and a new one created, even though some or all of the components remain the same.

Even many supposedly "permanent" buildings today are constructed on a modular plan so that interior walls and partitions may be shifted at will to form new enclosure patterns inside. The mobile partition, indeed, might well serve as a symbol of the transient society. One scarcely ever enters a large office today without tripping over a crew of workers busily moving desks and rearranging interior space by reorganizing the partitions. In Sweden a new triumph of modularism has recently been achieved: in a model apartment house in Uppsala *all* walls and closets are movable. The tenant needs only a screwdriver to transform his living space completely, to create, in effect, a new apartment.

Sometimes, however, modularity is directly combined with disposability. The simple, ubiquitous ballpoint pen provides an example. The original goosequill pen had a long life expectancy. Barring accident, it lasted a long time and could be resharpened (i.e., repaired) from time to time to extend its life. The fountain pen, however, was a great technological ad-

vance because it gave the user mobility. It provided a
writing tool that carried its own inkwell, thus vastly
increasing its range of usefulness. The invention of
the ball point consolidated and extended this advance.
It provided a pen that carried its own ink supply, but
that, in addition, was so cheap it could be thrown
away when empty. The first truly disposable pen-and-
ink combination had been created.

We have, however, not yet outgrown the psychological attitudes that accompany scarcity. Thus there
are still many people today who feel a twinge of
guilt at discarding even a spent ball-point pen. The
response of the pen industry to this psychological
reality was the creation of a ball-point pen built on
the modular principle—an outer frame that the user
could keep, and an inner ink module or cartridge that
he could throw away and replace. By making the ink
cartridge expendable, the whole structure is given
extended life at the expense of the sub-structure.

There are, however, more parts than wholes. And
whether he is shifting them around to create new
wholes or discarding and replacing them, the user experiences a more rapid through-put of things through
his life, a generalized decline in the average duration
of his relationship with things. The result is a new
fluidity, mobility and transience.

One of the most extreme examples of architecture
designed to embody these principles was the plan put
forward by the English theatrical producer Joan
Littlewood with the help of Frank Newby, a structural
engineer, Gordon Pask, a systems consultant, and
Cedric Price, the "thinkbelt" architect.

Miss Littlewood wanted a theater in which versatility might be maximized, in which she might present
anything from an ordinary play to a political rally,
from a performance of dance to a wrestling match—
preferably all at the same time. She wanted, as the
critic Reyner Banham has put it, a "zone of total
probability." The result was a fantastic plan for "The
Fun Palace," otherwise known as the "First Giant

Space Mobile in the World." The plan calls not for a multi-purpose building, but for what is, in effect, a larger than life-sized Erector Set, a collection of modular parts that can be hung together in an almost infinite variety of ways. More or less "permanent" vertical towers house various services—such as toilets and electronic control units—and are topped by gantry cranes that lift the modules into position and assemble them to form any temporary configuration desired. After an evening's entertainment, the cranes come out, disassemble the auditoria, exhibition halls and restaurants, and store them away.

Here is the way Reyner Banham describes it: ". . . the Fun Palace is a piece of ten-year-expendable urban equipment . . . Day by day this giant neo-Futurist machine will stir and reshuffle its movable parts—walls and floors, ramps and walks, steerable escalators, seating and roofing, stages and movie screens, lighting and sound systems—sometimes with only a small part walled in, but with the public poking about the exposed walks and stairs, pressing buttons to make things happen themselves.

"This, when it happens (and it is on the cards that it will, somewhere, soon) will be indeterminacy raised to a new power: no permanent monumental interior space or heroic silhouette against the sky will survive for posterity . . . For the only permanently visible elements of the Fun Palace will be the 'life-support' structure on which the transient architecture will be parasitic."

Proponents of what has become known as "plug-in" or "clip-on" architecture have designed whole cities based on the idea of "transient architecture." Extending the concepts on which the Fun Palace plan is based, they propose the construction of different types of modules which would be assigned different life expectancies. Thus the core of a "building" might be engineered to last twenty-five years, while the plug-in room modules are built to last only three years. Letting their imaginations roam still further, they have conjured up mobile skyscrapers that rest not on fixed foundations but on gigantic "ground effect" machines or hovercraft. The ultimate is an entire urban agglomeration freed of fixed position, floating on a cushion of air, powered by nuclear energy, and changing its inner shape even more rapidly than New York does today.

Whether or not precisely these visions become reality, the fact is that society is moving in this direction. The extension of the throw-away culture, the creation of more and more temporary structures, the spread of modularism are proceeding apace, and they all conspire toward the same psychological end: the ephemeralization of man's links with the things that surround him.

THE RENTAL REVOLUTION

Still another development is drastically altering the man-thing nexus: the rental revolution. The spread of rentalism, a characteristic of societies rocketing toward super-industrialism, is intimately connected with all the tendencies described above. The link between Hertz cars, disposable diapers, and Joan Littlewood's "Fun Palace," may seem obscure at first glance, but closer inspection reveals strong inner similarities. For rentalism, too, intensifies transience.

During the depression, when millions were jobless and homeless, the yearning for a home of one's own was one of the most powerful economic motivations in capitalist societies. In the United States today the desire for home ownership is still strong, but ever since the end of World War II the percentage of new housing devoted to rental apartments has been soaring. As late as 1955 apartments accounted for only 8 percent of new housing starts. By 1961 it reached 24 percent. By 1969, for the first time in the United States, more building permits were being issued for apartment construction than for private homes. Apart-

ment living, for a variety of reasons, is "in." It is particularly in among young people who, in the words of
MIT Professor Burnham Kelly, want "minimum-in-
volvement housing."

Minimum involvement is precisely what the user of
a throw-away product gets for his money. It is also
what temporary structures and modular components
foster. Commitments to apartments are, almost by
definition, shorter term commitments than those made
by a homeowner to his home. The trend toward residential renting thus underscores the tendency toward
ever-briefer relationships with the physical environment.*

More striking than this, however, has been the recent upsurge of rental activity in fields in which it was
all but unknown in the past. David Riesman has
written: "People are fond of their cars; they like to
talk about them—something that comes out very clearly in interviews—but their affection for any one in
particular rarely reaches enough intensity to become
long-term." This is reflected in the fact that the average car owner in the United States keeps his automobile only three and a half years; many of the more
affluent trade in their automobiles every year or two.
In turn, this accounts for the existence of a twenty-
billion-dollar used car business in the United States.
It was the automotive industry that first succeeded in
destroying the traditional notion that a major purchase
had to be a permanent commitment. The annual
model changeover, high-powered advertising, backed
by the industry's willingness to offer trade-in allow-
ances, made the purchase of a new (or new used)

---

* It might be noted that millions of American home "owners," having purchased a home with a down payment of 10
percent or less, are actually no more than surrogate owners for
banks and other lending institutions. For these families, the
monthly check to the bank is no different from the rent check
to the landlord. Their ownership is essentially metaphorical,
and since they lack a strong financial stake in their property,
they also frequently lack the homeowner's strong psychological
commitment to it.

car a relatively frequent occurrence in the life of the average American male. In effect, it shortened the interval between purchases, thereby shortening the duration of the relationship between an owner and any one vehicle.

In recent years, however, a spectacular new force has emerged to challenge many of the most deeply ingrained patterns of the automotive industry. This is the auto rental business. Today in the United States millions of motorists rent automobiles from time to time for periods of a few hours up to several months. Many big-city dwellers, especially in New York where parking is a nightmare, refuse to own a car, preferring to rent one for weekend trips to the country, or even for in-town trips that are inconvenient by public transit. Autos today can be rented with a minimum of red tape at almost any US airport, railroad station or hotel.

Moreover, Americans have carried the rental habit abroad with them. Nearly half a million of them rent cars while overseas each year. This figure is expected to rise to nearly a million by 1975, and the big American rental companies, operating now in some fifty countries around the globe, are beginning to run into foreign competitors. Simultaneously, European motorists are beginning to emulate the Americans. A cartoon in *Paris Match* shows a creature from outer space standing next to his flying saucer and asking a gendarme where he can rent an auto. The idea is catching on.

The rise of auto rentals, meanwhile, has been paralleled by the emergence in the United States of a new kind of general store—one which sells nothing but rents everything. There are now some 9000 such stores in the United States with an annual rental volume on the order of one billion dollars and a growth rate of from 10 to 20 percent per year. Virtually 50 percent of these stores were not in business five years ago. Today, there is scarcely a product that cannot be rented, from ladders and lawn equipment to mink coats and originals Rouaults.

In Los Angeles, rental firms provide live shrubs and trees for real estate developers who wish to landscape model homes temporarily. "Plants enhance —rent living plants," says the sign on the side of a truck in San Francisco. In Philadelphia one may rent shirts. Elsewhere, Americans now rent everything from gowns, crutches, jewels, TV sets, camping equipment, air conditioners, wheelchairs, linens, skis, tape recorders, champagne fountains, and silverware. A West Coast men's club rented a human skeleton for a demonstration, and an ad in the *Wall Street Journal* even urges: "Rent-a-Cow."

Not long ago the Swedish women's magazine *Svensk Damtidning* ran a five-part series about the world of 1985. Among other things, it suggested that by then "we will sleep in built-in sleeping furniture with buttons for when we eat breakfast or read, or else we will rent a bed at the same place that we rent the table and the paintings and the washing machine."

Impatient Americans are not waiting for 1985. Indeed, one of the most significant aspects of the booming rental business is the rise of furniture rental. Some manufacturers and many rental firms will now furnish entire small apartments for as little as twenty to fifty dollars per month, down to the drapes, rugs and ashtrays. "You arrive in town in the morning," says one airline stewardess, "and by evening you've got a swinging pad." Says a Canadian transferred to New York: "It's new, it's colorful, and I don't have to worry about carting it all over the world when I'm transferred."

William James once wrote that "lives based on having are less free than lives based either on doing or on being." The rise of rentalism is a move away from lives based on having and it reflects the increase in doing and being. If the people of the future live faster than the people of the past, they must also be far more flexible. They are like broken field runners—

and it is hard to sidestep a tackle when loaded down with possessions. They want the advantage of affluence and the latest that technology has to offer, but not the responsibility that has, until now, accompanied the accumulation of possessions. They recognize that to survive among the uncertainties of rapid change they must learn to travel light.

Whatever its broader effects, however, rentalism shortens still further the duration of the relationships between man and the things that he uses. This is made clear by asking a simple question: How many cars—rented, borrowed or owned—pass through the hands of the average American male in a lifetime? The answer for car owners might be in the range of twenty to fifty. For active car renters, however, the figure might run as high as 200 or more. While the buyer's average relationship with a particular vehicle extends over many months or years, the renter's average link with any one particular car is extremely short-lived.

Renting has the net effect of multiplying the number of people with successive relationships to the same object, and thus reducing, on average, the duration of such relationships. When we extend this principle to a very wide range of products, it becomes clear that the rise of rentalism parallels and reinforces the impact of throw-away items, temporary structures and modularism.

TEMPORARY NEEDS

It is important here to turn for a moment to the notion of obsolescence. For the fear of product obsolescence drives businessmen to innovation at the same time that it impels the consumer toward rented, disposable or temporary products. The very idea of obsolescence is disturbing to people bred on the ideal of permanence, and it is particularly upsetting when thought to be planned. Planned obsolescence has been the target of so much recent social criticism that the un-

wary reader might be led to regard it as the primary
or even exclusive cause of the trend toward shorter
relational durations.

There is no doubt that some businessmen conspire
to shorten the useful life of their products in order to
guarantee replacement sales. There is, similarly, no
doubt that many of the annual model changes with
which American (and other) consumers are increasingly familiar are not technologically substantive. Detroit's autos today deliver no more mileage per gallon
of gasoline than they did ten model changes back,
and the oil companies, for all the additives about
which they boast, still put a turtle, not a tiger, in the
tank. Moreover, it is incontestable that Madison
Avenue frequently exaggerates the importance of new
features and encourages consumers to dispose of partially worn-out goods to make way for the new.

It is therefore true that the consumer is sometimes
caught in a carefully engineered trap—an old product
whose death has been deliberately hastened by its
manufacturer, and the simultaneous appearance of a
"new improved" model advertised as the latest heaven-
sent triumph of advanced technology.

Nevertheless, these reasons by themselves cannot
begin to account for the fantastic rate of turnover of
the products in our lives. Rapid obsolescence is an
integral part of the entire accelerative process—a
process involving not merely the life span of spark-
plugs, but of whole societies. Bound up with the rise
of science and the speed-up in the acquisition of
knowledge, this historic process can hardly be attributed to the evil design of a few contemporary huck-
sters.

Clearly, obsolescence occurs with or without "planning." With respect to things, obsolescence occurs
under three conditions. It occurs when a product
literally deteriorates to the point at which it can no
longer fulfill its functions—bearings burn out, fabrics
tear, pipes rust. Assuming the same functions still need
to be performed for the consumer, the failure of a

product to perform these functions marks the point at which its replacement is required. This is obsolescence due to functional failure.

Obsolescence also occurs when some new product arrives on the scene to perform these functions more effectively than the old product could. The new antibiotics do a more effective job of curing infection than the old. The new computers are infinitely faster and cheaper to operate than the antique models of the early 1960's. This is obsolescence due to substantive technological advance.

But obsolescence also occurs when the needs of the consumer change, when the functions to be performed by the product are themselves altered. These needs are not as simply described as the critics of planned obsolescence sometimes assume. An object, whether a car or a can opener, may be evaluated along many different parameters. A car, for example, is more than a conveyance. It is an expression of the personality of the user, a symbol of status, a source of that pleasure associated with speed, a source of a wide variety of sensory stimuli—tactile, olfactory, visual, etc. The satisfaction a consumer gains from such factors may, depending upon his values, outweigh the satisfaction he might receive from improved gas consumption or pickup power.

The traditional notion that each object has a single easily definable function clashes with all that we now know about human psychology, about the role of values in decision-making, and with ordinary common sense as well. All products are multi-functional.

An excellent illustration of this occurred not long ago when I watched a little boy purchase half a dozen pink erasers at a little stationery store. Curious as to why he wanted so many of them, I picked one up for closer examination. "Do they erase well?" I asked the boy. "I don't know," he said, "but they sure smell good!" And, indeed, they did. They had been heavily perfumed by the Japanese manufacturer perhaps to mask an unpleasant chemical odor. In short, the needs filled by products vary by purchaser and through time.

In a society of scarcity, needs are relatively universal and unchanging because they are starkly related to the "gut" functions. As affluence rises, however, human needs become less directly linked to biological survival and more highly individuated. Moreover, in a society caught up in complex, high-speed change, the needs of the individual—which arise out of his interaction with the external environment—also change at relatively high speed. The more rapidly changing the society, the more temporary the needs. Given the general affluence of the new society, he can indulge many of these short-term needs.

Often, without even having a clear idea of what needs he wants served, the consumer has a vague feeling that he wants a change. Advertising encourages and capitalizes on this feeling, but it can hardly be credited with having created it single-handedly. The tendency toward shorter relational durations is thus built more deeply into the social structure than arguments over planned obsolescence or the manipulative effectiveness of Madison Avenue would suggest.

The rapidity with which consumers' needs shift is reflected in the alacrity with which buyers abandon product and brand loyalty. If Assistant Attorney General Donald F. Turner, a leading critic of advertising, is correct, one of the primary purposes of advertising is to create "durable preferences." If so, it is failing, for brand-switching is so frequent and common that it has become, in the words of one food industry publication, "one of the national advertiser's major headaches."

Many brands drop out of existence. Among brands that continue to exist there is a continual reshuffling of position. According to Henry M. Schachte, "In almost no major consumer goods category . . . is there a brand on top today which held that position ten years ago." Thus among ten leading American cigarettes, only one, Pall Mall, maintained in 1966 the same share of the market that it held in 1956. Camels plunged from 18 to 9 percent of the market; Lucky Strike declined even more sharply, from 14 to 6 percent. Other brands moved up, with Salem, for example, rising from 1 to 9 percent. Additional fluctuations have occurred since this survey.

However insignificant these shifts may be from the long-run view of the historian, this continual shuffling and reshuffling, influenced but not independently controlled by advertising, introduces into the short-run, everyday life of the individual a dazzling dynamism. It heightens still further the sense of speed, turmoil and impermanence in society.

THE FAD MACHINE

Fast-shifting preferences, flowing out of and interacting with high-speed technological change, not only lead to frequent changes in the popularity of products and brands, but also shorten the life cycle of products. Automation expert John Diebold never wearies of pointing out to businessmen that they must begin to think in terms of shorter life spans for their goods. Smith Brothers' Cough Drops, Calumet Baking Soda and Ivory Soap, have become American institutions by virtue of their long reign in the market place. In the days ahead, he suggests, few products will enjoy such longevity. Every consumer has had the experience of going to the supermarket or department store to replace some item, only to find that he cannot locate the same brand or product. In 1966 some 7000 new products turned up in American supermarkets. Fully 55 percent of all the items now sold there did not exist ten years ago. And of the products available then, 42 percent have faded away altogether. Each year the process repeats itself in more extreme form. Thus 1968 saw 9,500 new items in the consumer packaged-goods field alone, with only one in five meeting its sales target. A silent but rapid attrition kills off the old, and new products sweep in like a tide.

"Products that used to sell for twenty-five years," writes economist Robert Theobald, "now often count on no more than five. In the volatile pharmaceutical and electronic fields the period is often as short as six months." As the pace of change accelerates further, corporations may create new products knowing full well that they will remain on the market for only a matter of a few weeks.

Here, too, the present already provides us with a foretaste of the future. It lies in an unexpected quarter: the fads now sweeping over the high technology societies in wave after wave. In the past few years alone, in the United States, Western Europe and Japan, we have witnessed the sudden rise or collapse in popularity of "Bardot hairdos," the "Cleopatra look," James Bond, and Batman, not to speak of Tiffany lampshades, Super-Balls, iron crosses, pop sunglasses, badges and buttons with protest slogans or pornographic jokes, posters of Allen Ginsberg or Humphrey Bogart, false eyelashes, and innumerable other gimcracks and oddities that reflect—are tuned into—the rapidly changing pop culture.

Backed by mass media promotion and sophisticated marketing, such fads now explode on the scene virtually overnight—and vanish just as quickly. Sophisticates in the fad business prepare in advance for shorter and shorter product life cycles. Thus, there is in San Gabriel, California, a company entitled, with a kind of cornball relish, Wham-O Manufacturing Company. Wham-O specializes in fad products, having introduced the hula hoop in the fifties and the so-called Super-Ball more recently. The latter—a high-bouncing rubber ball—quickly became so popular with adults as well as children that astonished visitors saw several of them bouncing morrily on the floor of the Pacific Coast Stock Exchange. Wall Street executives gave them away to friends and one high broadcasting official complained that "All our executives are out in the halls with their Super-Balls." Wham-O, and other

companies like it, however, are not disconcerted when
sudden death overtakes their product; they anticipate
it. They are specialists in the design and manufacture
of "temporary" products.

The fact that fads are generated artificially, to a
large extent, merely underscores their significance.
Even engineered fads are not new to history. But
never before have they come fleeting across the consciousness in such rapid-fire profusion, and never has
there been such smooth coordination between those
who originate the fad, mass media eager to popularize
it, and companies geared for its instantaneous exploitation.

A well-oiled machinery for the creation and diffusion of fads is now an entrenched part of the modern
economy. Its methods will increasingly be adopted by
others as they recognize the inevitability of the ever-
shorter product cycle. The line between "fad" and
ordinary product will progressively blur. We are moving swiftly into the era of the temporary product,
made by temporary methods, to serve temporary
needs.

The turnover of things in our lives thus grows even
more frenetic. We face a rising flood of throw-away
items, impermanent architecture, mobile and modular
products, rented goods and commodities designed for
almost instant death. From all these directions, strong
pressures converge toward the same end: the inescapable ephemeralization of the man-thing relationship.

The foreshortening of our ties with the physical
environment, the stepped-up turnover of things, however, is only a small part of a much larger context. Let
us, therefore, press ahead in our exploration of life in
high transience society.

Chapter 5

PLACES:
THE NEW NOMADS

Every Friday afternoon at 4:30, a tall, graying Wall Street executive named Bruce Robe stuffs a mass of papers into his black leather briefcase, takes his coat off the rack outside his office, and departs. The routine has been the same for more than three years. First, he rides the elevator twenty-nine floors down to street level. Next he strides for ten minutes through crowded streets to the Wall Street Heliport. There he boards a helicopter which deposits him, eight minutes later, at John F. Kennedy Airport. Transferring to a Trans-World Airlines jet, he settles down for supper, as the giant craft swings out over the Atlantic, then banks and heads west. One hour and ten minutes later, barring delay, he steps briskly out of the terminal building at the airport in Columbus, Ohio, and enters a waiting automobile. In thirty more minutes he reaches his destination: he is home.

Four nights a week Robe lives at a hotel in Manhattan. The other three he spends with his wife and children in Columbus, 500 miles away. Claiming the best of two worlds, a job in the frenetic financial center of America and a family life in the comparatively tranquil Midwest countryside, he shuttles back and forth some 50,000 miles a year.

The Robe case is unusual—but not that unusual. In

California, ranch owners fly as much as 120 miles every morning from their homes on the Pacific Coast or in the San Bernardino Valley to visit their ranches in the Imperial Valley, and then fly back home again at night. One Pennsylvania teen-ager, son of a peripatetic engineer, jets regularly to an orthodontist in Frankfurt, Germany. A University of Chicago philosopher, Dr. Richard McKeon, commuted 1000 miles each way once a week for an entire semester in order to teach a series of classes at the New School for Social Research in New York. A young San Franciscoan and his girlfriend in Honolulu see each other every weekend, taking turns at crossing 2000 miles of Pacific Ocean. And at least one New England matron regularly swoops down on New York to visit her hairdresser.

Never in history has distance meant less. Never have man's relationships with place been more numerous, fragile and temporary. Throughout the advanced technological societies, and particularly among those I have characterized as "the people of the future," commuting, traveling, and regularly relocating one's family have become second nature. Figuratively, we "use up" places and dispose of them in much the same that we dispose of Kleenex or beer cans. We are witnessing a historic decline in the significance of place to human life. We are breeding a new race of nomads, and few suspect quite how massive, widespread and significant their migrations are.

THE 3,000,000-MILE CLUB

In 1914, according to Buckminster Fuller, the typical American averaged about 1,640 miles per year of total travel, counting some 1,300 miles of just plain everyday walking to and fro. This meant that he traveled only about 340 miles per year with the aid of horse or mechanical means. Using this 1,640 figure as a base, it is possible to estimate that the average American of that period moved a total of 88,560 miles in his lifetime.* Today, by contrast, the average American car owner drives 10,000 miles per year—and he lives longer than his father or grandfather. "At sixty-nine years of age," wrote Fuller a few years ago, ". . . I am one of a class of several million human beings who, in their lifetimes, have each covered 3,000,000 miles or more"—more than thirty times the total lifetime travel of the 1914 American.

The aggregate figures are staggering. In 1967, for instance, 108,000,000 Americans took 360,000,000 trips involving an overnight stay more than 100 miles from home. These trips alone accounted for 312,000,000,000 passenger miles.

Even if we ignore the introduction of fleets of jumbo jets, trucks, cars, trains, subways and the like, our social investment in mobility is astonishing. Paved roads and streets have been added to the American landscape at the incredible rate of more than 200 miles per day, every single day for at least the last twenty years. This adds up to 75,000 miles of new streets and roads every year, enough to girdle the globe three times. While United States population increased during this period by 38.5 percent, street and road mileage shot up 100 percent. Viewed another way, the figures are even more dramatic: passenger miles traveled within the United States have been increasing at a rate six times faster than population for at least twenty-five years.

This revolutionary step-up in per capita movement through space is paralleled, to greater or lesser degree, throughout the most technological nations. Anyone who has watched the rush hour traffic pileup on the once peaceful Strandvëg in Stockholm cannot help but be jolted by the sight. In Rotterdam and Amsterdam, streets built as recently as five years ago are

---

* This is based on a life expectancy of 54 years. Actual life expectancy for white males in the United States in 1920 was 54.1 years.

already horribly jammed: the number of automobiles has multiplied faster than anyone then thought possible.

In addition to the increase in everyday movement between one's home and various other nearby points, there is also a phenomenal increase in business and vacation travel involving overnight stays away from home. Nearly 1,500,000 Germans will vacation in Spain this summer, and hundreds of thousands more will populate beaches in Holland and Italy. Sweden annually welcomes more than 1,200,000 visitors from non-Scandinavian nations. More than a million foreigners visit the United States, while roughly 4,000,000 Americans travel overseas each year. A writer in *Le Figaro* justifiably refers to "gigantic human exchanges."

This busy movement of men back and forth over the landscape (and sometimes under it) is one of the identifying characteristics of super-industrial society. By contrast, pre-industrial nations seem congealed, frozen, their populations profoundly attached to a single place. Transportation expert Wilfred Owen talks about the "gap between the immobile and the mobile nations." He points out that for Latin America, Africa and Asia to reach the same ratio of road mileage to area that now prevails in the European Economic Community, they would have to pave some 40,000,000 miles of road. This contrast has profound economic consequences, but it also has subtle, largely overlooked cultural and psychological consequences. For migrants, travelers and nomads are not the same kind of people as those who stay put in one place.

FLAMENCO IN SWEDEN

Perhaps the most psychologically significant kind of movement that an individual can make is geographical relocation of his home. This dramatic form of geographical mobility is also strikingly evident in the United States and the other advanced nations. Speak-

ing of the United States, Peter Drucker has said: "The
largest migration in our history began during World
War II; and it has continued ever since with undimin-
ished momentum." And political scientist Daniel Elazar describes the great masses of Americans who "have
begun to move from place to place within each
[urban] belt . . . preserving a nomadic way of life
that is urban without being permanently attached to
any particular city . . ."

Between March 1967 and March 1968—in a single
year—36,600,000 Americans (not counting children
less than one year old) changed their place of residence. This is more than the total population of
Cambodia, Ghana, Guatemala, Honduras, Iraq, Israel,
Mongolia, Nicaragua and Tunisia combined. It is as if
the entire population of all these countries had suddenly been relocated. And movement on this massive
scale occurs every year in the United States. In each
year since 1948 one out of five Americans changed his
address, picking up his children, some household
effects, and starting life anew at a fresh place. Even
the great migrations of history, the Mongol hordes,
the westward movement of Europeans in the nineteenth century, seem puny by statistical comparison.

While this high rate of geographical mobility in the
United States is probably unmatched anywhere in the
world (available statistics, unfortunately, are spotty),
even in the more tradition-bound of the advanced
countries the age-old ties between man and place are
being shattered. Thus the *New Society*, a social science
journal published in London, reports that "The English
are a more mobile race than perhaps they thought . . .
No less than 11 percent of all the people in England
and Wales in 1961 had lived in their present usual
residence less than a year . . . In certain parts of
England, in fact, it appears that the migratory movements are nothing less than frenetic. In Kensington
over 25 percent had lived in their homes less than a
year, in Hampstead 20 percent, in Chelsea 19 percent."
And Anne Lapping, in another issue of the same

journal, states that "new houseowners expect to move house many more times than their parents. The average life of a mortgage is eight to nine years . . ." This is only slightly different than in the United States.

In France, a continuing housing shortage contrives to slow down internal mobility, but even there a study by demographer Guy Pourcher suggests that each year 8 to 10 percent of all Frenchmen shift homes. In Sweden, Germany, Italy and the Netherlands, the rate of domestic migration appears to be on the rise. And all Europe is experiencing a wave of international mass migration unlike anything since the disruptions of World War II. Economic prosperity in Northern Europe has created widespread labor shortages (except in England) and has attracted masses of unemployed agricultural workers from the Mediterranean and Middle Eastern countries.

They come by the thousands from Algeria, Spain, Portugal, Yugoslavia and Turkey. Every Friday afternoon 1000 Turkish workers in Istanbul clamber aboard a train heading north toward the promised lands. The cavernous rail terminal in Munich has become a debarkation point for many of them, and Munich now has its own Turkish-language newspaper. In Cologne, at the huge Ford factory, fully one-quarter of the workers are Turks. Other foreigners have fanned out through Switzerland, France, England, Denmark and as far north as Sweden. Not long ago, in the twelfth-century town of Pangbourne in England, my wife and I were served by Spanish waiters. And in Stockholm we visited the Vivel, a downtown restaurant that has become a meeting place for transplanted Spaniards who hunger for flamenco music with their dinner. There were no Swedes present; with the exception of a few Algerians and ourselves, everyone spoke Spanish. It was no surprise therefore to find that Swedish sociologists today are torn by debate over whether foreign worker populations should be assimilated into Swedish culture or encouraged to retain their own cultural traditions—precisely the same "melting pot" argument that excited American social scientists during the great period of open immigration in the United States.

MIGRATION TO THE FUTURE

There are, however, important differences between the kind of people who are on the move in the United States and those caught up in the European migrations. In Europe most of the new mobility can be attributed to the continuing transition from agriculture to industry; from the past to the present, as it were. Only a small part is as yet associated with the transition from industrialism to super-industrialism. In the United States, by contrast, the continuing redistribution of population is no longer primarily caused by the decline of agricultural employment. It grows, instead, out of the spread of automation and the new way of life associated with super-industrial society, the way of life of the future.

This becomes plain if we look at who is doing the moving in the United States. It is true that some technologically backward and disadvantaged groups, such as urban Negroes, are characterized by high rates of geographical mobility, usually within the same neighborhood or county. But these groups form only a relatively small slice of the total population, and it would be a serious mistake to assume that high rates of geographical mobility correlate only with poverty, unemployment or ignorance. In fact, we find that men with at least one year of college education (an ever increasing group) move more, and further, than those without. Thus we find that the professional and technical populations are among the most mobile of all Americans. And we find an increasing number of affluent executives who move far and frequently. (It is a house joke among executives of the International Business Machine Corporation that IBM stands for "I've Been Moved.") In the emerging super-industrialism it is precisely these groups—professional, technical and managerial—who increase in both absolute number and as a proportion of the total work force. They also give the society its characteristic flavor, as the denim-clad factory worker did in the past.

Just as millions of poverty-stricken and unemployed rural workers are flowing from the agricultural past into the industrial present in Europe, so thousands of European scientists, engineers and technicians are flowing into the United States and Canada, the most super-industrial of nations. In West Germany, Professor Rudolf Mossbauer, a Nobel prizewinner in physics, announces that he is thinking of migrating to America because of disagreements over administrative and budgetary policies at home. Europe's political ministers, worried over the "technology gap," have looked on helplessly as Westinghouse, Allied Chemical, Douglas Aircraft, General Dynamics and other major American corporations sent talent scouts to London or Stockholm to lure away everyone from astrophysicists to turbine engineers.

But there is a simultaneous "brain-drain" inside the United States, with thousands of scientists and engineers moving back and forth like particles in an atom. There are, in fact, well recognized patterns of movement. Two major streams, one from the North and the other from the South, both converge in California and the other Pacific Coast states, with a way station at Denver. Another major stream flows up from the South toward Chicago and Cambridge, Princeton and Long Island. A counter-stream carries men back to the space and electronics industries in Florida.

A typical young space engineer of my acquaintance quit his job with RCA at Princeton to go to work for General Electric. The house he had purchased only two years before was sold; his family moved into a rented house just outside Philadelphia, while a new one was built for them. They will move into this new house—the fourth in about five years—provided he is not transferred or offered a better job elsewhere. And all the time, California beckons.

There is a less obvious geographical pattern to the movement of management men, but, if anything, the turnover is heavier. A decade ago William Whyte, in *The Organization Man*, declared that "The man who leaves home is not the exception in American society but the key to it. Almost by definition, the organization man is a man who left home and . . . kept on going." His characterization, correct then, is even truer today. The *Wall Street Journal* refers to "corporate gypsies" in an article headlined "How Executive Family Adapts to Incessant Moving About Country." It describes the life of M. E. Jacobson, an executive with the Montgomery Ward retail chain. He and his wife, both forty-six at the time the story appeared, had moved twenty-eight times in twenty-six years of married life. "I almost feel like we're just camping," his wife tells her visitors. While their case is atypical, thousands like them move on the average of once every two years, and their numbers multiply. This is true not merely because corporate needs are constantly shifting, but also because top management regards frequent relocation of its potential successors as a necessary step in their training.

This moving of executives from house to house as if they were life-size chessmen on a continent-sized board has led one psychologist to propose facetiously a money-saving system called "The Modular Family." Under this scheme, the executive not only leaves his house behind, but his family as well. The company then finds him a matching family (personality characteristics carefully selected to duplicate those of the wife and children left behind) at the new site. Some other itinerant executive then "plugs into" the family left behind. No one appears to have taken the idea seriously—yet.

In addition to the large groups of professionals, technicians and executives who engage in a constant round of "musical homes," there are many other peculiarly mobile groupings in the society. A large military establishment includes tens of thousands of families who, peacetime and wartime, move again and again. "I'm not decorating any more houses," snaps the wife of an army colonel with irony in her voice: "The curtains never fit from one house to the next and the rug is always the wrong size or color. From now on I'm decorating my car." Tens of thousands of skilled construction workers add to the flow. On another level are the more than 750,000 students attending colleges away from their home state, plus the hundreds of thousands more who are away from home but still within their home state. For millions, and particularly for the "people of the future," home is where you find it.

SUICIDES AND HITCH-HIKERS

Such tidal movements of human beings produce all sorts of seldom-noticed side effects. Businesses that mail direct to the customer's home spend uncounted dollars keeping their address lists up to date. The same is true of telephone companies. Of the 885,000 listings in the Washington, D. C., telephone book in 1969, over half were different from the year before. Similarly, organizations and associations have a difficult time knowing where their members are. Within a single recent year fully one-third of the members of the National Society for Programmed Instruction, an organization of educational researchers, changed their addresses. Even friends have trouble keeping up with each other's whereabouts. One can sympathize with the plaint of poor Count Lanfranco Rasponi, who laments that travel and movement have destroyed "society." There is no social season any more, he says, because nobody is anywhere at the same time—except, of course, nobodies. The good Count has been quoted as saying: "Before this, if you wanted twenty for dinner, you'd have to ask forty—but now you first ask 200."

Despite such inconveniences, the overthrow of the tyranny of geography opens a form of freedom that proves exhilarating to millions. Speed, movement and even relocation carry positive connotations for many. This accounts for the psychological attachment that Americans and Europeans display toward automobiles —the technological incarnation of spatial freedom. Motivational researcher Ernest Dichter has unburdened himself of abundant Freudian nonsense in his time, but he is shrewdly insightful when he suggests that the auto is the "most powerful tool for mastery" available to the ordinary Western man. "The automobile has become the modern symbol of initiation. The license of the sixteen-year-old is a valid admission to adult society."

In the affluent nations, he writes, "most people have enough to eat and are reasonably well housed. Having achieved this thousand-year-old dream of humanity, they now reach out for further satisfactions. They want to travel, discover, be at least physically independent. The automobile is the mobile symbol of mobility . . ." In fact, the last thing that any family wishes to surrender, when hardpressed by financial hardship, is the automobile, and the worst punishment an American parent can mete out to a teen-ager is to "ground" him—i.e., deprive him of the use of an automobile.

Young girls in the United States, when asked what they regard as important about a boy, immediately list a car. Sixty-seven percent of those interviewed in a recent survey said a car is "essential," and a nineteen-year-old boy, Alfred Uranga of Albuquerque, N. M., confirmed gloomily that "If a guy doesn't have a car, he doesn't have a girl." Just how deep this passion for automobility runs among the youth is tragically illustrated by the suicide of a seventeen-year-old Wisconsin boy, William Nebel, who was "grounded" by his father after his driver's license was suspended for speeding. Before putting a .22 caliber rifle bullet in his brain, the boy penned a note that ended, "Without a license, I don't have my car, job or social life. So I think that it is better to end it all right now." It is clear that millions of young people all over the technological world agree with the poet Marinetti who, more than half a century ago, shouted: "A roaring racing car . . . is more beautiful than the Winged Victory."

Freedom from fixed social position is linked so closely with freedom from fixed geographical position, that when super-industrial man feels socially constricted his first impulse is to relocate. This idea seldom occurs to the peasant raised in his village or the coalminer toiling away in the black deeps. "A lot of problems are solved by migration. Go. Travel!" said a student of mine before rushing off to join the Peace Corps. But movement becomes a positive value in its own right, an assertion of freedom, not merely a response to or escape from outside pressures. A survey of 539 subscribers to *Redbook* magazine sought to determine why their addresses had changed in the previous year. Along with such reasons as "family grew too big for old home" or "pleasanter surroundings" fully ten percent checked off "just wanted a change."

An extreme manifestation of this urge to move is found among the female hitch-hikers who are beginning to form a recognizable sociological category of their own. Thus a young Catholic girl in England gives up her job selling advertising space for a magazine and goes off with a friend intending to hitchhike to Turkey. In Hamburg the girls split up. The first girl, Jackie, cruises the Greek Islands, reaches Istanbul, and at length returns to England, where she takes a job with another magazine. She stays only long enough to finance another trip. After that she comes back and works as a waitress, rejecting promotion to hostess on grounds that "I don't expect to be in England very long." At twenty-three Jackie is a confirmed hitchhiker, thumbing her way indefatigably all over Europe with a gas pistol in her rucksack, returning to England for six or eight months, then starting out again. Ruth, twenty-eight, has been living this way for years, her longest stay in any one place having been three years. Hitchhiking as a way of life, she says, is fine because while it is possible to meet people, "you don't get too involved."

Teen-age girls in particular—perhaps eager to escape restrictive home environments—are passionately keen travelers. A survey of girls who read *Seventeen*, for example, showed that 40.2 percent took one or more "major" trips during the summer before the survey. Sixty-nine percent of these trips carried the girl outside her home state, and nine percent took her abroad. But the itch to travel begins long before the teen years. Thus when Beth, the daughter of a New York psychiatrist, learned that a friend of her's had visited Europe, her tearful response was: "I'm nine years old already and I've never been to Europe!"

This positive attitude toward movement is reflected in survey findings that Americans tend to admire travelers. Thus researchers at the University of Michigan have found that respondents frequently term travelers "lucky" or "happy." To travel is to gain status, which explains why so many American travelers keep ragged airline tags on their luggage or attaché cases long after their return from a trip. One wag has suggested that someone set up a business washing and ironing old airline tags for status-conscious travelers.

Moving one's household, on the other hand, is a cause for commiseration rather than congratulations. Everyone makes ritual comments about the hardships of moving. Yet the fact is that those who have moved once are much more likely to move again than those who have never moved. The French sociologist Alain Touraine explains that "having already made one change and being less attached to the community, they are the readier to move again . . ." And a British trade-union official, R. Clark, not long ago told an international manpower conference that mobility might well be a habit formed in student days. He pointed out that those who spent their college years away from home move in less restricted circles than uneducated and more home-bound manual workers. Not only do these college people move more in later life, but he suggested, they pass on to their children attitudes that facilitate mobility. While for many worker families relocation is a dreaded necessity, a consequence of unemployment or other hardships, for the middle and upper classes moving is most often associated with the extension of the good life. For them, traveling is a joy, and moving out usually means moving up.

In short, throughout the nations in transition to super-industrialism, among the people of the future, movement is a way of life, a liberation from the con-strictions of the past, a step into the still more affluent future.

THE MOURNFUL MOVERS

Dramatically different attitudes, however, are evinced by the "immobiles." It is not only the agricultural villager in India or Iran who remains fixed in one place for most or all of his life. The same is true of millions of blue-collar workers, particularly those in backward industries. As technological change roars through the advanced economies, outmoding whole industries and creating new ones almost overnight, millions of unskilled and semiskilled workers find themselves compelled to relocate. The economy de-mands mobility, and most Western governments—no-tably Sweden, Norway, Denmark, and the United States—spend large sums to encourage workers to retrain for new jobs and leave their homes in pursuit of them. For coalminers in Appalachia or textile work-ers in the French provinces, however, this proves to be excruciatingly painful. Even for big-city workers uprooted by urban renewal and relocated quite near to their former homes, the disruption is often agoniz-ing.

"It is quite precise to speak of their reactions," says

Dr. Marc Fried of the Center for Community Studies, Massachusetts General Hospital, "as expressions of _grief_. These are manifest in the feelings of painful loss, the continued longing, the general depressive tone, frequent symptoms of psychological or social or somatic distress . . . the sense of helplessness, the occasional expressions of both direct and displaced anger, and tendencies to idealize the lost place." The responses, he declares, are "strikingly similar to mourning for a lost person."

Sociologist Monique Viot, of the French Ministry of Social Affairs, says: "The French are very attached to their geographical backgrounds. For jobs even thirty or forty kilometers away they are reluctant—extremely reluctant—to move. The unions call such moves 'deportations.'"

Even some educated and affluent movers show signs of distress when they are called upon to relocate. The author Clifton Fadiman, telling of his move from a restful Connecticut town to Los Angeles, reports that he was shortly "felled by a shotgun burst of odd physical and mental ailments . . . In the course of six months my illness got straightened out. The neurologist . . . diagnosed my trouble as 'culture shock' . . ." For relocation of one's home, even under the most favorable circumstances, entails a series of difficult psychological readjustments.

In a famous study of a Canadian suburb they call Crestwood Heights, sociologists J. R. Seeley, R. A. Sim, and E. W. Loosley, state: "The rapidity with which the transition has to be accomplished, and the depth to which change must penetrate the personality are such as to call for the greatest flexibility of behavior and stability of personality. Ideology, speech sometimes, food habits, and preferences in décor must be made over with relative suddonness and in the absence of unmistakable clues as to the behavior to be adopted."

The steps by which people make such adjustments have been mapped out by psychiatrist James S. Tyhurst of the University of British Columbia. "In field studies of individuals following immigration," he says, "a fairly consistent pattern can . . . be defined. Initially, the person is concerned with the immediate present, with an attempt to find work, make money, and find shelter. These features are often accompanied by restlessness and increased psychomotor activity . . ."

As the person's sense of strangeness or incongruity in the new surroundings grows, a second phase, "psychological arrival," takes place. "Characteristic of this are increasing anxiety and depression; increasing self-preoccupation, often with somatic preoccupations and somatic symptoms; general withdrawal from the society in contrast to previous activity; and some degree of hostility and suspicion. The sense of difference and helplessness becomes increasingly intense and the period is characterized by marked discomfort and turmoil. This period of more or less disturbance may last for . . . one to several months."

Only then does the third phase begin. This takes the form of relative adjustment to the new surroundings, a settling in, or else, in extreme cases, "the development of more severe disturbances manifested by more intense disorders of mood, the development of abnormal mental content and breaks with reality." Some people, in short, never do adjust adequately.

THE HOMING INSTINCT

Even when they do, however, they are no longer the same as before, for any relocation, of necessity, destroys a complex web-work of old relationships and establishes a set of new ones. It is this disruption that, especially if repeated more than once, breeds the "loss of commitment" that many writers have noted among the high mobiles. The man on the move is ordinarily in too much of a hurry to put down roots in any one place. Thus an airline executive is quoted as saying he avoids involvement in the political life of his community because "in a few years I won't even be living here. You plant a tree and you never see it grow."

This non-involvement or, at best, limited participation, has been sharply criticized by those who see in it a menace to the traditional ideal of grass-roots democracy. They overlook, however, an important reality: the possibility that those who refuse to involve themselves deeply in community affairs may be showing greater moral responsibility than those who do—and then move away. The movers boost a tax rate—but avoid paying the piper because they are no longer there. They help defeat a school bond issue—and leave the children of others to suffer the consequences. Does it not make more sense, is it not more responsible, to disqualify oneself in advance? Yet if one does withdraw from participation, refusing to join organizations, refusing to establish close ties with neighbors, refusing, in short, to commit oneself, what happens to the community and the self? Can individuals or society survive without commitment?

Commitment takes many forms. One of these is attachment to place. We can understand the significance of mobility only if we first recognize the centrality of fixed place in the psychological architecture of traditional man. This centrality is reflected in our culture in innumerable ways. Indeed, civilization, itself, began with agriculture—which meant settlement, an end, at last, to the dreary treks and migrations of the paleolithic nomad. The very word "rootedness" to which we pay so much attention today is agricultural in origin. The precivilized nomad listening to a discussion of "roots" would scarcely have understood the concept.

The notion of roots is taken to mean a fixed place, a permanently anchored "home." In a harsh, hungry and dangerous world, home, even when no more than a hovel, came to be regarded as the ultimate retreat, rooted in the earth, handed down from generation to generation, one's link with both nature and the past. The immobility of home was taken for granted, and literature overflows with reverent references to the importance of home. "Seek home for rest, For home is best" are lines from *Instructions to Housewifery*, a sixteenth-century manual by Thomas Tusser, and there are dozens of what one might, at the risk of a terrible pun, call "home-ilies" embedded in the culture. "A man's home is his castle . . ." "There's no place like home . . ." "Home, sweet home . . ." The syrupy glorification of home reached, perhaps, a climax in nineteenth-century England at precisely the time that industrialism was uprooting the rural folk and converting them into urban masses. Thomas Hood, the poet of the poor, tells us that "each heart is whispering, Home, Home at last . . ." and Tennyson paints a classically cloying picture of

An English home—gray twilight poured
On dewy pastures, dewy trees,
Softer than sleep—all things in order stored,
A haunt of ancient peace.

In a world churned by the industrial revolution, and in which all things were decidedly *not* "in order stored," home was the anchorage, the fixed point in the storm. If nothing else, at least *it* could be counted upon to stay in one place. Alas, this was poetry, not reality, and it could not hold back the forces that were to tear man loose from fixed location.

THE DEMISE OF GEOGRAPHY

The nomad of the past moved through blizzards and parching heat, always pursued by hunger, but he carried with him his buffalo-hide tent, his family *and* the rest of his tribe. He carried his social setting with him, and, as often as not, the physical structure that he called home. In contrast, the new nomads of today leave the physical structure behind. (It becomes an entry in the tables showing the turnover rate for things in their lives.) And they leave all but their family, the most immediate social setting, behind.

The downgrading of the importance of place, the decline in commitment to it, is expressed in scores of ways. A recent example was the decision of Ivy League colleges in the United States to de-emphasize geographical considerations in their admissions policies. These elite colleges traditionally applied geographical criteria to applicants, deliberately favoring boys from homes located far from their campuses, in the hopes of assembling a highly diversified student body. Between the 1930's and the 1950's, for example, Harvard cut in half the percentage of its students from homes in New England and New York. Today, says an official of the university, "We're pulling back on this geographical distribution thing."

Place, it is now recognized, is no longer a primary source of diversity. Differences between people no longer correlate closely with geographical background. The address on the application form may be purely temporary anyway. Many people no longer stay in one place long enough to acquire distinctive regional or local characteristics. Says the dean of admissions at Yale: "Of course, we still send our recruiting people to out-of-the-way places like Nevada, but there's really as much diversity in taking Harlem, Park Avenue and Queens." According to this official, Yale has virtually dropped geography altogether as a consideration in selection. And his counterpart at Princeton reports: "It is not the place they're from, really, but rather some sense of a different background that we're looking for."

Mobility has stirred the pot so thoroughly that the important differences between people are no longer strongly place related. So far has the decline in commitment to place gone, according to Prof. John Dyckman of the University of Pennsylvania, that "Allegiance to a city or state is even now weaker for many than allegiance to a corporation, a profession, or a voluntary association." Thus it might be said that commitments are shifting from place-related social structures (city, state, nation or neighborhood) to those (corporation, profession, friendship network) that are themselves mobile, fluid, and, for all practical purposes, place-less.

Commitment, however, appears to correlate with duration of relationship. Armed with a culturally conditioned set of durational expectancies, we have all learned to invest with emotional content those relationships that appear to us to be "permanent" or relatively long-lasting, while withholding emotion, as much as possible, from short-term relationships. There are, of course, exceptions; the swift summer romance is one. But, in general, across a broad variety of relationships, the correlation holds. The declining commitment to place is thus related not to mobility per se, but to a concomitant of mobility—the shorter duration of place relationships.

In seventy major United States cities, for example, including New York, average residence in one place is less than four years. Contrast this with the lifelong residence in one place characteristic of the rural villager. Moreover, residential relocation is critical in determining the duration of many other place relationships, so that when an individual terminates his relationship with a home, he usually also terminates his relationship with all kinds of "satellite" places in the neighborhood. He changes his supermarket, gas station, bus stop and barbershop, thus cutting short a series of other place relationships along with the home relationship. Across the board, therefore, we not only experience more places in the course of a lifetime, but, on average, maintain our link with each place for a shorter and shorter interval.

Thus we begin to see more clearly how the accelerative thrust in society affects the individual. For this telescoping of man's relationships with place precisely parallels the truncation of his relationship with things.

In both cases, the individual is forced to make and break his ties more rapidly. In both cases, the level of transience rises. In both cases, he experiences a quickening of the pace of life.

Chapter 6

PEOPLE:
THE MODULAR MAN

Each spring an immense lemming-like migration begins all over the Eastern United States. Singly and in groups, burdened with sleeping bags, blankets and bathing suits, some 15,000 American college students toss aside their texts and follow a highly accurate homing instinct that leads them to the sun-bleached shoreline of Fort Lauderdale, Florida. There, for approximately a week, this teeming, milling mass of sun and sex worshippers swims, sleeps, flirts, guzzles beer, sprawls and brawls in the sands. At the end of this period the bikini-clad girls and their bronzed admirers pack their kits and join in a mass exodus. Anyone near the booth set up by the resort city to welcome this rambunctious army can now hear the loudspeaker booming: "Car with two can take rider as far as Atlanta . . . Need ride to Washington . . . Leaving at 10:00 for Louisville . . ." In a few hours nothing is left of the great "beach-and-booze party" except butts and beer cans in the sand, and about $1.5 million in the cash registers of local merchants —who regard this annual invasion as a tainted blessing that threatens public sanity while it underwrites private profit.

What attracts the young people is more than an irrepressible passion for sunshine. Nor is it mere sex, a commodity available in other places as well. Rather, it is a sense of freedom without responsibility. In the words of a nineteen-year-old New York co-ed who made her way to the festivities recently: "You're not worried about what you do or say here because, frankly, you'll never see these people again."

What the Fort Lauderdale rite supplies is a transient agglomeration of people that makes possible a great diversity of temporary interpersonal relationships. And it is precisely this—temporariness—that increasingly characterizes human relations as we move further toward super-industrialism. For just as things and places flow through our lives at a faster clip, so, too, do people.

THE COST OF "INVOLVEMENT"

Urbanism—the city dweller's way of life—has preoccupied sociology since the turn of the century. Max Weber pointed out the obvious fact that people in cities cannot know all their neighbors as intimately as it was possible for them to do in small communities. Georg Simmel carried this idea one step further when he declared, rather quaintly, that if the urban individual reacted emotionally to each and every person with whom he came into contact, or cluttered his mind with information about them, he would be "completely atomized internally and would fall into an unthinkable mental condition."

Louis Wirth, in turn, noted the fragmented nature of urban relationships. "Characteristically, urbanites meet one another in highly segmental roles . . ." he wrote. "Their dependence upon others is confined to a highly fractionalized aspect of the other's round of activity." Rather than becoming deeply involved with the total personality of every individual we meet, he explained, we necessarily maintain superficial and partial contact with some. We are interested only in the efficiency of the shoe salesman in meeting our needs: we couldn't care less that his wife is an alcoholic.

What this means is that we form limited involvement relationships with most of the people around us. Consciously or not, we define our relationships with most people in functional terms. So long as we do not become involved with the shoe salesman's problems at home, or his more general hopes, dreams and frustrations, he is, for us, fully interchangeable with any other salesman of equal competence. In effect, we have applied the modular principle to human relationships. We have created the disposable person: Modular Man.

Rather than entangling ourselves with the whole man, we plug into a module of his personality. Each personality can be imagined as a unique configuration of thousands of such modules. Thus no whole person is interchangeable with any other. But certain modules are. Since we are seeking only to buy a pair of shoes, and not the friendship, love or hate of the salesman, it is not necessary for us to tap into or engage with all the other modules that form his personality. Our relationship is safely limited. There is limited liability on both sides. The relationship entails certain accepted forms of behavior and communication. Both sides understand, consciously or otherwise, the limitations and laws. Difficulties arise only when one or another party oversteps the tacitly understood limits, when he attempts to connect up with some module not relevant to the function at hand.

Today a vast sociological and psychological literature is devoted to the alienation presumed to flow from this fragmentation of relationships. Much of the rhetoric of existentialism and the student revolt decries this fragmentation. It is said that we are not sufficiently "involved" with our fellow man. Millions of young people go about seeking "total involvement."

Before leaping to the popular conclusion that modularization is all bad, however, it might be well to look more closely at the matter. Theologian Harvey Cox, echoing Simmel, has pointed out that in an urban environment the attempt to "involve" oneself fully with everyone can lead only to self-destruction and emotional emptiness. Urban man, he writes, "must have more or less impersonal relationships with most of the people with whom he comes in contact precisely in order to choose certain friendships to nourish and cultivate . . . His life represents a point touched by dozens of systems and hundreds of people. His capacity to know some of them better necessitates his minimizing the depth of his relationship to many others. Listening to the postman gossip becomes for the urban man an act of sheer graciousness, since he probably has no interest in the people the postman wants to talk about."

Moreover, before lamenting modularization, it is necessary to ask ourselves whether we really would prefer to return to the traditional condition of man in which each individual presumably related to the whole personality of a few people rather than to the personality modules of many. Traditional man has been so sentimentalized, so cloyingly romanticized, that we frequently overlook the consequences of such a return. The very same writers who lament fragmentation also demand freedom—yet overlook the unfreedom of people bound together in totalistic relationships. For any relationship implies mutual demands and expectations. The more intimately involved a relationship, the greater the pressure the parties exert on one another to fulfill these expectations. The tighter and more totalistic the relationship, the more modules, so to speak, are brought into play, and the more numerous are the demands we make.

In a modular relationship, the demands are strictly bounded. So long as the shoe salesman performs his rather limited service for us, thereby fulfilling our rather limited expectations, we do not insist that he believe in our God, or that he be tidy at home, or share our political values, or enjoy the same kind of food or music that we do. We leave him free in all other matters—as he leaves us free to be atheist or Jew, heterosexual or homosexual, John Bircher or Communist. This is not true of the total relationship and cannot be. To a certain point, fragmentation and freedom go together.

All of us seem to need some totalistic relationships in our lives. But to decry the fact that we cannot have *only* such relationships is nonsense. And to prefer a society in which the individual has holistic relationships with a few, *rather than* modular retionships with many, is to wish for a return to the imprisonment of the past—a past when individuals may have been more tightly bound to one another, but when they were also more tightly regimented by social conventions, sexual mores, political and religious restrictions.

This is not to say that modular relationships entail no risks or that this is the best of all possible worlds. There are, in fact, profound risks in the situation, as we shall attempt to show. Until now, however, the entire public and professional discussion of these issues has been badly out of focus. For it has overlooked a critical dimension of all interpersonal relationships: their duration.

THE DURATION OF HUMAN RELATIONSHIPS

Sociologists like Wirth have referred in passing to the transitory nature of human ties in urban society. But they have made no systematic effort to relate the shorter duration of human ties to shorter durations in other kinds of relationships. Nor have they attempted to document the progressive decline in these durations. Until we analyze the temporal character of human bonds, we will completely misunderstand the move toward super-industrialism.

For one thing, the decline in the *average* duration of human relationships is a likely corollary of the increase in the number of such relationships. The average urban individual today probably comes into contact with more people in a week than the feudal villager did in a year, perhaps even a lifetime. The villager's ties with other people no doubt included some transient relationships, but most of the people he knew were the same throughout his life. The urban man may have a core group of people with whom his interactions are sustained over long periods of time, but he also interacts with hundreds, perhaps thousands of people whom he may see only once or twice and who then vanish into anonymity.

All of us approach human relationships, as we approach other kinds of relationships, with a set of built-in durational expectancies. We expect that certain kinds of relationships will endure longer than others. It is, in fact, possible to classify relationships with other people in terms of their expected duration. These vary, of course, from culture to culture and from person to person. Nevertheless, throughout wide sectors of the population of the advanced technological societies something like the following order is typical:

Long-duration relationships. We expect ties with our immediate family, and to a lesser extent with other kin, to extend throughout the lifetimes of the people involved. This expectation is by no means always fulfilled, as rising divorce rates and family break-ups indicate. Nevertheless, we still theoretically marry "until death do us part" and the social ideal is a lifetime relationship. Whether this is a proper or realistic expectation in a society of high transience is debatable. The fact remains, however, that family links are expected to be long term, if not lifelong, and considerable guilt attaches to the person who breaks off such a relationship.

Medium-duration relationships. Four classes of relationships fall within this category. Roughly in order of descending durational expectancies, these are relationships with friends, neighbors, job associates, and co-members of churches, clubs and other voluntary organizations.

Friendships are traditionally supposed to survive almost, if not quite, as long as family ties. The culture places high value on "old friends" and a certain amount of blame attaches to dropping a friendship. One type of friendship relationship, however, acquaintanceship, is recognized as less durable.

Neighbor relationships are no longer regarded as long-term commitments—the rate of geographical turnover is too high. They are expected to last as long as the individual remains in a single location, an interval that is growing shorter and shorter on average. Breaking off with a neighbor may involve other difficulties, but it carries no great burden of guilt.

On-the-job relationships frequently overlap friendships, and less often, neighbor relationships. Traditionally, particularly among white-collar, professional and technical people, job relationships were supposed to last a relatively long time. This expectation, however, is also changing rapidly, as we shall see.

Co-membership relationships—links with people in church or civic organizations, political parties and the like—sometimes flower into friendship, but until that happens such individual associations are regarded as more perishable than either friendships, ties with neighbors or fellow workers.

Short-duration relationships. Most, though not all, service relationships fall into this category. These involve sales clerks, delivery people, gas station attendants, milkmen, barbers, hairdressers, etc. The turnover among these is relatively rapid and little or no shame attaches to the person who terminates such a relationship. Exceptions to the service patterns are professionals such as physicians, lawyers and accountants, with whom relationships are expected to be somewhat more enduring.

This categorization is hardly airtight. Most of us can cite some "service" relationship that has lasted longer than some friendship, job or neighbor relationship. Moreover, most of us can cite a number of quite long-lasting relationships in our own lives— perhaps we have been going to the same doctor for years or have maintained extremely close ties with a college friend. Such cases are hardly unusual, but they are relatively few in number in our lives. They are like long-stemmed flowers towering above a field of grass in which each blade represents a short-term relationship, a transient contact. It is the very durability of these ties that makes them noticeable. Such exceptions do not invalidate the rule. They do not change the key fact that, across the board, the *average* interpersonal relationship in our life is shorter and shorter in duration.

THE HURRY-UP WELCOME

Continuing urbanization is merely one of a number of pressures driving us toward greater "temporariness" in our human relationships. Urbanization, as suggested earlier, brings great masses of people into close proximity, thereby increasing the actual number of contacts made. This process is, however, strongly reinforced by the rising geographical mobility described in the last chapter. Geographical mobility not only speeds up the flow of places through our lives, but the flow of people as well.

The increase in travel brings with it a sharp increase in the number of transient, casual relationships with fellow passengers, with hotel clerks, taxi drivers, airline reservation people, with porters, maids, waiters, with colleagues and friends of friends, with customs officials, travel agents and countless others. The greater the mobility of the individual, the greater the number of brief, face-to-face encounters, human contacts, each one a relationship of sorts, fragmentary and, above all, compressed in time. (Such contacts appear natural and unimportant to us. We seldom stop to consider how few of the sixty-six billion human beings who preceded us on the planet ever experienced this high rate of transience in their human relationships.)

If travel increases the number of contacts—largely with service people of one sort or another—residential relocation also steps up the through-put of people in our lives. Moving leads to the termination of relationships in almost all categories. The young submarine engineer who is transferred from his job in the Navy Yard at Mare Island, California, to the installation at Newport News, Virginia, takes only his most immediate family with him. He leaves behind parents and in-laws, neighbors, service and tradespeople, as well as his associates on the job, and others. He cuts short his ties. In settling down in the new community, he, his wife and child must initiate a whole cluster of new (and once more temporary) relationships.

Here is how one young wife, a veteran of eleven moves in the past seventeen years, describes the process: "When you live in a neighborhood you watch a series of changes take place. One day a new mailman delivers the mail. A few weeks later the girl at the check-out counter at the supermarket disappears and a new one takes her place. Next thing you know, the mechanic at the gas station is replaced. Meanwhile, a neighbor moves out next door and a new family moves in. These changes are taking place all the time, but they are gradual. When you move, you break all these ties at once, and you have to start all over again. You have to find a new pediatrician, a new dentist, a new car mechanic who won't cheat you, and you quit all your organizations and start over again." It is the simultaneous rupture of a whole range of existing relationships that makes relocation psychologically taxing for many.

The more frequently this cycle repeats itself, of course, in the life of the individual, the shorter the duration of the relationships involved. Among significant sectors of the population this process is now occurring so rapidly that it is drastically altering tra-

ditional notions of time with respect to human relationships. "At a cocktail party on Frogtown Road
the other night," reads a story in *The New York
Times*, "the talk got around to how long those at the
party had lived in New Canaan. To nobody's surprise, it developed that the couple of longest residence had been there five years." In slower moving
times and places, five years constituted little more
than a breaking-in period for a family moved to a
new community. It took that long to be "accepted."
Today the breaking-in-period must be highly compressed in time.

Thus we have in many American suburbs a commercial "Welcome Wagon" service that accelerates
the process by introducing newcomers to the chief
stores and agencies in the community. A paid Welcome Wagon employee—usually a middle-aged lady—
visits the newcomers, answers questions about the
community, and leaves behind brochures and, sometimes, inexpensive gift certificates redeemable at local
stores. Since it affects only relationships in the service
category and is, actually, little more than a form of
advertising, the Welcome Wagon's integrative impact
is superficial.

The process of linking up with new neighbors and
friends is, however, often quite effectively accelerated by the presence of certain people—usually divorced or single older women—who play the role of
informal "integrator" in the community. Such people
are found in many established suburbs and housing
developments. Their function has been described by
urban sociologist Robert Gutman of Rutgers University, who notes that while the integrator herself is
frequently isolated from the mainstream of social life
in the community, she derives pleasure from serving
as a "bridge" for newcomers. She takes the initiative
by inviting them to parties and other gatherings. The
newcomers are duly flattered that an "oldtime" resident—in many communities "oldtime" means two
years—is willing to invite them. The newcomers, alas,

quickly learn that the integrator is herself an "outsider" whereupon, more often than not, they promptly disassociate themselves from her.

"Fortunately for the integrator," Gutman says, "by the time he or she managed to introduce the newcomer to the community and the newcomer in turn had gone on to abandon the integrator, there were new arrivals in the settlement to whom the integrator could once again proffer the hand of friendship."

Other people in the community also help speed the process of relationship formation. Thus, in developments, Gutman says, "Respondents reported that the real estate agents introduced them to neighbors before they had taken possession. In some cases, wives were called on by other wives in the neighborhood, sometimes individually and sometimes in groups. Neighboring wives, or husbands, encountered each other casually, while out gardening and cleaning up the yard or in tending children. And, of course, there were the usual meetings brought about by the children, who themselves often were the first to establish contact with the human population of the new environment."

Local organizations also play an important part in helping the individual integrate quickly into the community. This is more likely to be true among suburban homeowners than among housing development residents. Churches, political parties and women's organizations provide many of the human relationships that the newcomers seek. According to Gutman, "Sometimes a neighbor would inform the newcomer about the existence of the voluntary association, and might even take the newcomer to his first meeting; but even in these cases it was up to the migrant himself to find his own primary group within the association."

The knowledge that no move is final, that somewhere along the road the nomads will once more gather up their belongings and migrate, works against the development of relationships that are more than modular, and it means that if relationships are to be struck up at all, they had better be whipped into life quickly.

If, however, the breaking-in period is compressed in time, the leave-taking—the breaking-out—is also telescoped. This is particularly true of service relationships which, being unidimensional, can be both initiated and terminated with dispatch. "They come and they go," says the manager of a suburban food store. "You miss them one day and then you learn they've moved to Dallas." "Washington, D. C., retailers seldom have a chance to build long, enduring relationships with customers," observes a writer in *Business Week*. "Different faces all the time," says a conductor on the New Haven commuter line.

Even babies soon become aware of the transience of human ties. The "nanny" of the past has given way to the baby-sitter service which sends out a different person each time to mind the children. And the same trend toward time-truncated relationships is reflected in the demise of the family doctor. The late lamented family doctor, the general practitioner, did not have the refined narrow expertise of the specialist, but he did, at least, have the advantage of being able to observe the same patient almost from cradle to coffin. Today the patient doesn't stay put. Instead of enjoying a long-term relationship with a single physician, he flits back and forth between a variety of specialists, changing these relationships each time he relocates to a new community. Even within any single relationship, the contacts become shorter and shorter as well. Thus the authors of *Crestwood Heights*, discussing the interaction of experts and laymen, refer to "the short duration of any one exposure to each other . . . The nature of their contact, which is in turn a function of busy, time-pressed lives on both sides, means that any message must be collapsed into a very brief communiqué, and that there must not be too many of these . . ." The impact that this fragmentation and contraction of patient-doctor relationships has on health care ought to be more seriously explored.

FRIENDSHIPS IN THE FUTURE

Each time the family moves, it also tends to slough off a certain number of just plain friends and acquaintances. Left behind, they are eventually all but forgotten. Separation does not end all relationships. We maintain contact with, perhaps, one or two friends from the old location, and we tend to keep in sporadic touch with relatives. But with each move there is a deadly attrition. At first there is an eager flurry of letters back and forth. There may be occasional visits or telephone calls. But gradually these decrease in frequency. Finally, they stop coming. Says a typical English suburbanite after leaving London: "You can't forget it [London]. Not with all your family living there and that. We still got friends living in Plumstead and Eltham. We used to go back every weekend. But you can't keep that up."

John Barth has captured the sense of turnover among friendships in a passage from his novel *The Floating Opera*: "Our friends float past; we become involved with them; they float on, and we must rely on hearsay or lose track of them completely; they float back again, and we must either renew our friendship—catch up to date—or find that they and we don't comprehend each other any more." The only fault in this is its unspoken suggestion that the current upon which friendships bob and float is lazy and meandering. The current today is picking up speed. Friendship increasingly resembles a canoe shooting the rapids of the river of change. "Pretty soon," says Professor Eli Ginzberg of Columbia University, an expert on manpower mobility, "we're all going to be metropolitan-type people in this country without ties or commitments to long time friends and neighbors."

In a brilliant paper on "Friendships in the Future,"

psychologist Courtney Tall suggests that "Stability based on close relationships with a few people will be ineffective, due to the high mobility, wide interest range, and varying capacity for adaptation and change found among the members of a highly automated society . . . Individuals will develop the ability to form close 'buddy-type' relationships on the basis of common interests or sub-group affiliations, and to easily leave these friendships, moving either to another location and joining a similar interest group or to another interest group within the same location . . . Interests will change rapidly . . .

"This ability to form and then to drop, or lower to the level of acquaintanceship, close relationships quickly, coupled with increased mobility, will result in any given individual forming many more friendships than is possible for most in the present . . . Friendship patterns of the majority in the future will provide for many satisfactions, while substituting many close relationships of shorter durability for the few long-term friendships formed in the past."

MONDAY-TO-FRIDAY FRIENDS

One reason to believe that the trend toward temporary relationships will continue is the impact of new technology on occupations. Even if the push toward megalopolis stopped and people froze in their geographical tracks, there would still be a sharp increase in the number, and decrease in the duration of relationships as a consequence of job changes. For the introduction of advanced technology, whether we call it automation or not, is necessarily accompanied by drastic changes in the types of skills and personalities required by the economy.

Specialization increases the number of different occupations. At the same time, technological innovation reduces the life expectancy of any given occupation. "The emergence and decline of occupations will be so rapid," says economist Norman Anon, an expert in manpower problems, "that people will always be uncertain in them." The profession of airline flight engineer, he notes, emerged and then began to die out within a brief period of fifteen years.

A look at the "help wanted" pages of any major newspaper brings home the fact that new occupations are increasing at a mind-dazzling rate. Systems analyst, console operator, coder, tape librarian, tape handler, are only a few of those connected with computer operations. Information retrieval, optical scanning, thin-film technology all require new kinds of expertise, while old occupations lose importance or vanish altogether. When *Fortune* magazine in the mid-1960's surveyed 1,003 young executives employed by major American corporations, it found that fully one out of three held a job that simply had not existed until he stepped into it. Another large group held positions that had been filled by only one incumbent before them. Even when the name of the occupation stays the same, the content of the work is frequently transformed, and the people filling the jobs change.

Job turnover, however, is not merely a direct consequence of technological change. It also reflects the mergers and acquisitions that occur as industries everywhere frantically organize and reorganize themselves to adapt to the fast-changing environment, to keep up with myriad shifts in consumer preferences. Many other complex pressures also combine to stir the occupational mix incessantly. Thus a recent survey by the US Department of Labor revealed that the 71,000,000 persons in the American labor force had held their current jobs an average of 4.2 years. This compared with 4.6 years only three years earlier, a decline in duration of nearly 9 percent.

"Under conditions prevailing at the beginning of the 1960's," states another Labor Department report, "the average twenty-year-old man in the work force could be expected to change jobs about six or seven times." Thus instead of thinking in terms of a "career" the citizen of super-industrial society will think in terms of "serial careers."

Today, for manpower accounting purposes, men are classified according to their present jobs. A worker is a "machine operator" or a "sales clerk" or a "computer programmer." This system, born in a less dynamic period, is no longer adequate, according to many manpower experts. Efforts are now being made to characterize each worker not merely in terms of the present job held, but in terms of the particular "trajectory" that his career has followed. Each man's trajectory or career line will differ, but certain types of trajectories will recur. When asked "What do you *do?*" the super-industrial man will label himself not in terms of his present (transient) job, but in terms of his trajectory type, the overall pattern of his work life. Such labels are more appropriate to the super-industrial job market than the static descriptions used at present, which take no account of what the individual has done in the past, or of what he may be qualified to do in the future.

The high rate of job turnover now evident in the United States is also increasingly characteristic of Western European countries. In England, turnover in manufacturing industries runs an estimated 30 to 40 percent per year. In France about 20 percent of the total labor force is involved in job changes each year, and this figure, according to Monique Viot, is on the rise. In Sweden, according to Olof Gustafsson, director of the Swedish Manufacturing Association, "we count on an average turnover of 25 to 30 percent per year in the labor force . . . Probably the labor turnover in many places now reaches 35 to 40 percent."

Whether or not the statistically measurable rate of job turnover is rising, however, makes little difference, for the measurable changes are only part of the story. The statistics take no account of changes of job within the same company or plant, or shifts from one department to another. A. K. Rice of the Tavistock

Institute in London asserts that "Transfers from one department to another would appear to have the effect of the beginning of a 'new life' within the factory." The overall statistics on job turnover, by failing to take such changes into account, seriously underestimate the amount of shifting around that is actually taking place—each shift bringing with it the termination of old, and the initiation of new, human relationships.

Any change in job entails a certain amount of stress. The individual must strip himself of old habits, old ways of coping, and learn new ways of doing things. Even when the work task itself is similar, the environment in which it takes place is different. And just as is the case with moving to a new community, the newcomer is under pressure to form new relationships at high speed. Here, too, the process is accelerated by people who play the role of informal integrator. Here, too, the individual seeks out human relationships by joining organizations—usually informal and clique-like, rather than part of the company's table of organization. Here, too, the knowledge that no job is truly "permanent" means that the relationships formed are conditional, modular and, by most definitions, temporary.

RECRUITS AND DEFECTORS

In our discussion of geographical mobility we found that some individuals and groups are more mobile than others. With respect to occupational mobility, too, we find that some individuals or groups make more job changes than others. In a very crude sense, it is fair to say that people who are geographically mobile are quite likely to be occupationally mobile as well. Thus we once more find high turnover rates among some of the least affluent, least skilled groups in society. Exposed to the worst shocks and buffetings of an economy that demands educated, increasingly skilled workers, the poor bounce from job to job like a pinball between bumpers. They are the last hired and the first fired.

Throughout the middle range of education and affluence, we find people who, while certainly more mobile than agricultural populations, are nonetheless, relatively stable. And then, just as before, we find inordinately high and rising rates of turnover among those groups most characteristic of the future—the scientists and engineers, the highly educated professionals and technicians, the executives and managers.

Thus a recent study reveals that job turnover rates for scientists and engineers in the research and development industry in the United States are approximately twice as high as for the rest of American industry. The reason is easy to detect. This is precisely the speartip of technological change—the point at which the obsolescence of knowledge is most rapid. At Westinghouse, for example, it is believed that the so-called "half-life" of a graduate engineer is only ten years—meaning that fully one half of what he has learned will be outdated within a decade.

High turnover also characterizes the mass communications industries, especially advertising. A recent survey of 450 American advertising men found that 70 percent had changed their jobs within the last two years. Reflecting the rapid changes in consumer preferences, in art and copy styles, and in product lines, the same musical chairs game is played in England. There the circulation of personnel from one agency to another has occasioned cries of alarm within the industry, and many agencies refuse to list an employee as a regular until he has served for a full year.

But perhaps the most dramatic change has overtaken the ranks of management, once well insulated from the jolts of fate that afflicted the less fortunate. "For the first time in our history," says Dr. Harold Leavitt, professor of industrial administration and psychology, "obsolescence seems to be an imminent problem for management because for the first time, the relative advantage of experience over knowledge seems to be rapidly decreasing." Because it takes longer to train for modern management and the training itself becomes obsolete in a decade or so, as it does with engineers, Leavitt suggests that in the future "we may have to start planning careers that move downward instead of upward through time . . . Perhaps a man should reach his peak of responsibility very early in his career and then expect to be moved downward or outward into simpler, more relaxing, kinds of jobs."

Whether upward, downward or sideways, the future holds more, not less, turnover in jobs. This realization is already reflected in the altered attitudes of those doing the hiring. "I used to be concerned whenever I saw a résumé with several jobs in it," admits an official of the Celanese Corporation. "I would be afraid that the guy was a job-hopper or an opportunist. But I'm not concerned anymore. What I want to know is why he made each move. Even five or six jobs over twenty years could be a plus . . . In fact, if I had two equally qualified men, I'd take the man who moved a couple of times for valid reasons over the man who stayed in the same place. Why? I'd know he's adaptable." The director of executive personnel for International Telephone and Telegraph, Dr. Frank McCabe, says: "The more successful you are in attracting the comers, the higher your potential turnover rate is. The comers are movers."

The rising rate of turnover in the executive job market follows peculiar patterns of its own. Thus *Fortune* magazine reports: "The defection of a key executive starts not only a sequence of job changes in its own right but usually a series of collateral movements. When the boss moves, he is often flooded by requests from his immediate subordinates who want to go along; if he doesn't take them, they immediately begin to put out other feelers." No wonder a Stanford Research Institute report on the work environment of the year 1975 predicts that: "At upper white-collar levels, a great amount of turbulence and churning about is foreseen . . . the managerial work environment will be both unsettled and unsettling."

Behind all this job jockeying lies not merely the engine of technological innovation, but also the new affluence, which opens new opportunities and at the same time raises expectations for psychological self-fulfillment. "The man who came up thirty years ago," says the vice president of industrial relations for Philco, a subsidiary of the Ford Motor Company, "believed in hanging on to any job until he knew where he was going. But men today seem to feel there's another job right down the pike." And, for most, there is.

Not infrequently the new job involves not merely a new employer, a new location, and a new set of work associates, but a whole new way of life. Thus the "serial career" pattern is evidenced by the growing number of people who, once assured of reasonable comfort by the affluent economy, decide to make a full 180-degree turn in their career line at a time of life when others merely look forward to retirement. We learn of a real estate lawyer who leaves his firm to study social science. An advertising agency copy supervisor, after twenty-five years on Madison Avenue, concludes that "The phony glamour became stale and boring. I simply had to get away from it." She becomes a librarian. A sales executive in Long Island and an engineer in Illinois leave their jobs to become manual-training teachers. A top interior decorator goes back to school and takes a job with the poverty program.

RENT-A-PERSON

Each job change implies a step-up of the rate at which people pass through our lives, and as the rate of turnover increases, the duration of relationships declines. This is strikingly manifest in the rise to prominence of temporary help services—the human equivalent of the rental revolution. In the United States today nearly one out of every 100 workers is at some time during the year employed by a so-called "temporary help service" which, in turn, rents him or her out to industry to fill temporary needs.

Today some 500 temporary help agencies provide industry with an estimated 750,000 short-term workers ranging from secretaries and receptionists, to defense engineers. When the Lycoming Division of Avco Corporation needed 150 design engineers for hurry-up government contracts, it obtained them from a number of rental services. Instead of taking months to recruit them, it was able to assemble a complete staff in short order. Temporary employees have been used in political campaigns to man telephones and mimeograph machines. They have been called in for emergency duty in printing plants, hospitals and factories. They have been used in public relations activities. (In Orlando, Florida, temporaries were hired to give away dollar bills at a shopping center in an attempt to win publicity for the center.) More prosaically, tens of thousands of them fill routine office-work assignments to help the regular staff of large companies through peak-load periods. And one rental company, the Arthur Treacher Service System, advertises that it will rent maids, chauffeurs, butlers, cooks, handymen, babysitters, practical nurses, plumbers, electricians and other home service people. "Like Hertz and Avis rent cars" it adds.

The rental of temporary employees for temporary needs is, like the rental of physical objects, spreading all over the industrialized world. Manpower, Incorporated, the largest of the temporary help services, opened its operation in France in 1956. Since then it has doubled in size each year, and there are now some 250 such agencies in France.

Those employed by temporary help services express a variety of reasons for preferring this type of work. Says Hoke Hargett, an electromechanical engineer, "Every job I'm on is a crash job, and when the pressure is immense, I work better." In eight years, he has served in eleven different companies, meeting and then leaving behind hundreds of co-workers. For some skilled personnel organized job-hopping actually provides more job security than is available to supposedly permanent employees in highly volatile industries. In the defense industries sudden cut-backs and layoffs are so common, that the "permanent" employee is likely to find himself thrown on the street without much warning. The temporary help engineer simply moves off to another assignment when his project is completed.

More important for most temporary help workers is the fact that they can call their own turns. They can work very much when and where they wish. And for some it is a conscious way to broaden their circle of social contacts. One young mother, forced to move to a new city when her husband was transferred, found herself lonely during the long hours when her two children were away at school. Signing up with a temporary help service, she has worked eight or nine months a year since then and, by shifting from one company to another, has made contact with a large number of people from among whom she could select a few as friends.

HOW TO LOSE FRIENDS...

Rising rates of occupational turnover and the spread of rentalism into employment relationships will further increase the tempo at which human relationships are formed and forgotten. This speedup, however, affects different groups in society in different ways. Thus, in general, working-class individuals tend to live closer to, and depend more on their relatives than do middle- and upper-class groups. In the words of psychiatrist Leonard Duhl, "Their ties of kinship mean more to them, and with less money available distance is more of a handicap." Working-class people are generally less adept at the business of coping with temporary relationships. They take longer to establish ties and are more reluctant to let them go. Not surprisingly, this is reflected in a greater reluctance to move or change jobs. They go when they have to, but seldom from choice.

In contrast, psychiatrist Duhl points out, "The professional, academic and upper-managerial class [in the United States] is bound by interest ties across wide physical spaces and indeed can be said to have more functional relationships. Mobile individuals, easily duplicable relationships, and ties to interest problems depict this group."

What is involved in increasing the through-put of people in one's life are the abilities not only to make ties but to break them, not only to affiliate but to disaffiliate. Those who seem most capable of this adaptive skill are also among the most richly rewarded in society. Seymour Lipset and Reinhard Bendix in *Social Mobility in Industrial Society* declare that "the socially mobile among business leaders show an unusual capacity to break away from those who are liabilities and form relationships with those who can help them."

They support the findings of sociologist Lloyd Warner who suggests that "The most important component of the personalities of successful corporate managers and owners is that, their deep emotional identifications with their families of birth being dissolved, they no longer are closely intermeshed with the past, and, therefore, are capable of relating themselves easily to the present and future. They are people who have literally and spiritually left home . . . They can relate and disrelate themselves to others easily."

And again, in *Big Business Leaders in America*, a study he conducted with James Abegglen, Warner writes: "Before all, these are men on the move. They

left their homes, and all that this implies. They have
left behind a standard of living, level of income, and
style of life to adopt a way of living entirely different
from that into which they were born. The mobile
man first of all leaves the physical setting of his birth.
This includes the house he lived in, the neighborhood
he knew, and in many cases even the city, state and
region in which he was born.

"This physical departure is only a small part of
the total process of leaving that the mobile man must
undergo. He must leave behind people as well as
places. The friends of earlier years must be left, for
acquaintances of the lower-status past are incompatible with the successful present. Often the church
of his birth is left, along with the clubs and cliques
of his family and of his youth. But most important of
all, and this is the great problem of the man on the
move, he must, to some degree, leave his father,
mother, brothers, and sisters, along with the other
human relationships of his past."

This so, it is not so startling to read in a business
magazine a cooly detached guide for the newly promoted executive and his wife. It advises that he break
with old friends and subordinates gradually, in order
to minimize resentment. He is told to "find logical
excuses for not joining the group at coffee breaks or
lunch." Similarly, "Miss the department bowling or
card sessions, occasionally at first, then more frequently." Invitations to the home of a subordinate
may be accepted, but not reciprocated, except in the
form of an invitation to a whole group of subordinates at once. After a while all such interaction should
cease.

Wives are a special problem, we are informed,
because they "don't understand the protocol of office
organization." The successful man is advised to be
patient with his wife, who may adhere to old relationships longer than he does. But, as one executive
puts it, "a wife can be downright dangerous if she
insists on keeping close friendships with the wives of

her husband's subordinates. Her friendships will rub off on him, color his judgment about the people under him, jeopardize his job." Moreover, one personnel man points out, "When parents drift away from former friends, kids go too."

HOW MANY FRIENDS?

These matter-of-fact instructions on how to dis-relate send a chill down the spine of those raised on the traditional notion that friendships are for the long haul. But before accusing the business world of undue ruthlessness, it is important to recognize that precisely this pattern is employed, often beneath a veil of hypocritical regrets, in other strata of society as well. The professor who is promoted to dean, the military officer, the engineer who becomes a project leader, frequently play the same social game. Moreover, it is predictable that something like this pattern will soon extend far beyond the world of work and formal organization. For if friendship is based on shared interests or aptitudes, friendship relationships are bound to change when interests change—even when distinctions of social class are not involved. And in a society caught in the throes of the most rapid change in history, it would be astonishing if the interests of individuals did not also change kaleidoscopically.

Indeed, much of the social activity of individuals today can be described as search behavior—a relentless process of social discovery in which one seeks out new friends to replace those who are either no longer present or who no longer share the same interests. This turnover impels people, and especially educated people, toward cities and into temporary employment patterns. For the identification of people who share the same interests and aptitudes on the basis of which friendship may blossom is no simple procedure in a society in which specialization grows apace. The increase in specialization is present not merely in professional and work spheres, but even in leisure time pursuits. Seldom has any society offered so wide a range of acceptable and readily available leisure time activities. The greater the diversity available in both work and leisure, the greater the specialization, and the more difficult it is to find just the right friends.

Thus it has been estimated by Professor Sargant Florence in Britain that a minimum population of 1,000,000 is needed to provide a professional worker today with twenty interesting friends. The woman who sought temporary work as a strategy for finding friends was highly intelligent. By increasing the number of different people with whom she was thrown into work contact, she increased the mathematical probability of finding a few who share her interests and aptitudes.

We select our friends out of a very large pool of acquaintanceships. A study by Michael Gurevitch at the Massachusetts Institute of Technology asked a varied group to keep track of all the different people with whom they came in contact in a one hundred-day period. On average, each one listed some 500 names. Social psychologist Stanley Milgram, who has conducted a number of fascinating experiments dealing with communication through acquaintanceship networks, speaks of each American having a pool of acquaintanceships ranging from 500 to 2,500.

Actually, however, most people have far fewer friends than the twenty suggested by Professor Florence, and perhaps his definition was less restrictive than that employed in everyday use. A study of thirty-nine married middle-class couples in Lincoln, Nebraska, asked them to list their friends. The purpose was to determine whether husbands or wives are more influential in selecting friends for the family. The study showed that the average couple listed approximately seven "friendship units"—such a unit being either an individual or a married couple. This suggests that the number of individuals listed as friends by the average couple ranged from seven to fourteen. Of these, a considerable number were non-local, and the fact that wives seemed to list more non-local friends than their husbands suggests that they are less willing than their husbands to slough off a friendship after a move. Men, in short, seem to be more skilled at breaking off relationships than women.

TRAINING CHILDREN FOR TURNOVER

Today, however, training for disaffiliation or disrelating begins early. Indeed, this may well represent one of the major differences between the generations. For school children today are exposed to extremely high rates of turnover in their classrooms. According to the Educational Facilities Laboratories, Incorporated, an off-shoot of the Ford Foundation, "It is not unusual for city schools to have a turnover of more than half their student body in one school year." This phenomenal rate cannot but have some effect on the children.

William Whyte in *The Organization Man* pointed out that the impact of such mobility "is as severe on the teachers as on the children themselves, for the teachers are thereby robbed of a good bit of the feeling of achievement they get from watching the children develop." Today, however, the problem is compounded by the high rate of turnover among teachers too. This is true not only in the United States but elsewhere as well. Thus a report on England asserts: "Today it is not uncommon, even in grammar schools, for a child to be taught one subject by two or three different teachers in the course of one year. With teacher loyalty to the school so low, the loyalty of children cannot be summoned either. If a high proportion of teachers are preparing to move on to a better job, a better district, there will be less care, concern and commitment on their part." We can only speculate about the overall influence of this on the lives of the children.

A recent study of high school students by Harry R. Moore of the University of Denver indicated that the test scores of children who had moved across state or county lines from one to ten times were not substantially different from those of children who had not. But there was a definite tendency for the more nomadic children to avoid participation in the voluntary side of school life—clubs, sports, student government and other extra-curricular activities. It is as though they wished, where possible, to avoid new human ties that might only have to be broken again before long—as if they wished, in short, to slow down the flow-through of people in their lives.

How fast should children—or adults for that matter—be expected to make and break human relationships? Perhaps there is some optimum rate that we exceed at our peril? Nobody knows. However, if to this picture of declining durations we add the factor of diversity—the recognition that each new human relationship requires a different pattern of behavior from us—one thing becomes starkly clear: to be able to make these increasingly numerous and rapid on-off clicks in our interpersonal lives we must be able to operate at a level of adaptability never before asked of human beings.

Combine this with the accelerated through-put of places and things, as well as people, and we begin to glimpse the complexity of the coping behavior that we demand of people today. Certainly, the logical end of the direction in which we are now traveling is a society based on a system of temporary encounters, and a distinctly new morality founded on the belief, so succinctly expressed by the co-ed in Fort Lauderdale, that "frankly, you'll never see these people again." It would be absurd to assume that the future holds nothing more than a straight-line projection of present trends, that we must necessarily reach that ultimate degree of transience in human relations. But it is not absurd to recognize the direction in which we are moving.

Until now most of us have operated on the assumption that temporary relationships are superficial relationships, that only long-enduring ties can flower into real interpersonal involvement. Perhaps this assumption is false. Perhaps it is possible for holistic, non-modular relationships, to flower rapidly in a high transience society. It may prove possible to accelerate the formation of relationships, and to speed up the process of "involvement" as well. In the meantime, however, a haunting question remains:

"Is Fort Lauderdale the future?"

We have so far seen that with respect to all three of the tangible components of situations—people, places and things—the rate of turnover is rising. It is time now to look at those intangibles that are equally important in shaping experience, the information we use and the organizational frameworks within which we live.

Chapter 7

ORGANIZATIONS:
THE COMING AD-HOCRACY

One of the most persistent myths about the future
envisions man as a helpless cog in some vast organizational machine. In this nightmarish projection, each
man is frozen into a narrow, unchanging niche in a
rabbit-warren bureaucracy. The walls of this niche
squeeze the individuality out of him, smash his personality, and compel him, in effect, to conform or
die. Since organizations appear to be growing larger
and more powerful all the time, the future, according to this view, threatens to turn us all into that
most contemptible of creatures, spineless and faceless, the organization man.

It is difficult to overestimate the force with which
this pessimistic prophecy grips the popular mind,
especially among young people. Hammered into their
heads by a stream of movies, plays and books, fed by
a prestigious line of authors from Kafka and Orwell
to Whyte, Marcuse and Ellul, the fear of bureaucracy permeates their thought. In the United States
everyone "knows" that it is just such faceless bureaucrats who invent all-digit telephone numbers, who
send out cards marked "do not fold, spindle or muti-
late," who ruthlessly dehumanize students, and whom
you cannot fight at City Hall. The fear of being swal-

lowed up by this mechanized beast drives executives to orgies of self-examination and students to paroxysms of protest.

What makes the entire subject so emotional is the fact that organization is an inescapable part of all our lives. Like his links with things, places and people, man's organizational relationships are basic situational components. Just as every act in a man's life occurs in some definite geographical place, so does it also occur in an organizational place, a particular location in the invisible geography of human organization.

Thus, if the orthodox social critics are correct in predicting a regimented, super-bureaucratized future, we should already be mounting the barricades, punching random holes in our IBM cards, taking every opportunity to wreck the machinery of organization. If, however, we set our conceptual clichés aside and turn instead to the facts, we discover that bureaucracy, the very system that is supposed to crush us all under its weight, is itself groaning with change.

The kinds of organizations these critics project unthinkingly into the future are precisely those least likely to dominate tomorrow. For we are witnessing not the triumph, but the breakdown of bureaucracy. We are, in fact, witnessing the arrival of a new organizational system that will increasingly challenge, and ultimately supplant bureaucracy. This is the organization of the future. I call it "Ad-hocracy."

Man will encounter plenty of difficulty in adapting to this new style organization. But instead of being trapped in some unchanging, personality-smashing niche, man will find himself liberated, a stranger in a new free-form world of kinetic organizations. In this alien landscape, his position will be constantly changing, fluid, and varied. And his organizational ties, like his ties with things, places and people, will turn over at a frenetic and ever-accelerating rate.

CATHOLICS, CLIQUES AND COFFEE BREAKS

Before we can grasp the meaning of this odd term, Ad-hocracy, we need to recognize that not all organizations are bureaucracies. There are alternative ways of organizing people. Bureaucracy, as Max Weber pointed out, did not become the dominant mode of human organization in the West until the arrival of industrialism.

This is not the place for a detailed description of all the characteristics of bureaucracy, but it is important for us to note three basic facts. First, in this particular system of organization, the individual has traditionally occupied a sharply defined slot in a division of labor. Second, he fit into a vertical hierarchy, a chain of command running from the boss down to the lowliest menial. Third, his organizational relationships, as Weber emphasized, tended toward permanence.

Each individual, therefore, filled a precisely positioned slot, a fixed position in a more or less fixed environment. He knew exactly where his department ended and the next began; the lines between organizations and their sub-structures were anchored firmly in place. In joining an organization, the individual accepted a set of fixed obligations in return for a specified set of rewards. These obligations and rewards remained the same over relatively long spans of time. The individual thus stepped into a comparatively permanent web of relationships—not merely with other people (who also tended to remain in their slots for a long time)—but with the organizational framework, the structure, itself.

Some of these structures are more durable than others. The Catholic Church is a steel frame that has lasted for 2000 years, with some of its internal sub-structures virtually unchanged for centuries at a time. In contrast, the Nazi Party of Germany managed to bathe Europe in blood, yet it existed as a formal organization for less than a quarter of a century.

In turn, just as organizations endure for longer or shorter periods, so, too, does an individual's relationship with any specific organizational structure. Thus man's tie to a particular department, division, political party, regiment, club, or other such unit has a beginning and an end in time. The same is true of his membership in informal organizations—cliques, factions, coffee-break groups and the like. His tie begins when he assumes the obligations of membership by joining or being conscripted into an organization. His tie ends when he quits or is discharged from it—or when the organization, itself, ceases to be.

This is what happens, of course, when an organization disbands formally. It happens when the members simply lose interest and stop coming around. But the organization can "cease to be" in another sense, too. An organization, after all, is nothing more than a collection of human objectives, expectations, and obligations. It is, in other words, a structure of roles filled by humans. And when a reorganization sharply alters this structure by redefining or redistributing these roles, we can say that the old organization has died and a new one has sprung up to take its place. This is true even if it retains the old name and has the same members as before. The rearrangement of roles creates a new structure exactly as the rearrangement of mobile walls in a building converts *it* into a new structure.

A relationship between a person and an organization, therefore, is broken either by his departure from it, or by its dissolution, or by its transformation through reorganization. When the latter—reorganization—happens, the individual, in effect, severs his links with the old, familiar, but now no longer extant structure, and assumes a relationship to the new one that supersedes it.

Today there is mounting evidence that the duration of man's organizational relationships is shrinking, that

…elationships are turning over at a faster and
… rate. And we shall see that several powerful
forces, including this seemingly simple fact, doom
bureaucracy to destruction.

THE ORGANIZATIONAL UPHEAVAL

There was a time when a table of organization—sometimes familiarly known as a "T/O"—showed a neatly
arrayed series of boxes, each indicating an officer and
the organizational sub-units for which he was responsible. Every bureaucracy of any size, whether a corporation, a university or a government agency, had its
own T/O, providing its managers with a detailed map
of the organizational geography. Once drawn, such a
map became a fixed part of the organization's rule
book, remaining in use for years at a time. Today,
organizational lines are changing so frequently that a
three-month-old table is often regarded as an historic
artifact, something like the Dead Sea Scrolls.

Organizations now change their internal shape with
a frequency—and sometime a rashness—that makes
the head swim. Titles change from week to week.
Jobs are transformed. Responsibilities shift. Vast organizational structures are taken apart, bolted together again in new forms, then rearranged again.
Departments and divisions spring up overnight only
to vanish in another, and yet another, reorganization.

In part, this frenzied reshuffling arises from the tide
of mergers and "de-mergers" now sweeping through
industry in the United States and Western Europe.
The late sixties saw a tremendous rolling wave of
acquisitions, the growth of giant conglomerates and
diversified corporate monsters. The seventies may witness an equally powerful wave of divestitures and,
later, reacquisitions, as companies attempt to consoli-
date and digest their new subsidiaries, then trade off
troublesome components. Between 1967 and 1969 the
Questor Corporation (formerly Dunhill International,

Incorporated) bought eight companies and sold off
five. Scores of other corporations have similar stories
to tell. According to management consultant Alan J.
Zakon, "there will be a great deal more spinning off of
pieces." As the consumer marketplace churns and
changes, companies will be forced constantly to reposition themselves in it.

Internal reorganizations almost inevitably follow
such corporate swaps, but they may arise for a variety
of other reasons as well. Within a recent three-year
period fully sixty-six of the 100 largest industrial companies in the United States publicly reported major
organizational shake-ups. Actually, this was only the
visible tip of the proverbial iceberg. Many more reorganizations occur than are ever reported. Most companies try to avoid publicity when overhauling their
organization. Moreover, constant small and partial
reorganizations occur at the departmental or divisional
level or below, and are regarded as too small or unimportant to report.

"My own observation as a consultant," says D. R.
Daniel, an official of McKinsey & Company, a large
management consulting firm, "is that one major re-
structuring every two years is probably a conservative
estimate of the current rate of organizational change
among the largest industrial corporations. Our firm
has conducted over 200 organization studies for domestic corporate clients in the past year, and organization problems are an even larger part of our practice
outside the United States." What's more, he adds,
there are no signs of a leveling off. If anything, the
frequency of organizational upheavals is increasing.

These changes, moreover, are increasingly far-reaching in power and scope. Says Professor L. E. Greiner
of the Harvard Graduate School of Business Administration: "Whereas only a few years ago the target of
organization change was limited to a small work group
or a single department . . . the focus is now converg-
ing on the organization as a whole, reaching out to
include many divisions and levels at once, and even

the top managers themselves." He refers to "revolutionary attempts" to transform organization "at all levels of management."

If the once-fixed table of organization won't hold still in industry, much the same is increasingly true of the great government agencies as well. There is scarcely an important department or ministry in the governments of the technological nations that has not undergone successive organizational change in recent years. In the United States during the forty-year span from 1913 to 1953, despite depression, war and other social upheavals, not a single new cabinet-level department was added to the government. Yet in 1953 Congress created the Department of Health, Education and Welfare. In 1965 it established the Department of Housing and Urban Development. In 1967 it set up the Department of Transportation (thus consolidating activities formerly carried out in thirty different agencies,) and, at about the same time, the President called for a merger of the departments of Labor and Commerce.

Such changes within the structure of government are only the most conspicuous, for organizational tremors are similarly felt in all the agencies down below. Indeed, internal redesign has become a byword in Washington. In 1965 when John Gardner became Secretary of Health, Education and Welfare, a top-to-bottom reorganization shook that department. Agencies, bureaus and offices were realigned at a rate that left veteran employees in a state of mental exhaustion. (During the height of this reshuffling, one official, who happens to be a friend of mine, used to leave a note behind for her husband each morning when she left for work. The note consisted of her telephone number for *that* day. So rapid were the changes that she could not keep a telephone number long enough for it to be listed in the departmental directory.) Mr. Gardner's successors continued tinkering with organization, and by 1969, Robert Finch, after eleven months in office, was pressing for yet another major overhaul, having concluded in the meantime that the department was virtually unmanageable in the form in which he found it.

In *Self-Renewal*, an influential little book written before he entered the government, Gardner asserted that: "The farsighted administrator . . . reorganizes to break down calcified organizational lines. He shifts personnel . . . He redefines jobs to break them out of rigid categories." Elsewhere Gardner referred to the "crises of organization" in government and suggested that, in both the public and private sectors, "Most organizations have a structure that was designed to solve problems that no longer exist." The "self-renewing" organization, he defined as one that constantly changes its structure in response to changing needs.

Gardner's message amounts to a call for permanent revolution in organizational life, and more and more sophisticated managers are recognizing that in a world of accelerating change reorganization is, and must be, an on-going process, rather than a traumatic once-in-a-lifetime affair. This recognition is spreading outside the corporations and government agencies as well. Thus *The New York Times*, on the same day that it reports on proposed mergers in the plastics, plywood and paper industries, describes a major administrative upheaval at the British Broadcasting Corporation, a thorough renovation of the structure of Columbia University, and even a complete reorganization of that most conservative of institutions, the Metropolitan Museum of Art in New York. What is involved in all this activity is not a casual tendency but a historic movement. Organizational change—self-renewal, as Gardner puts it—is a necessary, an unavoidable response to the acceleration of change.

For the individual within these organizations, change creates a wholly new climate and a new set of problems. The turnover of organizational designs means that the individual's relationship to any one structure (with its implied set of obligations and rewards) is truncated, shortened in time. With each change, he must reorient himself. Today the average individual is frequently reassigned, shuffled about from one sub-structure to another. But even if he remains in the same department, he often finds that the department, itself, has been shifted on some fast-changing table of organization, so that his position in the overall maze is no longer the same.

The result is that man's organizational relationships today tend to change at a faster pace than ever before. The average relationship is less permanent, more temporary, than ever before.

THE NEW AD-HOCRACY

The high rate of turnover is most dramatically symbolized by the rapid rise of what executives call "project" or "task-force" management. Here teams are assembled to solve specific short-term problems. Then, exactly like the mobile playgrounds, they are disassembled and their human components reassigned. Sometimes these teams are thrown together to serve only for a few days. Sometimes they are intended to last a few years. But unlike the functional departments or divisions of a traditional bureaucratic organization, which are presumed to be permanent, the project or task-force team is temporary by design.

When Lockheed Aircraft Corporation won a controversial contract to build fifty-eight giant C-5A military air transports, it created a whole new 11,000-man organization specifically for that purpose. To complete the multi-billion-dollar job, Lockheed had to coordinate the work not only of its own people, but of hundreds of subcontracting firms. In all, 6000 companies are involved in producing the more than 120,000 parts needed for each of these enormous airplanes. The Lockheed project organization created for this purpose has its own management and its own complex internal structure.

The first of the C-5A's rolled out of the shop exactly

on schedule in March, 1969, twenty-nine months after award of the contract. The last of the fifty-eight transports was due to be delivered two years later. This meant that the entire imposing organization created for this job had a planned life span of five years. What we see here is nothing less than the creation of a disposable division—the organizational equivalent of paper dresses or throw-away tissues.

Project organization is widespread in the aerospace industries. When a leading manufacturer set out to win a certain large contract from the National Aeronautics and Space Agency, it assembled a team of approximately one hundred people borrowed from various functional divisions of the company. The project team worked for about a year and a half to gather data and analyze the job even before the government formally requested bids. When the time came to prepare a formal bid—a "proposal," as it is known in the industry —the "pre-proposal project team" was dissolved and its members sent back to their functional divisions. A new team was brought into being to write the actual proposal.

Proposal-writing teams often work together for a few weeks. Once the proposal is submitted, however, the proposal team is also disbanded. When the contract is won (if it is), new teams are successively established for development, and, ultimately, production of the goods required. Some individuals may move along with the job, joining each successive project team. Typically, however, people are brought in to work on only one or a few stages of the job.

While this form of organization is widely identified with aerospace companies, it is increasingly employed in more traditional industries as well. It is used when the task to be accomplished is non-routine, when it is, in effect, a one-time proposition.

"In just a few years," says *Business Week*, "the project manager has become commonplace." Indeed, project management has, itself, become recognized as a specialized executive art, and there is a small, but growing band of managers, both in the United States and Europe, who move from project to project, company to company, never settling down to run routine or long-term operations. Books on project and task-force management are beginning to appear. And the United States Air Force Systems Command at Dayton, Ohio, runs a school to train executives for project management.

Task forces and other *ad hoc* groups are now proliferating throughout the government and business bureaucracies, both in the United States and abroad. Transient teams, whose members come together to solve a specific problem and then separate, are particularly characteristic of science and help account for the kinetic quality of the scientific community. Its members are constantly on the move, organizationally, if not geographically.

George Kozmetsky, co-founder of Teledyne, Incorporated, and now dean of the school of business at the University of Texas, distinguishes between "routine" and "non-routine" organizations. The latter grapple most frequently with one-of-a-kind problems. He cites statistics to show that the non-routine sector, in which he brackets government and many of the advanced technology companies, is growing so fast that it will employ 65 percent of the total United States work force by the year 2001. Organizations in this sector are precisely the ones that rely most heavily on transient teams and task forces.

Clearly, there is nothing new about the idea of assembling a group to work toward the solution of a specific problem, then dismantling it when the task is completed. What is new is the frequency with which organizations must resort to such temporary arrangements. The seemingly permanent structures of many large organizations, often *because* they resist change, are now heavily infiltrated with these transient cells.

On the surface, the rise of temporary organization may seem insignificant. Yet this mode of operation plays havoc with the traditional conception of organi-

zation as consisting of more or less permanent structures. Throw-away organizations, *ad hoc* teams or
committees, do not necessarily replace permanent
functional structures, but they change them beyond
recognition, draining them of both people and power.
Today while functional divisions continue to exist,
more and more project teams, task forces and similar
organizational structures spring up in their midst, then
disappear. And people, instead of filling fixed slots in
the functional organization, move back and forth at a
high rate of speed. They often retain their functional
"home base" but are detached repeatedly to serve as
temporary team members.

We shall shortly see that this process, repeated often
enough, alters the loyalties of the people involved;
shakes up lines of authority; and accelerates the rate
at which individuals are forced to adapt to organizational change. For the moment, however, it is important to recognize that the rise of *ad hoc* organization
is a direct effect of the speed-up of change in society
as a whole.

So long as a society is relatively stable and unchanging, the problems it presents to men tend to be
routine and predictable. Organizations in such an
environment can be relatively permanent. But when
change is accelerated, more and more novel first-time
problems arise, and traditional forms of organization
prove inadequate to the new conditions. They can no
longer cope. As long as this is so, says Dr. Donald A.
Schon, president of the Organization for Social and
Technical Innovation, we need to create "self-destroy-
ing organizations . . . lots of autonomous, semi-at-
tached units which can be spun off, destroyed, sold
bye-bye, when the need for them has disappeared."

Traditional functional organization structures, created to meet predictable, non-novel conditions, prove
incapable of responding effectively to radical changes
in the environment. Thus temporary role structures are
created as the whole organization struggles to preserve

itself and keep growing. The process is exactly analogous to the trend toward modularism in architecture. We earlier defined modularism as the attempt to lend greater durability to a whole structure by shortening the life span of its components. This applies to organization as well, and it helps explain the rise of short-lived or throw-away, organization components.

As acceleration continues, organizational redesign becomes a continuing function. According to management consultant Bernard Muller-Thym, the new technology, combined with advanced management techniques, creates a totally new situation. "What is now within our grasp," he says, "is a kind of productive capability that is alive with intelligence, alive with information, so that at its maximum it is completely flexible; one could completely reorganize the plant from hour to hour if one wished to do so." And what is true of the plant is increasingly true of the organization as a whole.

In short, the organizational geography of super-industrial society can be expected to become increasingly kinetic, filled with turbulence and change. The more rapidly the environment changes, the shorter the life span of organization forms. In administrative structure, just as in architectural structure, we are moving from long-enduring to temporary forms, from permanence to transience. We are moving from bureaucracy to Ad-hocracy.

In this way, the accelerative thrust translates itself into organization. Permanence, one of the identifying characteristics of bureaucracy, is undermined, and we are driven to a relentless conclusion: man's ties with the invisible geography of organization turn over more and more rapidly, exactly as do his relationships with things, places, and the human beings who people these ever-changing organizational structures. Just as the new nomads migrate from place to place, man increasingly migrates from organizational structure to organizational structure.

THE COLLAPSE OF HIERARCHY

Something else is happening, too: a revolutionary shift in power relationships. Not only are large organizations forced both to change their internal structure and to create temporary units, but they are also finding it increasingly difficult to maintain their traditional chains-of-command.

It would be pollyannish to suggest that workers in industry or government today truly "participate" in the management of their enterprises—either in capitalist or, for that matter, in socialist and communist countries. Yet there is evidence that bureaucratic hierarchies, separating those who "make decisions" from those who merely carry them out, are being altered, side-stepped or broken.

This process is noticeable in industry where, according to Professor William H. Read of the Graduate School of Business at McGill University, "irresistible pressures" are battering hierarchical arrangements. "The central, crucial and important business of organizations," he declares, "is increasingly shifting from up and down to 'sideways.'" What is involved in such a shift is a virtual revolution in organizational structure—and human relations. For people communicating "sideways"—i.e., to others at approximately the same level of organization—behave differently, operate under very different pressures, than those who must communicate up and down a hierarchy.

To illustrate, let us look at a typical work setting in which a traditional bureaucratic hierarchy operates. While still a young man I worked for a couple of years as a millwright's helper in a foundry. Here, in a great dark cavern of a building, thousands of men labored to produce automobile crankcase castings. The scene was Dantesque—smoke and soot smeared our faces, black dirt covered the floors and filled the air, the pungent, choking smell of sulphur and burnt sand

seared our nostrils. Overhead a creaking conveyor
carried red hot castings and dripped hot sand on the
men below. There were flashes of molten iron, the
yellow flares of fires, and a lunatic cacophony of
noises: men shouting, chains rattling, pug mills hammering, compressed air shrieking.

To a stranger the scene appeared chaotic. But those
inside knew that everything was carefully organized.
Bureaucratic order prevailed. Men did the same job
over and over again. Rules governed every situation.
And each man knew exactly where he stood in a
vertical hierarchy that reached from the lowest-paid
core paster up to the unseen "they" who populated
the executive suites in another building.

In the immense shed where we worked, something
was always going wrong. A bearing would burn out, a
belt snap or a gear break. Whenever this happened
in a section, work would screech to a halt, and frantic
messages would begin to flow up and down the hierarchy. The worker nearest the breakdown would notify his foreman. He, in turn, would tell the production
supervisor. The production supervisor would send
word to the maintenance supervisor. The maintenance
supervisor would dispatch a crew to repair the damage.

Information in this system is passed by the worker
"upward" through the foreman to the production
supervisor. The production supervisor carries it "sideways" to a man occupying a niche at approximately
the same level in the hierarchy (the maintenance
supervisor), who, in turn, passes it "downward" to the
millwrights who actually get things going again. The
information thus must move a total of four steps up
and down the vertical ladder plus one stop sideways
before repairs can begin.

This system is premised on the unspoken assumption
that the dirty, sweaty men down below cannot make
sound decisions. Only those higher in the hierarchy are
to be trusted with judgment or discretion. Officials at
the top make the decisions; men at the bottom carry

them out. One group represents the brains of the organization; the other, the hands.

This typically bureaucratic arrangement is ideally suited to solving routine problems at a moderate pace. But when things speed up, or the problems cease to be routine, chaos often breaks loose. It is easy to see why.

First, the acceleration of the pace of life (and especially the speed-up of production brought about by automation) means that every minute of "down time" costs more in lost output than ever before. Delay is increasingly costly. Information must flow faster than ever before. At the same time, rapid change, by increasing the number of novel, unexpected problems, increases the amount of information needed. It takes more information to cope with a novel problem than one we have solved a dozen or a hundred times before. It is this combined demand for *more* information at *faster* speeds that is now undermining the great vertical hierarchies so typical of bureaucracy.

A radical speed-up could have been effected in the foundry described above simply by allowing the worker to report the breakdown directly to the maintenance supervisor or even to a maintenance crew, instead of passing the news along through his foreman and production supervisor. At least one and perhaps two steps could have been cut from the four-step communication process in this way—a saving of from 25 to 50 percent. Significantly, the steps that might be eliminated are the up-and-down steps, the vertical ones.

Today such savings are feverishly sought by managers fighting to keep up with change. Shortcuts that by-pass the hierarchy are increasingly employed in thousands of factories, offices, laboratories, even in the military. The cumulative result of such small changes is a massive shift from vertical to lateral communication systems. The intended result is speedier communication. This leveling process, however, represents a major blow to the once-sacred bureaucratic hierarchy, and it punches a jagged hole in the "brain and hand" analogy. For as the vertical chain of command is increasingly by-passed, we find "hands" beginning to make decisions, too. When the worker by-passes his foreman or supervisor and calls in a repair team, he makes a decision that in the past was reserved for these "higher ups."

This silent but significant deterioration of hierarchy, now occurring in the executive suite as well as at the ground level of the factory floor, is intensified by the arrival on the scene of hordes of experts—specialists in vital fields so narrow that often the men on top have difficulty understanding them. Increasingly, managers have to rely on the judgment of these experts. Solid state physicists, computer programmers, systems designers, operation researchers, engineering specialists—such men are assuming a new decision-making function. At one time, they merely consulted with executives who reserved unto themselves the right to make managerial decisions. Today, the managers are losing their monopoly on decision-making.

More and more, says Professor Read of McGill, the "specialists do not fit neatly together into a chain-of-command system" and "cannot wait for their expert advice to be approved at a higher level." With no time for decisions to wend their leisurely way up and down the hierarchy, "advisors" stop merely advising and begin to make decisions themselves. Often they do this in direct consultation with the workers and ground-level technicians.

As a result, says Frank Metzger, director of personnel planning for International Telephone and Telegraph Corporation, "You no longer have the strict allegiance to hierarchy. You may have five or six different levels of the hierarchy represented in one meeting. You try to forget about salary level and hierarchy, and organize to get the job done."

Such facts, according to Professor Read, "represent a staggering change in thinking, action, and decision-making in organizations." Quite possibly, he declares, "the only truly effective methods for preventing, or coping with, problems of coordination and communication in our changing technology will be found in new arrangements of people and tasks, in arrangements which sharply break with the bureaucratic tradition."

It will be a long time before the last bureaucratic hierarchy is obliterated. For bureaucracies are well suited to tasks that require masses of moderately educated men to perform routine operations, and, no doubt, some such operations will continue to be performed by men in the future. Yet it is precisely such tasks that the computer and automated equipment do far better than men. It is clear that in super-industrial society many such tasks will be performed by great self-regulating systems of machines, doing away with the need for bureaucratic organization. Far from fastening the grip of bureaucracy on civilization more tightly than before, automation leads to its overthrow.

As machines take over routine tasks and the accelerative thrust increases the amount of novelty in the environment, more and more of the energy of society (and its organizations) must turn toward the solution of non-routine problems. This requires a degree of imagination and creativity that bureaucracy, with its man-in-a-slot organization, its permanent structures, and its hierarchies, is not well equipped to provide. Thus it is not surprising to find that wherever organizations today are caught up in the stream of technological or social change, wherever research and development is important, wherever men must cope with first-time problems, the decline of bureaucratic forms is most pronounced. In these frontier organizations a new system of human relations is springing up.

To live, organizations must cast off those bureaucratic practices that immobilize them, making them less sensitive and less rapidly responsive to change. The result, according to Joseph A. Raffaele, Professor of Economics at Drexel Institute of Technology, is that we are moving toward a "working society of technical co-equals" in which the "line of demarcation between the leader and the led has become fuzzy."

Super-industrial Man, rather than occupying a permanent, cleanly-defined slot and performing mindless routine tasks in response to orders from above, finds increasingly that he must assume decision-making responsibility—and must do so within a kaleidoscopically changing organization structure built upon highly transient human relationships. Whatever else might be said, this is *not* the old, familiar Weberian bureaucracy at which so many of our novelists and social critics are still, belatedly, hurling their rusty javelins.

BEYOND BUREAUCRACY

If it was Max Weber who first defined bureaucracy and predicted its triumph, Warren Bennis may go down in sociological textbooks as the man who first convincingly predicted its demise and sketched the outlines of the organizations that are springing up to replace it. At precisely the moment when the outcry against bureaucracy was reaching its peak of shrillness on American campuses and elsewhere, Bennis, a social psychologist and professor of industrial management, predicted flatly that "in the next twenty-five to fifty years" we will all "participate in the end of bureaucracy." He urged us to begin looking "beyond bureaucracy."

Thus Bennis argues that "while various proponents of 'good human relations' have been fighting bureaucracy on humanistic grounds and for Christian values, bureaucracy seems most likely to founder on its inability to adapt to rapid change . . .

"Bureaucracy," he says, "thrives in a highly competitive undifferentiated and stable environment, such as the climate of its youth, the Industrial Revolution. A pyramidal structure of authority, with power concentrated in the hands of a few . . . was, and is, an eminently suitable social arrangement for routinized tasks. However, the environment has changed in just those ways which make the mechanism most problematic. Stability has vanished."

Each age produces a form of organization appropriate to its own tempo. During the long epoch of agricultural civilization, societies were marked by low transience. Delays in communication and transportation slowed the rate at which information moved. The pace of individual life was comparatively slow. And organizations were seldom called upon to make what we would regard as high-speed decisions.

The age of industrialism brought a quickened tempo to both individual and organizational life. Indeed, it was precisely for this reason that bureaucratic forms were needed. For all that they seem lumbering and inefficient to us, they were, on the average, capable of making better decisions faster than the loose and ramshackle organizations that preceded them. With all the rules codified, with a set of fixed principles indicating how to deal with various work problems, the flow of decisions could be accelerated to keep up with the faster pace of life brought by industrialism.

Weber was keen enough to notice this, and he pointed out that "The extraordinary increase in the speed by which public announcements, as well as economic and political facts are transmitted exerts a steady and sharp pressure in the direction of speeding up the tempo of administrative reaction . . ." He was mistaken, however, when he said "The optimum of such reaction time is normally attained only by a strictly bureaucratic organization." For it is now clear that the acceleration of change has reached so rapid a pace that even bureaucracy can no longer keep up. Information surges through society so rapidly, drastic changes in technology come so quickly that newer, even more instantly responsive forms of organization must characterize the future.

What, then, will be the characteristics of the organizations of super-industrial society? "The key word," says Bennis, "will be 'temporary'; there will be adap-

tive, rapidly changing *temporary systems.*" Problems
will be solved by task forces composed of "relative
strangers who represent a set of diverse professional
skills."

Executives and managers in this system will function as coordinators between the various transient
work teams. They will be skilled in understanding the
jargon of different groups of specialists, and they will
communicate across groups, translating and inter-
preting the language of one into the language of
another. People in this system will, according to
Bennis, "be differentiated not vertically, according to
rank and role, but flexibly and functionally, according to skill and professional training."

Because of the high rate of movement back and
forth from one transient team to another, he continues, "There will . . . be a reduced commitment to
work groups . . . While skills in human interaction
will become more important, due to the growing needs
for collaboration in complex tasks, there will be a
concomitant reduction in group cohesiveness . . .
People will have to learn to develop quick and intense
relationships on the job, and learn to bear the loss of
more enduring work relationships."

This then is a picture of the coming Ad-hocracy, the
fast-moving, information-rich, kinetic organization of
the future, filled with transient cells and extremely
mobile individuals. From this sketch, moreover, it is
possible to deduce some of the characteristics of the
human beings who will populate these new organizations—and who, to some extent, are already to be
found in the prototype organizations of today. What
emerges is dramatically different from the stereotype
of the organization man. For just as the acceleration
of change and increased novelty in the environment
demand a new form of organization, they demand,
too, a new kind of man.

Three of the outstanding characteristics of bureaucracy were, as we have seen, permanence, hierarchy,

and a division of labor. These characteristics molded the human beings who manned the organizations.

Permanence—the recognition that the link between man and organization would endure through time—brought with it a commitment to the organization. The longer the man stayed within its embrace, the more he saw his past as an investment in the organization, the more he saw his personal future as dependent upon that of the organization. Longevity bred loyalty. In work organizations, this natural tendency was powerfully reinforced by the knowledge that termination of one's links with the organization very often meant a loss of the means of economic survival. In a world wracked by scarcity for the many, a job was precious. The bureaucrat was thus immobile and deeply oriented toward economic security. To keep his job, he willingly subordinated his own interests and convictions to those of the organization.

Power-laden hierarchies, through which authority flowed, wielded the whip by which the individual was held in line. Knowing that his relationship with the organization would be relatively permanent (or at least hoping that it would be) the organization man looked within for approval. Rewards and punishments came down the hierarchy to the individual, so that the individual, habitually looking upward at the next rung of the hierarchical ladder, became conditioned to subservience. Thus: the wishy-washy organization man—the man without personal convictions (or without the courage to make them evident). It paid to conform.

Finally, the organization man needed to understand his place in the scheme of things; he occupied a well-defined niche, performed actions that were also well-defined by the rules of the organization, and he was judged by the precision with which he followed the book. Faced by relatively routine problems, he was encouraged to seek routine answers. Unorthodoxy, creativity, venturesomeness were discouraged, for they interfered with the predictability required by the organization of its component parts.

The embryonic Ad-hocracies of today demand a radically different constellation of human characteristics. In place of permanence, we find transience—high mobility between organizations, never-ending reorganizations within them, and a constant generation and decay of temporary work groupings. Not surprisingly, we witness a decline in old-fashioned "loyalty" to the organization and its sub-structures.

Writing about young executives in American industry today, Walter Guzzardi, Jr., declares: "The agreements between modern man and modern organization are not like the laws of the Medes and the Persians. They were not made to stand forever . . . The man periodically examines his own attitude toward the organization, and gauges its attitude toward him. If he doesn't like what he sees, he tries to change it. If he can't change it, he moves." Says executive recruiter George Peck: "The number of top executives with their résumés in their desk drawer is amazing."

The old loyalty felt by the organization man appears to be going up in smoke. In its place we are watching the rise of professional loyalty. In all of the techno-societies there is a relentless increase in the number of professional, technical and other specialists. In the United States between 1950 and 1969 alone, their number has more than doubled and this class continues to grow more rapidly than any other group in the work force. Instead of operating as individual, entrepreneurial free lancers, millions of engineers, scientists, psychologists, accountants and other professionals have entered the ranks of organization. What has happened as a result is a neat dialectical reversal. Veblen wrote about the industrialization of the professional. Today we are observing the professionalization of industry.

Thus John Gardner declares: "The loyalty of the professional man is to his profession and not to the organization that may house him at any given moment.

Compare the chemist or electronics engineer in a local plant with the non-professional executives in the same plant. The men the chemist thinks of as his colleagues are not those who occupy neighboring offices, but his fellow professionals wherever they may be throughout the country, even throughout the world. Because of his fraternal ties with widely dispersed contemporaries, he himself is highly mobile. But even if he stays in one place his loyalty to the local organization is rarely of the same quality as that of the true organization man. He never quite believes in it.

"The rise of the professions means that modern large-scale organization has been heavily infiltrated by men who have an entirely different concept of what organization is about . . ." In effect, these men are "outsiders" working within the system.

At the same time, the term "profession" is itself taking on new meaning. Just as the vertical hierarchies of bureaucracy break down under the combined impact of new technology, new knowledge, and social change, so too, do the horizontal hierarchies that have until now divided human knowledge. The old boundaries between specialties are collapsing. Men increasingly find that the novel problems thrust at them can be solved only by reaching beyond narrow disciplines.

The traditional bureaucrat put electrical engineers in one compartment and psychologists in another. Indeed, engineers and psychologists in their own professional organizations assumed an airtight distinction between their spheres of knowledge and competence. Today, however, in the aerospace industry, in education, and in other fields, engineers and psychologists are frequently thrown together in transient teams. New organizations reflecting these sometimes exotic intellectual mergers are springing up all around the basic professions, so that we begin to find sub-groupings of bio-mathematicians, psycho-pharmacologists, engineer-librarians and computer-musicians. Distinctions between the disciplines do not disappear; but they become finer, more porous, and there is a constant reshuffling process.

In this situation, even professional loyalties turn into short-term commitments, and the work itself, the task to be done, the problem to be solved, begins to elicit the kind of commitment hitherto reserved for the organization. Professional specialists, according to Bennis, "seemingly derive their rewards from inward standards of excellence, from their professional societies, and from the intrinsic satisfaction of their task. In fact, they are committed to the task, not the job; to their standards, not their boss. And because they have degrees, they travel. They are not good 'company men'; they are uncommitted except to the challenging environments where they can 'play with problems.'"

These men of the future already man some of the Ad-hocracies that exist today. There is excitement and creativity in the computer industry, in educational technology, in the application of systems techniques to urban problems, in the new oceanography industry, in government agencies concerned with environmental health, and elsewhere. In each of these fields, more representative of the future than the past, there is a new venturesome spirit which stands in total contrast to the security-minded orthodoxy and conformity associated with the organization man.

The new spirit in these transient organizations is closer to that of the entrepreneur than the organization man. The free-swinging entrepreneur who started up vast enterprises unafraid of defeat or adverse opinion, is a folk hero of industrialism, particularly in the United States. Pareto labeled the entrepreneurs "adventurous souls, hungry for novelty . . . not at all alarmed at change."

It is conventional wisdom to assert that the age of the entrepreneur is dead, and that in his place there now stand only organization men or bureaucrats. Yet what is happening today is a resurgence of entrepreneurialism within the heart of large organizations. The secret behind this reversal is the new transience and the death of economic insecurity for large masses of educated men. With the rise of affluence has come a new willingness to take risks. Men are willing to risk failure because they cannot believe they will ever starve. Thus says Charles Elwell, director of industrial relations for Hunt Foods: "Executives look at themselves as individual entrepreneurs who are selling their knowledge and skills." Indeed, as Max Ways has pointed out in *Fortune:* "The professional man in management has a powerful base of independence—perhaps a firmer base than the small businessman ever had in his property rights."

Thus we find the emergence of a new kind of organization man—a man who, despite his many affiliations, remains basically uncommitted to any organization. He is willing to employ his skills and creative energies to solve problems with equipment provided by the organization, and within temporary groups established by it. But he does so only so long as the problems interest *him*. He is committed to his own career, his own self-fulfillment.

It is no accident, in light of the above, that the term "associate" seems suddenly to have become extremely popular in large organizations. We now have "associate marketing directors" and "research associates," and even government agencies are filled with "associate directors" and "associate administrators." The word associate implies co-equal, rather than subordinate, and its spreading use accurately reflects the shift from vertical and hierarchical arrangements to the new, more lateral, communication patterns.

Where the organization man was subservient to the organization, Associative Man is almost insouciant toward it. Where the organization man was immobilized by concern for economic security, Associative Man increasingly takes it for granted. Where the organization man was fearful of risk, Associative Man welcomes it (knowing that in an affluent and fast-changing society even failure is transient). Where the

organization man was hierarchy-conscious, seeking
status and prestige within the organization, Associative Man seeks it without. Where the organization man
filled a predetermined slot, Associative Man moves
from slot to slot in a complex pattern that is largely
self-motivated. Where the organization man dedicated
himself to the solution of routine problems according
to well-defined rules, avoiding any show of unorthodoxy or creativity, Associative Man, faced by novel
problems, is encouraged to innovate. Where the organization man had to subordinate his own individuality
to "play ball on the team," Associative Man recognizes
that the team, itself, is transient. He may subordinate
his individuality for a while, under conditions of his
own choosing; but it is never a permanent submer-
gence.

In all this, Associative Man bears with him a secret
knowledge: the very temporariness of his relationships with organization frees him from many of the
bonds that constricted his predecessor. Transience, in
this sense, is liberating.

Yet there is another side of the coin, and he knows
this, as well. For the turnover of relationships with
formal organizational structures brings with it an
increased turnover of informal organization and a
faster through-put of people as well. Each change
brings with it a need for new learning. He must learn
the rules of the game. But the rules keep changing.
The introduction of Ad-hocracy increases the adaptability of organizations; but it strains the adaptability
of men. Thus Tom Burns, after a study of the British
electronics industry, finds a disturbing contrast between managers in stable organizational structures
and those who find themselves where change is most
rapid. Frequent adaptation, he reports, "happened at
the cost of personal satisfaction and adjustment. The
difference in the personal tension of people in the top
management positions and those of the same age who
had reached a similar position in a more stable situation was marked." And Bennis declares: "Coping with

rapid change, living in the temporary work systems, setting up (in quick-step time) meaningful relations —and then breaking them—all augur social strains and psychological tensions."

It is possible that for many people, in their organizational relationships as in other spheres, the future is arriving too soon. For the individual, the move toward Ad-hocracy means a sharp acceleration in the turnover of organizational relationships in his life. Thus another piece falls into place in our study of high-transience society. It becomes clear that acceleration telescopes our ties with organization in much the same way that it truncates our relationships with things, places and people. The increased turnover of all these relationships places a heavy adaptive burden on individuals reared and educated for life in a slower-paced social system.

It is here that the danger of future shock lies. This danger, as we shall now see, is intensified by the impact of the accelerative thrust in the realm of information.

Chapter 8

INFORMATION:
THE KINETIC IMAGE

In a society in which instant food, instant education and even instant cities are everyday phenomena, no product is more swiftly fabricated or more ruthlessly destroyed than the instant celebrity. Nations advancing toward super-industrialism sharply step up their output of these "psycho-economic" products. Instant celebrities burst upon the consciousness of millions like an image-bomb—which is exactly what they are.

Within less than one year from the time a Cockney girl-child nicknamed "Twiggy" took her first modelling job, millions of human beings around the globe stored mental images of her in their brain. A dewy-eyed blonde with minimal mammaries and pipestem legs, Twiggy exploded into celebrityhood in 1967. Her winsome face and malnourished figure suddenly appeared on the covers of magazines in Britain, America, France, Italy and other countries. Overnight, Twiggy eyelashes, mannikins, perfumes and clothes began to gush from the fad mills. Critics pontificated about her social significance. Newsmen accorded her the kind of coverage normally reserved for a peace treaty or a papal election.

By now, however, our stored mental images of Twiggy have been largely erased. She has all but vanished from public view. Reality has confirmed her own shrewd estimate that "I may not be around here for another six months." For images, too, have become increasingly transient—and not only the images of models, athletes or entertainers. Not long ago I asked a highly intelligent teenager whether she and her classmates had any heroes. I said, "Do you regard John Glenn, for example, as a hero?" (Glenn being, lest the reader has forgotten, the first American astronaut to orbit in space.) The child's response was revealing. "No," she said, "he's too old."

At first I thought she regarded a man in his forties as being too old to be a hero. Soon I realized this was mistaken. What she meant was that Glenn's exploits had taken place too long ago to be of interest. (John H. Glenn's history-making flight occurred in February, 1962.) Today Glenn has receded from the foreground of public attention. In effect, his image has decayed.

Twiggy, the Beatles, John Glenn, Billie Sol Estes, Bob Dylan, Jack Ruby, Norman Mailer, Eichmann, Jean-Paul Sartre, Georgi Malenkov, Jacqueline Kennedy—thousands of "personalities" parade across the stage of contemporary history. Real people, magnified and projected by the mass media, they are stored as images in the minds of millions of people who have never met them, never spoken to them, never seen them "in person." They take on a reality almost as (and sometimes even more) intense than that of many people with whom we do have "in-person" relationships.

We form relationships with these "vicarious people," just as we do with friends, neighbors and colleagues. And just as the through-put of real, in-person people in our lives is increasing, and the duration of our average relationship with them decreasing, the same is true of our ties with the vicarious people who populate our minds.

Their rate of flow-through is influenced by the real rate of change in the world. Thus, in politics, for example, we find that the British prime ministership has been turning over since 1922 at a rate some 13 percent faster than in the base period 1721–1922. In sports, the heavyweight boxing championship now changes hands twice as fast as it did during our father's youth.* Events, moving faster, constantly throw new personalities into the charmed circle of celebrity-hood, and old images in the mind decay to make way for the new.

The same might be said for the fictional characters spewed out from the pages of books, from television screens, theaters, movies and magazines. No previous generation in history has had so many fictional characters flung at it. Commenting on the mass media, historian Marshall Fishwick wryly declares: "We may not even get used to Super-Hero, Captain Nice and Mr. Terrific before they fly off our television screens forever."

These vicarious people, both live and fictional, play a significant role in our lives, providing models for behavior, acting out for us various roles and situations from which we draw conclusions about our own lives. We deduce lessons from their activities, consciously or not. We learn from their triumphs and tribulations. They make it possible for us to "try on" various roles or life styles without suffering the consequences that might attend such experiments in real life. The accelerated flow-through of vicarious people cannot but contribute to the instability of personality patterns among many real people who have difficulty in finding a suitable life style.

These vicarious people, however, are not independent of one another. They perform their roles in a vast, complexly organized "public drama" which is, in the words of sociologist Orrin Klapp, author of a

---

* Between 1882 and 1932, there were ten new world heavy-weight boxing champions, each holding the crown an average of 5 years. Between 1932 and 1951, there were 7 champions, each with an average tenure of 3.2 years. From 1951 to 1967, when the World Boxing Association declared the title vacant, 7 men held the championship for an average of 2.3 years each.

fascinating book called *Symbolic Leaders*, largely a product of the new communications technology. This public drama, in which celebrities upstage and replace celebrities at an accelerating rate, has the effect, according to Klapp, of making leadership "more unstable than it would be otherwise. Contretemps, upsets, follies, contests, scandals, make a feast of entertainment or a spinning political roulette wheel. Fads come and go at a dizzying pace . . . A country like the United States has an open public drama, in which new faces appear daily, there is always a contest to steal the show, and almost anything can happen and often does." What we are observing, says Klapp, is a "rapid turnover of symbolic leaders."

This can be extended, however, into a far more powerful statement: what is happening is not merely a turnover of real people or even fictional characters, but a more rapid turnover of the images and image-structures in our brains. Our relationships with these images of reality, upon which we base our behavior, are growing, on average, more and more transient. The entire knowledge system in society is undergoing violent upheaval. The very concepts and codes in terms of which we think are turning over at a furious and accelerating pace. We are increasing the rate at which we must form and forget our images of reality.

TWIGGY AND THE K-MESONS

Every person carries within his head a mental model of the world—a subjective representation of external reality. This model consists of tens upon tens of thousands of images. These may be as simple as a mental picture of clouds scudding across the sky. Or they may be abstract inferences about the way things are organized in society. We may think of this mental model as a fantastic internal warehouse, an image emporium in which we store our inner portraits of Twiggy, Charles De Gaulle or Cassius Clay, along with such sweeping propositions as "Man is basically good" or "God is dead."

Any person's mental model will contain some images that approximate reality closely, along with others that are distorted or inaccurate. But for the person to function, even to survive, the model must bear some overall resemblance to reality. As V. Gordon Childe has written in *Society and Knowledge*, "Every reproduction of the external world, constructed and used as a guide to action by an historical society, must in some degree correspond to that reality. Otherwise the society could not have maintained itself; its members, if acting in accordance with totally untrue propositions, would not have succeeded in making even the simplest tools and in securing therewith food and shelter from the external world."

No man's model of reality is a purely personal product. While some of his images are based on first-hand observation, an increasing proportion of them today are based on messages beamed to us by the mass media and the people around us. Thus the degree of accuracy in his model to some extent reflects the general level of knowledge in society. And as experience and scientific research pump more refined and accurate knowledge into society, new concepts, new ways of thinking, supersede, contradict, and render obsolete older ideas and world views.

If society itself were standing still, there might be little pressure on the individual to update his own supply of images, to bring them in line with the latest knowledge available in the society. So long as the society in which he is embedded is stable or slowly changing, the images on which he bases his behavior can also change slowly. But to function in a fast-changing society, to cope with swift and complex change, the individual must turn over his own stock of images at a rate that in some way correlates with the pace of change. His model must be updated. To the degree that it lags, his responses to change become inappropriate; he becomes increasingly thwarted, ineffective. Thus there is intense pressure on the individual to keep up with the generalized pace.

Today change is so swift and relentless in the techno-societies that yesterday's truths suddenly become today's fictions, and the most highly skilled and intelligent members of society admit difficulty in keeping up with the deluge of new knowledge—even in extremely narrow fields.

"You can't possibly keep in touch with all you want to," complains Dr. Rudolph Stohler, a zoologist at the University of California at Berkeley. "I spend 25 percent to 50 percent of my working time trying to keep up with what's going on," says Dr. I. E. Wallen, chief of oceanography at the Smithsonian Institution in Washington. Dr. Emilio Segre, a Nobel prizewinner in physics, declares: "On K-mesons alone, to wade through all the papers is an impossibility." And another oceanographer, Dr. Arthur Stump, admits: "I don't really know the answer unless we declare a moratorium on publications for ten years."

New knowledge either extends or outmodes the old. In either case it compels those for whom it is relevant to reorganize their store of images. It forces them to relearn today what they thought they knew yesterday. Thus Lord James, vice-chancellor of the University of York, says, "I took my first degree in chemistry at Oxford in 1931." Looking at the questions asked in chemistry exams at Oxford today, he continues, "I realize that not only can I not do them, but that I never *could* have done them, since at least two-thirds of the questions involve knowledge that simply did not exist when I graduated." And Dr. Robert Hilliard, the top educational broadcasting specialist for the Federal Communications Commission, presses the point further: "At the rate at which knowledge is growing, by the time the child born today graduates from college, the amount of knowledge in the world will be four times as great. By the time that same child is fifty years old, it will be thirty-two times as great, and 97 percent of everything known in the world will have been learned since the time he was born."

Granting that definitions of "knowledge" are vague and that such statistics are necessarily hazardous, there still can be no question that the rising tide of new knowledge forces us into ever-narrower specialization and drives us to revise our inner images of reality at ever-faster rates. Nor does this refer merely to abstruse scientific information about physical particles or genetic structure. It applies with equal force to various categories of knowledge that closely affect the everyday life of millions.

THE FREUDIAN WAVE

Much new knowledge is admittedly remote from the immediate interests of the ordinary man in the street. He is not intrigued or impressed by the fact that a noble gas like xenon can form compounds—something that until recently most chemists swore was impossible. While even this knowledge may have an impact on him when it is embodied in new technology, until then, he can afford to ignore it. A good bit of new knowledge, on the other hand, is directly related to his immediate concerns, his job, his politics, his family life, even his sexual behavior.

A poignant example is the dilemma that parents find themselves in today as a consequence of successive radical changes in the image of the child in society and in our theories of childrearing.

At the turn of the century in the United States, for example, the dominant theory reflected the prevailing scientific belief in the primacy of heredity in determining behavior. Mothers who had never heard of Darwin or Spencer raised their babies in ways consistent with the world views of these thinkers. Vulgarized and simplified, passed from person to person, these world views were reflected in the conviction of millions of ordinary people that "bad children are a result of bad stock," that "crime is hereditary," etc.

In the early decades of the century, these attitudes fell back before the advance of environmentalism. The belief that environment shapes personality, and that the early years are the most important, created a new image of the child. The work of Watson and Pavlov began to creep into the public ken. Mothers reflected the new behaviorism, refusing to feed infants on demand, refusing to pick them up when they cried, weaning them early to avoid prolonged dependency.

A study by Martha Wolfenstein has compared the advice offered parents in seven successive editions of *Infant Care*, a handbook issued by the United States Children's Bureau between 1914 and 1951. She found distinct shifts in the preferred methods for dealing with weaning, thumb-sucking, masturbation, bowel and bladder training. It is clear from this study that by the late thirties still another image of the child had gained ascendancy. Freudian concepts swept in like a wave and revolutionized childrearing practices. Suddenly, mothers began to hear about "the rights of infants" and the need for "oral gratification." Permissiveness became the order of the day.

Parenthetically, at the same time that Freudian images of the child were altering the behavior of parents in Dayton, Dubuque and Dallas, the image of the psychoanalyst changed, too. Psychoanalysts became culture heroes. Movies, television scripts, novels and magazine stories represented them as wise and sympathetic souls, wonder-workers capable of remaking damaged personalities. From the appearance of the movie *Spellbound* in 1945, through the late fifties, the analyst was painted in largely positive terms by the mass media.

By the mid-sixties, however, he had already turned into a comical creature. Peter Sellers in *What's New Pussycat?* played a psychoanalyst much crazier than most of his patients, and "psychoanalyst jokes" began to circulate not merely among New York and California sophisticates, but through the population at large, helped along by the same mass media that created the myth of the analyst in the first place.

This sharp reversal in the public image of the psychoanalyst (the public image being no more than the weighted aggregate of private images in the society) reflected changes in research as well. For evidence was piling up that psychoanalytic therapy did not live up to the claims made for it, and new knowledge in the behavioral sciences, and particularly in psychopharmacology, made many Freudian therapeutic measures seem quaintly archaic. At the same time, there was a great burst of research in the field of learning theory, and a new swing in childrearing, this time toward a kind of neo-behaviorism, got under way.

At each stage of this development a widely held set of images was attacked by a set of counter-images. Individuals holding one set were assailed by reports, articles, documentaries, and advice from authorities, friends, relatives and even casual acquaintances who accepted conflicting views. The same mother, turning to the same authorities at two different times in the course of raising her child, would receive, in effect, somewhat different advice based on different inferences about reality. While for the people of the past, childrearing patterns remained stable for centuries at a time, for the people of the present and the future, it has, like so many other fields, become an arena in which successive waves of images, many of them generated by scientific research, do battle.

In this way, new knowledge alters old. The mass media instantly and persuasively disseminate new images, and ordinary individuals, seeking help in coping with an ever more complex social environment, attempt to keep up. At the same time, events—as distinct from research as such—also batter our old image structures. Racing swiftly past our attention screen, they wash out old images and generate new ones. After the freedom rides and the riots in black ghettos only the pathological could hang on to the long-cherished notion that blacks are "happy children" content with their poverty. After the Israeli blitz victory over the Arabs in 1967, how many still cling to the image of the Jew as a cheek-turning pacifist or a battlefield coward?

In education, in politics, in economic theory, in medicine, in international affairs, wave after wave of new images penetrate our defenses, shake up our mental models of reality. The result of this image bombardment is the accelerated decay of old images, a faster intellectual through-put, and a new, profound sense of the impermanence of knowledge, itself.

A BLIZZARD OF BEST SELLERS

This impermanence is reflected in society in many subtle ways. A single dramatic example is the impact of the knowledge explosion on that classic knowledge-container, the book.

As knowledge has become more plentiful and less permanent, we have witnessed the virtual disappearance of the solid old durable leather binding, replaced at first by cloth and later by paper covers. The book itself, like much of the information it holds, has become more transient.

A decade ago, communications systems designer Sol Cornberg, a radical prophet in the field of library technology, declared that reading would soon cease to be a primary form of information intake. "Reading and writing," he suggested, "will become obsolete skills." (Ironically, Mr. Cornberg's wife is a novelist.)

Whether or not he is correct, one fact is plain: the incredible expansion of knowledge implies that each book (alas, this one included) contains a progressively smaller fraction of all that is known. And the paperback revolution, by making inexpensive editions available everywhere, lessens the scarcity value of the book at precisely the very moment that the increasingly rapid obsolescence of knowledge lessens its long-term informational value. Thus, in the United States a paperback appears simultaneously on more than 100,000 newsstands, only to be swept away by another tidal wave of publications delivered a mere thirty days later. The book thus approaches the transience of the monthly magazine. Indeed, many books are no more than "one-shot" magazines.

At the same time, the public's span of interest in a book—even a very popular book—is shrinking. Thus, for example, the life span of best sellers on *The New York Times* list is rapidly declining. There are marked irregularities from year to year, and some books manage to buck the tide. Nevertheless, if we examine the first four years for which full data on the subject is available, 1953–1956, and compare this with a similar period one decade later, 1963–1966, we find that the average best seller in the earlier period remained on the list a full 18.8 weeks. A decade later this had shrunk to 15.7 weeks. Within a ten-year-period, the life expectancy of the average best seller had shrunk by nearly one-sixth.

We can understand such trends only if we grasp the elemental underlying truth. We are witnessing an historic process that will inevitably change man's psyche. For across the board, from cosmetics to cosmology, from Twiggy-type trivia to the triumphant facts of technology, our inner images of reality, responding to the acceleration of change outside ourselves, are becoming shorter-lived, more temporary. We are creating and using up ideas and images at a faster and faster pace. Knowledge, like people, places, things and organizational forms, is becoming disposable.

THE ENGINEERED MESSAGE

If our inner images of reality appear to be turning over more and more rapidly, one reason may well be an increase in the rate at which image-laden messages are being hurled at our senses. Little effort has been made to investigate this scientifically, but there is evidence that we are increasing the exposure of the individual to image-bearing stimuli.

To understand why, we need first to examine the basic sources of imagery. Where do the thousands of images filed in our mental model come from? The external environment showers stimuli upon us. Signals originating outside ourselves—sound waves, light, etc. —strike our sensory organs. Once perceived, these signals are converted, through a still mysterious process, into symbols of reality, into images.

These incoming signals are of several types. Some might be called *uncoded*. Thus, for example, a man walks along a street and notices a leaf whipped along the sidewalk by the wind. He perceives this event through his sensory apparatus. He hears a rustling sound. He sees movement and greenness. He feels the wind. From these sensory perceptions he somehow forms a mental image. We can refer to these sensory signals as a message. But the message was not, in any ordinary sense of the term, man-made. It was not designed by anyone to communicate anything, and the man's understanding of it does not depend directly on a social code—a set of socially agreed-upon signs and definitions. We are all surrounded by and participate in such events. When they occur within range of our senses, we may pick up uncoded messages from them and convert these messages into mental images. In fact, some proportion of the images in every individual's mental model are derived from such uncoded messages.

But we also receive *coded* messages from outside ourselves. Coded messages are any which depend upon social convention for their meaning. All languages, whether based on words or gestures, drumbeats or dancesteps, hieroglyphs, pictographs or the arrangement of knots in a string, are codes. All messages conveyed by means of such languages are coded. We may speculate with some safety that as societies have grown larger and more complex, proliferating codes for the transmission of images from person to person, the ratio of uncoded messages received by the ordinary person has declined in favor of coded messages. We may guess, in other words, that today more of our imagery derives from man-made messages than from personal observation of raw, "uncoded" events.

Furthermore, we can discern a subtle but significant shift in the type of coded messages as well. For the illiterate villager in an agricultural society of the past, most of the incoming messages were what might be called casual or "do-it-yourself" communications. The peasant might engage in ordinary household conversation, banter, cracker-barrel or tavern talk, griping, complaining, boasting, baby talk, (and, in the same sense, animal talk), etc. This determined the nature of most of the coded messages he received, and one characteristic of this sort of communication is its loose, unstructured, garrulous or unedited quality.

Compare this message input with the kind of coded messages received by the ordinary citizen of the present-day industrial society. In addition to all of the above, he also receives messages—mainly from the mass media—that have been artfully fashioned by communications experts. He listens to the news; he watches carefully scripted plays, telecasts, movies; he hears much more music (a highly disciplined form of communication); he hears frequent speeches. Above all, he does something his peasant ancestor could not do: He reads—thousands of words every day, all of them carefully edited in advance.

The industrial revolution, bringing with it the enormous elaboration of the mass media, thus alters radically the nature of the messages received by the ordinary individual. In addition to receiving uncoded messages from the environment, and coded but casual messages from the people around him, the individual now begins to receive a growing number of coded but pre-engineered messages as well.

These engineered messages differ from the casual

or do-it-yourself product in one crucial respect: Instead of being loose or carelessly framed, the engineered product tends to be tighter, more condensed, less redundant. It is highly purposive, preprocessed to eliminate unnecessary repetition, consciously designed to maximize informational content. It is, as communications theorists say, "information-rich."

This highly significant but often overlooked fact can be observed by anyone who takes the trouble to compare a tape recorded sample of 500 words of ordinary household conversation (i.e., coded, but casual) with 500 words of newspaper text or movie dialogue (also coded, but engineered). Casual conversation tends to be filled with repetition and pauses. Ideas are repeated several times, often in identical words, but if not, then varied only slightly.

In contrast, the 500 words of newspaper copy or movie dialogue are carefully pre-edited, streamlined. They convey relatively non-repetitive ideas. They tend to be more grammatically accurate than ordinary conversation and, if presented orally, they tend to be enunciated more clearly. Waste material has been trimmed away. Editor, writer, director—everyone involved in the production of the engineered message —fights to "keep the story moving" or to produce "fast-paced action." It is no accident that books, movies, television plays, are so frequently advertised as "high-speed adventure," "fast-reading," or "breathless." No publisher or movie producer would dare advertise his work as "repetitive" or "redundant."

Thus, as radio, television, newspapers, magazines and novels sweep through society, as the proportion of engineered messages received by the individual rises (and the proportion of uncoded and coded casual messages correspondingly declines), we witness a profound change: a steady speed-up in the average pace at which image-producing messages are presented to the individual. The sea of coded information that surrounds him begins to beat at his senses with new urgency.

This helps account for the sense of hurry in everyday affairs. But if industrialism is marked by a communication's speed-up, the transition to super-industrialism is marked by intense efforts to accelerate the process even further. The waves of coded information turn into violent breakers and come at a faster and faster clip, pounding at us, seeking entry, as it were, to our nervous system.

MOZART ON THE RUN

In the United States today the median time spent by adults reading newspapers is fifty-two minutes per day. The same person who commits nearly an hour to newspapers also spends time reading magazines, books, signs, billboards, recipes, instructions, labels on cans, advertising on the back of breakfast food boxes, etc. Surrounded by print, he "ingests" between 10,000 and 20,000 edited words per day of the several times that many to which he is exposed. The same person also probably spends an hour and a quarter per day listening to the radio—more if he owns an FM receiver. If he listens to news, commercials, commentary or other such programs, he will, during this period, hear about 11,000 pre-processed words. He also spends several hours watching television—add another 10,000 words or so, plus a sequence of carefully arranged, highly purposive visuals.*

Nothing, indeed, is quite so purposive as advertising, and today the average American adult is assaulted by a minimum of 560 advertising messages each day. Of the 560 to which he is exposed, however, he only notices seventy-six. In effect, he blocks out 484 adver-

---

* This is not to suggest that only words and pictures convey or evoke images. Music, too, sets the internal image machinery working, although the images produced may be completely non-verbal.

tising messages a day to preserve his attention for other matters.

All this represents the press of engineered messages against his senses. And the pressure is rising. In an effort to transmit even richer image-producing messages at an even faster rate, communications people, artists and others consciously work to make each instant of exposure to the mass media carry a heavier informational and emotional freight.

Thus we see the widespread and increasing use of symbolism for compacting information. Today advertising men, in a deliberate attempt to cram more messages into the individual's mind within a given moment of time, make increasing use of the symbolic techniques of the arts. Consider the "tiger" that is allegedly put in one's tank. Here a single word transmits to the audience a distinct visual image that has been associated since childhood with power, speed, and force. The pages of advertising trade magazines like *Printer's Ink* are filled with sophisticated technical articles about the use of verbal and visual symbolism to accelerate image-flow. Indeed, today many artists might learn new image-accelerating techniques from the advertising men.

If the ad men, who must pay for each split second of time on radio or television, and who fight for the reader's fleeting attention in magazines and newspapers, are busy trying to communicate maximum imagery in minimum time, there is evidence, too, that at least some members of the public want to increase the rate at which they can receive messages and process images. This explains the phenomenal success of speed-reading courses among college students, business executives, politicians and others. One leading speed-reading school claims it can increase almost anyone's input speed three times, and some readers report the ability to read literally tens of thousands of words per minute—a claim roundly disputed by many reading experts. Whether or not such speeds are possible, the clear fact is that the rate of communication is accelerating. Busy people wage a desperate battle each day to plow through as much information as possible. Speed-reading presumably helps them do this.

The impulse toward acceleration in communications is, however, by no means limited to advertising or to the printed word. A desire to maximize message content in minimum time explains, for example, the experiments conducted by psychologists at the American Institutes for Research who played taped lectures at faster than normal speeds and then tested the comprehension of listeners. Their purpose: to discover whether students would learn more if lecturers talked faster.

The same intent to accelerate information flow explains the recent obsession with split-screen and multi-screen movies. At the Montreal World's Fair, viewers in pavilion after pavilion were confronted not with a traditional movie screen on which ordered visual images appear in sequence, but with two, three, or five screens, each of them hurling messages at the viewer at the same time. On these, several stories play themselves out at the same time, demanding of the viewer the ability to accept many more messages simultaneously than any movie-goer in the past, or else to censor out, or block, certain messages to keep the rate of message-input, or image-stimulation, within reasonable limits.

The author of an article in *Life*, entitled "A Film Revolution to Blitz Man's Mind," accurately describes the experience in these words: "Having to look at six images at the same time, having to watch in twenty minutes the equivalent of a full length movie, excites and crams the mind." Elsewhere he suggests that another multi-screen film "by putting more into a moment, condenses time."

Even in music the same accelerative thrust is increasingly evident. A conference of composers and computer specialists held in San Francisco not long ago was informed that for several centuries music has been undergoing "an increase in the amoun tory information transmitted during a given of time," and there is evidence also that n ....ans today play the music of Mozart, Bach and Haydn at a faster tempo than that at which the same music was performed at the time it was composed. We are getting Mozart on the run.

THE SEMI-LITERATE SHAKESPEARE

If our images of reality are changing more rapidly, and the machinery of image-transmission is being speeded up, a parallel change is altering the very codes we use. For language, too, is convulsing. According to lexicographer Stuart Berg Flexner, senior editor of the *Random House Dictionary of the English Language*, "The words we use are changing faster today—and not merely on the slang level, but on every level. The rapidity with which words come and go is vastly accelerated. This seems to be true not only of English, but of French, Russian and Japanese as well."

Flexner illustrated this with the arresting suggestion that, of the estimated 450,000 "usable" words in the English language today, only perhaps 250,000 would be comprehensible to William Shakespeare. Were Shakespeare suddenly to materialize in London or New York today, he would be able to understand, on the average, only five out of every nine words in our vocabulary. The Bard would be a semi-literate.

This implies that if the language had the same number of words in Shakespeare's time as it does today, at least 200,000 words—perhaps several times that many—have dropped out and been replaced in the intervening four centuries. Moreover, Flexner conjectures that a full third of this turnover has occurred within the last fifty years alone. This, if correct, would mean that words are now dropping out of the language and being replaced at a rate at least ree times faster than during the base period 1564 to 1914.

This high turnover rate reflects changes in things, processes, and qualities in the environment. Some new words come directly from the world of consumer products and technology. Thus, for example, words like "fast-back," "wash-and-wear" or "flashcube" were all propelled into the language by advertising in recent years. Other words come from the headlines. "Sit-in" and "swim-in" are recent products of the civil rights movement; "teach-in" a product of the campaign against the Vietnam war; "be-in" and "love-in" products of the hippie subculture. The LSD cult has brought with it a profusion of new words—"acid-head," "psychedelic," etc.

At the level of slang, the turnover rate is so rapid that it has forced dictionary makers to change their criteria for word inclusion. "In 1954," says Flexner, "when I started work on the *Dictionary of American Slang*, I would not consider a word for inclusion unless I could find three uses of the word over a five-year period. Today such a criterion would be impossible. Language, like art, is increasingly becoming a fad proposition. The slang terms 'fab' and 'gear,' for example, didn't last a single year. They entered the teen-age vocabulary in about 1966; by 1967 they were out. You cannot use a time criterion for slang any more."

One fact contributing to the rapid introduction and obsolescence of words is the incredible speed with which a new word can be injected into wide usage. In the late 1950's and early sixties one could actually trace the way in which certain scholarly jargon words such as "rubric" or "subsumed" were picked up from academic journals, used in small-circulation periodicals like the *New York Review of Books* or *Commentary*, then adopted by *Esquire* with its then circulation of 800,000 to 1,000,000, and finally diffused through the larger society by *Time*, *Newsweek* and the larger mass magazines. Today the process has been telescoped. The editors of mass magazines no longer pick up vocabulary from the intermediate intellectual publications alone; they, too, lift directly from the scholarly press in their hurry to be "on top of things."

When Susan Sontag disinterred the word "camp" and used it as the basis of an essay in *Partisan Review* in the fall of 1964, *Time* waited only a few weeks before devoting an article to the word and its rejuvenator. Within a matter of a few additional weeks, the term was cropping up in newspapers and other mass media. Today the word has virtually dropped out of usage. "Teenybopper" is another word that came and went with blinding speed.

A more significant example of language turnover can be seen in the sudden shift of meaning associated with the ethnic term "black." For years, dark-skinned Americans regarded the term as racist. Liberal whites dutifully taught their children to use the term "Negro" and to capitalize the "N." Shortly after Stokely Carmichael proclaimed the doctrine of Black Power in Greenwood, Mississippi in June, 1966, however, "black" became a term of pride among both blacks and whites in the movement for racial justice. Caught off guard, liberal whites went through a period of confusion, uncertain as to whether to use Negro or black. Black was quickly legitimated when the mass media adopted the new meaning. Within a few months, black was "in," Negro "out."

Even faster cases of diffusion are on record. "The Beatles," says lexicographer Flexner, "at the height of their fame could make up any word they like, slip it into a record, and within a month it would be part of the language. At one time perhaps no more than fifty people in NASA used the word 'A-OK.' But when an astronaut used it during a televised flight, the word became part of the language in a single day. The same has been true of other space terms, too—lik 'sputnik' or 'all systems go.'"

As new words sweep in, old words vanish. A pic-

ture of a nude girl nowadays is no longer a "pin-up"
or a "cheesecake shot," but a "playmate." "Hep" has
given way to "hip"; "hipster" to "hippie." "Go-go"
rushed eagerly into the language at breakneck speed,
but it is already gone-gone among those who are
truly "with it."

The turnover of language would even appear to
involve non-verbal forms of communication as well.
We have slang gestures, just as we have slang words
—thumbs up or down, thumb to nose, the "shame on
you" gesture used by children, the hand moving
across the neck to suggest a throat-slitting. Professionals who watch the development of the gestural
language suggest that it, too, may be changing more
rapidly.

Some gestures that were regarded as semi-obscene
have become somewhat more acceptable as sexual
values have changed in the society. Others that were
used only by a few have achieved wider usage. An
example of diffusion, Flexner observes, is the wider
use today of that gesture of contempt and defiance
—the fist raised and screwed about. The invasion of
Italian movies that hit the United States in the
fifties and sixties probably contributed to this. Similarly, the upraised finger—the "up yours" gesture—
appears to be gaining greater respectability and
currency than it once had. At the same time, other gestures have virtually vanished or been endowed with
radically changed meaning. The circle formed by the
thumb and forefinger to suggest that all goes well
appears to be fading out; Churchill's "V for Victory"
sign is now used by protesters to signify something
emphatically different: "peace" *not* "victory."

There was a time when a man learned the language
of his society and made use of it, with little change,
throughout his lifetime. His "relationship" with each
learned word or gesture was durable. Today, to an
astonishing degree, it is not.

ART: CUBISTS AND KINETICISTS

Art, like gesture, is a form of non-verbal expression and a prime channel for the transmission of images. Here the evidences of ephemeralization are, if anything, even more pronounced. If we regard each school of art as though it were a word-based language, we are witnessing the successive replacement not of words, but of whole languages at once. In the past one rarely saw a fundamental change in an art style within a man's lifetime. A style or school endured, as a rule, for generations at a time. Today the pace of turnover in art is vision-blurring—the viewer scarcely has time to "see" a school develop, to learn its language, so to speak, before it vanishes.

Bursting on the scene in the last quarter of the nineteenth century, Impressionism was only the first of a sequence of shattering changes. It came at a time when industrialism was beginning its climactic forward surge, bringing with it a notable step-up in the tempo of everyday life. "It is above all the furious speed of [technological] development and the way the pace is forced that seems pathological, particularly when compared with the rate of progress in earlier periods in the history of art and culture," writes the art historian Arnold Hauser in describing the turnover of art styles. "For the rapid development of technology not only accelerates the change of fashion, but also the shifting emphases in the criteria of aesthetic taste. . . . The continual and increasingly rapid replacement of old articles in everyday use by new ones . . . readjusts the speed at which philosophical and artistic revaluations occur . . ."

If we roughly date the Impressionist interval from 1875 to 1910, we see a period of dominance lasting approximately thirty-five years. Since then no school or style, from Futurism to Fauvism, from Cubism to Surrealism, has dominated the scene for even that

long. One after another, styles supplant one another.
The most enduring twentieth-century school, Abstract
Expressionism, held sway for at most twenty years,
from 1940 to 1960, then to be followed by a wild
succession—"Pop" lasting perhaps five years, "Op"
managing to grip the public's attention for two or
three years, then the emergence, appropriately
enough, of "Kinetic Art" whose very *raison d'être* is
transience.

This phantasmagoric turnover is evident not merely
in New York or San Francisco, but in Paris, in Rome,
in Stockholm and London—wherever painters are
found. Thus Robert Hughes writes in the *New Society*: "Hailing the new painters is now one of the
annual sports in England . . . The enthusiasm for
discovering a new direction in English art once a
year has become a mania—an euphoric, almost hysterical belief in renewal." Indeed, he suggests, the
expectation that each year will bring a new mode
and a new crop of artists is "a significant parody of
what is, in itself, a parodical situation—the accelerated turnover in the avant-garde today."

If schools of art may be likened to languages, then
individual works of art may be compared to words.
If we make this transposition, we find in art a process
exactly analogous to that now occurring in the verbal
language. Here, too, "words"—i.e., individual works
of art—are coming into use and then dropping out
of the vocabulary at heightened speeds. Individual
works flash across our consciousness in galleries or
in the pages of mass magazines; the next time we look
they are gone. Sometimes the work itself quite literally disappears—many are collages or constructions
built of fragile materials that simply fall apart after a
short time.

Much of the confusion in the art world today arises
from the failure of the cultural establishment to recognize, once and for all, that elitism and permanence
are dead—so, at least, contends John McHale, the
imaginative Scot, half artist/half social scientist, who

heads the Center for Integrative Studies, State University of New York at Binghamton. In a forceful essay entitled *The Plastic Parthenon*, McHale points out that "traditional canons of literary and artistic judgment . . . tend to place high value on permanence, uniqueness and the enduring universal value of chosen artifacts." Such aesthetic standards, he argues, were appropriate enough in a world of handcrafted goods and relatively small taste-making elites. These same standards, however, "in no way enable one to relate adequately to our present situation in which astronomical numbers of artifacts are mass produced, circulated and consumed. These may be identical, or only marginally different. In varying degree, they are expendable, replaceable, and lack any unique 'value' or intrinsic 'truth.'"

Today's artists, McHale suggests, neither work for a tiny elite nor take seriously the idea that permanence is a virtue. The future of art, he says, "seems no longer to lie with the creation of enduring masterworks." Rather, artists work for the short term. McHale concludes that: "Accelerated changes in the human condition require an array of symbolic images of man which will match up to the requirements of constant change, fleeting impression and a high rate of obsolescence." We need, he says, "a replaceable, expendable series of ikons."

One may quarrel with McHale's contention that transience in art is desirable. Perhaps the flight from permanence is a tactical error. It can even be argued that our artists are employing homeopathic magic, behaving like primitives who, awed by a force they do not comprehend, attempt to exert control over it by simple-mindedly imitating it. But whatever one's attitude toward contemporary art, transience remains an implacable fact, a social and historic tendency so central to our times that it cannot be ignored. And it is clear that artists are reacting to it.

The impulse toward transience in art explains the whole development of that most transient of art works, the "happening." Allan Kaprow, who is often credited with originating the happening, has explicitly suggested its relationship to the throw-away culture within which we live. The happening, according to its proponents, is ideally performed once and once only. The happening is the Kleenex tissue of art.

This so, kinetic art can be considered the aesthetic embodiment of modularism. Kinetic sculptures or constructions crawl, whistle, whine, swing, twitch, rock or pulsate, their lights blinking, their magnetic tapes whirling, their plastic, steel, glass and copper components arranging and rearranging themselves into evanescent patterns within a given, though sometimes concealed, framework. Here the wiring and connections tend to be the least transient part of the structure, just as the gantry cranes and service towers in Joan Littlewood's Fun Palace are designed to outlive any particular arrangement of the modular components. The intent of the kinetic work, however, is to create maximum variability and maximum transience. Jean Clay has pointed out that in a traditional work of art "the relationship of parts to a whole had been decided forever." In kinetic art, he says, the "balance of forms is in flux."

Many artists are working with engineers and scientists today, in the hope of exploiting the latest technical processes for their own purpose, the symbolization of the accelerative thrust in society. "Speed," writes Francastel, the French art critic, "has become something undreamt-of, and constant movement every man's intimate experience." Art reflects this new reality.

Thus we find artists from France, England, the United States, Scotland, Sweden, Israel and elsewhere creating kinetic images. Their creed is perhaps best expressed by Yaacov Agam, an Israeli kineticist, who says: "We are different from what we were three moments ago, and in three minutes more, we will again be different . . . I try to give this approach a plastic expression by creating a visual form that doesn't exist. The image appears and disappears, but nothing is retained."

The final culmination of such efforts, of course, is the creation of those new and quite real "fun palaces" —so-called total environment nightclubs in which the fun-seeker plunges into a space in which lights, colors and sounds change their patterns constantly. In effect, the patron steps inside a work of kinetic art. Here again the framework, the building itself, is only the longest lasting part of the whole, while its interior is designed to produce transient combinations of sensory in-puts. Whether one regards this as fun or not depends on the individual, perhaps; but the over-all direction of such movements is clear. In art, as in language, we are racing toward impermanence. Man's relationships with symbolic imagery are growing more and more temporary.

THE NEURAL INVESTMENT

Events speed past us, compelling us to reassess our assumptions—our previous formed images of reality. Research topples older conceptions of man and nature. Ideas come and go at a frenetic rate. (A rate, that, in science at least, has been estimated to be twenty to one hundred times faster than a mere century ago.) Image-laden messages hammer at our senses. Meanwhile, language and art, the codes through which we transfer image-bearing messages to one another, are themselves turning over more rapidly.

All this cannot—and does not—leave us unchanged. It accelerates the rate at which the individual must process his imagery if he is to adapt successfully to the churning environment. Nobody really knows how we convert signals from outside into images within. Yet psychology and the information sciences cast some light on what happens once the image is born. They suggest, to begin with, that the mental model is organized into many highly complex image-structures, and that new images are, in effect, filed away in these structures according to several classificatory principles. A newly generated image is filed away with other images pertaining to the same subject matter. Smaller and more limited inferences are ranged under larger and more inclusive generalizations. The image is checked out for its consistency with those already in file. (There is evidence of the existence of a specific neural mechanism that carries out this consistency-checking procedure.) We make a decision, with respect to the image, as to whether it is closely relevant to our goals, or whether, instead, it is remote and hence, for us, unimportant. Each image is also evaluated—is it "good" or "bad" for us? Finally, whatever else we do with the new image, we also judge its truth. We decide just how much faith to place in it. Is it an accurate reflection of reality? Can it be believed? Can we base action on it?

A new image that clearly fits somewhere into a subject matter slot, and which is consistent with images already stored there, gives us little difficulty. But if, as happens increasingly, the image is ambiguous, if it is inconsistent, or, worse yet, if it flies in the face of our previous inferences, the mental model has to be forcibly revised. Large numbers of images may have to be reclassified, shuffled, changed again until a suitable integration is found. Sometimes whole groups of image-structures have to be torn down and rebuilt. In extreme cases, the basic shape of the whole model has to be drastically overhauled.

Thus the mental model must be seen not as a static library of images, but as a living entity, tightly charged with energy and activity. It is not a "given" that we passively receive from outside. Rather, it is something we actively construct and reconstruct from moment to moment. Restlessly scanning the outer world with our senses, probing for information relevant to our needs and desires, we engage in a constant process of rearrangement and updating.

At any given instant, innumerable images are decaying, dropping into the black immensity of the forgotten. Others are entering the system, being processed and filed. At the same time, we are retrieving images, "using them," and returning them to file, perhaps in a different place. We are constantly comparing images, associating them, cross-referencing them in new ways, and repositioning them. This is what is meant by the term "mental activity." And like muscular activity, it is a form of work. It requires high energy to keep the system operating.

Change, roaring through society, widens the gap between what we believe and what really is, between the existing images and the reality they are supposed to reflect. When this gap is only moderate, we can cope more or less rationally with change, we can react sanely to new conditions, we have a grip on reality. When this gap grows too wide, however, we find ourselves increasingly unable to cope, we respond inappropriately, we become ineffectual, withdraw or simply panic. At the final extreme, when the gap grows too wide, we suffer psychosis—or even death.

To maintain our adaptive balance, to keep the gap within manageable proportions, we struggle to refresh our imagery, to keep it up-to-date, to relearn reality. Thus the accelerative thrust outside us finds a corresponding speed-up in the adapting individual. Our image-processing mechanisms, whatever they may be, are driven to operate at higher and higher speeds.

This has consequences that have been as yet largely overlooked. For when we classify an image, any image, we make a definite, perhaps even measurable, energy-investment in a specific organizational pattern in the brain. Learning requires energy; and relearning requires even more. "All the researches on learning," writes Harold D. Lasswell of Yale, "seem to confirm the view that 'energies' are bound in support of past learning, and that new energies are essential to unbind the old . . ." At the neurological level, he continues, "Any established system appears to include exceedingly intricate arrangements of cell material, electrical charges and chemical elements. At any cross section in time . . . the somatic structure represents a tremendous investment of fixed forms and potentials . . ." What this means in brief is very simple: there are costs involved in relearning—or, in our terminology, reclassifying imagery.

In all the talk about the need for continuing education, in all the popular discussions of retraining, there is an assumption that man's potentials for re-education are unlimited. This is, at best, an assumption, not a fact, and it is an assumption that needs close and scientific scrutiny. The process of image formation and classification is, in the end, a physical process, dependent upon finite characteristics of nerve cells and body chemicals. In the neural system as now constituted there are, in all likelihood, inherent limits to the amount and speed of image processing that the individual can accomplish. How fast and how continuously can the individual revise his inner images before he smashes up against these limits?

Nobody knows. It may well be that the limits stretch so far beyond present needs, that such gloomy speculations are unjustified. Yet one salient fact commands attention: by speeding up change in the outer world, we compel the individual to relearn his environment at every moment. This, in itself, places a new demand on the nervous system. The people of the past, adapting to comparatively stable environments, maintained longer-lasting ties with their own inner conceptions of "the-way-things-are." We, moving into high-transience society, are forced to truncate these relationships. Just as we must make and break our relationships with things, places, people and organizations at an ever more rapid pace, so, too, must we turn over our conceptions of reality, our mental images of the world at shorter and shorter intervals.

Transience, then, the forcible abbreviation of man's

relationships, is not merely a condition of the external world. It has its shadow within us as well. New discoveries, new technologies, new social arrangements in the external world erupt into our lives in the form of increased turnover rates—shorter and shorter relational durations. They force a faster and faster pace of daily life. They demand a new level of adaptability. And they set the stage for that potentially devastating social illness—future shock.

Part Three:

NOVELTY

Chapter 9

THE SCIENTIFIC TRAJECTORY

We are creating a new society. Not a changed society. Not an extended, larger-than-life version of our present society. But a new society.

This simple premise has not yet begun to tincture our consciousness. Yet unless we understand this, we shall destroy ourselves in trying to cope with tomorrow.

A revolution shatters institutions and power relationships. This is precisely what is happening today in all the high-technology nations. Students in Berlin and New York, in Turin and Tokyo, capture their deans and chancellors, bring great clanking education factories to a grinding halt, and even threaten to topple governments. Police stand aside in the ghettos of New York, Washington and Chicago as ancient property laws are openly violated. Sexual standards are overthrown. Great cities are paralyzed by strikes, power failures, riots. International power alliances are shaken. Financial and political leaders secretly tremble—not out of fear that communist (or capitalist) revolutionaries will oust them, but that the entire system is somehow flying out of control.

These are indisputable signs of a sick social structure, a society that can no longer perform even its most basic functions in the accustomed ways. It

is a society caught in the agony of revolutionary
change. In the 1920's and 1930's, communists used
to speak of the "general crisis of capitalism." It is
now clear that they were thinking small. What is
occurring now is not a crisis of capitalism, but of
industrial society itself, regardless of its political
form. We are simultaneously experiencing a youth
revolution, a sexual revolution, a racial revolution, a
colonial revolution, an economic revolution, and the
most rapid and deep-going technological revolution
in history. We are living through the general crisis
of industrialism. In a word, we are in the midst of
the super-industrial revolution.

If failure to grasp this fact impairs one's ability to
understand the present, it also leads otherwise intelligent men into total stupidity when they talk about
the future. It encourages them to think in simple-
minded straight lines. Seeing evidence of bureaucracy today, they naïvely assume there will be *more*
bureaucracy tomorrow. Such linear projections characterize most of what is said or written about the
future. And it causes us to worry about precisely
the wrong things.

One needs imagination to confront a revolution.
For revolution does not move in straight lines alone.
It jerks, twists and backtracks. It arrives in the form
of quantum jumps and dialectical reversals. Only by
accepting the premise that we are racing toward a
wholly new stage of eco-technological development—
the super-industrial stage—can we make sense of our
era. Only by accepting the revolutionary premise can
we free our imaginations to grapple with the future.

Revolution implies novelty. It sends a flood of newness into the lives of countless individuals, confronting them with unfamiliar institutions and first-time
situations. Reaching deep into our personal lives, the
enormous changes ahead will transform traditional
family structures and sexual attitudes. They will
smash conventional relationships between old and
young. They will overthrow our values with respect

to money and success. They will alter work, play and education beyond recognition. And they will do all this in a context of spectacular, elegant, yet frightening scientific advance.

If transience is the first key to understanding the new society, therefore, novelty is the second. The future will unfold as an unending succession of bizarre incidents, sensational discoveries, implausible conflicts, and wildly novel dilemmas. This means that many members of the super-industrial society will never "feel at home" in it. Like the voyager who takes up residence in an alien country, only to find, once adjusted, that he must move on to another, and yet another, we shall come to feel like "strangers in a strange land."

The super-industrial revolution can erase hunger, disease, ignorance and brutality. Moreover, despite the pessimistic prophecies of the straight-line thinkers, super-industrialism will not restrict man, will not crush him into bleak and painful uniformity. In contrast, it will radiate new opportunities for personal growth, adventure and delight. It will be vividly colorful and amazingly open to individuality. The problem is not whether man can survive regimentation and standardization. The problem, as we shall see, is whether he can survive freedom.

Yet for all this, man has never truly inhabited a novelty-filled environment before. Having to live at an accelerating pace is one thing when life situations are more or less familiar. Having to do so when faced by unfamiliar, strange or unprecedented situations is distinctly another. By unleashing the forces of novelty, we slam men up against the non-routine, the unpredicted. And, by so doing, we escalate the problems of adaptation to a new and dangerous level. For transience and novelty are an explosive mix.

If all this seems doubtful, let us contemplate some of the novelties that lie in store for us. Combining rational intelligence with all the imagination we can command, let us project ourselves forcefully into the

future. In doing so, let us not fear occasional error—
the imagination is only free when fear of error is
temporarily laid aside. Moreover, in thinking about
the future, it is better to err on the side of daring,
than the side of caution.

One sees why the moment one begins listening to
the men who are even now creating that future.
Listen, as they describe some of the developments
waiting to burst from their laboratories and factories.

THE NEW ATLANTIS

"Within fifty years," says Dr. F. N. Spiess, head of
the Marine Physical Laboratory of the Scripps Institution of Oceanography, "man will move onto and
into the sea—occupying it and exploiting it as an integral part of his use of this planet for recreation,
minerals, food, waste disposal, military and transportation operations, and, as populations grow, for
actual living space."

More than two-thirds of the planet's surface is
covered with ocean—and of this submerged terrain
a bare five percent is well mapped. However, this
underwater land is known to be rich with oil, gas,
coal, diamonds, sulphur, cobalt, uranium, tin, phos-
phates and other minerals. It teems with fish and
plant life.

These immense riches are about to be fought over
and exploited on a staggering scale. Today in the
United States alone more than 600 companies, including such giants as Standard Oil and Union Car-
bide, are readying themselves for a monumental
competitive struggle under the seas.

The race will intensify year by year—with far-
reaching impacts on society. Who "owns" the bottom
of the ocean and the marine life that covers it? As
ocean mining becomes feasible and economically
advantageous, we can expect the resource balance
among nations to shift. The Japanese already extract

10,000,000 tons of coal each year from underwater mines; tin is already being ocean-mined by Malaysia, Indonesia and Thailand. Before long nations may go to war over patches of ocean bottom. We may also find sharp changes in the rate of industrialization of what are now resource-poor nations.

Technologically, novel industries will rise to process the output of the oceans. Others will produce sophisticated and highly expensive tools for working the sea—deep-diving research craft, rescue submarines, electronic fish-herding equipment and the like. The rate of obsolescence in these fields will be swift. The competitive struggle will spur ever accelerating innovation.

Culturally, we can expect new words to stream rapidly into the language. "Aqua-culture"—the term for scientific cultivation of the ocean's food resources—will take its place alongside "Agriculture." "Water," itself a term freighted with symbolic and emotional associations, will take on wholly new connotations. Along with a new vocabulary will come new symbols in poetry, painting, film and the other arts. Representations of oceanic life forms will find their way into graphic and industrial design. Fashions will reflect dependence on the ocean. New textiles, new plastics and other materials will be discovered. New drugs will be found to cure illness or alter mental states.

Most important, increased reliance on the oceans for food will alter the nutrition of millions—a change that, itself, carries significant unknowns in its wake. What happens to the energy level of people, to their desire for achievement, not to speak of their biochemistry, their average height and weight, their rate of maturation, their life span, their characteristic diseases, even their psychological responses, when their society shifts from a reliance on agri- to aquaculture?

The opening of the sea may also bring with it a new frontier spirit—a way of life that offers adventure, danger, quick riches or fame to the initial explorers. Later, as man begins to colonize the continental shelves, and perhaps even the deeper reaches, the pioneers may well be followed by settlers who build artificial cities beneath the waves—work cities, science cities, medical cities, and play cities, complete with hospitals, hotels and homes.

If all this sounds too far off, it is sobering to note that Dr. Walter L. Robb, a scientist at General Electric, has already kept a hamster alive under water by enclosing it in a box that is, in effect, an artificial gill—a synthetic membrane that extracts air from the surrounding water while keeping the water out. Such membranes formed the top, bottom and two sides of a box in which the hamster was submerged in water. Without the gill, the animal would have suffocated. With it, it was able to breathe under water. Such membranes, G.E. claims, may some day furnish air for the occupants of underwater experimental stations. They might eventually be built into the walls of undersea apartment houses, hotels and other structures, or even—who knows?— into the human body itself.

Indeed, the old science fiction speculations about men with surgically implanted gills no longer seem quite so impossibly far-fetched as they once did. We may create (perhaps even breed) specialists for ocean work, men and women who are not only mentally, but physically equipped for work, play, love and sex under the sea. Even if we do not resort to such dramatic measures in our haste to conquer the underwater frontier, it seems likely that the opening of the oceans will generate not merely new professional specialties, but new life styles, new ocean-oriented subcultures, and perhaps even new religious sects or mystical cults to celebrate the seas.

One need not push speculation so far, however, to recognize that the novel environments to which man will be exposed will, of necessity, bring with them altered perceptions, new sensations, new sensitivities to color and form, new ways of thinking and feeling. Moreover, the invasion of the sea, the first wave of which we shall witness long before the arrival of A.D. 2000, is only one of a series of closely tied scientific-technological trends that are now racing forward —all of them crammed with novel social and psychological implications.

SUNLIGHT AND PERSONALITY

The conquest of the oceans links up directly with the advance toward accurate weather prediction and, ultimately, climate control. What we call weather is largely a consequence of the interaction of sun, air and ocean. By monitoring ocean currents, salinity and other factors, by placing weather-watch satellites in the skies, we will greatly increase our ability to forecast weather accurately. According to Dr. Walter Orr Roberts, past president of the American Association for the Advancement of Science, "We foresee bringing the entire globe under continuous weather observation by the mid-1970's—and at reasonable cost. And we envision, from this, vastly improved forecasting of storms, freezes, droughts, smog episodes— with attendant opportunities to avert disaster. But we can also see lurking in the beyond-knowledge of today an awesome potential weapon of war—the deliberate manipulation of weather for the benefit of the few and the powerful, to the detriment of the enemy, and perhaps of the bystanders as well."

In a science fiction story entitled *The Weather Man*, Theodore L. Thomas depicts a world in which the central political institution is a "Weather Council." In it, representatives of the various nations hammer out weather policy and control peoples by adjusting climate, imposing a drought here or a storm there to enforce their edicts. We may still be a long way from having such carefully calibrated control. But there is no question that the day is past when man simply had to take whatever heaven deigned to give in the way of weather. In the blunt words of the American Meteorological Society: "Weather modification today is a reality."

This represents one of the turning points in history and provides man with a weapon that could radically affect agriculture, transportation, communication, recreation. Unless wielded with extreme care, however, the gift of weather control can prove man's undoing. The earth's weather system is an integrated whole; a minute change at one point can touch off massive consequences elsewhere. Even without aggressive intent, there is danger that attempts to control a drought on one continent could trigger a tornado on another.

Moreover, the unknown socio-psychological consequences of weather manipulation could be enormous. Millions of us, for example, hunger for sunshine, as our mass migrations to Florida, California or the Mediterranean coast indicate. We may well be able to produce sunshine—or a facsimile of it—at will. The National Aeronautics and Space Administration is studying the concept of a giant orbiting space mirror capable of reflecting the sun's light downward on night-shrouded parts of the earth. A NASA official, George E. Mueller, has testified before Congress that the United States will have the capacity to launch huge sun-reflecting satellites by mid-1970. (By extension, it should not be impossible to loft satellites that would block out sunlight over preselected regions, plunging them into at least semi-darkness.)

The present natural light-dark cycle is tied to human biological rhythms in ways that are, as yet, unexplored. One can easily imagine the use of orbiting sun-mirrors to alter the hours of light for agricultural, industrial or even psychological reasons. For example, the introduction of longer days into Scandinavia could have a strong influence on the culture and personality types now characteristic of that region. To put the matter only half-facetiously, what happens to Ingmar Bergman's brooding art when Stockholm's brooding darkness is lifted? Could *The Seventh Seal* or *Winter Light* have been conceived in another climate?

The increasing ability to alter weather, the development of new energy sources, new materials (some of them almost surrealistic in their properties), new transportation means, new foods (not only from the sea, but from huge hydroponic food-growing factories)—all these only begin to hint at the nature of the accelerating changes that lie ahead.

THE VOICE OF THE DOLPHIN

In *War With the Newts*, Karel Capek's marvelous but little-known novel, man brings about the destruction of civilization through his attempt to domesticate a variety of salamander. Today, among other things, man is learning to exploit animals and fish in ways that would have made Capek smile wryly. Trained pigeons are used to identify and eliminate defective pills from drug factory assembly lines. In the Ukraine, Soviet scientists employ a particular species of fish to clear the algae off the filters in pumping stations. Dolphins have been trained to carry tools to "aquanauts" submerged off the coast of California, and to ward off sharks who approach the work zone. Others have been trained to ram submerged mines, thereby detonating them and committing suicide on man's behalf—a use that provoked a slight furor over inter-species ethics.

Research into communication between man and the dolphin may prove to be extremely useful if, and when, man makes contact with extra-terrestrial life—a possibility that many reputable astronomers regard as almost inevitable. In the meantime, dolphin research is yielding new data on the ways in which man's sensory apparatus differs from that of other animals. It suggests some of the outer limits within which the human organism operates—feelings, moods, perceptions not available to man because of his own biological make-up can be at least analyzed or described.

Existing animal species, however, are by no means all we have to work with. A number of writers have suggested that new animal forms be bred for specialized purposes. Sir George Thomson notes that "with advancing knowledge of genetics very large modifications in the wild species can no doubt be made." Arthur Clarke has written about the possibility that we can "increase the intelligence of our domestic animals, or evolve wholly new ones with much higher I.Q.'s than any existing now." We are also developing the capacity to control animal behavior by remote control. Dr. José M. R. Delgado, in a series of experiments terrifying in their human potential, implanted electrodes in the skull of a bull. Waving a red cape, Delgado provoked the animal to charge. Then, with a signal emitted from a tiny hand-held radio transmitter, he made the beast turn aside in mid-lunge and trot docilely away.

Whether we grow specialized animals to serve us or develop household robots depends in part on the uneven race between the life sciences and the physical sciences. It may be cheaper to make machines for our purposes, than to raise and train animals. Yet the biological sciences are developing so rapidly that the balance may well tip within our lifetimes. Indeed, the day may even come when we begin to grow our machines.

THE BIOLOGICAL FACTORY

Raising and training animals may be expensive, but what happens when we go down the evolutionary scale to the level of bacteria, viruses and other microorganisms? Here we can harness life in its primitive forms just as we once harnessed the horse. Today a new science based on this principle is rapidly emerging and it promises to change the very nature of industry as we know it.

"Our ancestors domesticated various plant and animal species in the prehistoric past," says biochemist Marvin J. Johnson of the University of Wisconsin. But "microorganisms were not domesticated until very recently, primarily because man did not know of their existence." Today he does, and they are already used in the large-scale production of vitamins, enzymes, antibiotics, citric acid and other useful compounds. By the year 2000, if the pressure for food continues to intensify, biologists will be growing microorganisms for use as animal feed and, eventually, human food.

At Uppsala University in Sweden, I had the opportunity to discuss this with Arne Tiselius, the Nobel prizewinning biochemist who is now president of the Nobel Foundation itself. "Is it conceivable," I asked, "that one day we shall create, in effect, biological machines—systems that can be used for productive purposes and will be composed not of plastic or metal parts, but of living organisms?" His answer was roundabout, but unequivocal: "We are already there. The great future of industry will come from biology. In fact, one of the most striking things about the tremendous technological development of Japan since the war has been not only its shipbuilding, but its microbiology. Japan is now the greatest power in the world in industry based on microbiology . . . Much of their food and food industry is based on processes in which bacteria are used. Now they produce all sorts of useful things—amino acids, for example. In Sweden everybody now talks about the need to strengthen our position in microbiology.

"You see, one need not think in terms of bacteria and viruses alone . . . The industrial processes, in general, are based on man-made processes. You make steel by a reduction of iron ore with coal. Think of the plastic industries, artificial products made originally from petroleum. Yet it is remarkable that even today, with the tremendous development of chemistry and chemical technology, there is no single foodstuff produced industrially which can compete with what the farmers grow.

"In this field, and in a great many fields, nature is far superior to man, even to the most advanced chemical engineers and researchers. Now what is the consequence of that? When we gradually get to know how nature makes these things, and when we can imitate nature, we will have processes of an entirely new kind. These will form the basis for industries of a new kind—a sort of bio-technical factory, a biological technology.

"The green plants make starch with the aid of carbon dioxide from the atmosphere and the sun. This is an extremely efficient machine . . . The green leaf is a marvelous machine. We know a great deal more about it today than two or three years ago. But not enough to imitate it yet. There are many such 'machines' in nature." Such processes, Tiselius continued, will be put to work. Rather than trying to synthesize products chemically, we will, in effect, grow them to specification.

One might even conceive of biological components in machines—in computers, for example. "It is quite obvious," Tiselius continued, "that computers so far are just bad imitations of our brains. Once we learn more about how the brain acts, I would be surprised if we could not construct a sort of biological computer . . . Such a computer might have electronic components modeled after biological components in the real brain. And at some distant point in the future it is conceivable that biological elements themselves might be parts of the machine." Precisely such ideas have led Jean Fourastié, the French economist and planner, to state flatly: "Man is on the path toward integrating living tissue in the processes of physical mechanisms . . . We shall have in the near future machines constituted at one and the same time of metal and of living substances . . ." In the light of this, he says, "The human body itself takes on new meaning."

THE PRE-DESIGNED BODY

Like the geography of the planet, the human body has until now represented a fixed point in human experience, a "given." Today we are fast approaching the day when the body can no longer be regarded as fixed. Man will be able, within a reasonably short period, to redesign not merely individual bodies, but the entire human race.

In 1962 Drs. J. D. Watson and F. H. C. Crick received the Nobel prize for describing the DNA molecule. Since then advances in genetics have come tripping over one another at a rapid pace. Molecular biology is now about to explode from the laboratories. New genetic knowledge will permit us to tinker with human heredity and manipulate the genes to create altogether new versions of man.

One of the more fantastic possibilities is that man will be able to make biological carbon copies of himself. Through a process known as "cloning" it will be possible to grow from the nucleus of an adult cell a new organism that has the same genetic characteristics of the person contributing the cell nucleus. The resultant human "copy" would start life with a genetic endowment identical to that of the donor, although cultural differences might thereafter alter the personality or physical development of the clone.

Cloning would make it possible for people to see themselves born anew, to fill the world with twins of themselves. Cloning would, among other things, provide us with solid empirical evidence to help us resolve, once and for all, the ancient controversy over "nature *vs.* nurture" or "heredity *vs.* environment." The solution of this problem, through the determination of the role played by each, would be one of the great milestones of human intellectual development. Whole libraries of philosophical speculation could, by a single stroke, be rendered irrelevant. An answer to this question would open the way for speedy, qualitative advances in psychology, moral philosophy and a dozen other fields.

But cloning could also create undreamed of complications for the race. There is a certain charm to the idea of Albert Einstein bequeathing copies of himself to posterity. But what of Adolf Hitler? Should there be laws to regulate cloning? Nobel Laureate Joshua Lederberg, a scientist who takes his social responsibility very seriously, believes it conceivable that those most likely to replicate themselves will be those who are most narcissistic, and that the clones they produce will also be narcissists.

Even if narcissism, however, is culturally rather than biologically transmitted, there are other eerie difficulties. Thus Lederberg raises a question as to whether human cloning, if permitted, might not "go critical." "I use that phrase," he told me, "in almost exactly the same sense that is involved in nuclear energy. It *will* go critical if there is a sufficient positive advantage to doing so . . . This has to do with whether the efficiency of communication, particularly along educational lines, is increased as between identical genotypes or not. The similarity of neurological hardware might make it easier for identical copies to transmit technical and other insights from one generation to the next."

How close is cloning? "It has already been done in amphibia," says Lederberg, "and somebody may be doing it right now with mammals. It wouldn't surprise me if it comes out any day now. When someone will have the courage to try it in a man, I haven't the foggiest idea. But I put the time scale on that anywhere from zero to fifteen years from now. Within fifteen years."

During those same fifteen years scientists will also

learn how the various organs of the body develop, and they will, no doubt, begin to experiment with various means of modifying them. Says Lederberg: "Things like the size of the brain and certain sensory qualities of the brain are going to be brought under direct developmental control . . . I think this is very near."

It is important for laymen to understand that Lederberg is by no means a lone worrier in the scientific community. His fears about the biological revolution are shared by many of his colleagues. The ethical, moral and political questions raised by the new biology simply boggle the mind. Who shall live and who shall die? What is man? Who shall control research into these fields? How shall new findings be applied? Might we not unleash horrors for which man is totally unprepared? In the opinion of many of the world's leading scientists the clock is ticking for a "biological Hiroshima."

Imagine, for example, the implications of biological breakthroughs in what might be termed "birth technology." Dr. E. S. E. Hafez, an internationally respected biologist at Washington State University, has publicly suggested, on the basis of his own astonishing work on reproduction, that within a mere ten to fifteen years a woman will be able to buy a tiny frozen embryo, take it to her doctor, have it implanted in her uterus, carry it for nine months, and then give birth to it as though it had been conceived in her own body. The embryo would, in effect, be sold with a guarantee that the resultant baby would be free of genetic defect. The purchaser would also be told in advance the color of the baby's eyes and hair, its sex, its probable size at maturity and its probable IQ.

Indeed, it will be possible at some point to do away with the female uterus altogether. Babies will be conceived, nurtured and raised to maturity outside the human body. It is clearly only a matter of years before the work begun by Dr. Daniele Petrucci in Bologna and other scientists in the United States and the Soviet Union, makes it possible for women to have babies without the discomfort of pregnancy.

The potential applications of such discoveries raise memories of *Brave New World* and *Astounding Science Fiction*. Thus Dr. Hafez, in a sweep of his imagination, suggests that fertilized human eggs might be useful in the colonization of the planets. Instead of shipping adults to Mars, we could ship a shoebox full of such cells and grow them into an entire city-size population of humans. "When you consider how much it costs in fuel to lift every pound off the launch pad," Dr. Hafez observes, "why send full-grown men and women aboard space ships? Instead, why not ship tiny embryos, in the care of a competent biologist . . . We miniaturize other spacecraft components. Why not the passengers?"

Long before such developments occur in outer space, however, the impact of the new birth technology will strike home on earth, splintering our traditional notions of sexuality, motherhood, love, child-rearing, and education. Discussions about the future of the family that deal only with The Pill overlook the biological witches' brew now seething in the laboratories. The moral and emotional choices that will confront us in the coming decades are mind-staggering.

A fierce controversy is already raging today among biologists over the problems and ethical issues arising out of eugenics. Should we try to breed a better race? If so, exactly what is "better?" And who is to decide? Such questions are not entirely new. Yet the techniques soon to be available smash the traditional limits of the argument. We can now imagine remaking the human race not as a farmer slowly and laboriously "breeds up" his herd, but as an artist might, employing a brilliant range of unfamiliar colors, shapes and forms.

Not far from Route 80, outside the little town of Hazard, Kentucky, is a place picturesquely known as

Valley of Troublesome Creek. In this tiny backwoods community lives a family whose members, for generations, have been marked by a strange anomaly: blue skin. According to Dr. Madison Cawein of the University of Kentucky College of Medicine, who tracked the family down and traced its story, the blue-skinned people seem perfectly normal in other respects. Their unusual color is caused by a rare enzyme deficiency that has been passed from one generation to the next.

Given our new, fast-accumulating knowledge of genetics, we shall be able to breed whole new races of blue people—or, for that matter, green, purple or orange. In a world still suffering from the moral lesion of racism, this is a thought to be conjured with. Should we strive for a world in which all people share the same skin color? If we want that, we shall no doubt have the technical means for bringing it about. Or should we, instead, work toward even greater diversity than now exists? What happens to the entire concept of race? To standards of physical beauty? To notions of superiority or inferiority?

We are hurtling toward the time when we will be able to breed both super- and sub-races. As Theodore J. Gordon put it in *The Future*, "Given the ability to tailor the race, I wonder if we would "create all men equal,' or would we choose to manufacture apartheid? Might the races of the future be: a superior group, the DNA controllers; the humble servants; special athletes for the 'games'; research scientists with 200 IQ and diminutive bodies . . ." We shall have the power to produce races of morons or of mathematical savants.

We shall also be able to breed babies with supernormal vision or hearing, supernormal ability to detect changes in odor, or supernormal muscular or musical skills. We will be able to create sexual superathletes, girls with super-mammaries (and perhaps more or less than the standard two), and countless other varieties of the previously monomorphic human being.

Ultimately, the problems are not scientific or technical, but ethical and political. Choice—and the criteria for choice—will be critical. The eminent science fiction author William Tenn once mused about the possibilities of genetic manipulation and the difficulties of choice. "Assuming hopefully for the moment that no dictator, self-righteous planning board or omnipotent black box is going to make genetic selections for the coming generation, then who or what is? Not parents, certainly . . ." he said, "they'll take the problem to their friendly neighborhood Certified Gene Architect.

"It seems inevitable to me that there will also be competitive schools of genetic architecture . . . the Functionalists will persuade parents to produce babies fitted for the present needs of society; the Futurists will suggest children who will have a niche in the culture as it will have evolved in twenty years; the Romantics will insist that each child be bred with at least one outstanding talent; and the Naturalists will advise the production of individuals so balanced genetically as to be in almost perfect equilibrium . . . Human body styles, like human clothing styles, will become *outré,* or *à la mode* as the genetic *couturiers* who designed them come into and out of vogue."

Buried behind this tongue-in-cheek are serious issues, made more profound by the immensity of the possibilities—some of them so grotesque that they appear to leap at us from the canvases of Hieronymus Bosch. Mention was made earlier of the idea of breeding men with gills or implanting gills in them for efficiency in underwater environments. At a meeting of world renowned biologists in London, J. B. S. Haldane began to expatiate about the possibility of creating new, far-out forms of man for space exploration. "The most obvious abnormalities in extra-terrestrial environments," Haldane observed, "are differences in gravitation, temperature, air pressure, air composition, and radiation ... Clearly a gibbon is better preadapted than a man for life in a low gravitational field, such as that of a space ship, an asteroid, or perhaps even the moon. A platyrrhine with a prehensile tail is even more so. Gene grafting may make it possible to incorporate such features into the human stocks."

While the scientists at this meeting devoted much of their attention to the moral consequences and perils of the biological revolution, no one challenged Haldane's suggestion that we shall someday make men with tails if we want them. Indeed, Lederberg merely observed that there might well be non-genetic ways to accomplish the same ends more easily. "We are going to modify man experimentally through physiological and embryological alterations, and by the substitution of machines for his parts," Lederberg declared. "If we want a man without legs, we don't have to breed him, we can chop them off; if we want a man with a tail, we will find a way of grafting it on to him."

At another meeting of scientists and scholars, Dr. Robert Sinsheimer, a Caltech biophysicist, put the challenge squarely:

"How will you choose to intervene in the ancient designs of nature for man? Would you like to control the sex of your offspring? It will be as you wish. Would you like your son to be six feet tall—seven feet? Eight feet? What troubles you?—allergy, obesity, arthritic pain? These will be easily handled. For cancer, diabetes, phenylketonuria there will be genetic therapy. The appropriate DNA will be provided in the appropriate dose. Viral and microbial disease will be easily met. Even the timeless patterns of growth and maturity and aging will be subject to our design. We know of no intrinsic limits to the life span. How long would you like to live?"

Lest his audience mistake him, Sinsheimer asked: "Do these projections sound like LSD fantasies, or the view in a distorted mirror? None transcends the potential of what we now know. They may not be developed in the way one might now anticipate, but they *are* feasible, they *can* be brought to reality, and sooner rather than later."

Not only *can* such wonders be brought to reality, but the odds are they *will*. Despite profound ethical questions about whether they *should*, the fact remains that scientific curiosity is, itself, one of the most powerful driving forces in our society. In the words of Dr. Rollin D. Hotchkiss of the Rockefeller Institute: "Many of us feel instinctive revulsion at the hazards of meddling with the finely balanced and far-reaching systems that make an individual what he is. Yet I believe it will surely be done or attempted. The pathway will be built from a combination of altruism, private profit and ignorance." To this list, worse yet, he might have added political conflict and bland unconcern. Thus Dr. A. Neyfakh, chief of the research laboratory of the Institute of Development Biology of the Soviet Academy of Sciences, predicts with a frightening lack of anxiety that the world will soon witness a genetic equivalent of the arms race. He bases his argument on the notion that the capitalist powers are engaged in a "struggle for brains." To make up for the brain drain, one or another of the "reactionary governments" will be "compelled" to employ genetic engineering to increase its output of geniuses and gifted individuals. Since this will occur "regardless of their intention," an international genetics race is inevitable. And this being so, he implies, the Soviet Union ought to be ready to jump the gun.

Criticized by the Soviet philosopher A. Petropavlovsky for his seeming willingness, even enthusiasm, to participate in such a race, Neyfakh shrugged aside the horrors that might be unleashed by hasty application of the new biology, replying merely that the advance of science is, and ought to be, unstoppable. If Neyfakh's political logic leaves something to be desired, his appeal to cold war passions as a justification for genetic tinkering is terrifying.

In short, it is safe to say that, unless specific counter-measures are taken, if something *can* be done, someone, somewhere *will* do it. The nature of what can and will be done exceeds anything that man is as yet psychologically or morally prepared to live with.

THE TRANSIENT ORGAN

We steadfastly refuse to face such facts. We avoid them by stubbornly refusing to recognize the speed of change. It makes us feel better to defer the future. Even those closest to the cutting edge of scientific research can scarcely believe the reality. Even they routinely underestimate the speed at which the future is breaking on our shores. Thus Dr. Richard J. Cleveland, speaking before a conference of organ transplant specialists, announced in January, 1967, that the first human heart transplant operation will occur "within five years." Yet before the same year was out Dr. Christiaan Barnard had operated on a fifty-five-year-old grocer named Louis Washkansky, and a staccato sequence of heart transplant operations exploded like a string of firecrackers into the world's awareness. In the meantime, success rates are rising steadily in kidney transplants. Successful liver, pancreas and ovary transplants are also reported.

Such accelerating medical advances must compel profound changes in our ways of thinking, as well as our way of caring for the sick. Startling new legal, ethical and philosophical issues arise. What, for instance, is death? Does death occur when the heart stops beating, as we have traditionally believed? Or does it occur when the brain stops functioning? Hospitals are becoming more and more familiar with cases of patients kept alive through advanced medical techniques, but doomed to exist as unconscious vegetables. What are the ethics of condemning such a person to death to obtain a healthy organ needed for transplant to save the life of a person with a better prognosis?

Lacking guidelines or precedents, we flounder over the moral and legal questions. Ghoulish rumors race through the medical community. *The New York Times* and *Komsomolskaya Pravda* both speculate about the possibility of "future murder rings supplying healthy organs for black-market surgeons whose patients are unwilling to wait until natural sources have supplied the heart or liver or pancreas they need." In Washington, the National Academy of Sciences, backed by a grant from the Russell Sage Foundation, begins a study of social policy issues springing from advances in the life sciences. At Stanford, a symposium, also funded by Russell Sage, examines methods for setting up transplant organ banks, the economics of an organ market, and evidences of class or racial discrimination in organ availability.

The possibility of cannibalizing bodies or corpses for usable transplant organs, grisly as it is, will serve to accelerate further the pace of change by lending urgency to research in the field of artificial organs—plastic or electronic substitutes for the heart or liver or spleen. (Eventually, even these may be made unnecessary when we learn how to regenerate damaged organs or severed limbs, growing new ones as the lizard now grows a tail.)

The drive to develop spare parts for failing human bodies will be stepped up as demand intensifies. The development of an economical artificial heart, Professor Lederberg says, "is only a few transient failures away." Professor R. M. Kenedi of the bio-engineering group at the University of Strathclyde in Glasgow believes that "by 1984, artificial replacements for tissues and organs may well have become commonplace." For some organs, this date is, in fact, conservative. Already more than 13,000 cardiac patients in the United States—including a Supreme Court justice—are alive because they carry, stitched into their chest cavity, a tiny "pacemaker"—a device that sends pulses of electricity to activate the heart.*

Another 10,000 pioneers are already equipped with artificial heart valves made of dacron mesh. Implantable hearing aids, artificial kidneys, arteries, hip joints, lungs, eye sockets and other parts are all in various stages of early development. We shall, before many decades are past, implant tiny, aspirin-sized sensors in the body to monitor blood pressure, pulse, respiration and other functions, and tiny transmitters to emit a signal when something goes wrong. Such signals will feed into giant diagnostic computer centers upon which the medicine of the future will be based. Some of us will also carry a tiny platinum plate and a dime-sized "stimulator" attached to the spine. By turning a midget "radio" on and off we will be able to activate the stimulator and kill pain. Initial work on these pain-control mechanisms is already under way at the Case Institute of Technology. Pushbutton pain killers are already being used by certain cardiac patients.

Such developments will lead to vast new bio-engineering industries, chains of medical-electronic repair stations, new technical professions and a reorganization of the entire health system. They will change life expectancy, shatter insurance company life tables, and bring about important shifts in the

---

* At a major Midwest hospital not long ago a patient appeared at the emergency room in the middle of the night. He was hiccupping violently, sixty times a minute. The patient, it turned out, was an early pacemaker wearer. A fast-thinking resident realized what had happened: a pacemaker wire, instead of stimulating the heart, had broken loose and become lodged in the diaphragm. Its jolts of electricity were causing the hiccupping. Acting swiftly, the resident inserted a needle into the patient's chest near the pacemaker, ran a wire out from the needle and grounded it to the hospital plumbing. The hiccupping stopped, giving doctors a chance to operate and reposition the faulty wire. A foretaste of tomorrow's medicine?

human outlook. Surgery will be less frightening to the average individual; implantation routine. The human body will come to be seen as modular. Through application of the modular principle—preservation of the whole through systematic replacement of transient components—we may add two or three decades to the average life span of the population. Unless, however, we develop far more advanced understanding of the brain than we now have, this could lead to one of the greatest ironies in history. Sir George Pickering, Regius professor of medicine at Oxford, has warned that unless we watch out, "those with senile brains will form an ever increasing fraction of the inhabitants of the earth. I find this," he added rather unnecessarily, "a terrifying prospect." Just such terrifying prospects will drive us toward more accelerated research into the brain—which, in turn, will generate still further radical changes in the society.

Today we struggle to make heart valves or artificial plumbing that imitate the original they are designed to replace. We strive for functional equivalence. Once we have mastered the basic problems, however, we shall not merely install plastic aortas in people because their original aorta is about to fail. We shall install specially-designed parts that are *better* than the original, and then we shall move on to install parts that provide the user with capabilities that were absent in the first place. Just as genetic engineering holds out the promise of producing "super-people," so, too, does organ technology suggest the possibility of track stars with extra-capacity lungs or hearts; sculptors with a neural device that intensifies sensitivity to texture; lovers with sex-intensifying neural machinery. In short, we shall no longer implant merely to save a life, but to enhance it—to make possible the achievement of moods, states, conditions or ecstasies that are presently beyond us.

Under these circumstances, what happens to our age-old definitions of "human-ness?" How will it feel to be part protoplasm and part transistor? Exactly what possibilities will it open? What limitations will it place on work, play, sex, intellectual or aesthetic responses? What happens to the mind when the body is changed? Questions like these cannot be long deferred, for advanced fusions of man and machine—called "Cyborgs"—are closer than most people suspect.

THE CYBORGS AMONG US

Today the man with a pacemaker or a plastic aorta is still recognizably a man. The inanimate part of his body is still relatively unimportant in terms of his personality and consciousness. But as the proportion of machine components rises, what happens to his awareness of self, his inner experience? If we assume that the brain is the seat of consciousness and intelligence, and that no other part of the body affects personality or self very much, then it is possible to conceive of a disembodied brain—a brain without arms, legs, spinal cord or other equipment—as a self, a personality, an embodiment of awareness. It may then become possible to combine the human brain with a whole set of artificial sensors, receptors and effectors, and to call *that* tangle of wires and plastic a human being.

All this may seem to resemble medieval speculation about the number of angels who can pirouette on a pinhead, yet the first small steps toward some form of man-machine symbiosis are already being taken. Moreover, they are being taken not by a lone mad scientist, but by thousands of highly trained engineers, mathematicians, biologists, surgeons, chemists, neurologists and communications specialists.

Dr. W. G. Walter's mechanical "tortoises" are machines that behave as though they had been psychologically conditioned. These tortoises were early specimens of a growing breed of robots ranging from the "Perceptron" which could learn (and even generalize) to the more recent "Wanderer," a robot capable of exploring an area, building up in its memory an "image" of the terrain, and able even to indulge in certain operations comparable, at least in some respects, to "contemplative speculation" and "fantasy." Experiments by Ross Ashby, H. D. Block, Frank Rosenblatt and others demonstrate that machines can learn from their mistakes, improve their performance, and, in certain limited kinds of learning, outstrip human students. Says Block, professor of Applied Mathematics at Cornell University: "I don't think there's a task you can name that a machine can't do—in principle. If you can define a task and a human can do it, then a machine can, at least in theory, also do it. The converse, however, is not true." Intelligence and creativity, it would appear, are not a human monopoly.

Despite setbacks and difficulties, the roboteers are moving forward. Recently they enjoyed a collective laugh at the expense of one of the leading critics of the robot-builders, a former RAND Corporation computer specialist named Hubert L. Dreyfus. Arguing that computers would never be able to match human intelligence, Dreyfus wrote a lengthy paper heaping vitriolic scorn on those who disagreed with him. Among other things, he declared, "No chess program can play even amateur chess." In context, he appeared to be saying that none ever would. Less than two years later, a graduate student at MIT, Richard Greenblatt, wrote a chess-playing computer program, challenged Dreyfus to a match, and had the immense satisfaction of watching the computer annihilate Dreyfus to the cheers of the "artificial intelligence" researchers.

In a quite different field of robotology there is progress, too. Technicians at Disneyland have created extremely life-like computer-controlled humanoids capable of moving their arms and legs, grimacing, smiling, glowering, simulating fear, joy and a wide range of other emotions. Built of clear plastic that, according to one reporter, "does everything but bleed," the robots chase girls, play music, fire pistols, and so closely resemble human forms that visitors routinely shriek with fear, flinch and otherwise react as though they were dealing with real human beings. The purposes to which these robots are put may seem trivial, but the technology on which they are based is highly sophisticated. It depends heavily on knowledge acquired from the space program—and this knowledge is accumulating rapidly.

There appears to be no reason, in principle, why we cannot go forward from these present primitive and trivial robots to build humanoid machines capable of extremely varied behavior, capable even of "human" error and seemingly random choice—in short, to make them behaviorally indistinguishable from humans except by means of highly sophisticated or elaborate tests. At that point we shall face the novel sensation of trying to determine whether the smiling, assured humanoid behind the airline reservation counter is a pretty girl or a carefully wired robot.*

The likelihood, of course, is that she will be both.

The thrust toward some form of man-machine symbiosis is furthered by our increasing ingenuity in communicating with machines. A great deal of much-publicized work is being done to facilitate the interaction of men and computers. But quite apart from this, Russian and American scientists have both been experimenting with the placement or implantation

---

* This raises a number of half-amusing, half-serious problems about the relationships between men and machines, including emotional and even sexual relationships. Professor Block at Cornell speculates that man-machine sexual relationships may not be too far distant. Pointing out that men often develop emotional attachments to the machines they use, he suggests that we shall have to give attention to the "ethical" questions arising from our treatment of "these mechanical objects of our affection and passion." A serious inquiry into these issues is to be found in an article by Roland Puccetti in the British *Journal of the Philosophy of Science*, 18 (1967) 39–51.

of detectors that pick up signals from the nerve ends at the stub of an amputated limb. These signals are then amplified and used to activate an artificial limb, thereby making a machine directly and sensitively responsive to the nervous system of a human being. The human need not "think out" his desires; even involuntary impulses are transmittable. The responsive behavior of the machine is as automatic as the behavior of ones' own hand, eye or leg.

In *Flight to Arras*, Antoine de Saint-Exupéry, novelist, poet and pioneer aviator, described buckling himself into the seat of a fighter plane during World War II. "All this complication of oxygen tubes, heating equipment; these speaking tubes that form the 'intercom' running between the members of the crew. This mask through which I breathe. I am attached to the plane by a rubber tube as indispensable as an umbilical cord. Organs have been added to my being, and they seem to intervene between me and my heart . . ." We have come far since those distant days. Space biology is marching irresistibly toward the day when the astronaut will not merely be buckled into his capsule, but become a part of it in the full symbiotic sense of the phrase.

One aim is to make the craft itself a wholly self-sufficient universe, in which algae is grown for food, water is recovered from body waste, air is recycled to purge it of the ammonia entering the atmosphere from urine, etc. In this totally enclosed fully regenerative world, the human being becomes an integral part of an on-going micro-ecological process whirling through the vastnesses of space. Thus Theodore Gordon, author of *The Future* and himself a leading space engineer, writes: "Perhaps it would be simpler to provide life support in the form of machines that plug into the astronaut. He could be fed intravenously using a liquid food compactly stored in a remote pressurized tank. Perhaps direct processing of body liquid wastes, and conversion to water, could be accomplished by a new type of artificial kidney built in as part of the spaceship. Perhaps sleep could be induced electronically . . . to lower his metabolism . . ." *Und so weiter.* One after another, the body functions of the human become interwoven with, dependent on, and part of, the machine functions of the capsule.

The ultimate extension of such work, however, is not necessarily to be found in the outer reaches of space; it may well become a common part of everyday life here on the mother planet. This is the direct link-up of the human brain—stripped of its supporting physical structures—with the computer. Indeed, it may be that the biological component of the supercomputers of the future may be massed human brains. The possibility of enhancing human (and machine) intelligence by linking them together organically opens enormous and exciting probabilities, so exciting that Dr. R. M. Page, director of the Naval Research Laboratory in Washington, has publicly discussed the feasibility of a system in which human thoughts are fed automatically into the storage unit of a computer to form the basis for machine decision-making. Participants in a RAND Corporation study conducted several years ago were asked when this development might occur. Answers ranged from as soon as 1990 to "never." But the median date given was 2020—well within the lifetime of today's teen-agers.

In the meantime, research from countless sources contributes toward the eventual symbiosis. In one of the most fascinating, frightening and intellectually provocative experiments ever recorded, Professor Robert White, director of neurosurgery at the Metropolitan General Hospital in Cleveland, has given evidence that the brain *can* be isolated from its body and kept alive after the "death" of the rest of the organism. The experiment, described in a brilliant article by Oriana Fallaci, saw a team of neurosurgeons cut the brain out of a rhesus monkey, discard the body, then hook the brain's carotid arteries up to another monkey, whose blood then continued to bathe the disembodied organ, keeping it alive.

Said one of the members of the medical team, Dr. Leo Massopust, a neurophysiologist: "The brain activity is largely better than when the brain had a body . . . No doubt about it. I even suspect that without his senses, he can think more quickly. What kind of thinking, I don't know. I guess he is primarily a memory, a repository for information stored when he had his flesh; he cannot develop further because he no longer has the nourishment of experience. Yet this, too, is a new experience."

The brain survived for five hours. It could have lasted much longer, had it served the purposes of research. Professor White has successfully kept other brains alive for days, using machinery, rather than a living monkey, to keep the brain washed with blood. "I don't think we have reached the stage," he told Miss Fallaci, "where you can turn men into robots, obedient sheep. Yet . . . it could happen, it isn't impossible. If you consider that we can transfer the head of a man onto the trunk of another man, if you consider that we can isolate the brain of a man and make it work without its body . . . To me, there is no longer any gap between science fiction and science . . . We could keep Einstein's brain alive and make it function normally."

Not only, Professor White implies, can we transfer the head of one man to the shoulders of another, not only can we keep a head or a brain "alive" and functioning, but it can all be done, with "existing techniques." Indeed, he declares, "The Japanese will be the first to [keep an isolated human head alive]. I will not, because I haven't resolved as yet this dilemma: Is it right or not?" A devout Catholic, Dr. White is deeply troubled by the philosophical and moral implications of his work.

As the brain surgeons and the neurologists probe further, as the bio-engineers and the mathematicians, the communications experts and robot-builders become more sophisticated, as the space men and their capsules grow closer and closer to one another, as machines begin to embody biological components and men come bristling with sensors and mechanical organs, the ultimate symbiosis approaches. The work converges. Yet the greatest marvel of all is not organ transplantation or symbiosis or underwater engineering. It is not technology, nor science itself.

The greatest and most dangerous marvel of all is the complacent past-orientation of the race, its unwillingness to confront the reality of acceleration. Thus man moves swiftly into an unexplored universe, into a totally new stage of eco-technological development, firmly convinced that "human nature is eternal" or that "stability will return." He stumbles into the most violent revolution in human history muttering, in the words of one famous, though myopic sociologist, that "the processes of modernization . . . have been more or less 'completed.'" He simply refuses to imagine the future.

THE DENIAL OF CHANGE

In 1865 a newspaper editor told his readers that "Well-informed people know that it is impossible to transmit the voice over wires and that, were it possible to do so, the thing would be of no practical value." Barely a decade later, the telephone erupted from Mr. Bell's laboratory and changed the world.

On the very day that the Wright brothers took wing, newspapers refused to report the event because their sober, solid, feet-on-the-ground editors simply could not bring themselves to believe it had happened. After all, a famous American astronomer, Simon Newcomb, had not long before assured the world that "No possible combination of known substances, known forms of machinery and known forms of force, can be united in a practical machine by which man shall fly long distances."

Not long after this, another expert announced publicly that it was "nothing less than feeblemindedness
to expect anything to come of the horseless carriage
movement." Six years later the one-millionth Ford
rolled off an assembly line. And then there was the
great Rutherford, himself, the discoverer of the atom,
who said in 1933 that the energy in the atom's nucleus
would never be released. Nine years later: the first
chain reaction.

Again and again the human brain—including the
first class scientific brain—has blinded itself to the novel
possibilities of the future, has narrowed its field of
concern to gain momentary reassurance, only to be
rudely shaken by the accelerative thrust.

This is not to imply that *all* the scientific or technological advances so far discussed will necessarily
materialize. Still less does it imply that they will all
occur between now and the turn of the century. Some
will, no doubt, die a-borning. Some may represent
blind alleys. Others will succeed in the lab, but turn
out to be impractical for one reason or another. Yet
all this is unimportant. For even if none of these developments occur, others, perhaps even more unsettling, will.

We have scarcely touched on the computer revolution and the far-ramifying changes that must follow
in its churning wake. We have barely mentioned the
implications of the thrust into outer space, an adventure that could, before the new millennium arrives,
change all our lives and attitudes in radical and as yet
unpredicted ways. (What would happen if an astronaut or space vehicle returned to earth contaminated
with some fast-multiplying, death-dealing microorga-
nism?) We have said nothing about the laser, the
holograph, the powerful new instruments of personal
and mass communication, the new technologies of
crime and espionage, new forms of transport and construction, the developing horror of chemical and bac-
teriological warfare techniques, the radiant promise of

solar energy, the coming discovery of life in a test tube, the startling new tools and techniques for education, and an endless list of other fields in which high-impact changes lie just ahead.

In the coming decades, advances in all these fields will fire off like a series of rockets carrying us out of the past, plunging us deeper into the new society. Nor will this new society quickly settle into a steady state. It, too, will quiver and crack and roar as it suffers jolt after jolt of high-energy change. For the individual who wishes to live in his time, to be a part of the future, the super-industrial revolution offers no surcease from change. It offers no return to the familiar past. It offers only the highly combustible mixture of transience and novelty.

This massive injection of speed and novelty into the fabric of society will force us not merely to cope more rapidly with familiar situations, events and moral dilemmas, but to cope at a progressively faster rate with situations that are, for us, decidedly unfamiliar, "first-time" situations, strange, irregular, unpredictable.

This will significantly alter the balance that prevails in any society between the familiar and unfamiliar elements in the daily life of its people, between the routine and non-routine, the predictable and the unpredictable. The relationship between these two kinds of daily-life elements can be called the "novelty ratio" of the society, and as the level of newness or novelty rises, less and less of life appears subject to our routine forms of coping behavior. More and more, there is a growing weariness and wariness, a pall of pessimism, a decline in our sense of mastery. More and more, the environment comes to seem chaotic, beyond human control.

Thus two great social forces converge: the relentless movement toward transience is reinforced and made more potentially dangerous by a rise in the novelty ratio. Nor, as we shall next see, is this novelty to be found solely in the technological arrangements of the society-to-be. In its social arrangements, too, we can anticipate the unprecedented, the unfamiliar, the bizarre.

Chapter 10

THE EXPERIENCE MAKERS

The year 2000 is closer to us in time than the great depression, yet the world's economists, traumatized by that historic disaster, remain frozen in the attitudes of the past. Economists, even those who talk the language of revolution, are peculiarly conservative creatures. If it were possible to pry from their brains their collective image of the economy of, say, the year 2025, it would look very much like that of 1970—only more so.

Conditioned to think in straight lines, economists have great difficulty imagining alternatives to communism and capitalism. They see in the growth of large-scale organization nothing more than a linear expansion of old-fashioned bureaucracy. They see technological advance as a simple, non-revolutionary extension of the known. Born of scarcity, trained to think in terms of limited resources, they can hardly conceive of a society in which man's basic material wants have been satisfied.

One reason for their lack of imagination is that when they think about technological advance, they concentrate solely on the *means* of economic activity. Yet the super-industrial revolution challenges the ends as well. It threatens to alter not merely the "how" of production but the "why." It will, in short, transform the very purposes of economic activity.

Before such an upheaval, even the most sophisticated tools of today's economists are helpless. Input-output tables, econometric models—the whole paraphernalia of analysis that economists employ simply do not come to grips with the external forces—political, social and ethical—that will transform economic life in the decades before us. What does "productivity" or "efficiency" mean in a society that places a high value on psychic fulfillment? What happens to an economy when, as is likely, the entire concept of property is reduced to meaninglessness? How are economies likely to be affected by the rise of supra-national planning, taxing and regulatory agencies or by a kind of dialectical return to "cottage industry" based on the most advanced cybernetic technologies? Most important, what happens when "no growth" replaces "growth" as an economic objective, when GNP ceases to be the holy grail?

Only by stepping outside the framework of orthodox economic thought and examining these possibilities can we begin to prepare for tomorrow. And among these, none is more central than the shift in values that is likely to accompany the super-industrial revolution.

Under conditions of scarcity, men struggle to meet their immediate material needs. Today under more affluent conditions, we are reorganizing the economy to deal with a new level of human needs. From a system designed to provide material satisfaction, we are rapidly creating an economy geared to the provision of psychic gratification. This process of "psychologization," one of the central themes of the super-industrial revolution, has been all but overlooked by the economists. Yet it will result in a novel, surprise-filled economy unlike any man has ever experienced. The issues raised by it will reduce the great conflict of the twentieth century, the conflict between capitalism and communism, to comparative insignificance. For these issues sweep far beyond economic or political dogma. They involve, as we shall see, nothing less than sanity, the human organism's ability to distinguish illusion from reality.

THE PSYCHIC CAKE-MIX

Much excitement has accompanied the discovery that once a techno-society reaches a certain stage of industrial development, it begins to shift energies into the production of services, as distinct from goods. Many experts see in the services the wave of the future. They suggest that manufacturing will soon be outstripped by service activity in all the industrial nations —a prophecy already on its way toward fulfillment.

What the economists, however, have not done, is to ask the obvious question. Where does the economy go next? After the services, what?

The high technology nations must, in coming years, direct vast resources to rehabilitating their physical environment and improving what has come to be called "the quality of life." The fight against pollution, aesthetic blight, crowding, noise and dirt will clearly absorb tremendous energies. But, in addition to the provision of these public goods, we can also anticipate a subtle change in the character of production for private use.

The very excitement aroused by the mushrooming growth of the service sector has diverted professional attention from another shift that will deeply affect both goods *and* services in the future. It is this shift that will lead to the next forward movement of the economy, the growth of a strange new sector based on what can only be called the "experience industries." For the key to the post-service economy lies in the psychologization of all production, beginning with manufacture.

One of the curious facts about production in all the techno-societies today, and especially the United

States, is that goods are increasingly designed to yield psychological "extras" for the consumer. The manufacturer adds a "psychic load" to his basic product, and the consumer gladly pays for this intangible benefit.

A classic example is the case of the appliance or auto manufacturer who adds buttons, knobs or dials to the control panel or dashboard, even when these have seemingly no significance. The manufacturer has learned that increasing the number of gadgets, up to a point, gives the operator of the machine the sense of controlling a more complex device, and hence a feeling of increased mastery. This psychological payoff is designed into the product.

Conversely, pains are taken not to deprive the consumer of an existing psychological benefit. Thus a large American food company proudly launched a labor-saving, add-water-only cake mix. The company was amazed when women rejected the product in favor of mixes that require extra labor—the addition of an egg along with the water. By inserting powdered egg in the factory, the company had oversimplified the task of the housewife, depriving her of the sense of creatively participating in the cake-baking process. The powdered egg was hastily eliminated, and women went happily back to cracking their own eggs. Once again a product was modified to provide a psychic benefit.

Examples like these can be multiplied endlessly in almost any major industry, from soap and cigarettes to dishwashers and diet colas. According to Dr. Emanuel Demby, president of Motivational Programmers, Incorporated, a research firm employed in the United States and Europe by such blue-chip corporations as General Electric, Caltex and IBM, "The engineering of psychological factors into manufactured goods will be a hallmark of production in the future—not only in consumer goods, but in industrial hardware.

"Even the big cranes and derricks built today embody this principle. Their cabs are streamlined, slick, like something out of the twenty-first century. Caterpillar, International Harvester, Ferguson—all of them. Why? These mechanical monsters don't dig better or hoist better because the cab is aesthetically improved. But the contractor who buys them likes it better. The men who work on them like it better. The contractor's customers like it better. So even the manufacturers of earthmoving equipment begin to pay attention to non-utilitarian—i.e., psychological—factors."

Beyond this, Demby asserts, manufacturers are devoting more attention to reducing tensions that accompany the use of certain products. Manufacturers of sanitary napkins, for example, know that women have a fear of stopping up the toilet when disposing of them. "A new product has been developed," he says, "that instantly dissolves on contact with water. It doesn't perform its basic function any better. But it relieves some of the anxiety that went with it. This is psychological engineering if ever there was any!"

Affluent consumers are willing and able to pay for such niceties. As disposable income rises, they become progressively less concerned with price, progressively more insistent on what they call "quality." For many products quality can still be measured in the traditional terms of workmanship, durability and materials. But for a fast-growing class of products, such differences are virtually undetectable. Blindfolded, the consumer cannot distinguish Brand A from Brand B. Nevertheless, she often argues fiercely that one is superior to another.

This paradox vanishes once the psychic component of production is taken into account. For even when they are otherwise identical, there are likely to be marked psychological differences between one product and another. Advertisers strive to stamp each product with its own distinct image. These images are functional: they fill a need on the part of the consumer. The need is psychological, however, rather than utilitarian in the ordinary sense. Thus we find that the term "quality" increasingly refers to the ambience, the status associations—in effect, the psychological connotations of the product.

As more and more of the basic material needs of the consumer are met, it is strongly predictable that even more economic energy will be directed at meeting the consumer's subtle, varied and quite personal needs for beauty, prestige, individuation, and sensory delight. The manufacturing sector will channel ever greater resources into the conscious design of psychological distinctions and gratifications. The psychic component of goods production will assume increasing importance.

"SERVING WENCHES" IN THE SKY

This, however, is only the first step toward the psychologization of the economy. The next step will be the expansion of the psychic component of the services.

Here, again, we are already moving in the predictable direction, as a glance at air travel demonstrates. Once flying was simply a matter of getting from here to there. Before long, the airlines began to compete on the basis of pretty stewardesses, food, luxurious surroundings, and in-flight movies. Trans-World Airlines recently carried this process one step further by offering what it called "foreign accent" flights between major American cities.

The TWA passenger may now choose a jet on which the food, the music, the magazines, the movies, and the stewardess' miniskirt are all French. He may choose a "Roman" flight on which the girls wear togas. He may opt for a "Manhattan Penthouse" flight. Or he may select the "Olde English" flight on which the girls are called "serving wenches" and the decor supposedly suggests that of an English pub.

It is clear that TWA is no longer selling transportation, as such, but a carefully designed psychological package as well. We can expect the airlines before long to make use of lights and multi-media projections to create total, but temporary, environments providing the passenger with something approaching a theatrical experience.

The experience may, in fact, soon go beyond theater. British Overseas Airways Corporation recently pointed a wavering finger at the future when it announced a plan to provide unmarried American male passengers with "scientifically chosen" blind dates in London. In the event the computer-selected date failed to show up, an alternate would be provided. Moreover, a party would be arranged to which "several additional Londoners of both sexes of varying ages" would be invited so that the traveler, who would also be given a tour of discothèques and restaurants, would under no circumstances be alone. The program, called "The Beautiful Singles of London," was abruptly called off when the government-owned airline came under Parliamentary criticism. Nevertheless, we can anticipate further colorful attempts to paint a psychic coating on many consumer service fields, including retailing.

Anyone who has strolled through Newport Center, an incredibly lavish new shopping plaza in Newport Beach, California, cannot fail to be impressed by the attention paid by its designers to aesthetic and psychological factors. Tall white arches and columns outlined against a blue sky, fountains, statues, carefully planned illumination, a pop art playground, and an enormous Japanese wind-bell are all used to create a mood of casual elegance for the shopper. It is not merely the affluence of the surroundings, but their programmed pleasantness that makes shopping there a quite memorable experience. One can anticipate fantastic variations and elaborations of the same principles in the planning of retail stores in the future. We shall go far beyond any "functional" necessity, turning the service, whether it is shopping, dining, or having one's hair cut, into a pre-fabricated experience. We shall watch movies or listen to chamber music as we have our hair cut, and the mechanical bowl that fits over the skull of a woman in the beauty parlor will do more than simply dry her hair. By directing electronic waves to her brain, it may, quite literally, tickle her fancy.

Bankers and brokers, real estate and insurance companies will employ the most carefully chosen decor, music, closed circuit color television, engineered tastes and smells, along with the most advanced mixed-media equipment to heighten (or neutralize) the psychological charge that accompanies even the most routine transaction. No important service will be offered to the consumer before it has been analyzed by teams of behavioral engineers to improve its psychic loading.

EXPERIENTIAL INDUSTRIES

Reaching beyond these simple elaborations of the present, we shall also witness a revolutionary expansion of certain industries whose sole output consists not of manufactured goods, nor even of ordinary services, but of pre-programmed "experiences." The experience industry could turn out to be one of the pillars of super-industrialism, the very foundation, in fact, of the post-service economy.

As rising affluence and transience ruthlessly undercut the old urge to possess, consumers begin to collect experiences as consciously and passionately as they once collected things. Today, as the airline example suggests, experiences are sold as an adjunct to some more traditional service. The experience is, so to speak, the frosting on the cake. As we advance into the future, however, more and more experiences will be sold strictly on their own merits, exactly as if they *were* things.

Precisely this is beginning to happen, in fact. This accounts for the high growth rate visible in certain industries that have always been, at least partly, engaged in the production of experiences for their own sake. The arts are a good example. Much of the "culture industry" is devoted to the creation or staging of specialized psychological experiences. Today we find art-based "experience industries" booming in virtually all the techno-societies. The same is true of recreation, mass entertainment, education, and certain psychiatric services, all of which participate in what might be called experiential production.

When Club Méditerranée sells a package holiday that takes a young French secretary to Tahiti or Israel for a week or two of sun and sex, it is manufacturing an experience for her quite as carefully and systematically as Renault manufactures cars. Its advertisements underscore the point. Thus a two-page spread in *The New York Times Magazine* begins with the headline: "Take 300 men and women. Strand them on an exotic island. And strip them of every social pressure." Based in France, Club Méditerranée now operates thirty-four vacation "villages" all over the world.

Similarly, when the Esalen Institute in Big Sur, California, offers weekend seminars in "body-awareness" and "non-verbal communication," at seventy dollars per person, or five-day workshops at $180, it promises not simply to teach, but to plunge its affluent customers into "joyous" new interpersonal experiences —a phrase some readers take to mean adventures with sex or LSD. Group therapy and sensitivity training sessions are packaged experiences. So are certain classes. Thus, going to an Arthur Murray or Fred Astaire studio to learn the latest dance step may provide the student with a skill that will bring enjoyment in the future, but it also provides a pleasurable here-and-now experience for the lonely bachelor or spinster. The learning experience, itself, is a major attraction for the customer.

All these, however, provide only the palest clue as to the nature of the experience industry of the future and the great psychological corporations, or psych-corps, that will dominate it.

SIMULATED ENVIRONMENTS

One important class of experiential products will be based on simulated environments that offer the customer a taste of adventure, danger, sexual titillation or other pleasure without risk to his real life or reputation. Thus computer experts, roboteers, designers, historians, and museum specialists will join to create experiential enclaves that reproduce, as skillfully as sophisticated technology will permit, the splendor of ancient Rome, the pomp of Queen Elizabeth's court, the "sexoticism" of an eighteenth-century Japanese geisha house, and the like. Customers entering these pleasure domes will leave their everyday clothes (and cares) behind, don costumes, and run through a planned sequence of activities intended to provide them with a first-hand taste of what the original—i.e., unsimulated—reality must have felt like. They will be invited, in effect, to live in the past or perhaps even in the future.

Production of such experiences is closer than one might think. It is clearly foreshadowed in the participatory techniques now being pioneered in the arts. Thus "happenings" in which the members of the audience take part may be regarded as a first stumbling step toward these simulations of the future. The same is true of more formal works as well. When *Dionysus in 69* was performed in New York, a critic summed up the theories of its playwright, Richard Schechner, in the following words. "Theater has traditionally said to an audience, 'Sit down and I'll tell you a story.' Why can't it also say, 'Stand up and we'll play a game?'" Schechner's work, based loosely on Euripides, says precisely this, and the audience is literally invited to join in dancing to celebrate the rites of Dionysus.

Artists also have begun to create whole "environments"—works of art into which the audience may actually walk, and inside which things happen. In

Sweden the Moderna Museet has exhibited an immense papier-mâché lady called "Hon" ("She"), into whose innards the audience entered via a vaginal portal. Once inside, there were ramps, stairways, flashing lights, odd sounds, and something called a "bottle smashing machine." Dozens of museums and galleries around the United States and Europe now display such "environments." *Time* magazine's art critic suggests that their intention is to bombard the spectator with "wacky sights, weirdo sounds and otherworldly sensations, ranging from the feeling of weightlessness to hopped-up, psychedelic hallucinations." The artists who produce these are really "experiential engineers."

In a deceptively shabby storefront on a Lower Manhattan street lined with factories and warehouses, I visited Cerebrum, an "electronic studio of participation" where, for an hourly fee, guests are admitted into a startling white, high-ceilinged room. There they strip off their clothing, don semi-transparent robes, and sprawl comfortably on richly padded white platforms. Attractive male and female "guides," similarly nude under their veils, offer each guest a stereophonic headset, a see-through mask, and, from time to time, balloons, kaleidoscopes, tambourines, plastic pillows, mirrors, pieces of crystal, marshmallows, slides and slide projectors. Folk and rock music, interspersed with snatches of television commercials, street noises and a lecture by or about Marshall McLuhan fill the ears. As the music grows more excited, guests and guides begin to dance on the platforms and the carpeted white walkways that connect them. Bubbles drift down from machines in the ceiling. Hostesses float through, spraying a variety of fragrances into the air. Lights change color and random images wrap themselves around the walls, guests and guides. The mood shifts from cool at first to warm, friendly, and mildly erotic.

Still primitive both artistically and technologically, Cerebrum is a pale forerunner of the "$25,000,000 'super' Environmental Entertainment Complex" its builders enthusiastically talk of creating some day. Whatever their artistic merit, experiments such as these point to far more sophisticated enclave-building in the future. Today's young artists and environmental entrepreneurs are performing research and development for the psych-corps of tomorrow.

LIVE ENVIRONMENTS

Knowledge gained for this research will permit the construction of fantastic simulations. But it will also lead to complex live environments that subject the customer to significant risks and rewards. The African safari today is a colorless example. Future experience designers will, for example, create gambling casinos in which the customer plays not for money, but for experiential payoffs—a date with a lovely and willing lady if he wins, perhaps a day in solitary confinement if he loses. As the stakes rise, more imaginative payoffs and punishments will be designed.

A loser may have to serve (by voluntary pre-agreement) as a "slave" to a winner for several days. A winner may be rewarded by ten free minutes of electronic pleasure-probing of his brain. A player may risk flogging or its psychological equivalent—participation in a day-long session during which winners are permitted to work off their aggressions and hostilities by sneering, shouting at, reviling, or otherwise attacking the ego of the loser.

High rollers may play to win a free heart or lung transplant at some later date, should it prove to be necessary. Losers may have to forego a kidney. Such payoffs and punishments may be escalated in intensity and varied endlessly. Experiential designers will study the pages of Krafft-Ebing or the Marquis de Sade for ideas. Only imagination, technological capability, and the constraints of a generally relaxed morality limit the possibilities. Experiential gambling cities will rise to overshadow Las Vegas or Deauville, combining in a single place some of the features of Disneyland, the World's Fair, Cape Kennedy, the Mayo Clinic, and the honky-tonks of Macao.*

Once again, present-day developments foreshadow the future. Thus certain American television programs, such as *The Dating Game*, already pay players off in experiential rewards, as does the contest recently discussed in the Swedish Parliament. In this contest, a pornographic magazine awarded one of its readers a week in Majorca with one of its "topless" models. A Conservative M.P. challenged the propriety of such goings-on. Presumably, he felt better when he was assured by the Finance Minister, Gunnar Sträng, that the transaction was taxable.

Simulated and non-simulated experiences will also be combined in ways that will sharply challenge man's grasp of reality. In Ray Bradbury's vivid novel, *Fahrenheit 451*, suburban couples desperately save their money to enable them to buy three-wall or four-wall video sets that permit them to enter into a kind of televised psycho-drama. They become actor-participants in soap operas that continue for weeks or months. Their participation in these stories is highly involving. We are, in fact, beginning to move toward the actual development of such "interactive" films with the help of advanced communications technology. The combination of simulations and "reals" will vastly multiply the number and variety of experiential products.

But the great psych-corps of tomorrow will not only sell individual, discrete experiences. They will offer sequences of experiences so organized that their very juxtaposition with one another will contribute color, harmony or contrast to lives that lack these qualities. Beauty, excitement, danger or delicious sen-

---

* For a brilliant and provocative insight into experiential gambling and its philosophical implications, see "The Lottery in Babylon," by Jorge Luis Borges, the Argentinian philosopher-essayist. This short work is found in Borges' collection entitled *Labyrinths*.

suality will be programmed to enhance one another. By offering such experiential chains or sequences, the psych-corps (working closely, no doubt, with community mental health centers) will provide partial frameworks for those whose lives are otherwise too chaotic and unstructured. In effect, they will say: "Let us plan (part of) your life for you." In the transient, change-filled world of tomorrow, that proposition will find many eager takers.

The packaged experiences offered in the future will reach far beyond the imagination of the average consumer, filling the environment with endless novelties. Companies will vie with one another to create the most outlandish, most gratifying experiences. Indeed, some of these experiences—as in the case of topless Swedish models—will even reach beyond tomorrow's broadened boundaries of social acceptability. They may be offered to the public covertly by unlicensed, underground psych-corps. This will simply add the thrill of "illicitude" to the experience itself.

(One very old experiential industry has traditionally operated covertly: prostitution. Many other illegal activities also fit within the experience industry. For the most part, however, all these reveal a paucity of imagination and a lack of technical resources that will be remedied in the future. They are trivial compared with the possibilities in a society that will, by the year 2000 or sooner, be armed with robots, advanced computers, personality-altering drugs, brain-stimulating pleasure probes, and similar technological goodies.)

The diversity of novel experiences arrayed before the consumer will be the work of experience-designers, who will be drawn from the ranks of the most creative people in the society. The working motto of this profession will be: "If you can't serve it up real, find a vicarious substitute. If you're good, the customer will never know the difference!" This implied blurring of the line between the real and the unreal will confront the society with serious problems, but it will not prevent or even slow the emergence of the "psyche-service industries" and "psych-corps." Great globe-girdling syndicates will create super-Disneylands of a variety, scale, scope, and emotional power that is hard for us to imagine.

We can thus sketch the dim outlines of the super-industrial economy, the post-service economy of the future. Agriculture and the manufacture of goods will have become economic backwaters, employing fewer and fewer people. Highly automated, the making and growing of goods will be relatively simple. The design of new goods and the process of coating them with stronger, brighter, more emotion-packed psychological connotations, however, will challenge the ingenuity of tomorrow's best and most resourceful entrepreneurs.

The service sector, as defined today, will be vastly enlarged, and once more the design of psychological rewards will occupy a growing percentage of corporate time, energy and money. Investment services, such as mutual funds, for example, may introduce elements of experiential gambling to provide both additional excitement and non-economic payoffs to their shareholders. Insurance companies may offer not merely to pay death benefits, but to care for the widow or widower for several months after bereavement, providing nurses, psychological counseling and other assistance. Based on banks of detailed data about their customers, they may offer a computerized mating service to help the survivor locate a new life partner. Services, in short, will be greatly elaborated. Attention will be paid to the psychological overtones of every step or component of the product.

Finally, we shall watch the irresistible growth of companies already in the experiential field, and the formation of entirely new enterprises, both profit and non-profit, to design, package and distribute planned or programmed experiences. The arts will expand, becoming as Ruskin or Morris might have said, the handmaiden of industry. Psych-corps and other businesses will employ actors, directors, musicians and designers in large numbers. Recreational industries will grow, as the whole nature of leisure is redefined in experiential terms. Education, already exploding in size, will become one of the key experience industries as it begins to employ experiential techniques to convey both knowledge and values to students. The communications and computer industries will find in experiential production a major market for their machines and for their soft-ware as well. In short, those industries that in one way or another associate themselves with behavioral technology, those industries that transcend the production of tangible goods and traditional services, will expand most rapidly. Eventually, the experience-makers will form a basic—if not *the* basic—sector of the economy. The process of psychologization will be complete.

THE ECONOMICS OF SANITY

The essence of tomorrow's economy, declares the Stanford Research Institute in a report by its Long Range Planning Service, will be an "emphasis upon the inner as well as the material needs of individuals and groups." This new emphasis, SRI suggests, will arise not merely from the demands of the consumer, but from the very need of the economy to survive. "In a nation where all essential material needs can be filled by perhaps no more than three-fourths or even half of the productive capacity, a basic adjustment is required to keep the economy healthy."

It is this convergence of pressures—from the consumer and from those who wish to keep the economy growing—that will propel the techno-societies toward the experiential production of the future.

The movement in this direction can be delayed. The poverty-stricken masses of the world may not stand idly by as the world's favored few traverse the path toward psychological self-indulgence. There is something morally repellent about one group seeking to gratify itself psychologically, pursuing novel and rarified pleasures, while the majority of mankind lives in wretchedness or starvation. The techno-societies could defer the arrival of experientialism, could maintain a more conventional economy for a time by maximizing traditional production, shifting resources to environmental quality control, and then launching absolutely massive anti-poverty and foreign aid programs.

By creaming off "excess" productivity and, in effect, giving it away, the factories can be kept running, the agricultural surpluses used up, and the society can continue to focus on the satisfaction of material wants. A fifty-year campaign to erase hunger from the world, for example, would not only make excellent moral sense, but would buy the techno-societies badly needed time for an easier transition to the economy of the future.

Such a pause might give us time to contemplate the philosophical and psychological impact of experiential production. If consumers can no longer distinguish clearly between the real and the simulated, if whole stretches of one's life may be commercially programmed, we enter into a set of psycho-economic problems of breathtaking complexity. These problems challenge our most fundamental beliefs, not merely about democracy or economics, but about the very nature of rationality and sanity.

One of the great unasked questions of our time has to do with the balance between vicarious and non-vicarious experience in our lives. No previous generation has been exposed to one-tenth the amount of vicarious experiences that we lavish on ourselves and our children today, and no one, anywhere, has any real idea about the impact of this monumental shift on personality. Our children mature physically more rapidly than we did. The age of first menstruation continues to drop four to six months every decade. The population grows taller sooner. It is clear that many of our young people, products of television and instant access to oceans of information, also become precocious intellectually. But what happens to emotional development as the ratio of vicarious experience to "real" experience rises? Does the step-up of vicariousness contribute to emotional maturity? Or does it, in fact, retard it?

And what, then, happens when an economy in search of a new purpose, seriously begins to enter into the production of experiences for their own sake, experiences that blur the distinction between the vicarious and the non-vicarious, the simulated and the real? One of the definitions of sanity, itself, is the ability to tell real from unreal. Shall we need a new definition?

We must begin to reflect on these problems, for unless we do—and perhaps even *if* we do—service will in the end triumph over manufacture, and experiential production over service. The growth of the experiential sector might just be an inevitable consequence of affluence. For the satisfaction of man's elemental material needs opens the way for new, more sophisticated gratifications. We are moving from a "gut" economy to a "psyche" economy because there is only so much gut to be satisfied.

Beyond this, we are also moving swiftly in the direction of a society in which objects, things, physical constructs, are increasingly transient. Not merely man's relationships with them, but the very things themselves. It may be that experiences are the only products which, once bought by the consumer, cannot be taken away from him, cannot be disposed of like non-returnable soda pop bottles or nicked razor blades.

For the ancient Japanese nobility every flower, every serving bowl or obi, was freighted with surplus meaning; each carried a heavy load of coded symbolism and ritual significance. The movement toward the psychologization of manufactured goods takes us in this direction; but it collides with the powerful thrust toward transience that makes the objects themselves so perishable. Thus we shall find it easier to adorn our services with symbolic significance than our products. And, in the end, we shall pass beyond the service economy, beyond the imagination of today's economists; we shall become the first culture in history to employ high technology to manufacture that most transient, yet lasting of products: the human experience.

Chapter 11

THE FRACTURED FAMILY

The flood of novelty about to crash down upon us will spread from universities and research centers to factories and offices, from the marketplace and mass media into our social relationships, from the community into the home. Penetrating deep into our private lives, it will place absolutely unprecedented strains on the family itself.

The family has been called the "giant shock absorber" of society—the place to which the bruised and battered individual returns after doing battle with the world, the one stable point in an increasingly flux-filled environment. As the super-industrial revolution unfolds, this "shock absorber" will come in for some shocks of its own.

Social critics have a field day speculating about the family. The family is "near the point of complete extinction," says Ferdinand Lundberg, author of *The Coming World Transformation*. "The family is dead except for the first year or two of child raising," according to psychoanalyst William Wolf. "This will be its only function." Pessimists tell us the family is racing toward oblivion—but seldom tell us what will take its place.

Family optimists, in contrast, contend that the family, having existed all this time, will continue to exist.

Some go so far as to argue that the family is in for a Golden Age. As leisure spreads, they theorize, families will spend more time together and will derive great satisfaction from joint activity. "The family that plays together, stays together," etc.

A more sophisticated view holds that the very turbulence of tomorrow will drive people deeper into their families. "People will marry for stable structure," says Dr. Irwin M. Greenberg, Professor of Psychiatry at the Albert Einstein College of Medicine. According to this view, the family serves as one's "portable roots," anchoring one against the storm of change. In short, the more transient and novel the environment, the more important the family will become.

It may be that both sides in this debate are wrong. For the future is more open than it might appear. The family may neither vanish *nor* enter upon a new Golden Age. It may—and this is far more likely—break up, shatter, only to come together again in weird and novel ways.

THE MYSTIQUE OF MOTHERHOOD

The most obviously upsetting force likely to strike the family in the decades immediately ahead will be the impact of the new birth technology. The ability to pre-set the sex of one's baby, or even to "program" its IQ, looks and personality traits, must now be regarded as a real possibility. Embryo implants, babies grown *in vitro*, the ability to swallow a pill and guarantee oneself twins or triplets or, even more, the ability to walk into a "babytorium" and actually purchase embryos—all this reaches so far beyond any previous human experience that one needs to look at the future through the eyes of the poet or painter, rather than those of the sociologist or conventional philosopher.

It is regarded as somehow unscholarly, even frivolous, to discuss these matters. Yet advances in science and technology, or in reproductive biology alone, could, within a short time, smash all orthodox ideas about the family and its responsibilities. When babies can be grown in a laboratory jar what happens to the very notion of maternity? And what happens to the self-image of the female in societies which, since the very beginnings of man, have taught her that her primary mission is the propagation of and nurture of the race?

Few social scientists have begun as yet to concern themselves with such questions. One who has is psychiatrist Hyman G. Weitzen, director of Neuropsychiatric Service at Polyclinic Hospital in New York. The cycle of birth, Dr. Weitzen suggests, "fulfills for most women a major creative need . . . Most women are proud of their ability to bear children . . . The special aura that glorifies the pregnant woman has figured largely in the art and literature of both East and West."

What happens to the cult of motherhood, Weitzen asks, if "her offspring might literally not be hers, but that of a genetically 'superior' ovum, implanted in her womb from another woman, or even grown in a Petri dish?" If women are to be important at all, he suggests, it will no longer be because they alone can bear children. If nothing else, we are about to kill off the mystique of motherhood.

Not merely motherhood, but the concept of parenthood itself may be in for radical revision. Indeed, the day may soon dawn when it is possible for a child to have more than two biological parents. Dr. Beatrice Mintz, a developmental biologist at the Institute for Cancer Research in Philadelphia, has grown what are coming to be known as "multi-mice"—baby mice each of which has more than the usual number of parents. Embryos are taken from each of two pregnant mice. These embryos are placed in a laboratory dish and nurtured until they form a single growing mass. This is then implanted in the womb of a third female mouse. A baby is born that clearly shares the genetic characteristics of both sets of donors. Thus a typical multi-mouse, born of two pairs of parents, has white fur and whiskers on one side of its face, dark fur and whiskers on the other, with alternating bands of white and dark hair covering the rest of the body. Some 700 multi-mice bred in this fashion have already produced more than 35,000 offspring themselves. If multi-mouse is here, can "multi-man" be far behind?

Under such circumstances, what or who is a parent? When a woman bears in her uterus an embryo conceived in another woman's womb, who is the mother? And just exactly who is the father?

If a couple can actually purchase an embryo, then parenthood becomes a legal, not a biological matter. Unless such transactions are tightly controlled, one can imagine such grotesqueries as a couple buying an embryo, raising it *in vitro*, then buying another in the name of the first, as though for a trust fund. In that case, they might be regarded as legal "grandparents" before their first child is out of its infancy. We shall need a whole new vocabulary to describe kinship ties.

Furthermore, if embryos are for sale, can a corporation buy one? Can it buy ten thousand? Can it resell them? And if not a corporation, how about a noncommercial research laboratory? If we buy and sell living embryos, are we back to a new form of slavery? Such are the nightmarish questions soon to be debated by us. To continue to think of the family, therefore, in purely conventional terms is to defy all reason.

Faced by rapid social change and the staggering implications of the scientific revolution, super-industrial man may be forced to experiment with novel family forms. Innovative minorities can be expected to try out a colorful variety of family arrangements. They will begin by tinkering with existing forms.

THE STREAMLINED FAMILY

One simple thing they will do is streamline the family. The typical pre-industrial family not only had a good many children, but numerous other dependents as well—grandparents, uncles, aunts, and cousins. Such "extended" families were well suited for survival in slow-paced agricultural societies. But such families are hard to transport or transplant. They are immobile.

Industrialism demanded masses of workers ready and able to move off the land in pursuit of jobs, and to move again whenever necessary. Thus the extended family gradually shed its excess weight and the so-called "nuclear" family emerged—a stripped-down, portable family unit consisting only of parents and a small set of children. This new style family, far more mobile than the traditional extended family, became the standard model in all the industrial countries.

Super-industrialism, however, the next stage of eco-technological development, requires even higher mobility. Thus we may expect many among the people of the future to carry the streamlining process a step further by remaining childless, cutting the family down to its most elemental components, a man and a woman. Two people, perhaps with matched careers, will prove more efficient at navigating through education and social shoals, through job changes and geographic relocations, than the ordinary child-cluttered family. Indeed, anthropologist Margaret Mead has pointed out that we may already be moving toward a system under which, as she puts it, "parenthood would be limited to a smaller number of families whose principal functions would be childrearing," leaving the rest of the population "free to function—for the first time in history—as individuals."

A compromise may be the postponement of children, rather than childlessness. Men and women today arc often torn in conflict between a commitment to career and a commitment to children. In the future, many couples will sidestep this problem by deferring the entire task of raising children until after retirement.

This may strike people of the present as odd. Yet once childbearing is broken away from its biological base, nothing more than tradition suggests having children at an early age. Why not wait, and buy your embryos later, after your work career is over? Thus childlessness is likely to spread among young and middle-aged couples; sexagenarians who raise infants may be far more common. The post-retirement family could become a recognized social institution.

BIO-PARENTS AND PRO-PARENTS

If a smaller number of families raise children, however, why do the children have to be their own? Why not a system under which "professional parents" take on the childrearing function for others?

Raising children, after all, requires skills that are by no means universal. We don't let "just anyone" perform brain surgery or, for that matter, sell stocks and bonds. Even the lowest ranking civil servant is required to pass tests proving competence. Yet we allow virtually anyone, almost without regard for mental or moral qualification, to try his or her hand at raising young human beings, so long as these humans are biological offspring. Despite the increasing complexity of the task, parenthood remains the greatest single preserve of the amateur.

As the present system cracks and the super-industrial revolution rolls over us, as the armies of juvenile delinquents swell, as hundreds of thousands of youngsters flee their homes, and students rampage at universities in all the techno-societies, we can expect vociferous demands for an end to parental dilettantism.

There are far better ways to cope with the problems of youth, but professional parenthood is certain to be proposed, if only because it fits so perfectly with the society's overall push toward specialization. Moreover, there is a powerful, pent-up demand for this social innovation. Even now millions of parents, given the opportunity, would happily relinquish their pa-

rental responsibilities—and not necessarily through irresponsibility or lack of love. Harried, frenzied, up
against the wall, they have come to see themselves as
inadequate to the tasks. Given affluence and the existence of specially-equipped and licensed professional
parents, many of today's biological parents would not
only gladly surrender their children to them, but would
look upon it as an act of love, rather than rejection.

Parental professionals would not be therapists, but
actual family units assigned to, and well paid for,
rearing children. Such families might be multi-genera-
tional by design, offering children in them an opportunity to observe and learn from a variety of adult
models, as was the case in the old farm homestead.
With the adults paid to be professional parents, they
would be freed of the occupational necessity to relocate repeatedly. Such families would take in new
children as old ones "graduate" so that age-segrega-
tion would be minimized.

Thus newspapers of the future might well carry
advertisements addressed to young married couples:
"Why let parenthood tie you down? Let us raise your
infant into a responsible, successful adult. Class A
Pro-family offers: father age 39, mother, 36, grand-
mother, 67. Uncle and aunt, age 30, live in, hold part-
time local employment. Four-child-unit has opening
for one, age 6–8. Regulated diet exceeds government
standards. All adults certified in child development
and management. Bio-parents permitted frequent visits. Telephone contact allowed. Child may spend summer vacation with bio-parents. Religion, art, music
encouraged by special arrangement. Five year contract, minimum. Write for further details."

The "real" or "bio-parents" could, as the ad suggests,
fill the role presently played by interested godparents,
namely that of friendly and helpful outsiders. In such
a way, the society could continue to breed a wide
diversity of genetic types, yet turn the care of children over to mother-father groups who are equipped,

both intellectually and emotionally, for the task of caring for kids.

COMMUNES AND HOMOSEXUAL DADDIES

Quite a different alternative lies in the communal family. As transience increases the loneliness and alienation in society, we can anticipate increasing experimentation with various forms of group marriage. The banding together of several adults and children into a single "family" provides a kind of insurance against isolation. Even if one or two members of the household leave, the remaining members have one another. Communes are springing up modeled after those described by psychologist B. F. Skinner in *Walden Two* and by novelist Robert Rimmer in *The Harrad Experiment and Proposition 31*. In the latter work, Rimmer seriously proposes the legalization of a "corporate family" in which from three to six adults adopt a single name, live and raise children in common, and legally incorporate to obtain certain economic and tax advantages.

According to some observers, there are already hundreds of open or covert communes dotting the American map. Not all, by any means, are composed of young people or hippies. Some are organized around specific goals—like the group, quietly financed by three East Coast colleges—which has taken as its function the task of counseling college freshmen, helping to orient them to campus life. The goals may be social, religious, political, even recreational. Thus we shall before long begin to see communal families of surfers dotting the beaches of California and Southern France, if they don't already. We shall see the emergence of communes based on political doctrines and religious faiths. In Denmark, a bill to legalize group marriage has already been introduced in the Folketing (Parliament). While passage is not imminent, the act of introduction is itself a significant symbol of change.

In Chicago, 250 adults and children already live together in "family-style monasticism" under the auspices of a new, fast-growing religious organization, the Ecumenical Institute. Members share the same quarters, cook and eat together, worship and tend children in common, and pool their incomes. At least 60,000 people have taken "EI" courses and similar communes have begun to spring up in Atlanta, Boston, Los Angeles and other cities. "A brand-new world is emerging," says Professor Joseph W. Mathews, leader of the Ecumenical Institute, "but people are still operating in terms of the old one. We seek to re-educate people and give them the tools to build a new social context."

Still another type of family unit likely to win adherents in the future might be called the "geriatric commune"—a group marriage of elderly people drawn together in a common search for companionship and assistance. Disengaged from the productive economy that makes mobility necessary, they will settle in a single place, band together, pool funds, collectively hire domestic or nursing help, and proceed—within limits—to have the "time of their lives."

Communalism runs counter to the pressure for ever greater geographical and social mobility generated by the thrust toward super-industrialism. It presupposes groups of people who "stay put." For this reason, communal experiments will first proliferate among those in the society who are free from the industrial discipline—the retired population, the young, the dropouts, the students, as well as among self-employed professional and technical people. Later, when advanced technology and information systems make it possible for much of the work of society to be done at home via computer-telecommunication hookups, communalism will become feasible for larger numbers.

We shall, however, also see many more "family" units consisting of a single unmarried adult and one or more children. Nor will all of these adults be women. It is already possible in some places for unmarried men to adopt children. In 1965 in Oregon, for example, a thirty-eight-year-old musician named Tony Piazza became the first unmarried man in that state, and perhaps in the United States, to be granted the right to adopt a baby. Courts are more readily granting custody to divorced fathers, too. In London, photographer Michael Cooper, married at twenty and divorced soon after, won the right to raise his infant son, and expressed an interest in adopting other children. Observing that he did not particularly wish to remarry, but that he liked children, Cooper mused aloud: "I wish you could just ask beautiful women to have babies for you. Or any woman you liked, or who had something you admired. Ideally, I'd like a big house full of children—all different colors, shapes and sizes." Romantic? Unmanly? Perhaps. Yet attitudes like these will be widely held by men in the future.

Two pressures are even now softening up the culture, preparing it for acceptance of the idea of child-rearing by men. First, adoptable children are in oversupply in some places. Thus, in California, disc jockeys blare commercials: "We have many wonderful babies of all races and nationalities waiting to bring love and happiness to the right families . . . Call the Los Angeles County Bureau of Adoption." At the same time, the mass media, in a strange non-conspiratorial fashion, appear to have decided simultaneously that men who raise children hold special interest for the public. Extremely popular television shows in recent seasons have glamorized womanless households in which men scrub floors, cook, and, most significantly, raise children. *My Three Sons, The Rifleman, Bonanza* and *Bachelor Father* are four examples.

As homosexuality becomes more socially acceptable, we may even begin to find families based on homosexual "marriages" with the partners adopting children. Whether these children would be of the same or opposite sex remains to be seen. But the rapidity with which homosexuality is winning respectability in the techno-societies distinctly points in this direction. In Holland not long ago a Catholic priest "married" two homosexuals, explaining to critics that "they are among the faithful to be helped." England has rewritten its relevant legislation; homosexual relations between consenting adults are no longer considered a crime. And in the United States a meeting of Episcopal clergymen concluded publicly that homosexuality might, under certain circumstances, be adjudged "good." The day may also come when a court decides that a couple of stable, well educated homosexuals might make decent "parents."

We might also see the gradual relaxation of bars against polygamy. Polygamous families exist even now, more widely than generally believed, in the midst of "normal" society. Writer Ben Merson, after visiting several such families in Utah where polygamy is still regarded as essential by certain Mormon fundamentalists, estimated that there are some 30,000 people living in underground family units of this type in the United States. As sexual attitudes loosen up, as property rights become less important because of rising affluence, the social repression of polygamy may come to be regarded as irrational. This shift may be facilitated by the very mobility that compels men to spend considerable time away from their present homes. The old male fantasy of the Captain's Paradise may become a reality for some, although it is likely that, under such circumstances, the wives left behind will demand extramarital sexual rights. Yesterday's "captain" would hardly consider this possibility. Tomorrow's may feel quite differently about it.

Still another family form is even now springing up in our midst, a novel childrearing unit that I call the "aggregate family"—a family based on relationships between divorced and remarried couples, in which all the children become part of "one big family." Though sociologists have paid little attention as yet to this phenomenon, it is already so prevalent that it formed the basis for a hilarious scene in a recent American movie entitled _Divorce American Style_. We may expect aggregate families to take on increasing importance in the decades ahead.

Childless marriage, professional parenthood, post-retirement childrearing, corporate families, communes, geriatric group marriages, homosexual family units, polygamy—these, then, are a few of the family forms and practices with which innovative minorities will experiment in the decades ahead. Not all of us, however, will be willing to participate in such experimentation. What of the majority?

THE ODDS AGAINST LOVE

Minorities experiment; majorities cling to the forms of the past. It is safe to say that large numbers of people will refuse to jettison the conventional idea of marriage or the familiar family forms. They will, no doubt, continue searching for happiness within the orthodox format. Yet, even they will be forced to innovate in the end, for the odds against success may prove overwhelming.

The orthodox format presupposes that two young people will "find" one another and marry. It presupposes that the two will fulfill certain psychological needs in one another, and that the two personalities will develop over the years, more or less in tandem, so that they continue to fulfill each other's needs. It further presupposes that this process will last "until death do us part."

These expectations are built deeply into our culture. It is no longer respectable, as it once was, to marry for anything but love. Love has changed from a peripheral concern of the family into its primary justification. Indeed, the pursuit of love through family life has become, for many, the very purpose of life itself.

Love, however, is defined in terms of this notion of shared growth. It is seen as a beautiful mesh of complementary needs, flowing into and out of one another, fulfilling the loved ones, and producing feel-

ings of warmth, tenderness and devotion. Unhappy
husbands often complain that they have "left their
wives behind" in terms of social, educational or intellectual growth. Partners in successful marriages are
said to "grow together."

This "parallel development" theory of love carries
endorsement from marriage counsellors, psychologists
and sociologists. Thus, says sociologist Nelson Foote,
a specialist on the family, the quality of the relationship between husband and wife is dependent upon
"the degree of matching in their phases of distinct
but comparable development."

If love is a product of shared growth, however, and
we are to measure success in marriage by the degree
to which matched development actually occurs, it
becomes possible to make a strong and ominous prediction about the future.

It is possible to demonstrate that, even in a relatively stagnant society, the mathematical odds are
heavily stacked against any couple achieving this
ideal of parallel growth. The odds for success posi-
tively plummet, however, when the rate of change in
society accelerates, as it now is doing. In a fast-moving
society, in which many things change, not once, but
repeatedly, in which the husband moves up and down
a variety of economic and social scales, in which the
family is again and again torn loose from home and
community, in which individuals move further from
their parents, further from the religion of origin, and
further from traditional values, it is almost miraculous
if two people develop at anything like comparable
rates.

If, at the same time, average life expectancy rises
from, say, fifty to seventy years, thereby lengthening
the term during which this acrobatic feat of matched
development is supposed to be maintained, the odds
against success become absolutely astronomical. Thus,
Nelson Foote writes with wry understatement: "To
expect a marriage to last indefinitely under modern

conditions is to expect a lot." To ask love to last indefinitely is to expect even more. Transience and novelty are both in league against it.

TEMPORARY MARRIAGE

It is this change in the statistical odds against love that accounts for the high divorce and separation rates in most of the techno-societies. The faster the rate of change and the longer the life span, the worse these odds grow. Something has to crack.

In point of fact, of course, something has already cracked—and it is the old insistence on permanence. Millions of men and women now adopt what appears to them to be a sensible and conservative strategy. Rather than opting for some offbeat variety of the family, they marry conventionally, they attempt to make it "work," and then, when the paths of the partners diverge beyond an acceptable point, they divorce or depart. Most of them go on to search for a new partner whose developmental stage, at that moment, matches their own.

As human relationships grow more transient and modular, the pursuit of love becomes, if anything, more frenzied. But the temporal expectations change. As conventional marriage proves itself less and less capable of delivering on its promise of lifelong love, therefore, we can anticipate open public acceptance of temporary marriages. Instead of wedding "until death us do part," couples will enter into matrimony knowing from the first that the relationship is likely to be short-lived.

They will know, too, that when the paths of husband and wife diverge, when there is too great a discrepancy in developmental stages, they may call it quits—without shock or embarrassment, perhaps even without some of the pain that goes with divorce today. And when the opportunity presents itself, they will marry again . . . and again . . . and again.

Serial marriage—a pattern of successive temporary marriages—is cut to order for the Age of Transience in which all man's relationships, all his ties with the environment, shrink in duration. It is the natural, the inevitable outgrowth of a social order in which automobiles are rented, dolls traded in, and dresses discarded after one-time use. It is the mainstream marriage pattern of tomorrow.

In one sense, serial marriage is already the best kept family secret of the techno-societies. According to Professor Jessie Bernard, a world-prominent family sociologist, "Plural marriage is more extensive in our society today than it is in societies that permit polygamy—the chief difference being that we have institutionalized plural marriage serially or sequentially rather than contemporaneously." Remarriage is already so prevalent a practice that nearly one out of every four bridegrooms in America has been to the altar before. It is so prevalent that one IBM personnel man reports a poignant incident involving a divorced woman, who, in filling out a job application, paused when she came to the question of marital status. She put her pencil in her mouth, pondered for a moment, then wrote: "Unremarried."

Transience necessarily affects the durational expectancies with which persons approach new situations. While they may yearn for a permanent relationship, something inside whispers to them that it is an increasingly improbable luxury.

Even young people who most passionately seek commitment, profound involvement with people and causes, recognize the power of the thrust toward transience. Listen, for example, to a young black American, a civil-rights worker, as she describes her attitude toward time and marriage:

"In the white world, marriage is always billed as 'the end'—like in a Hollywood movie. I don't go for that. I can't imagine myself promising my whole lifetime away. I might want to get married now, but how about next year? That's not disrespect for the institution [of marriage], but the deepest respect. In The [civil rights] Movement, you need to have a feeling for the temporary—of making something as good as you can, while it lasts. In conventional relationships, time is a prison."

Such attitudes will not be confined to the young, the few, or the politically active. They will whip across nations as novelty floods into the society and catch fire as the level of transience rises still higher. And along with them will come a sharp increase in the number of temporary—then serial—marriages.

The idea is summed up vividly by a Swedish magazine, *Svensk Damtidning*, which interviewed a number of leading Swedish sociologists, legal experts, and others about the future of man-woman relationships. It presented its findings in five photographs. They showed the same beautiful bride being carried across the threshold five times—by five different bridegrooms.

MARRIAGE TRAJECTORIES

As serial marriages become more common, we shall begin to characterize people not in terms of their present marital status, but in terms of their marriage career or "trajectory." This trajectory will be formed by the decisions they make at certain vital turning points in their lives.

For most people, the first such juncture will arrive in youth, when they enter into "trial marriage." Even now the young people of the United States and Europe are engaged in a mass experiment with probationary marriage, with or without benefit of ceremony. The staidest of United States universities are beginning to wink at the practice of co-ed housekeeping among their students. Acceptance of trial marriage is even growing among certain religious philosophers. Thus we hear the German theologian Siegfried Keil of Marburg University urge what he terms "recognized premarriage." In Canada, Father Jacques Lazure has publicly proposed "probationary marriages" of three to eighteen months.

In the past, social pressures and lack of money restricted experimentation with trial marriage to a relative handful. In the future, both these limiting forces will evaporate. Trial marriage will be the first step in the serial marriage "careers" that millions will pursue.

A second critical life juncture for the people of the future will occur when the trial marriage ends. At this point, couples may choose to formalize their relationship and stay together into the next stage. Or they may terminate it and seek out new partners. In either case, they will then face several options. They may prefer to go childless. They may choose to have, adopt or "buy" one or more children. They may decide to raise these children themselves or to farm them out to professional parents. Such decisions will be made, by and large, in the early twenties—by which time many young adults will already be well into their second marriages.

A third significant turning point in the marital career will come, as it does today, when the children finally leave home. The end of parenthood proves excruciating for many, particularly women who, once the children are gone, find themselves without a *raison d'être*. Even today divorces result from the failure of the couple to adapt to this traumatic break in continuity.

Among the more conventional couples of tomorrow who choose to raise their own children in the time-honored fashion, this will continue to be a particularly painful time. It will, however, strike earlier. Young people today already leave home sooner than their counterparts a generation ago. They will probably depart even earlier tomorrow. Masses of youngsters will move off, whether into trial marriage or not, in their mid-teens. Thus we may anticipate that the middle and late thirties will be another important breakpoint in the marital careers of millions. Many at that juncture will enter into their third marriage.

This third marriage will bring together two people for what could well turn out to be the longest uninterrupted stretch of matrimony in their lives—from, say, the late thirties until one of the partners dies. This may, in fact, turn out to be the only "real" marriage, the basis of the only truly durable marital relationship. During this time two mature people, presumably with well-matched interests and complementary psychological needs, and with a sense of being at comparable stages of personality development, will be able to look forward to a relationship with a decent statistical probability of enduring.

Not all these marriages will survive until death, however, for the family will still face a fourth crisis point. This will come, as it does now for so many, when one or both of the partners retires from work. The abrupt change in daily routine brought about by this development places great strain on the couple. Some couples will go the path of the post-retirement family, choosing this moment to begin the task of raising children. This may overcome for them the vacuum that so many couples now face after reaching the end of their occupational lives. (Today many women go to work when they finish raising children; tomorrow many will reverse that pattern, working first and childrearing next.) Other couples will overcome the crisis of retirement in other ways, fashioning both together a new set of habits, interests and activities. Still others will find the transition too difficult, and will simply sever their ties and enter the pool of "in-betweens"—the floating reserve of temporarily unmarried persons.

Of course, there will be some who, through luck, interpersonal skill and high intelligence, will find it possible to make long-lasting monogamous marriages work. Some will succeed, as they do today, in marrying for life and finding durable love and affection. But others will fail to make even sequential marriages

endure for long. Thus some will try two or even three
partners within, say, the final stage of marriage. Across
the board, the average number of marriages per capita
will rise—slowly but relentlessly.

Most people will probably move forward along this
progression, engaging in one "conventional" temporary marriage after another. But with widespread
familial experimentation in the society, the more daring or desperate will make side forays into less conventional arrangements as well, perhaps experimenting
with communal life at some point, or going it alone
with a child. The net result will be a rich variation
in the types of marital trajectories that people will
trace, a wider choice of life-patterns, an endless opportunity for novelty of experience. Certain patterns will
be more common than others. But temporary marriage
will be a standard feature, perhaps the dominant
feature, of family life in the future.

THE DEMANDS OF FREEDOM

A world in which marriage is temporary rather than
permanent, in which family arrangements are diverse
and colorful, in which homosexuals may be acceptable
parents and retirees start raising children—such a
world is vastly different from our own. Today all boys
and girls are expected to find life-long partners. In
tomorrow's world, being single will be no crime. Nor
will couples be forced to remain imprisoned, as so
many still are today, in marriages that have turned
rancid. Divorce will be easy to arrange, so long as
responsible provision is made for children. In fact, the
very introduction of professional parenthood could
touch off a great liberating wave of divorces by making it easier for adults to discharge their parental
responsibilities without necessarily remaining in the
cage of a hateful marriage. With this powerful external pressure removed, those who stay together
would be those who wish to stay together, those for

whom marriage is actively fulfilling—those, in short, who are in love.

We are also likely to see, under this looser, more variegated family system, many more marriages involving partners of unequal age. Increasingly, older men will marry young girls or vice versa. What will count will not be chronological age, but complementary values and interests and, above all, the level of personal development. To put it another way, partners will be interested not in age, but in stage.

Children in this super-industrial society will grow up with an ever enlarging circle of what might be called "semi-siblings"—a whole clan of boys and girls brought into the world by their successive sets of parents. What becomes of such "aggregate" families will be fascinating to observe. Semi-sibs may turn out to be like cousins, today. They may help one another professionally or in time of need. But they will also present the society with novel problems. Should semi-sibs marry, for example?

Surely, the whole relationship of the child to the family will be dramatically altered. Except perhaps in communal groupings, the family will lose what little remains of its power to transmit values to the younger generation. This will further accelerate the pace of change and intensify the problems that go with it.

Looming over all such changes, however, and even dwarfing them in significance is something far more subtle. Seldom discussed, there is a hidden rhythm in human affairs that until now has served as one of the key stabilizing forces in society: the family cycle.

We begin as children; we mature; we leave the parental nest; we give birth to children who, in turn, grow up, leave and begin the process all over again. This cycle has been operating so long, so automatically, and with such implacable regularity, that men have taken it for granted. It is part of the human landscape. Long before they reach puberty, children learn the part they are expected to play in keeping this great cycle turning. This predictable succession of family events has provided all men, of whatever tribe or society, with a sense of continuity, a place in the temporal scheme of things. The family cycle has been one of the sanity-preserving constants in human existence.

Today this cycle is accelerating. We grow up sooner, leave home sooner, marry sooner, have children sooner. We space them more closely together and complete the period of parenthood more quickly. In the words of Dr. Bernice Neugarten, a University of Chicago specialist on family development, "The trend is toward a more rapid rhythm of events through most of the family cycle."

But if industrialism, with its faster pace of life, has accelerated the family cycle, super-industrialism now threatens to smash it altogether. With the fantasies that the birth scientists are hammering into reality, with the colorful familial experimentation that innovative minorities will perform, with the likely development of such institutions as professional parenthood, with the increasing movement toward temporary and serial marriage, we shall not merely run the cycle more rapidly; we shall introduce irregularity, suspense, unpredictability—in a word, novelty—into what was once as regular and certain as the seasons.

When a "mother" can compress the process of birth into a brief visit to an embryo emporium, when by transferring embryos from womb to womb we can destroy even the ancient certainty that childbearing took nine months, children will grow up into a world in which the family cycle, once so smooth and sure, will be jerkily arhythmic. Another crucial stabilizer will have been removed from the wreckage of the old order, another pillar of sanity broken.

There is, of course, nothing inevitable about the developments traced in the preceding pages. We have it in our power to shape change. We may choose one future over another. We cannot, however, maintain the past. In our family forms, as in our economics, science, technology and social relationships, we shall be forced to deal with the new.

The Super-industrial Revolution will liberate men from many of the barbarisms that grew out of the restrictive, relatively choiceless family patterns of the past and present. It will offer to each a degree of freedom hitherto unknown. But it will exact a steep price for that freedom.

As we hurtle into tomorrow, millions of ordinary men and women will face emotion-packed options so unfamiliar, so untested, that past experience will offer little clue to wisdom. In their family ties, as in all other aspects of their lives, they will be compelled to cope not merely with transience, but with the added problem of novelty as well.

Thus, in matters both large and small, in the most public of conflicts and the most private of conditions, the balance between routine and non-routine, predictable and non-predictable, the known and the unknown, will be altered. The novelty ratio will rise.

In such an environment, fast-changing and unfamiliar, we shall be forced, as we wend our way through life, to make our personal choices from a diverse array of options. And it is to the third central characteristic of tomorrow, *diversity*, that we must now turn. For it is the final convergence of these three factors—transience, novelty and diversity—that sets the stage for the historic crisis of adaptation that is the subject of this book: future shock.

Part Four:

DIVERSITY

Chapter 12

THE ORIGINS OF OVERCHOICE

The Super-industrial Revolution will consign to the archives of ignorance most of what we now believe about democracy and the future of human choice.

Today in the techno-societies there is an almost ironclad consensus about the future of freedom. Maximum individual choice is regarded as the democratic ideal. Yet most writers predict that we shall move further and further from this ideal. They conjure up a dark vision of the future, in which people appear as mindless consumer-creatures, surrounded by standardized goods, educated in standardized schools, fed a diet of standardized mass culture, and forced to adopt standardized styles of life.

Such predictions have spawned a generation of future-haters and technophobes, as one might expect. One of the most extreme of these is a French religious mystic, Jacques Ellul, whose books are enjoying a campus vogue. According to Ellul, man was far freer in the past when "Choice was a real possibility for him." By contrast, today, "The human being is no longer in any sense the agent of choice." And, as for tomorrow: "In the future, man will apparently be confined to the role of a recording device." Robbed of choice, he will be acted upon, not active. He will live,

Ellul warns, in a totalitarian state run by a velvet-gloved Gestapo.

This same theme—the loss of choice—runs through much of the work of Arnold Toynbee. It is repeated by everyone from hippie gurus to Supreme Court justices, tabloid editorialists and existentialist philosophers. Put in its simplest form, this Theory of Vanishing Choice rests on a crude syllogism: Science and technology have fostered standardization. Science and technology will advance, making the future even more standardized than the present. *Ergo:* Man will progressively lose his freedom of choice.

If instead of blindly accepting this syllogism, we stop to analyze it, however, we make an extraordinary discovery. For not only is the logic itself faulty, the entire idea is premised on sheer factual ignorance about the nature, the meaning and the direction of the Super-industrial Revolution.

Ironically, the people of the future may suffer not from an absence of choice, but from a paralyzing surfeit of it. They may turn out to be victims of that peculiarly super-industrial dilemma: overchoice.

DESIGN-A-MUSTANG

No person traveling across Europe or the United States can fail to be impressed by the architectural similarity of one gas station or airport to another. Anyone thirsting for a soft drink will find one bottle of Coca-Cola to be almost identical with the next. Clearly a consequence of mass production techniques, the uniformity of certain aspects of our physical environment has long outraged intellectuals. Some decry the Hiltonization of our hotels; others charge that we are homogenizing the entire human race.

Certainly, it would be difficult to deny that industrialism has had a leveling effect. Our ability to produce millions of nearly identical units is the crowning achievement of the industrial age. Thus, when intellectuals bewail the sameness of our material goods, they accurately reflect the state of affairs under industrialism.

In the same breath, however, they reveal shocking ignorance about the character of super-industrialism. Focused on what society was, they are blind to what it is fast becoming. For the society of the future will offer not a restricted, standardized flow of goods, but the greatest variety of *unstandardized* goods and services any society has ever seen. We are moving not toward a further extension of material standardization, but toward its dialectical negation. .

The end of standardization is already in sight. The pace varies from industry to industry, and from country to country. In Europe, the peak of standardization has not yet been crested. (It may take another twenty or thirty years to run its course.) But in the United States, there is compelling evidence that a historic corner has been turned.

Some years ago, for example, an American marketing expert named Kenneth Schwartz made a surprising discovery. "It is nothing less than a revolutionary transformation that has come over the mass consumer market during the past five years," he wrote. "From a single homogenous unit, the mass market has exploded into a series of segmented, fragmented markets, each with its own needs, tastes and way of life." This fact has begun to alter American industry beyond recognition. The result is an astonishing change in the actual outpouring of goods offered to the consumer.

Philip Morris, for example, sold a single major brand of cigarettes for twenty-one years. Since 1954 by contrast, it has introduced six new brands and so many options with respect to size, filter and menthol that the smoker now has a choice among sixteen different variations. This fact would be trivial, were it not duplicated in virtually every major product field. Gasoline? Until a few years ago, the American motorist took his pick of either "regular" or "premium." Today he drives up to a Sunoco pump and is asked to choose among eight different blends and mixes. Groceries? Between 1950 and 1963 the number of different soaps and detergents on the American grocery shelf increased from sixty-five to 200; frozen foods from 121 to 350; baking mixes and flour from eighty-four to 200. Even the variety of pet foods increased from fifty-eight to eighty-one.

One major company, Corn Products, produces a pancake syrup called Karo. Instead of offering the same product nationally, however, it sells two different viscosities, having found that Pennsylvanians, for some regional reason, prefer their syrup thicker than other Americans. In the field of office décor and furniture, the same process is at work. "There are ten times the new styles and colors there were a decade ago," says John A. Saunders, president of General Fireproofing Company, a major manufacturer in the field. "Every architect wants his own shade of green." Companies, in other words, are discovering wide variations in consumer wants and are adapting their production lines to accommodate them. Two economic factors encourage this trend: first, consumers have more money to lavish on their specialized wants; second, and even more important, *as technology becomes more sophisticated, the cost of introducing variations declines.*

This is the point that our social critics—most of whom are technologically naive—fail to understand: it is only primitive technology that imposes standardization. Automation, in contrast, frees the path to endless, blinding, mind-numbing diversity.

"The rigid uniformity and long runs of identical products which characterize our traditional mass production plants are becoming less important" reports industrial engineer Boris Yavitz. "Numerically controlled machines can readily shift from one product model or size to another by a simple change of programs . . . Short product runs become economically feasible." According to Professor Van Court Hare, Jr., of the Columbia University Graduate School of

Business, "Automated equipment . . . permits the production of a wide variety of products in short runs at almost 'mass production' costs." Many engineers and business experts foresee the day when diversity will cost no more than uniformity.

The finding that pre-automation technology yields standardization, while advanced technology permits diversity is borne out by even a casual look at that controversial American innovation, the supermarket. Like gas stations and airports, supermarkets tend to look alike whether they are in Milan or Milwaukee. By wiping out thousands of little "mom and pop" stores they have without doubt contributed to uniformity in the architectural environment. Yet the array of goods they offer the consumer is incomparably more diverse than any corner store could afford to stock. Thus at the very moment that they encourage architectural sameness, they foster gastronomic diversity.

The reason for this contrast is simple: Food and food packaging technology is far more advanced than construction techniques. Indeed, construction has scarcely reached the level of mass production; it remains, in large measure, a pre-industrial craft. Strangled by local building codes and conservative trade unions, the industry's rate of technological advance is far below that of other industries. The more advanced the technology, the cheaper it is to introduce variation in output. We can safely predict, therefore, that when the construction industry catches up with manufacture in technological sophistication, gas stations, airports, and hotels, as well as supermarkets, will stop looking as if they had been poured from the same mold. Uniformity will give way to diversity.[*]

---

[*] Where the process has begun, the results are striking. In Washington, D.C., for example, there is a computer-designed apartment house—Watergate East—in which no two floors are alike. Of 240 apartments, 167 have different floor plans. And there are no continuous straight lines in the building anywhere.

While certain parts of Europe and Japan are still building their first all-purpose supermarkets, the United States has already leaped to the next stage—the creation of specialized super-stores that widen still further (indeed, almost beyond belief) the variety of goods available to the consumer. In Washington, D.C., one such store specializes in foreign foods, offering such delicacies as hippopotamus steak, alligator meat, wild snow hare, and thirty-five different kinds of honey.

The idea that primitive industrial techniques foster uniformity, while advanced automated techniques favor diversity, is dramatized by recent changes in the automobile industry. The widespread introduction of European and Japanese cars into the American market in the late 1950's opened many new options for the buyer—increasing his choice from half a dozen to some fifty makes. Today even this wide range of choice seems narrow and constricted.

Faced with foreign competition, Detroit took a new look at the so-called "mass consumer." It found not a single uniform mass market, but an aggregation of transient mini-markets. It also found, as one writer put it, that "customers wanted custom-like cars that would give them an illusion of having one-of-a-kind." To provide that illusion would have been impossible with the old technology; the new computerized assembly systems, however, make possible not merely the illusion, but even—before long—the reality.

Thus the beautiful and spectacularly successful Mustang is promoted by Ford as "the one you design yourself," because, as critic Reyner Banham explains, there "isn't a dung-regular Mustang any more, just a stockpile of options to meld in combinations of 3 (bodies) × 4 (engines) × 3 (transmissions) × 4 (basic sets of high-performance engine modifications) − 1 (rock-bottom six cylinder car to which these modifications don't apply) + 2 (Shelby grand-touring and racing set-ups applying to only one body shell and not all engine/transmission combinations)."

This does not even take into account the possible variations in color, upholstery and optional equipment.

Both car buyers and auto salesmen are increasingly disconcerted by the sheer multiplicity of options. The buyer's problem of choice has become far more complicated, the addition of each option creating the need for more information, more decisions and subdecisions. Thus, anyone who has attempted to buy a car lately, as I have, soon finds that the task of learning about the various brands, lines, models and options (even within a fixed price range) requires days of shopping and reading. In short, the auto industry may soon reach the point at which its technology can economically produce more diversity than the consumer needs or wants.

Yet we are only beginning the march toward destandardization of our material culture. Marshall McLuhan has noted that "Even today, most United States automobiles are, in a sense, custom-produced. Figuring all possible combinations of styles, options and colors available on a certain new family sports car, for example, a computer expert came up with 25,000,000 different versions of it for a buyer . . . When automated electronic production reaches full potential, it will be just about as cheap to turn out a million differing objects as a million exact duplicates. The only limits on production and consumption will be the human imagination." Many of McLuhan's other assertions are highly debatable. This one is not. He is absolutely correct about the direction in which technology is moving. The material goods of the future will be many things; but they will not be standardized. We are, in fact, racing toward "overchoice"—the point at which the advantages of diversity and individualization are cancelled by the complexity of the buyer's decision-making process.

COMPUTERS AND CLASSROOMS

Does any of this matter? Some people argue that diversity in the material environment is insignificant so long as we are racing toward cultural or spiritual homogeneity. "It's what's inside that counts," they say, paraphrasing a well-known cigarette commercial.

This view gravely underestimates the importance of material goods as symbolic expressions of human personality differences, and it foolishly denies a connection between the inner and outer environment. Those who fear the standardization of human beings should warmly welcome the destandardization of goods. For by increasing the diversity of goods available to man we increase the mathematical probability of differences in the way men actually live.

More important, however, is the very *premise* that we are racing toward cultural homogeneity, since a close look at this also suggests that just the opposite is true. It is unpopular to say this, but we are moving swiftly toward fragmentation and diversity not only in material production, but in art, education and mass culture as well.

One highly revealing test of cultural diversity in any literate society has to do with the number of different books published per million of population. The more standardized the tastes of the public, the fewer titles will be published per million; the more diverse these tastes, the greater the number of titles. The increase or decrease of this figure over time is a significant clue to the direction of cultural change in the society. This was the reasoning behind a study of world book trends published by UNESCO. Conducted by Robert Escarpit director of the Center for the Sociology of Literature at the University of Bordeaux, it provided dramatic evidence of a powerful international shift toward cultural destandardization.

Thus, between 1952 and 1962 the index of diversity rose in fully twenty-one of the twenty-nine chief book-producing nations. Among the countries registering the highest shifts toward literary diversity were Canada, the United States and Sweden, all with increases in excess of 50 percent or more. The United Kingdom, France, Japan and the Netherlands all moved from 10 to 25 percent in the same direction. The eight countries that moved in the opposite direction—i.e., toward greater standardization of literary output—were India, Mexico, Argentina, Italy, Poland, Yugoslavia, Belgium, and Austria. In short, the more advanced the technology in a country, the greater the likelihood that it would be moving in the direction of literary diversity and away from uniformity.

The same push toward pluralism is evident in painting, too, where we find an almost incredibly wide spectrum of production. Representationalism, expressionism, surrealism, abstract expressionism, hard-edge, pop, kinetic, and a hundred other styles are pumped into the society at the same time. One or another may dominate the galleries temporarily, but there are no universal standards or styles. It is a pluralistic marketplace.

When art was a tribal-religious activity, the painter worked for the whole community. Later he worked for a single small aristocratic elite. Still later the audience appeared as a single undifferentiated mass. Today he faces a large audience split into a milling mass of sub-groups. According to John McHale: "The most uniform cultural contexts are typically primitive enclaves. The most striking feature of our contemporary 'mass' culture is the vast range and diversity of its alternative cultural choices . . . The 'mass,' on even cursory examination, breaks down into many different 'audiences.'"

Indeed, artists no longer attempt to work for a universal public. Even when they think they are doing so, they are usually responding to the tastes and styles preferred by one or another sub-group in the society. Like the manufacturers of pancake syrup and automobiles, artists, too, produce for "mini-markets." And as these markets multiply, artistic output diversifies.

The push for diversity, meanwhile, is igniting bitter conflict in education. Ever since the rise of industrialism, education in the West, and particularly in the United States, has been organized for the mass production of basically standardized educational packages. It is not accidental that at the precise moment when the consumer has begun to demand and obtain greater diversity, the same moment when new technology promises to make destandardization possible, a wave of revolt has begun to sweep the college campus. Though the connection is seldom noticed, events on the campus and events in the consumer market are intimately connected.

One basic complaint of the student is that he is not treated as an individual, that he is served up an undifferentiated gruel, rather than a personalized product. Like the Mustang buyer, the student wants to design his own. The difference is that while industry is highly responsive to consumer demand, education typically has been indifferent to student wants. (In one case we say, "the customer knows best"; in the other, we insist that "Papa—or his educational surrogate—knows best.") Thus the student-consumer is forced to fight to make the education industry responsive to his demand for diversity.

While most colleges and universities have greatly broadened the variety of their course offerings, they are still wedded to complex standardizing systems based on degrees, majors and the like. These systems lay down basic tracks along which all students must progress. While educators are rapidly multiplying the number of alternative paths, the pace of diversification is by no means swift enough for the students. This explains why young people have set up "para-universities"—experimental colleges and so-called free universities—in which each student is free to choose what he wishes from a mind-shattering smorgasbord of courses that range from guerrilla tactics and stock market techniques to Zen Buddhism and "underground theater."

Long before the year 2000, the entire antiquated structure of degrees, majors and credits will be a shambles. No two students will move along exactly the same educational track. For the students now pressuring higher education to destandardize, to move toward super-industrial diversity, will win their battle.

It is significant, for example, that one of the chief results of the student strike in France was a massive decentralization of the university system. Decentralization makes possible greater regional diversity, local authority to alter curriculum, student regulations and administrative practices.

A parallel revolution is brewing in the public schools as well. It has already flared into open violence. Like the disturbance at Berkeley that initiated the worldwide wave of student protest, it has begun with something that appears at first glimpse to be a purely local issue.

Thus New York City, whose public education system encompasses nearly 900 schools and is responsible for one out of every forty American public school pupils, has suffered the worst teachers' strike in history—precisely over the issue of decentralization. Teacher picket lines, parent boycotts, and near riot have become everyday occurrences in the city's schools. Angered by the ineffectiveness of the schools, and by what they rightfully regard as blatant race prejudice, black parents, backed by various community forces, have demanded that the entire school system be cut up into smaller "community-run" school systems.

In effect, New York's black population, having failed to achieve racial integration and quality education, wants its own school system. It wants courses in Negro history. It wants greater parental involvement with the schools than is possible in the present large, bureaucratic and ossified system. It claims, in short, the right to be different.

The essential issues far transcend racial prejudice, however. Until now the big urban school systems in the United States have been powerful homogenizing influences. By fixing city-wide standards and curricula, by choosing texts and personnel on a city-wide basis, they have imposed considerable uniformity on the schools.

Today, the pressure for decentralization, which has already spread to Detroit, Washington, Milwaukee, and other major cities in the United States (and which will, in different forms, spread to Europe as well), is an attempt not simply to improve the education of Negroes, but to smash the very idea of centralized, city-wide school policies. It is an attempt to generate local variety in public education by turning over control of the schools to local authorities. It is, in short, part of a larger struggle to diversify education in the last third of the twentieth century. That the effort has been temporarily blocked in New York, largely through the stubborn resistance of an entrenched trade union, does not mean that the historic forces pushing toward destandardization will forever be contained.

Failure to diversify education *within* the system will simply lead to the growth of alternative educational opportunities *outside* the system. Thus we have today the suggestions of prominent educators and sociologists, including Kenneth B. Clark and Christopher Jencks, for the creation of new schools outside of, and competitive with, the official public school systems. Clark has called for regional and state schools, federal schools, schools run by colleges, trade unions, corporations and even military units. Such competing schools would, he contends, help create the diversity that education desperately needs. Simultaneously, in a less formal way, a variety of "paraschools" are already being established by hippie communes and other groups who find the mainstream educational system too homogeneous.

We see here, therefore, a major cultural force in the society—education—being pushed to diversify its output, exactly as the economy is doing. And here, exactly as in the realm of material production, the new technology, rather than fostering standardization, carries us toward super-industrial diversity.

Computers, for example, make it easier for a large school to schedule more flexibly. They make it easier for the school to cope with independent study, with a wider range of course offerings and more varied extracurricular activities. More important, computer-assisted education, programmed instruction and other such techniques, despite popular misconceptions, radically enhance the possibility of diversity in the classroom. They permit each student to advance at his own purely personal pace. They permit him to follow a custom-cut path toward knowledge, rather than a rigid syllabus as in the traditional industrial era classroom.

Moreover, in the educational world of tomorrow, that relic of mass production, the centralized work place, will also become less important. Just as economic mass production required large numbers of workers to be assembled in factories, educational mass production required large numbers of students to be assembled in schools. This itself, with its demands for uniform discipline, regular hours, attendance checks and the like, was a standardizing force. Advanced technology will, in the future, make much of this unnecessary. A good deal of education will take place in the student's own room at home or in a dorm, at hours of his own choosing. With vast libraries of data available to him via computerized information retrieval systems, with his own tapes and video units, his own language laboratory and his own electronically equipped study carrel, he will be freed, for much of the time, of the restrictions and unpleasantness that dogged him in the lockstep classroom.

The technology upon which these new freedoms will be based will inevitably spread through the schools in the years ahead—aggressively pushed, no doubt, by major corporations like IBM, RCA, and Xerox. Within thirty years, the educational systems of the United States, and several Western European countries as well, will have broken decisively with the mass production pedagogy of the past, and will have advanced into an era of educational diversity based on the liberating power of the new machines.

In education, therefore, as in the production of material goods, the society is shifting irresistibly away from, rather than toward, standardization. It is not simply a matter of more varied automobiles, detergents and cigarettes. The social thrust toward diversity and increased individual choice affects our mental, as well as our material surroundings.

"DRAG QUEEN" MOVIES

Of all the forces accused of homogenizing the modern mind, few have been so continuously and bitterly criticized as the mass media. Intellectuals in the United States and Europe have lambasted television, in particular, for standardizing speech, habits, and tastes. They have pictured it as a vast lawnroller flattening out our regional differences, crushing the last vestiges of cultural variety. A thriving academic industry has leveled similar charges against magazines and movies.

While there is truth in some of these charges, they overlook critically important counter-trends that generate diversity, not standardization. Television, with its high costs of production and its limited number of channels, is still necessarily dependent upon very large audiences. But in almost every other communications medium we can trace a decreasing reliance on mass audiences. Everywhere the "market segmentation" process is at work.

A generation ago, American movie-goers saw almost nothing but Hollywood-made films aimed at capturing the so-called mass audience. Today in cities across the country these "mainstream" movies are supplemented by foreign movies, art films, sex movies, and a whole stream of specialized motion pictures consciously designed to appeal to sub-markets—surfers, hot-rodders, motorcyclists, and the like. Output is so specialized that it is even possible, in New York at least, to find a theater patronized almost exclusively by homosexuals who watch the antics of transvestites and "drag queens" filmed especially for them.

All this helps account for the trend toward smaller movie theaters in the United States and Europe. According to the *Economist*, "The days of the 4000-seater Trocadero . . . are over . . . The old-style mass cinema audience of regular once-a-weekers has gone for good." Instead, multiple small audiences turn out for particular kinds of films, and the economics of the industry are up-ended. Thus Cinecenta has opened a cluster of four 150-seat theaters on a single site in London, and other exhibitors are planning midget movie houses. Once again, advanced technology fosters dehomogenization: the development of in-flight movies has led to new low-cost 16 mm. projection systems that are made to order for the mini-movie. They require no projectionist and only a single machine, instead of the customary two. United Artists is marketing these "cineautomats" on a franchise basis.

Radio, too, though still heavily oriented toward the mass market, shows some signs of differentiation. Some American stations beam nothing but classical music to upper-income, high education listeners, while others specialize in news, and still others in rock music. (Rock stations are rapidly subdividing into still finer categories: some aim their fare for the under-eighteen market; others for a somewhat older group; still others for Negroes.) There are even rudimentary attempts to set up radio stations programming solely for a single profession—physicians, for example. In the future, we can anticipate networks that broadcast for such specialized occupational groups as engineers, accountants and attorneys. Still later, there will be market segmentation not simply along occupational lines, but along socio-economic and psycho-social lines as well.

It is in publishing, however, that the signs of de-standardization are most unmistakable. Until the rise of television, mass magazines were the chief standardizing media in most countries. Carrying the same fiction, the same articles and the same advertisements to hundreds of thousands, even millions of homes, they rapidly spread fashions, political opinions and styles. Like radio broadcasters and moviemakers, publishers tended to seek the largest and most universal audience.

The competition of television killed off a number of major American magazines such as *Collier's* and *Woman's Home Companion*. Those mass market publications that have survived the post-TV shake-up have done so, in part, by turning themselves into a collection of regional and segmentalized editions. Between 1959 and 1969, the number of American magazines offering specialized editions jumped from 126 to 235. Thus every large circulation magazine in the United States today prints slightly different editions for different regions of the country—some publishers offering as many as one hundred variations. Special editions are also addressed to occupational and other groups. The 80,000 physicians and dentists who receive *Time* each week get a somewhat different magazine than that received by teachers whose edition, in turn, is different from that sent to college students. These "demographic editions" are growing increasingly refined and specialized. In short, mass magazine publishers are busily destandardizing, diversifying their output exactly as the automakers and appliance manufacturers have done.

Furthermore, the rate of new magazine births has

shot way up. According to the Magazine Publishers Association, approximately four new magazines have come into being for every one that died during the past decade. Every week sees a new small-circulation magazine on the stands or in the mails, magazines aimed at mini-markets of surfers, scuba-divers and senior citizens, at hot-rodders, credit-card holders, skiers and jet passengers. A varied crop of teenage magazines has sprung up, and most recently we have witnessed something no "mass society" pundit would have dared predict a few years ago: a rebirth of local monthlies. Today scores of American cities such as Phoenix, Philadelphia, San Diego and Atlanta, boast fat, slick, well-supported new magazines devoted entirely to local or regional matters. This is hardly a sign of the erosion of differences. Rather, we are getting a richer mix, a far greater choice of magazines than ever before. And, as the UNESCO survey showed, the same is true of books.

The number of different titles published each year has risen so sharply, and is now so large (more than 30,000 in the United States) that one suburban matron has complained, "It's getting hard to find someone who's read the same book as you. How can you even carry on a conversation about reading?" She may be overstating the case, but book clubs, for example, are finding it increasingly more difficult to choose monthly selections that appeal to large numbers of divergent readers.

Nor is the process of media differentiation confined to commercial publishing alone. Non-commercial literary magazines are proliferating. "Never in American history have there been as many such magazines as there are today," reports *The New York Times Book Review*. Similarly, "underground newspapers" have sprung up in dozens of American and European cities. There are at least 200 of these in the United States, many of them supported by advertising placed by leading record manufacturers. Appealing chiefly to hippies, campus radicals and the rock audience, they have become a tangible force in the formation of opinion among the young. From London's *IT* and the *East Village Other* in New York, to the *Kudzu* in Jackson, Mississippi, they are heavily illustrated, often color-printed, and jammed with ads for "psychedelicatessens" and dating services. Underground papers are even published in high schools. To observe the growth of these grass-roots publications and to speak of "mass culture" or "standardization" is to blind oneself to the new realities.

Significantly, this thrust toward media diversity is based not on affluence alone, but, as we have seen before, on the new technology—the very machines that are supposedly going to homogenize us and crush all vestiges of variety. Advances in offset printing and xerography have radically lowered the costs of short-run publishing, to the point at which high school students can (and do) finance publication of their underground press with pocket money. Indeed, the office copying machine—some versions selling now for as little as thirty dollars—makes possible such extremely short production runs that, as McLuhan puts it, every man can now be his own publisher. In America, where the office copying machine is almost as universal as the adding machine, it would appear that every man *is*. The rocketing number of periodicals that land on one's desk is dramatic testimony to the ease of publication.

Meanwhile, hand-held cameras and new video-tape equipment are similarly revolutionizing the ground rules of cinema. New technology has put camera and film into the hands of thousands of students and amateurs, and the underground movie—crude, colorful, perverse, highly individualized and localized—is flourishing even more than the underground press.

These technological advances have their analog in audio communications, too, where the omnipresence of tape recorders permits every man to be his own "broadcaster." André Moosmann, chief Eastern European expert for Radio-Television Française, reports the existence of widely known pop singers in Russia and Poland who have never appeared on radio or television, but whose songs and voices have been popularized through the medium of tape recordings alone. Tapings of Bulat Okudzava's songs, for example, pass from hand to hand, each listener making his own duplicate—a process that totalitarian governments find difficult to prevent or police. "It goes quickly," says Moosmann, "if a man makes one tape and a friend makes two, the rate of increase can be very fast."

Radicals have often complained that the means of communication are monopolized by a few. Sociologist C. Wright Mills went so far, if my memory is correct, as to urge cultural workers to take over the means of communication. This turns out to be hardly necessary. The advance of communications technology is quietly and rapidly de-monopolizing communications without a shot being fired. The result is a rich destandardization of cultural output.

Television, therefore, may still be homogenizing taste; but the other media have already passed beyond the technological state at which standardization is necessary. When technical breakthroughs alter the economics of television by providing more channels and lowering costs of production, we can anticipate that that medium, too, will begin to fragment its output and cater to, rather than counter, the increasing diversity of the consuming public. Such breakthroughs are, in fact, closer than the horizon. The invention of electronic video recording, the spread of cable television, the possibility of broadcasting direct from satellite to cable systems, all point to vast increases in program variety. For it should now be clear that tendencies toward uniformity represent only one stage in the development of any technology. A dialectical process is at work, and we are on the edge of a long leap toward unparalleled cultural diversity.

The day is already in sight when books, magazines,

newspapers, films and other media will, like the Mustang, be offered to the consumer on a design-it-yourself basis. Thus in the mid-sixties, Joseph Naughton, a mathematician and computer specialist at the University of Pittsburgh, suggested a system that would store a consumer's profile—data about his occupation and interests—in a central computer. Machines would then scan newspapers, magazines, video tapes, films and other material, match them against the individual's interest profile, and instantaneously notify him when something appears that concerns him. The system could be hitched to facsimile machines and TV transmitters that would actually display or print out the material in his own living room. By 1969 the Japanese daily *Asahi Shimbun* was publicly demonstrating a low cost "Telenews" system for printing newspapers in the home, and Matsushita Industries of Osaka was displaying a competitive system known as TV Fax (H). These are the first steps toward the newspaper of the future —a peculiar newspaper, indeed, offering no two viewer-readers the same content. Mass communication, under a system like this, is "de-massified." We move from homogeneity to heterogeneity.

It is obstinate nonsense to insist, in the face of all this, that the machines of tomorrow will turn us into robots, steal our individuality, eliminate cultural variety, etc., etc. Because primitive mass production imposed certain uniformities, does not mean that super-industrial machines will do the same. The fact is that the entire thrust of the future carries away from standardization—away from uniform goods, away from homogenized art, mass produced education and "mass" culture. We have reached a dialectical turning point in the technological development of society. And technology, far from restricting our individuality, will multiply our choices—and our freedom—exponentially.

Whether man is prepared to cope with the increased choice of material and cultural wares available to him is, however, a totally different question. For there comes a time when choice, rather than freeing the individual, becomes so complex, difficult and costly, that it turns into its opposite. There comes a time, in short, when choice turns into overchoice and freedom into un-freedom.

To understand why, we must go beyond this examination of our expanding material and cultural choice. We must look at what is happening to social choice as well.

Chapter 13

A SURFEIT OF SUBCULTS

Thirty miles north of New York City, within easy reach of its towers, its traffic and its urban temptations, lives a young taxicab driver, a former soldier, who boasts 700 surgical stitches in his body. These stitches are not the result of combat wounds, nor of an accident involving his taxi. Instead, they are the result of his chief recreation: rodeo riding.

On a cab driver's modest salary, this man spends more than $1,200 a year to own a horse, stable it, and keep it in perfect trim. Periodically hitching a horse-trailer to his auto, he drives a little over one hundred miles to a place outside Philadelphia called "Cow Town." There, with others like himself, he participates in roping, steer wrestling, bronco busting, and other strenuous contests, the chief prize of which have been repeated visits to a hospital emergency ward.

Despite its proximity, New York holds no fascination for this fellow. When I met him he was twenty-three, and he had visited it only once or twice in his life. His entire interest is focused on the cow ring, and he is a member of a tiny group of rodeo fanatics who form a little-known underground in the United States. They are not professionals who earn a living from this atavistic sport. Nor are they simply people who affect Western-style boots, hats, denim jackets

284

and leather belts. They are a tiny, but authentic subcult lost within the vastness and complexity of the most highly technological civilization in the world.

This odd group not only engages the cab driver's passion, it consumes his time and money. It affects his family, his friends, his ideas. It provides a set of standards against which he measures himself. In short, it rewards him with something that many of us have difficulty finding: an identity.

The techno-societies, far from being drab and homogenized, are honeycombed with just such colorful groupings—hippies and hot rodders, theosophists and flying saucer fans, skin-divers and sky-divers, homosexuals, computerniks, vegetarians, body-builders and Black Muslims.

Today the hammerblows of the super-industrial revolution are literally splintering the society. We are multiplying these social enclaves, tribes and mini-cults among us almost as fast as we are multiplying automotive options. The same destandardizing forces that make for greater individual choice with respect to products and cultural wares, are also destandardizing our social structures. This is why, seemingly over-night, new subcults like the hippies burst into being. We are, in fact, living through a "subcult explosion."

The importance of this cannot be overstated. For we are all deeply influenced, our identities are shaped, by the subcults with which we choose, un-consciously or not, to identify ourselves. It is easy to ridicule a hippie or an uneducated young man who is willing to suffer 700 stitches in an effort to test and "find" himself. Yet we are all rodeo riders or hippies in one sense: we, too, search for identity by attaching ourselves to informal cults, tribes or groups of various kinds. And the more numerous the choices, the more difficult the quest.

SCIENTISTS AND STOCKBROKERS

The proliferation of subcults is most evident in the world of work. Many subcults spring up around occupational specialties. Thus, as the society moves toward greater specialization, it generates more and more subcultural variety.

The scientific community, for example, is splitting into finer and finer fragments. It is criss-crossed with formal organizations and associations whose specialized journals, conferences and meetings are rapidly multiplying in number. But these "open" distinctions according to subject matter are matched by "hidden" distinctions as well. It is not simply that cancer researchers and astronomers do different things; they talk different languages, tend to have different personality types; they think, dress and live differently. (So marked are these distinctions that they often interfere with interpersonal relationships. Says a woman scientist: "My husband is a microbiologist and I am a theoretical physicist, and sometimes I wonder if we mutually exist.")

Scientists within a specialty tend to hang together with their own kind, forming themselves into tight little subcultural cells, to which they turn for approval and prestige, as well as for guidance about such things as dress, political opinions, and life style.

As science expands and the scientific population grows, new specialties spring up, fostering more and still more diversity at this "hidden" or informal level. In short, specialization breeds subcults.

This process of cellular division within a profession is dramatically marked in finance. Wall Street was once a relatively homogeneous community. "It used to be," says one prominent sociological observer of the money men, "that you came down here from St. Paul's and you made a lot of money and belonged to the Racquet Club and you had an estate on the North

Shore, and your daughters were debutantes. You did it all by selling bonds to your ex-classmates." The remark is perhaps slightly exaggerated, but Wall Street was, in fact, one big White Anglo-Saxon Protestant subcult, and its members did tend to go to the same schools, join the same clubs, engage in the same sports (tennis, golf and squash), attend the same churches (Presbyterian and Episcopalian), and vote for the same party (Republican).

Anybody who still thinks of Wall Street in these terms, however, is getting his ideas from the novels of Auchincloss or Marquand rather than from the new, fast-changing reality. Today, Wall Street has splintered, and a young man entering the business has a choice of a whole clutch of competing subcultural affiliations. In investment banking the old conservative WASP grouping still lingers on. There are still some old-line "white shoe" firms of which it is said "They'll have a black partner before they hire a Jew." Yet in the mutual fund field, a relatively new specialized segment of the financial industry, Greek, Jewish and Chinese names abound, and some star salesmen are black. Here the entire style of life, the implicit values of the group, are quite different. Mutual fund people are a separate tribe.

"Not everyone even wants to be a WASP any more," says a leading financial writer. Indeed, many young, aggressive Wall Streeters, even when they do happen to be WASP in origin, reject the classical Wall Street subcult and identify themselves instead with one or more of the pluralistic social groupings that now swarm and sometimes collide in the canyons of Lower Manhattan.

As specialization continues, as research extends into new fields and probes more deeply into old ones, as the economy continues to create new technologies and services, subcults will continue to multiply. Those social critics who inveigh against "mass society" in one breath and denounce "over-specialization" in the next are simply flapping their tongues. Specialization means a movement away from sameness.

Despite much loose talk about the need for "generalists," there is little evidence that the technology of tomorrow can be run without armies of highly trained specialists. We are rapidly changing the types of expertise needed. We are demanding more "multi-specialists" (men who know one field deeply, but who can cross over into another as well) rather than rigid, "mono-specialists." But we shall continue to need and breed ever more refined work specialties as the technical base of society increases in complexity. For this reason alone, we must expect the variety and number of subcults in the society to increase.

THE FUN SPECIALISTS

Even if technology were to free millions of people from the need to work in the future, we would find the same push toward diversity operating among those who are left free to play. For we are already producing large numbers of "fun specialists." We are rapidly multiplying not merely types of work, but types of play as well.

The number of acceptable pastimes, hobbies, games, sports and entertainments is climbing rapidly, and the growth of a distinct subcult built around surfing, for example, demonstrates that, at least for some, a leisure-time commitment can also serve as the basis for an entire life style. The surfing subcult is a signpost pointing to the future.

"Surfing has already developed a kind of symbolism that gives it the character of a secret fraternity or a religious order," writes Remi Nadeau. "The identifying sign is a shark's tooth, St. Christopher medal, or Maltese cross hung loosely about one's neck . . . For a long time, the most accepted form of transportation has been a wood-paneled Ford station wagon of ancient vintage." Surfers display sores and nodules on their knees and feet as proud proof of their involvement. Suntan is *de rigeur*. Hair is styled in a distinctive way. Members of the tribe spend endless hours debating the prowess of such in-group heroes as J. J. Moon, and his followers buy J. J. Moon T-shirts, surfboards, and fan club memberships.

Surfers are only one of many such play-based subcults. Among skydivers, for example, the name J. J. Moon is virtually unknown, and so are the peculiar rituals and fashions of the wave-cresters. Skydivers talk, instead, about the feat of Rod Pack, who not long ago jumped from an airplane without a parachute, was handed one by a companion in mid-air, put it on, opened it, and landed safely. Skydivers have their own little world, as do glider enthusiasts, scuba-divers, hot rodders, drag racers and motorcyclists. Each of these represents a leisure-based subcult organized around a technological device. As the new technology makes new sports possible, we can anticipate the formation of highly varied new play cults.

Leisure-time pursuits will become an increasingly important basis for differences between people, as the society itself shifts from a work orientation toward greater involvement in leisure. In the United States, since the turn of the century alone, the society's measurable commitment to work has plummeted by nearly a third. This is a massive redeployment of the society's time and energy. As this commitment declines further, we shall advance into an era of breathtaking fun specialism—much of it based on sophisticated technology.

We can anticipate the formation of subcults built around space activity, holography, mind-control, deep-sea diving, submarining, computer gaming and the like. We can even see on the horizon the creation of certain anti-social leisure cults—tightly organized groups of people who will disrupt the workings of society not for material gain, but for the sheer sport of "beating the system"—a development foreshadowed in such films as *Duffy* and *The Thomas Crown Af-*

fair. Such groups may attempt to tamper with governmental or corporate computer programs, re-route mail, intercept and alter radio and television broadcasts, perform elaborately theatrical hoaxes, tinker with the stock market, corrupt the random samples upon which political or other polls are based, and even, perhaps, commit complexly plotted robberies and assassinations. Novelist Thomas Pynchon in *The Crying of Lot 49* describes a fictional underground group who have organized their own private postal system and maintained it for generations. Science fiction writer Robert Sheckley has gone so far as to propose, in a terrifying short story called *The Seventh Victim,* the possibility that society might legalize murder among certain specified "players" who hunt one another and are, in turn, hunted. This ultimate game would permit those who are dangerously violent to work off their aggressions within a managed framework.

Bizarre as some of this may sound, it would be well not to rule out the seemingly improbable, for the realm of leisure, unlike that of work, is little constrained by practical considerations. Here imagination has free play, and the mind of man can conjure up incredible varieties of "fun." Given enough time, money and, for some of these, technical skill, the men of tomorrow will be capable of playing in ways never dreamed of before. They will play strange sexual games. They will play games with the mind. They will play games with society. And in so doing, by choosing among the unimaginably broad options, they will form subcults and further set themselves off from one another.

THE YOUTH GHETTO

Subcults are multiplying—the society is cracking—along age lines, too. We are becoming "age specialists" as well as work and play specialists. There was a time when people were divided roughly into children, "young persons," and adults. It wasn't until the forties that the loosely defined term "young persons" began to be replaced by the more restrictive term "teenager," referring specifically to the years thirteen to nineteen. (In fact, the word was virtually unknown in England until after World War II.)

Today this crude, three-way division is clearly inadequate, and we are busy inventing far more specific categories. We now have a classification called "pre-teens" or "sub-teens" that sits perched between childhood and adolescence. We are also beginning to hear of "post-teens" and, after that, "young marrieds." Each of these terms is a linguistic recognition of the fact that we can no longer usefully lump all "young persons" together. Increasingly deep cleavages separate one age group from another. So sharp are these differences that sociologist John Lofland of the University of Michigan predicts they will become the "conflict equivalent of southerner and northerner, capitalist and worker, immigrant and 'native stock,' suffragette and male, white and Negro."

Lofland supports this startling suggestion by documenting the rise of what he calls the "youth ghetto"—large communities occupied almost entirely by college students. Like the Negro ghetto, the youth ghetto is often characterized by poor housing, rent and price gouging, very high mobility, unrest and conflict with the police. Like the Negro ghetto, it, too, is quite heterogeneous, with many subcults competing for the attention and allegiance of the ghettoites.

Robbed of adult heroes or role models other than their own parents, children of streamlined, nuclear families are increasingly flung into the arms of the only other people available to them—other children. They spend more time with one another, and they become more responsive to the influence of peers than ever before. Rather than idolizing an uncle, they idolize Bob Dylan or Donovan or whomever else the peer group holds up for a life style model. Thus we are beginning to form not only a college student ghetto, but even semi-ghettos of pre-teens and teen-agers, each with its own peculiar tribal characteristics, its own fads, fashions, heroes and villains.

We are simultaneously segmenting the adult population along age lines, too. There are suburbs occupied largely by young married couples with small children, or by middle-aged couples with teenagers, or by older couples whose children have already left home. We have specially-designed "retirement communities" for retirees. "There may come a day," Professor Lofland warns, ". . . when some cities will find that their politics revolve around the voting strength of various age category ghettos, in the same way that Chicago politics has long revolved around ethnic and racial enclaves."

This emergence of age-based subcultures can now be seen as part of a stunning historical shift in the basis of social differentiation. Time is becoming more important as a source of differences among men; space is becoming less so.

Thus communications theorist James W. Carey of the University of Illinois, points out that "among primitive societies and in the earlier stages of western history, relatively small discontinuities in space led to vast differences in culture . . . Tribal societies separated by a hundred miles could have . . . grossly dissimilar systems of expressive symbolism, myth and ritual." Within these same societies, however, there was "great continuity . . . over generations . . . vast differences between societies but relatively little variation between generations within a given society."

Today, he continues, space "progressively disappears as a differentiating factor." But if there has been some reduction in regional variation, Carey takes pains to point out, "one must not assume that differences between groups are being obliterated . . . as some mass society theorists [suggest]." Rather, Carey points out, "the axis of diversity shifts from a spatial . . . to a temporal or generational dimension."

Thus we get jagged breaks between the generations —and Mario Savio summed it up with the revolutionary slogan, "Don't trust anyone over thirty!" In no previous society could such a slogan have caught on so quickly.

Carey explains this shift from spatial to temporal differentiation by calling attention to the advance of communications and transportation technology which spans great distances, and, in effect, conquers space. Yet there is another, easily overlooked factor at work: the acceleration of change. For as the pace of change in the external environment steps up, the inner differences between young and old become necessarily more marked. In fact, the pace of change is already so blinding that even a few years can make a great difference in the life experience of the individual. This is why some brothers and sisters, separated in age by a mere three or four years, subjectively feel themselves to be members of quite different "generations." It is why among those radicals who participated in the strike at Columbia University, seniors spoke of the "generation gap" that separated them from sophomores.

MARITAL TRIBES

Splintering along occupational, recreational and age lines, the society is also fragmenting along sexual-familial lines. Even now, however, we are already creating distinctive new subcults based on marital status. Once people might be loosely classified as either single, married or widowed. Today this three-way categorization is no longer adequate. Divorce rates are so high in most of the techno-societies today that a distinct new social grouping has emerged— those who are no longer married or who are between marriages. Thus Morton Hunt, an authority on the subject, describes what he terms "the world of the formerly married."

This group, says Hunt, is a "subculture . . . with its own mechanisms for bringing people together, its own patterns of adjustment to the separated or divorced life, its own opportunities for friendship, social life and love." As its members break away from their married friends, they become progressively isolated from those still in "married life" and "ex-marrieds," like "teen-agers" or "surfers," tend to form social enclaves of their own with their own favored meeting places, their own attitudes toward time, their own distinct sexual codes and conventions.

Strong trends make it likely that this particular social category will swell in the future. And when this happens, the world of the formerly married will, in turn, split into multiple worlds, more and still more sub-cultural groupings. For the bigger a subcult becomes, the more likely it is to fragment and give birth to new subcults.

If the first clue to the future of social organization lies, therefore, in the idea of proliferating subcults, the second lies in sheer size. This basic principle is largely overlooked by those who are most exercised over "mass society," and it helps explain the persistence of diversity even under extreme standardizing pressures. Because of in-built limitations in social communication, size itself acts as a force pushing toward diversity of organization. The larger the population of a modern city, for example, the more numerous—and diverse—the subcults within it. Similarly, the larger the subcult, the higher the odds that it will fragment and diversify. The hippies provide a perfect example.

HIPPIES, INCORPORATED

In the mid-fifties, a small group of writers, artists and assorted hangers-on coalesced in San Francisco and around Carmel and Big Sur on the California coast.

Quickly dubbed "beats" or "beatniks," they pieced
together a distinctive way of life.

Its most conspicuous elements were the glorification of poverty—jeans, sandals, pads and hovels; a
predilection for Negro jazz and jargon; an interest in
Eastern mysticism and French existentialism; and a
general antagonism to technologically based society.

Despite extensive press coverage, the beats remained a tiny sect until a technological innovation—
lysergic acid, better known as LSD—appeared on the
scene. Pushed by the messianic advertising of Timothy Leary, Allen Ginsberg and Ken Kesey, distributed
free to thousands of young people by irresponsible
enthusiasts, LSD soon began to claim a following on
the American campus, and almost as quickly spread
to Europe as well. The infatuation with LSD was accompanied by a new interest in marijuana, a drug
with which the beats had long experimented. Out of
these two sources, the beat subcult of the mid-fifties
and the "acid" subcult of the early sixties, sprang a
larger group—a new subcult that might be described
as a corporate merger of the two: the hippie movement. Blending the blue jeans of the beats with the
beads and bangles of the acid crowd, the hippies
became the newest and most hotly publicized subcult
on the American scene.

Soon, however, the pressures of growth proved too
much for it. Thousands of teen-agers joined the ranks;
millions of pre-teens watched their television sets,
read magazine articles about the movement, and un-
dulated in sympathy; some suburban adults even became "plastic" or weekend hippies. The result was
predictable. The hippie subcult—exactly like General
Motors or General Electric—was forced to division-
alize, to break down into subsidiaries. Thus out of the
hippie subcult came a shower of progeny.

To the eye of the uninitiated, all young people with
long hair seemed alike. Yet important sub-units
emerged within the movement. According to David
Andrew Seeley, an acute young observer, there were

at its height "perhaps a score of recognizable and distinct groups." These varied not only by certain subtleties of dress but by interest. Thus, Seeley reported, their activities ranged "from beer parties to poetry readings, from pot-smoking to modern dance—and often those who indulge in one wouldn't touch the other." Seeley then proceeded to explain the differences that set apart such groups as the teeny-boppers (now largely vanished from the scene), the political activist beatniks, the folk beatniks, and then, and only then, the original hippies *per se*.

Members of these subcultural subsidiaries wore identifying badges that held meaning for insiders. Teeny-boppers, for example, were beardless, many, in fact, being too young to shave. Sandals were "in" with the folk set, but not some of the others. The tightness of one's trousers varied according to subcult.

At the level of ideas, there were many common complaints about the dominant culture. But sharp differences emerged with respect to political and social action. Attitudes ranged from the conscious withdrawal of the acid hippie, through the ignorant unconcern of the teeny-bopper, to the intense involvement of the New Left activist and the politics-of-the-absurd activities of groupings like the Dutch provos, the Crazies, and the guerrilla theater crowd.

The hippie corporation, so to speak, grew too large to handle all its business in a standardized way. It had to diversify and it did. It spawned a flock of fledgling subcultural enterprises.

TRIBAL TURNOVER

Even as this happened, however, the movement began to die. The most passionate LSD advocates of yesterday began to admit that "acid was a bad scene" and various underground newspapers began warning followers against getting too involved with "tripsters." A mock funeral was held in San Francisco to "bury" the hippie subcult, and its favored locations, Haight-Ashbury and the East Village turned into tourist meccas as the original movement writhed and disintegrated, forming new and odder, but smaller and weaker subcults and mini-tribes. Then, as though to start the process all over again, yet another subcult, the "skinheads," surfaced. Skinheads had their own characteristic outfits—suspenders, boots, short haircuts—and an unsettling predilection for violence.

The death of the hippie movement and the rise of the skinheads provide a crucial new insight into the subcultural structure of tomorrow's society. For we are not merely multiplying subcults. We are turning them over more rapidly. The principle of transience is at work here, too. As the rate of change accelerates in all other aspects of the society, subcults, too, grow more ephemeral.

Evidence pointing toward a decrease in the life span of subcults also lies in the disappearance of that violent subcult of the fifties, the fighting street gang. Throughout that decade certain streets in New York were regularly devastated by a peculiar form of urban warfare called the "rumble." During a rumble, scores, if not hundreds, of youths would attack one another with flailing chains, switchblade knives, broken bottles and zip-guns. Rumbles occurred in Chicago, Philadelphia, Los Angeles, and even as far away as London and Tokyo.

While there was no direct connection between these far-flung outbreaks, rumbles were by no means chance events. They were planned and carried out with military precision by highly organized "bopping gangs." In New York these gangs affected colorful names—Cobras, Corsair Lords, Apaches, Egyptian Kings and the like. They fought one another for dominance in their "turf"—the specific geographic area they staked out for themselves.

At their peak there were some 200 such gangs in New York alone, and in a single year, 1958, they accounted for no fewer than eleven homicides. Yet by

1966, according to police officials, the bopping gangs had virtually vanished. Only one gang was left in New York, and *The New York Times* reported: "No one knows on what garbage strewn street . . . the last rumble took place. But it happened four or five years ago [which would date the death of the rumble a mere two or three years after the 1958 peak]. Then, suddenly, after a decade of mounting violence the era of the fighting gangs of New York came to an end." The same appeared to be true in Washington, Newark, Philadelphia and elsewhere as well.

The disappearance of the violent street gangs has not, of course, led to an era of urban tranquility. The aggressive passions that led poor Puerto Rican and Negro youths in New York to wage war on rival gangs is now directed at the social system itself, and totally new kinds of social organizations, subcults and life style groupings are emerging in the ghetto.

What we sense, therefore, is a process by which subcults multiply at an ever accelerating rate, and in turn die off to make room for still more and newer subcults. A kind of metabolic process is taking place in the bloodstream of the society, and it is speeding up exactly as other aspects of social interaction are quickening.

For the individual, this raises the problems of choice to a totally new level of intensity. It is not simply that the number of tribes is expanding rapidly. It is not even that these tribes or subcults are bouncing off one another, shifting and changing their relationships to one another more and more rapidly. It is also that many of them will not hold still long enough to permit an individual to make a rational investigation of the presumed advantages or disadvantages of affiliation.

The individual searching for some sense of belonging, looking for the kind of social connection that confers some sense of identity, moves through a blurry environment in which the possible targets of affiliation are all in high-speed motion. He must choose from among a growing number of moving targets. The problems of choice thus escalate not arithmetically, but geometrically.

At the very instant when his choices among material goods, education, culture consumption, recreation and entertainment are all multiplying, he is also given a bewildering array of social choices. And just as there is a limit to how much choice he may *wish* to exercise in buying a car—at a certain point the addition of options requires more decision-making than they are worth—so, too, we may soon approach the moment of social overchoice.

The level of personality disorder, neurosis, and just plain psychological distress in our society suggests that it is already difficult for many individuals to create a sensible, integrated, and reasonably stable personal style. Yet there is every evidence that the thrust toward social diversity, paralleling that at the level of goods and culture, is just beginning. We face a tempting and terrifying extension of freedom.

THE IGNOBLE SAVAGE

The more subcultural groupings in a society, the greater the potential freedom of the individual. This is why pre-industrial man, despite romantic myths to the contrary, suffered so bitterly from lack of choice.

While sentimentalists prattle about the supposedly unfettered freedom of the primitive, evidence collected by anthropologists and historians contradicts them. John Gardner puts the matter tersely: "The primitive tribe or pre-industrial community has usually demanded far more profound submission of the individual to the group than has any modern society." As an Australian social scientist was told by a Temne tribesman in Sierra Leone: "When Temne people choose a thing, we must all agree with the decision —this is what we call cooperation."

This is, of course, what *we* call conformity.

The reason for the crushing conformity required of pre-industrial man, the reason the Temne tribesman has to "go along" with his fellows, is precisely that he has nowhere else to go. His society is monolithic, not yet broken into a liberating multiplicity of components. It is what sociologists call "undifferentiated."

Like a bullet smashing into a pane of glass, industrialism shatters these societies, splitting them up into thousands of specialized agencies—schools, corporations, government bureaus, churches, armies—each subdivided into smaller and still more specialized subunits. The same fragmentation occurs at the informal level, and a host of subcults spring up: rodeo riders, Black Muslims, motorcyclists, skinheads and all the rest.

This split-up of the social order is precisely analogous to the process of growth in biology. Embryos differentiate as they develop, forming more and more specialized organs. The entire march of evolution, from the virus to man, displays a relentless advance toward higher and higher degrees of differentiation. There appears to be a seemingly irresistible movement of living beings and social groups from less to more differentiated forms.

Thus it is not accidental that we witness parallel trends toward diversity—in the economy, in art, in education and mass culture, in the social order itself. These trends all fit together forming part of an immensely larger historic process. The Super-industrial Revolution can now be seen for what, in large measure, it is—the advance of human society to its next higher stage of differentiation.

This is why it often seems to us that our society is cracking at the seams. It is. This is why everything grows increasingly complex. Where once there stood 1000 organizational entities, there now stand 10,000 —interconnected by increasingly transient links. Where once there were a few relatively permanent subcults with which a person might identify, there now are thousands of temporary subcults milling

about, colliding and multiplying. The powerful bonds
that integrated industrial society—bonds of law, common values, centralized and standardized education
and cultural production—are breaking down.

All this explains why cities suddenly seem to be
"unmanageable" and universities "ungovernable." For
the old ways of integrating a society, methods based
on uniformity, simplicity, and permanence, are no
longer effective. A new, more finely fragmented social
order—a super-industrial order—is emerging. It is
based on many more diverse and short-lived components than any previous social system—and we
have not yet learned how to link them together, how
to integrate the whole.

For the individual, this leap to a new level of differentiation holds awesome implications. But not
the ones most people fear. We have been told so often
that we are heading for faceless uniformity that we
fail to appreciate the fantastic opportunities for individuality that the Super-industrial Revolution brings
with it. And we have hardly begun to think about the
dangers of over-individualization that are also implicit in it.

The "mass society" theorists are obsessed by a reality that has already begun to pass us by. The Cassan-
dras who blindly hate technology and predict an
ant-heap future are still responding in knee-jerk
fashion to the conditions of industrialism. Yet this
system is already being superseded.

To denounce the conditions that imprison the industrial worker today is admirable. To project these
conditions into the future, and predict the death of
individualism, diversity and choice, is to utter dangerous clichés.

The people of both past and present are still locked
into relatively choiceless life ways. The people of the
future, whose number increases daily, face not choice
but overchoice. For them there comes an explosive
extension of freedom.

And this freedom comes not in spite of the new

technology but very largely because of it. For if the early technology of industrialism required mindless, robot-like men to perform endlessly repetitive tasks, the technology of tomorrow takes over precisely these tasks, leaving for men only those functions that require judgment, interpersonal skills and imagination. Super-industrialism requires, and will create, not identical "mass men," but people richly different from one another, individuals, not robots.

The human race, far from being flattened into monotonous conformity, will become far more diverse socially than it ever was before. The new society, the super-industrial society now beginning to take form, will encourage a crazy-quilt pattern of evanescent life styles.

Chapter 14

A DIVERSITY
OF LIFE STYLES

In San Francisco, executives lunch at restaurants where they are served by bare-breasted waitresses. In New York, however, a kooky girl cellist is arrested for performing avant garde music in a topless costume. In St. Louis, scientists hire prostitutes and others to copulate under a camera as part of a study of the physiology of the orgasm. But in Columbus, Ohio, civic controversy erupts over the sale of so-called "Little Brother" dolls that come from the factory equipped with male genitalia. In Kansas City, a conference of homosexual organizations announces a campaign to lift a Pentagon ban on homosexuals in the armed forces and, in fact, the Pentagon discreetly does so. Yet American jails are well populated with men arrested for the crime of homosexuality.

Seldom has a single nation evinced greater confusion over its sexual values. Yet the same might be said for other kinds of values as well. America is tortured by uncertainty with respect to money, property, law and order, race, religion, God, family and self. Nor is the United States alone in suffering from a kind of value vertigo. All the techno-societies are caught up in the same massive upheaval. This collapse of the values of the past has hardly gone unnoticed. Every priest, politician and parent is reduced to head-shaking anxiety by it. Yet most discussions of value change are barren for they miss two essential points. The first of these is acceleration.

Value turnover is now faster than ever before in history. While in the past a man growing up in a society could expect that its public value system would remain largely unchanged in his lifetime, no such assumption is warranted today, except perhaps in the most isolated of pre-technological communities.

This implies temporariness in the structure of both public and personal value systems, and it suggests that *whatever* the content of values that arise to replace those of the industrial age, they will be shorter-lived, more ephemeral than the values of the past. There is no evidence whatsoever that the value systems of the techno-societies are likely to return to a "steady state" condition. For the foreseeable future, we must anticipate still more rapid value change.

Within this context, however, a second powerful trend is unfolding. For the fragmentation of societies brings with it a diversification of values. We are witnessing the crack-up of consensus.

Most previous societies have operated with a broad central core of commonly shared values. This core is now contracting, and there is little reason to anticipate the formation of a new broad consensus within the decades ahead. The pressures are outward toward diversity, not inward toward unity.

This accounts for the fantastically discordant propaganda that assails the mind in the techno-societies. Home, school, corporation, church, peer group, mass media—and myriad subcults—all advertise varying sets of values. The result for many is an "anything goes" attitude—which is, itself, still another value position. We are, declares *Newsweek* magazine, "a society that has lost its consensus . . . a society that cannot agree on standards of conduct, language and manners, on what can be seen and heard."

This picture of a cracked consensus is confirmed by

the findings of Walter Gruen, social science research coordinator at Rhode Island Hospital, who has conducted a series of statistical studies of what he terms "the American core culture." Rather than the monolithic system of beliefs attributed to the middle class by earlier investigators, Gruen found—to his own surprise—that "diversity in beliefs was more striking than the statistically supported uniformities. It is," he concluded, "perhaps already misleading to talk of an 'American' culture complex."

Gruen suggests that particularly among the affluent, educated group, consensus is giving way to what he calls "pockets" of values. We can expect that, as the number and variety of subcults continues to expand, these pockets will proliferate, too.

Faced with colliding value systems, confronted with a blinding array of new consumer goods, services, educational, occupational and recreational options, the people of the future are driven to make choices in a new way. They begin to "consume" life styles the way people of an earlier, less choice-choked time consumed ordinary products.

MOTORCYCLISTS AND INTELLECTUALS

During Elizabethan times, the term "gentleman" referred to a whole way of life, not simply an accident of birth. Appropriate lineage may have been a prerequisite, but to be a gentleman one had also to live in a certain style: to be better educated, have better manners, wear better clothes than the masses; to engage in certain recreations (and not others); to live in a large, well-furnished house; to maintain a certain aloofness with subordinates; in short, never to lose sight of his class "superiority."

The merchant class had its own preferred life style and the peasantry still another. These life styles, like that of the gentleman, were pieced together out of many different components, ranging from residence, occupation and dress to jargon, gesture and religion.

Today we still create our life styles by forming a mosaic of components. But much has changed. Life style is no longer simply a manifestation of class position. Classes themselves are breaking up into smaller units. Economic factors are declining in importance. Thus today it is not so much one's class base as one's ties with a subcult that determine the individual's style of life. The working-class hippie and the hippie who dropped out of Exeter or Eton share a common style of life but no common class.

Since life style has become the way in which the individual expresses his identification with this or that subcult, the explosive multiplication of subcults in society has brought with it an equally explosive multiplication of life styles. Thus the stranger launched into American or English or Japanese or Swedish society today must choose not among four or five class-based styles of life, but among literally hundreds of diverse possibilities. Tomorrow, as subcults proliferate, this number will be even larger.

How we choose a life style, and what it means to us, therefore, looms as one of the central issues of the psychology of tomorrow. For the selection of a life style, whether consciously done or not, powerfully shapes the individual's future. It does this by imposing order, a set of principles or criteria on the choices he makes in his daily life.

This becomes clear if we examine how such choices are actually made. The young couple setting out to furnish their apartment may look at literally hundreds of different lamps—Scandinavian, Japanese, French Provincial, Tiffany lamps, hurricane lamps, American colonial lamps—dozens, scores of different sizes, models and styles before selecting, say, the Tiffany lamp. Having surveyed a "universe" of possibilities, they zero in on one. In the furniture department, they again scan an array of alternatives, then settle on a Victorian end table. This scan-and-select procedure is repeated with respect to rugs, sofa, drapes, dining room chairs, etc. In fact, something like this same procedure is followed not merely in furnishing their home, but also in their adoption of ideas, friends, even the vocabulary they use and the values they espouse.

While the society bombards the individual with a swirling, seemingly patternless set of alternatives, the selections made are anything but random. The consumer (whether of end tables or ideas) comes armed with a pre-established set of tastes and preferences. Moreover, no choice is wholly independent. Each is conditioned by those made earlier. The couple's selection of an end table has been conditioned by their previous choice of a lamp. In short, there is a certain consistency, an attempt at personal style, in all our actions—whether consciously recognized or not.

The American male who wears a button-down collar and garter-length socks probably also wears wing-tip shoes and carries an attaché case. If we look closely, chances are we shall find a facial expression and brisk manner intended to approximate those of the stereotypical executive. The odds are astronomical that he will not let his hair grow wild in the manner of rock musician Jimi Hendrix. He knows, as we do, that certain clothes, manners, forms of speech, opinions and gestures hang together, while others do not. He may know this only by "feel," or "intuition," having picked it up by observing others in the society, but the knowledge shapes his actions.

The black-jacketed motorcyclist who wears steel-studded gauntlets and an obscene swastika dangling from his throat completes his costume with rugged boots, not loafers or wing-tips. He is likely to swagger as he walks and to grunt as he mouths his anti-authoritarian platitudes. For he, too, values consistency. He knows that any trace of gentility or articulateness would destroy the integrity of his style.

STYLE-SETTERS AND MINI-HEROES

Why do the motorcyclists wear black jackets? Why not brown or blue? Why do executives in America prefer attaché cases, rather than the traditional briefcase? It is as though they were following some model, trying to attain some ideal laid down from above.

We know little about the origin of life style models. We do know, however, that popular heroes and celebrities, including fictional characters (James Bond, for example), have something to do with it.

Marlon Brando, swaggering in a black jacket as a motorcyclist, perhaps originated, and certainly publicized a life style model. Timothy Leary, robed, beaded, and muttering mystic pseudo profundities about love and LSD, provided a model for thousands of youths. Such heroes, as the sociologist Orrin Klapp puts it, help to "crystallize a social type." He cites the late James Dean who depicted the alienated adolescent in the movie *Rebel Without a Cause* or Elvis Presley who initially fixed the image of the guitar-twanging rock-'n'-roller. Later came the Beatles with their (at that time) outrageous hair and exotic costumes. "One of the prime functions of popular favorites," says Klapp, "is to make types visible, which in turn make new life styles and new tastes visible."

Yet the style-setter need not be a mass media idol. He may be almost unknown outside a particular subcult. Thus for years Lionel Trilling, an English professor at Columbia, was the father figure for the West Side Intellectuals, a New York subcult well known in literary and academic circles in the United States. The mother figure was Mary McCarthy, long before she achieved popular fame.

An acute article by John Speicher in a youth magazine called *Cheetah* listed some of the better-known life style models to which young people were responding in the late sixties. They ranged from Ché

Guevara to William Buckley, from Bob Dylan and Joan Baez to Robert Kennedy. "The American youth bag," wrote Speicher, lapsing into hippie jargon, "is overcrowded with heroes." And, he adds, "where heroes are, there are followers, cultists."

To the subcult member, its heroes provide what Speicher calls the "crucial existential necessity of psychological identity." This is, of course, hardly new. Earlier generations identified with Charles Lindbergh or Theda Bara. What is new and highly significant, however, is the fabulous proliferation of such heroes and mini-heroes. As subcults multiply and values diversify, we find, in Speicher's words, "a national sense of identity hopelessly fragmented." For the individual, he says, this means greater choice: "There is a wide range of cults available, a wide range of heroes. You can do comparison shopping."

LIFE STYLE FACTORIES

While charismatic figures may become style-setters, styles are fleshed out and marketed to the public by the sub-societies or tribe-lets we have termed subcults. Taking in raw symbolic matter from the mass media, they somehow piece together odd bits of dress, opinion, and expression and form them into a coherent package: a life style model. Once they have assembled a particular model, they proceed, like any good corporation, to merchandise it. They find customers for it.

Anyone doubting this is advised to read the letters of Allen Ginsberg to Timothy Leary, the two men most responsible for creating the hippie life style, with its heavy accent on drug use.

Says poet Ginsberg: "Yesterday got on TV with N. Mailer and Ashley Montagu and gave big speech . . . recommending everybody get high . . . Got in touch with all the liberal pro-dope people I know to have [a certain pro-drug report] publicized and circulated . . . I wrote a five-page summary of the situation to this friend Kenny Love on *The New York Times* and he said he'd perhaps do a story (newswise) . . . which could then be picked up by U.P. friend on national wire. Also gave copy to Al Aronowitz on New York *Post* and Rosalind Constable at *Time* and Bob Silvers on *Harper's* . . ."

No wonder LSD and the whole hippie phenomenon received the immense mass media publicity it did. This partial account of Ginsberg's energetic press agentry, complete with the Madison Avenue suffix "-wise" (as in newswise), reads precisely like an internal memo from Hill and Knowlton or any of the other giant public relations corporations whom hippies love to flagellate for manipulating public opinion. The successful "sale" of the hippie life style model to young people all over the techno-societies, is one of the classic merchandising stories of our time.

Not all subcults are so aggressive and talented at flackery, yet their cumulative power in the society is enormous. This power stems from our almost universal desperation to "belong." The primitive tribesman feels a strong attachment to his tribe. He knows that he "belongs" to it, and may even have difficulty imagining himself apart from it. The techno-societies are so large, however, and their complexities so far beyond the comprehension of any individual, that it is only by plugging in to one or more of their subcults, that we maintain some sense of identity and contact with the whole. Failure to identify with some such group or groups condemns us to feelings of loneliness, alienation and ineffectuality. We begin to wonder "who we are."

In contrast, the sense of belonging, of being part of a social cell larger than ourselves (yet small enough to be comprehensible) is often so rewarding that we feel deeply drawn, sometimes even against our own better judgment, to the values, attitudes and most-favored life style of the group.

However, we pay for the benefits we receive. For once we psychologically affiliate with a subcult, it begins to exert pressures on us. We find that it pays to "go along" with the group. It rewards us with warmth, friendship and approval when we conform to its life style model. But it punishes us ruthlessly with ridicule, ostracism or other tactics when we deviate from it.

Hawking their preferred life style models, subcults clamor for our attention. In so doing, they act directly on our most vulnerable psychological property, our self-image. "Join us," they whisper, "and you become a bigger, better, more effective, more respected and less lonely person." In choosing among the fast-pro-liferating subcults we may only vaguely sense that our identity will be shaped by our decision, but we feel the hot urgency of their appeals and counter-appeals. We are buffeted back and forth by their psychological promises.

At the moment of choice among them, we resemble the tourist walking down Bourbon Street in New Or-leans. As he strolls past the honky-tonks and clip joints, doormen grab him by the arm, spin him around, and open a door so he can catch a titillating glimpse of the naked flesh of the strippers on the platform behind the bar. Subcults reach out to capture us and appeal to our most private fantasies in ways far more power-ful and subtle than any yet devised by Madison Avenue.

What they offer is not simply a skin show or a new soap or detergent. They offer not a product, but a super-product. It is true they hold out the promise of human warmth, companionship, respect, a sense of' community. But so do the advertisers of deodorants and beer. The "miracle ingredient," the exclusive com-ponent, the one thing that subcults offer that other hawkers cannot, is a respite from the strain of over-choice. For they offer not a single product or idea, but a way of organizing all products and ideas, not a single commodity but a whole style, a set of guidelines that help the individual reduce the increasing com-plexity of choice to manageable proportions.

Most of us are desperately eager to find precisely such guidelines. In the welter of conflicting moralities, in the confusion occasioned by overchoice, the most powerful, most useful "super-product" of all is an organizing principle for one's life. This is what a life style offers.

THE POWER OF STYLE

Of course, not just any life style will do. We live in a Cairo bazaar of competing models. In this psychological phantasmagoria we search for a style, a way of ordering our existence, that will fit our particular temperament and circumstances. We look for heroes or mini-heroes to emulate. The style-seeker is like the lady who flips through the pages of a fashion magazine to find a suitable dress pattern. She studies one after another, settles on one that appeals to her, and decides to create a dress based on it. Next she begins to collect the necessary materials—cloth, thread, piping, buttons, etc. In precisely the same way, the life style creator acquires the necessary props. He lets his hair grow. He buys art nouveau posters and a paperback of Guevara's writings. He learns to discuss Marcuse and Frantz Fanon. He picks up a particular jargon, using words like "relevance" and "establishment."

None of this means that his political actions are insignificant, or that his opinions are unjust or foolish. He may (or may not) be accurate in his views of society. Yet the particular way in which he chooses to express them is inescapably part of his search for personal style.

The lady, in constructing her dress, alters it here and there, deviating from the pattern in minor ways to make it fit her more perfectly. The end product is truly custom-made; yet it bears a striking resemblance to others sewn from the same design. In quite the same way we individualize our style of living, yet it usually winds up bearing a distinct resemblance to some life style model previously packaged and marketed by a subcult.

Often we are unaware of the moment when we commit ourselves to one life style model over all others. The decision to "be" an Executive or a Black Militant or a West Side Intellectual is seldom the result of purely logical analysis. Nor is the decision always made cleanly, all at once. The research scientist who switches from cigarettes to a pipe may do so for health reasons without recognizing that the pipe is part of a whole life style toward which he finds himself drawn. The couple who choose the Tiffany lamp think they are furnishing an apartment; they do not necessarily see their actions as an attempt to flesh out an overall style of life.

Most of us, in fact, do not think of our own lives in terms of life style, and we often have difficulty in talking about it objectively. We have even more trouble when we try to articulate the structure of values implicit in our style. The task is doubly hard because many of us do not adopt a single integrated style, but a composite of elements drawn from several different models. We may emulate both Hippie and Surfer. We may choose a cross between West Side Intellectual and Executive—a fusion that is, in fact, chosen by many publishing officials in New York. When one's personal style is a hybrid, it is frequently difficult to disentangle the multiple models on which it is based.

Once we commit ourselves to a particular model, however, we fight energetically to build it, and perhaps even more so to preserve it against challenge. For the style becomes extremely important to us. This is doubly true of the people of the future, among whom concern for style is downright passionate. This intense concern for style is not, however, what literary critics mean by formalism. It is not simply an interest in outward appearances. For style of life involves not merely the external forms of behavior, but the values implicit in that behavior, and one cannot change one's life style without working some change in one's self-image. The people of the future are not "style conscious" but "life style conscious."

This is why little things often assume great significance for them. A single small detail of one's life may be charged with emotional power if it challenges a hard-won life style, if it threatens to break up the integrity of the style. Aunt Ethel gives us a wedding present. We are embarrassed by it, for it is in a style alien to our own. It irritates and upsets us, even though we know that "Aunt Ethel doesn't know any better." We banish it hastily to the top shelf of the closet.

Aunt Ethel's toaster or tablewear is not important, in and of itself. But it is a message from a different subcultural world, and unless we are weak in commitment to our own style, unless we happen to be in transition between styles, it represents a potent threat. The psychologist Leon Festinger coined the term "cognitive dissonance" to mean the tendency of a person to reject or deny information that challenges his preconceptions. We don't want to hear things that may upset our carefully worked out structure of beliefs. Similarly, Aunt Ethel's gift represents an element of "stylistic dissonance." It threatens to undermine our carefully worked out style of life.

Why does the life style have this power to preserve itself? What is the source of our commitment to it? A life style is a vehicle through which we express ourselves. It is a way of telling the world which particular subcult or subcults we belong to. Yet this hardly accounts for its enormous importance to us. The real reason why life styles are so significant—and increasingly so as the society diversifies—is that, above all else, the choice of a life style model to emulate is a crucial strategy in our private war against the crowding pressures of overchoice.

Deciding, whether consciously or not, to be "like" William Buckley or Joan Baez, Lionel Trilling or his surfer equivalent, J. J. Moon, rescues us from the need to make millions of minute life-decisions. Once a commitment to a style is made, we are able to rule out many forms of dress and behavior, many ideas and attitudes, as inappropriate to our adopted style. The college boy who chooses the Student Protester Model wastes little energy agonizing over whether to vote for Wallace, carry an attaché case, or invest in mutual funds.

By zeroing in on a particular life style we exclude a vast number of alternatives from further consideration. The fellow who opts for the Motorcyclist Model need no longer concern himself with the hundreds of types of gloves available to him on the open market, but which violate the spirit of his style. He need only choose among the far smaller repertoire of glove types that fit within the limits set by his model. And what is said of gloves is equally applicable to his ideas and social relationships as well.

The commitment to one style of life over another is thus a super-decision. It is a decision of a higher order than the general run of everyday life-decisions. It is a decision to narrow the range of alternatives that will concern us in the future. So long as we operate within the confines of the style we have chosen, our choices are relatively simple. The guidelines are clear. The subcult to which we belong helps us answer any questions; it keeps the guidelines in place.

But when our style is suddenly challenged, when something forces us to reconsider it, we are driven to make another super-decision. We face the painful need to transform not only ourselves, but our self-image as well.

It is painful because, freed of our commitment to any given style, cut adrift from the subcult that gave rise to it, we no longer "belong." Worse yet, our basic principles are called into question and we must face each new life-decision afresh, alone, without the security of a definite, fixed policy. We are, in short, confronted with the full, crushing burden of overchoice again.

A SUPERABUNDANCE OF SELVES

To be "between styles" or "between subcults" is a life-crisis, and the people of the future spend more time in this condition, searching for styles, than do the people of the past or present. Altering his identity as he goes, super-industrial man traces a private trajectory through a world of colliding subcults. This is the social mobility of the future: not simply movement from one economic class to another, but from one tribal grouping to another. Restless movement from subcult to ephemeral subcult describes the arc of his life.

There are plenty of reasons for this restlessness. It is not merely that the individual's psychological needs change more often than in the past; the subcults also change. For these and other reasons, as subcult membership becomes ever more unstable, the search for a personal style will become increasingly intense, even frenetic in the decades to come. Again and again, we shall find ourselves bitter or bored, vaguely dissatisfied with "the way things are"—upset, in other words, with our present style. At that moment, we begin once more to search for a new principle around which to organize our choices. We arrive again at the moment of super-decision.

At this moment, if anyone studied our behavior closely, he would find a sharp increase in what might be called the Transience Index. The rate of turnover of things, places, people, organizational and informational relationships spurts upward. We get rid of that silk dress or tie, the old Tiffany lamp, that horror of a claw-footed Victorian end table—all those symbols of our links with the subcult of the past. We begin, bit by bit, to replace them with new items emblematic of our new identification. The same process occurs in our social lives—the through-put of people speeds up. We begin to reject ideas we have held (or to explain them or rationalize them in new ways). We are suddenly free of all the constraints that our subcult or style imposed on us. A Transience Index would prove a sensitive indicator of those moments in our lives when we are most free—but, at the same time, most lost.

It is in this interval that we exhibit the wild oscillation engineers call "searching behavior." We are most vulnerable now to the messages of new subcults, to the claims and counterclaims that rend the air. We lean this way and that. A powerful new friend, a new fad or idea, a new political movement, some new hero rising from the depths of the mass media—all these strike us with particular force at such a moment. We are more "open," more uncertain, more ready for someone or some group to tell us what to do, how to behave.

Decisions—even little ones—come harder. This is not accidental. To cope with the press of daily life we need more information about far more trivial matters than when we were locked into a firm life style. And so we feel anxious, pressured, alone, and we move on. We choose or allow ourselves to be sucked into a new subcult. We put on a new style.

As we rush toward super-industrialism, therefore, we find people adopting and discarding life styles at a rate that would have staggered the members of any previous generation. For the life style itself has become a throw-away item.

This is no small or easy matter. It accounts for the much lamented "loss of commitment" that is so characteristic of our time. As people shift from subcult to subcult, from style to style, they are conditioned to guard themselves against the inevitable pain of disaffiliation. They learn to armor themselves against the sweet sorrow of parting. The extremely devout Catholic who throws over his religion and plunges into the life of a New Left activist, then throws himself into some other cause or movement or subcult, cannot go on doing so forever. He becomes, to adapt Graham Greene's term, a "burnt out case." He learns from past disappointment never to lay too much of his old self on the line.

And so, even when he seemingly adopts a subcult or style, he withholds some part of himself. He conforms to the group's demands and revels in the belonging-ness that it gives him. But this belongingness is never the same as it once was, and secretly he remains ready to defect at a moment's notice. What this means is that even when he seems most firmly plugged in to his group or tribe, he listens, in the dark of night, to the short-wave signals of competing tribes.

In this sense, his membership in the group is shal-low. He remains constantly in a posture of non-com-mitment, and without strong commitment to the values and styles of some group he lacks the explicit set of criteria that he needs to pick his way through the burgeoning jungle of overchoice.

The super-industrial revolution, consequently, forces the whole problem of overchoice to a qualitatively new level. It forces us now to make choices not merely among lamps and lampshades, but among lives, not among life style *components*, but among whole life *styles*.

This intensification of the problem of overchoice presses us toward orgies of self-examination, soul-searching and introversion. It confronts us with that most popular of contemporary illnesses, the "identity crisis." Never before have masses of men faced a more complex set of choices. The hunt for identity arises not out of the supposed choicelessness of "mass so-ciety," but precisely from the plenitude and complex-ity of our choices.

Each time we make a style choice, a super-decision, each time we link up with some particular subcultural group or groups, we make some change in our self-image. We become, in some sense, a different person, and we perceive ourselves as different. Our old friends, those who knew us in some previous incarnation, raise their eyebrows. They have a harder and harder time recognizing us, and, in fact, we experience in-

creasing difficulty in identifying with, or even sympa-
thizing with, our own past selves.

The hippie becomes the straight-arrow executive,
the executive becomes the skydiver without noting the
exact steps of transition. In the process, he discards
not only the externals of his style, but many of his
underlying attitudes as well. And one day the question
hits him like a splash of cold water in a sleep-sodden
face: "What remains?" What is there of "self" or "personality" in the sense of a continuous, durable internal
structure? For some, the answer is very little. For they
are no longer dealing in "self" but in what might be
called "serial selves."

The Super-industrial Revolution thus requires a basic change in man's conception of himself, a new
theory of personality that takes into account the discontinuities in men's lives, as well as the continuities.

The Super-industrial Revolution also demands a new
conception of freedom—a recognition that freedom,
pressed to its ultimate, negates itself. Society's leap to
a new level of differentiation necessarily brings with
it new opportunities for individuation, and the new
technology, the new temporary organizational forms,
cry out for a new breed of man. This is why, despite
"backlash" and temporary reversals, the line of social
advance carries us toward a wider tolerance, a more
easy acceptance of more and more diverse human
types.

The sudden popularity of the slogan "do your thing"
is a reflection of this historic movement. For the more
fragmented or differentiated the society, the greater
the number of varied life styles it promotes. And the
more socially accepted life style models put forth by
the society, the closer that society approaches a condition in which, in fact, each man does his own,
unique thing.

Thus, despite all the anti-technological rhetoric of
the Elluls and Fromms, the Mumfords and Marcuses,
it is precisely the super-industrial society, the most
advanced technological society ever, that extends the

range of freedom. The people of the future enjoy greater opportunities for self-realization than any previous group in history.

The new society offers few roots in the sense of truly enduring relationships. But it does offer more varied life niches, more freedom to move in and out of these niches, and more opportunity to create one's own niche, than all earlier societies put together. It also offers the supreme exhilaration of riding change, cresting it, changing and growing with it—a process infinitely more exciting than riding the surf, wrestling steers, playing "knock hubcaps" on an eight-lane speedway, or the pursuit of pharmaceutical kicks. It presents the individual with a contest that requires self-mastery and high intelligence. For the individual who comes armed with these, and who makes the necessary effort to understand the fast-emerging superindustrial social structure, for the person who finds the "right" life pace, the "right" sequence of subcults to join and life style models to emulate, the triumph is exquisite.

Undeniably, these grand words do not apply to the majority of men. Most people of the past and present remain imprisoned in life niches they have neither made nor have much hope, under present conditions, of ever escaping. For most human beings, the options remain excruciatingly few.

This imprisonment must—and will—be broken. Yet it will not be broken by tirades against technology. It will not be broken by calls for a return to passivity, mysticism and irrationality. It will not be broken by "feeling" or "intuiting" our way into the future while derogating empirical study, analysis, and rational effort. Rather than lashing out, Luddite-fashion, against the machine, those who genuinely wish to break the prison-hold of the past and present would do well to hasten the controlled—selective—arrival of tomorrow's technologies. To accomplish this, however, intuition and "mystical insights" are hardly enough. It will take exact scientific knowledge, expertly applied to the crucial, most sensitive points of social control.

Nor does it help to offer the principle of the maximization of choice as the key to freedom. We must consider the possibility, suggested here, that choice may become overchoice, and freedom unfreedom.

THE FREE SOCIETY

Despite romantic rhetoric, freedom cannot be absolute. To argue for total choice (a meaningless concept) or total individuality is to argue against any form of community or society altogether. If each person, busily doing his thing, were to be wholly different from every other, no two humans would have any basis for communication. It is ironic that the people who complain most loudly that people cannot "relate" to one another, or cannot "communicate" with one another, are often the very same people who urge greater individuality. The sociologist Karl Mannheim recognized this contradiction when he wrote: "The more individualized people are, the more difficult it is to attain identification."

Unless we are literally prepared to plunge backward into pre-technological primitivism, and accept all the consequences—a shorter, more brutal life, more disease, pain, starvation, fear, superstition, xenophobia, bigotry and so on—we shall move forward to more and more differentiated societies. This raises severe problems of social integration. What bonds of education, politics, culture must we fashion to tie the super-industrial order together into a functioning whole? Can this be accomplished? "This integration," writes Bertram M. Gross of Wayne State University, "must be based upon certain commonly accepted values or some degree of perceived interdependence, if not mutually acceptable objectives."

A society fast fragmenting at the level of values and life styles challenges all the old integrative mech-

anisms and cries out for a totally new basis for recon-
stitution. We have by no means yet found this basis.
Yet if we shall face disturbing problems of social integration, we shall confront even more agonizing problems of individual integration. For the multiplication
of life styles challenges our ability to hold the very
self together.

Which of many potential selves shall we choose to
be? What sequence of serial selves will describe us?
How, in short, must we deal with overchoice at this,
the most intensely personal and emotion-laden level
of all? In our headlong rush for variety, choice and
freedom, we have not yet begun to examine the awesome implications of diversity.

When diversity, however, converges with transience
and novelty, we rocket the society toward an historical
crisis of adaptation. We create an environment so
ephemeral, unfamiliar and complex as to threaten millions with adaptive breakdown. This breakdown is
future shock.

Part Five:

THE LIMITS OF ADAPTABILITY

Chapter 15

FUTURE SHOCK:
THE PHYSICAL DIMENSION

Eons ago the shrinking seas cast millions of unwilling aquatic creatures onto the newly created beaches. Deprived of their familiar environment, they died, gasping and clawing for each additional instant of eternity. Only a fortunate few, better suited to amphibian existence, survived the shock of change. Today, says sociologist Lawrence Suhm of the University of Wisconsin, "We are going through a period as traumatic as the evolution of man's predecessors from sea creatures to land creatures ... Those who can adapt will; those who can't will either go on surviving somehow at a lower level of development or will perish—washed up on the shores."

To assert that man must adapt seems superfluous. He has already shown himself to be among the most adaptable of life forms. He has survived Equatorial summers and Antarctic winters. He has survived Dachau and Vorkuta. He has walked the lunar surface. Such accomplishments give rise to the glib notion that his adaptive capabilities are "infinite." Yet nothing could be further from the truth. For despite all his heroism and stamina, man remains a biological organism, a "biosystem," and all such systems operate within inexorable limits.

Temperature, pressure, caloric intake, oxygen and

carbon dioxide levels, all set absolute boundaries beyond which man, as presently constituted, cannot venture. Thus when we hurl a man into outer space, we surround him with an exquisitely designed microenvironment that maintains all these factors within livable limits. How strange, therefore, that when we hurl a man into the future, we take few pains to protect him from the shock of change. It is as though NASA had shot Armstrong and Aldrin naked into the cosmos.

It is the thesis of this book that there are discoverable limits to the amount of change that the human organism can absorb, and that by endlessly accelerating change without first determining these limits, we may submit masses of men to demands they simply cannot tolerate. We run the high risk of throwing them into that peculiar state that I have called future shock.

We may define future shock as the distress, both physical and psychological, that arises from an overload of the human organism's physical adaptive systems and its decision-making processes. Put more simply, future shock is the human response to overstimulation.

Different people react to future shock in different ways. Its symptoms also vary according to the stage and intensity of the disease. These symptoms range all the way from anxiety, hostility to helpful authority, and seemingly senseless violence, to physical illness, depression and apathy. Its victims often manifest erratic swings in interest and life style, followed by an effort to "crawl into their shells" through social, intellectual and emotional withdrawal. They feel continually "bugged" or harassed, and want desperately to reduce the number of decisions they must make.

To understand this syndrome, we must pull together from such scattered fields as psychology, neurology, communications theory and endocrinology, what science can tell us about human adaptation. There is, as yet, no science of adaptation *per se*. Nor is there any systematic listing of the diseases of adaptation. Yet evidence now sluicing in from a variety of disciplines makes it possible to sketch the rough outlines of a theory of adaptation. For while researchers in these disciplines often work in ignorance of each other's efforts, their work is elegantly compatible. Forming a distinct and exciting pattern, it provides solid underpinning for the concept of future shock.

LIFE-CHANGE AND ILLNESS

What actually happens to people when they are asked to change again and again? To understand the answer, we must begin with the body, the physical organism, itself. Fortunately, a series of startling, but as yet unpublicized, experiments have recently cast revealing light on the relationship of change to physical health.

These experiments grow out of the work of the late Dr. Harold G. Wolff at the Cornell Medical Center in New York. Wolff repeatedly emphasized that the health of the individual is intimately bound up with the adaptive demands placed on him by the environment. One of Wolff's followers, Dr. Lawrence E. Hinkle, Jr., has termed this the "human ecology" approach to medicine, and has argued passionately that disease need not be the result of any single, specific agent, such as a germ or virus, but a consequence of many factors, including the general nature of the environment surrounding the body. Hinkle has worked for years to sensitize the medical profession to the importance of environmental factors in medicine.

Today, with spreading alarm over air pollution, water pollution, urban crowding and other such factors, more and more health authorities are coming around to the ecological notion that the individual needs to be seen as part of a total system, and that his health is dependent upon many subtle external factors.

It was another of Wolff's colleagues, however, Dr. Thomas H. Holmes, who came up with the idea that change, itself—not this or that specific change but the general rate of change in a person's life—could be one of the most important environmental factors of all. Originally from Cornell, Holmes is now at the University of Washington School of Medicine, and it was there, with the help of a young psychiatrist named Richard Rahe, that he created an ingenious research tool named the Life-Change Units Scale. This was a device for measuring how much change an individual has experienced in a given span of time. Its development was an important methodological breakthrough, making it possible, for the first time, to qualify, at least crudely, the rate of change in individual life.

Reasoning that different kinds of life-changes strike us with different force, Holmes and Rahe began by listing as many such changes as they could. A divorce, a marriage, a move to a new home—such events affect each of us differently. Moreover, some carry greater impact than others. A vacation trip, for example, may represent a pleasant break in the routine. Yet it can hardly compare in impact with, say, the death of a parent.

Holmes and Rahe next took their list of life-changes to thousands of men and women in many walks of life in the United States and Japan. Each person was asked to rank order the specific items on the list according to how much impact each had. Which changes required a great deal of coping or adjustment? Which ones were relatively minor?

To Holmes' and Rahe's surprise, it turned out that there is widespread agreement among people as to which changes in their lives require major adaptations and which ones are comparatively unimportant. This agreement about the "impact-fullness" of various life events extends even across national and language barriers.* People tend to *know* and to *agree* on which changes hit the hardest.

Given this information, Holmes and Rahe were able to assign a numerical weight to each type of life change. Thus each item on their list was ranked by its magnitude and given a score accordingly. For example, if the death of one's spouse is rated as one hundred points, then moving to a new home is rated by most people as worth only twenty points, a vacation thirteen. (The death of a spouse, incidentally, is almost universally regarded as the single most impactful change that can befall a person in the normal course of his life.)

Now Holmes and Rahe were ready for the next step. Armed with their Life-Change Units Scale, they began to question people about the actual pattern of change in their lives. The scale made it possible to compare the "changefulness" of one person's life with that of another. By studying the amount of change in a person's life, could we learn anything about the influence of change itself on health?

To find out, Holmes, Rahe and other researchers compiled the "life change scores" of literally thousands of individuals and began the laborious task of comparing these with the medical histories of these same individuals. Never before had there been a way to correlate change and health. Never before had there been such detailed data on patterns of change in individual lives. And seldom were the results of an experiment less ambiguous. In the United States and Japan, among servicemen and civilians, among pregnant women and the families of leukemia victims, among college athletes and retirees, the same striking pattern was present: those with high life change scores were more likely than their fellows to be ill in the following year. For the first time, it was possible to show in dramatic form that the rate of change in a person's

---

* The work in the United States and Japan is now being supplemented by studies in France, Belgium and the Netherlands.

life—his pace of life—is closely tied to the state of his health.

"The results were so spectacular," says Dr. Holmes, "that at first we hesitated to publish them. We didn't release our initial findings until 1967."

Since then, the Life-Change Units Scale and the Life Changes Questionnaire have been applied to a wide variety of groups from unemployed blacks in Watts to naval officers at sea. In every case, the correlation between change and illness has held. It has been established that "alterations in life style" that require a great deal of adjustment and coping, correlate with illness—whether or not these changes are under the individual's own direct control, whether or not he sees them as undesirable. Furthermore, the higher the degree of life change, the higher the risk that subsequent illness will be severe. So strong is this evidence, that it is becoming possible, by studying life change scores, actually to predict levels of illness in various populations.

Thus in August, 1967, Commander Ransom J. Arthur, head of the United States Navy Medical Neuropsychiatric Research Unit at San Diego, and Richard Rahe, now a Captain in Commander Arthur's group, set out to forecast sickness patterns in a group of 3000 Navy men. Drs. Arthur and Rahe began by distributing a Life Changes Questionnaire to the sailors on three cruisers in San Diego harbor. The ships were about to depart and would be at sea for approximately six months each. During this time it would be possible to maintain exact medical records on each crew member. Could information about a man's life change pattern tell us in advance the likelihood of his falling ill during the voyage?

Each crew member was asked to tell what changes had occurred in his life during the year preceding the voyage. The questionnaire covered an extremely broad spectrum of topics. Thus it asked whether the man had experienced either more or less trouble with superiors during the twelve-month period. It asked about alterations in his eating and sleeping habits. It inquired about change in his circle of friends, his dress, his forms of recreation. It asked whether he had experienced any change in his social activities, in family get-togethers, in his financial condition. Had he been having more or less trouble with his in-laws? More or fewer arguments with his wife? Had he gained a child through birth or adoption? Had he suffered the death of his wife, a friend or relative?

The questionnaire went on to probe such issues as the number of times he had moved to a new home. Had he been in trouble with the law over traffic violations or other minor infractions? Had he spent a lot of time away from his wife as a result of job-related travel or marital difficulties? Had he changed jobs? Won awards or promotions? Had his living conditions changed as a consequence of home remodeling or the deterioration of his neighborhood? Had his wife started or stopped working? Had he taken out a loan or mortgage? How many times had he taken a vacation? Was there any major change in his relations with his parents as a result of death, divorce, remarriage, etc.?

In short, the questionnaire tried to get at the kind of life changes that are part of normal existence. It did not ask whether a change was regarded as "good" or "bad," simply whether or not it had occurred.

For six months, the three cruisers remained at sea. Just before they were scheduled to return, Arthur and Rahe flew new research teams out to join the ships. These teams proceeded to make a fine-tooth survey of the ships' medical records. Which men had been ill? What diseases had they reported? How many days had they been confined to sick bay?

When the last computer runs were completed, the linkage between changefulness and illness was nailed down more firmly than ever. Men in the upper ten percent of life change units—those who had had to adapt to the most change in the preceding year—turned out to suffer from one-and-a-half to two times as much illness as those in the bottom ten percent. Moreover, once again, the higher the life change score, the more severe the illness was likely to be. The study of life change patterns—of change as an environmental factor—contributed significantly to success in predicting the amount and severity of illness in widely varied populations.

"For the first time," says Dr. Arthur, appraising life change research, "we have an index of change. If you've had many changes in your life within a short time, this places a great challenge on your body . . . An enormous number of changes within a short period might overwhelm its coping mechanisms.

"It is clear," he continues, "that there is a connection between the body's defenses and the demands for change that society imposes. We are in a continuous dynamic equilibrium . . . Various 'noxious' elements, both internal and external, are always present, always seeking to explode into disease. For example, certain viruses live in the body and cause disease only when the defenses of the body wear down. There may well be generalized body defense systems that prove inadequate to cope with the flood of demands for change that come pulsing through the nervous and endocrine systems."

The stakes in life-change research are high, indeed, for not only illness, but death itself, may be linked to the severity of adaptational demands placed on the body. Thus a report by Arthur, Rahe, and a colleague, Dr. Joseph D. McKean, Jr., begins with a quotation from Somerset Maugham's literary autobiography, *The Summing Up:*

> My father . . . went to Paris and became solicitor to the British Embassy. . . . After my mother's death, her maid became my nurse. . . . I think my father had a romantic mind. He took it into his head to build a house to live in during the summer. He bought a piece of land on the top of a hill at Suresnes. . . . It was to be like a villa on the Bosphorous and on

the top floor it was surrounded by loggias. . . . It was a white house and the shutters were painted red. The garden was laid out. The rooms were furnished and then my father died.

"The death of Somerset Maugham's father," they write, "seems at first glance to have been an abrupt unheralded event. However, a critical evaluation of the events of a year or two prior to the father's demise reveals changes in his occupation, residence, personal habits, finances and family constellation." These changes, they suggest, may have been precipitating events.

This line of reasoning is consistent with reports that death rates among widows and widowers, during the first year after loss of a spouse, are higher than normal. A series of British studies have strongly suggested that the shock of widowhood weakens resistance to illness and tends to accelerate aging. The same is true for men. Scientists at the Institute of Community Studies in London, after reviewing the evidence and studying 4,486 widowers, declare that "the excess mortality in the first six months is almost certainly real . . . [Widowerhood] appears to bring in its wake a sudden increment in mortality-rates of something like 40 percent in the first six months."

Why should this be true? It is speculated that grief, itself, leads to pathology. Yet the answer may lie not in the state of grief at all, but in the very high impact that loss of a spouse carries, forcing the survivor to make a multitude of major life changes within a short period after the death takes place.

The work of Hinkle, Holmes, Rahe, Arthur, McKean and others now probing the relationship of change to illness is still in its early stages. Yet one lesson already seems vividly clear: change carries a physiological price tag with it. And the more radical the change, the steeper the price.

RESPONSE TO NOVELTY

"Life," says Dr. Hinkle, ". . . implies a constant inter-action between organism and environment." When we speak of the change brought about by divorce or a death in the family or a job transfer or even a vacation, we are talking about a major life event. Yet, as everyone knows, life consists of tiny events as well, a constant stream of them flowing into and out of our experience. Any major life change *is* major only because it forces us to make many little changes as well, and these, in turn, consist of still smaller and smaller changes. To grapple with the meaning of life in the accelerative society, we need to see what happens at the level of these minute, "micro-changes" as well. .

What happens when something in our environment is altered? All of us are constantly bathed in a shower of signals from our environment—visual, auditory, tactile, etc. Most of these come in routine, repetitive patterns. When something changes within the range of our senses, the pattern of signals pouring through our sensory channels into our nervous system is modified. The routine, repetitive patterns are interrupted —and to this interruption we respond in a particularly acute fashion.

Significantly, when some new set of stimuli hits us, both body and brain know almost instantly that they *are* new. The change may be no more than a flash of color seen out of the corner of an eye. It may be that a loved one brushing us tenderly with the fingertips momentarily hesitates. Whatever the change, an enormous amount of physical machinery comes into play.

When a dog hears a strange noise, his ears prick, his head turns. And we do much the same. The change in stimuli triggers what experimental psychologists call an "orientation response." The orientation response or OR is a complex, even massive bodily operation. The pupils of the eyes dilate. Photochemical changes occur in the retina. Our hearing becomes momentarily more acute. We involuntarily use our muscles to direct our sense organs toward the incoming stimuli—we lean toward the sound, for example, or squint our eyes to see better. Our general muscle tone rises. There are changes in our pattern of brain waves. Our fingers and toes grow cold as the veins and arteries in them constrict. Our palms sweat. Blood rushes to the head. Our breathing and heart rate alter.

Under certain circumstances, we may do all of this—and more—in a very obvious fashion, exhibiting what has been called the "startle reaction." But even when we are unaware of what is going on, these changes take place every time we perceive novelty in our environment.

The reason for this is that we have, apparently built into our brains, a special novelty-detection apparatus that has only recently come to the attention of neurologists. The Soviet scientist E. N. Sokolov, who has put forward the most comprehensive explanation of how the orientation response works, suggests that neural cells in the brain store information about the intensity, duration, quality, and sequence of incoming stimuli. When new stimuli arrive, these are matched against the "neural models" in the cortex. If the stimuli are novel, they do not match any existing neural model, and the OR takes place. If, however, the matching process reveals their similarity to previously stored models, the cortex shoots signals to the reticular activating system, instructing it, in effect, to hold its fire.

In this way, the level of novelty in our environment has direct physical consequences. Moreover, it is vital to recognize that the OR is not an unusual affair. It takes place in most of us literally thousands of times in the course of a single day as various changes occur in the environment around us. Again and again the OR fires off, even during sleep.

"The OR is big!" says research psychologist Ardie Lubin, an expert on sleep mechanisms. "The whole body is involved. And when you increase novelty in the environment—which is what a lot of change means —you get continual ORs with it. This is probably very stressful for the body. It's a helluva load to put on the body.

"If you overload an environment with novelty, you get the equivalent of anxiety neurotics—people who have their systems continually flooded with adrenalin, continual heart pumping, cold hands, increased muscle tone and tremors—all the usual OR characteristics."

The orientation response is no accident. It is nature's gift to man, one of his key adaptive mechanisms. The OR has the effect of sensitizing him to take in more information—to see or hear better, for instance. It readies his muscles for sudden exertion, if necessary. In short, it prepares him for fight or flight. Yet each OR, as Lubin underscores, takes its toll in wear and tear on the body, for it requires energy to sustain it.

Thus one result of the OR is to send a surge of anticipatory energy through the body. Stored energy exists in such sites as the muscles and the sweat glands. As the neural system pulses in response to novelty, its synaptic vesicles discharge small amounts of adrenalin and nor-adrenalin. These, in turn, trigger a partial release of the stored energy. In short, each OR draws not only upon the body's limited supply of quick energy, but on its even more limited supply of energy-releasers.

It needs to be emphasized, moreover, that the OR occurs not merely in response to simple sensory inputs. It happens when we come across novel ideas or information as well as novel sights or sounds. A fresh bit of office gossip, a unifying concept, even a new joke or an original turn of phrase can trigger it.

The OR is particularly stressing when a novel event or fact challenges one's whole preconceived world view. Given an elaborate ideology, Catholicism, Marxism or whatever, we quickly recognize (or think we recognize) familiar elements in otherwise novel stimuli, and this puts us at ease. Indeed, ideologies may be regarded as large mental filing cabinets with vacant drawers or slots waiting to accept new data. For this reason, ideologies serve to reduce the intensity and frequency of the OR.

It is only when a new fact fails to fit, when it resists filing, that the OR occurs. A classical example is that of the religious person who is brought up to believe in the goodness of God and who is suddenly faced by what strikes him as a case of overwhelming, senseless evil. Until the new fact can be reconciled or his world view altered, he suffers acute agitation and anxiety.

The OR is so inherently stressing that we enjoy a vast sense of relief when it is over. At the level of ideas or cognition, this is the "a-hah!" reaction we experience at a moment of revelation, when we finally understand something that has been puzzling us. We may be aware of the "a-hah" reaction on rare occasions only, but OR's and "a-hah's" are continually occurring just below the level of consciousness.

Novelty, therefore—any perceptible novelty—touches off explosive activity within the body, and especially the nervous system. OR's fire off like flashbulbs within us, at a rate determined by what is happening outside us. Man and environment are in constant, quivering interplay.

THE ADAPTIVE REACTION

While novelty in the environment raises or lowers the rate at which OR's occur, some novel conditions call forth even more powerful responses. We are driving along a monotonous turnpike, listening to the radio and beginning to daydream. Suddenly, a car speeds by, forcing us to swerve out of our lane. We react automatically, almost instantaneously, and the OR is very pronounced. We can feel our heart pumping and our hands shaking. It takes a while before the tension subsides.

But what if it does not subside? What happens when

we are placed in a situation that demands a complex set of physical and psychological reactions and in which the pressure is sustained? What happens if, for example, the boss breathes hotly down our collar day after day? What happens when one of our children is seriously ill? Or when, on the other hand, we look forward eagerly to a "big date" or to closing an important business deal?

Such situations cannot be handled by the quick spurt of energy provided by the OR, and for these we have what might be termed the "adaptive reaction." This is closely related to the OR. Indeed, the two processes are so intertwined that the OR can be regarded as part of, or the initial phase of, the larger, more encompassing adaptive reaction. But while the OR is primarily based on the nervous system, the adaptive reaction is heavily dependent upon the endocrine glands and the hormones they shoot into the bloodstream. The first line of defense is neural; the second is hormonal.

When individuals are forced to make repeated adaptations to novelty, and especially when they are compelled to adapt to certain situations involving conflict and uncertainty, a pea-sized gland called the pituitary pumps out a number of substances. One of these, ACTH, goes to the adrenals. This causes them, in turn, to manufacture certain chemicals termed corticosteroids. When these are released, they speed up body metabolism. They raise blood pressure. They send anti-inflammatory substances through the blood to fight infection at wound sites, if any. And they begin turning fat and protein into dispersible energy, thus tapping into the body's reserve tank of energy. The adaptive reaction provides a much more potent and sustained flush of energy than the OR.

Like the orientation response, the adaptive reaction is no rarity. It takes longer to arouse and it lasts longer, but it happens countless times even within the course of a single day, responding to changes in our physical and social environment. The adaptive reaction, sometimes known by the more dramatic term "stress," can be touched off by shifts and changes in the psychological climate around us. Worry, upset, conflict, uncertainty, even happy anticipation, hilarity and joy, all set the ACTH factory working. The very anticipation of change can trigger the adaptive reaction. The need to alter one's way of life, to trade an old job for a new one, social pressures, status shifts, life style modifications, in fact, anything that forces us to confront the unknown, can switch on the adaptive reaction.

Dr. Lennart Levi, director of the Clinical Stress Laboratory at the Karolinska Hospital in Stockholm, has shown, for example, that even quite small changes in the emotional climate or in interpersonal relationships can produce marked changes in body chemistry. Stress is frequently measured by the amount of corticosteroids and catecholamines (adrenalin and noradrenalin, for example) found in the blood and urine. In one series of experiments Levi used films to generate emotions and plotted the resultant chemical changes.

A group of Swedish male medical students were shown film clips depicting murders, fights, torture, execution and cruelty to animals. The adrenalin component of their urine rose an average 70 percent as measured before and after. Nor-adrenalin rose an average 35 percent. Next a group of young female office workers were shown four different films on successive nights. The first was a bland travelog. They reported feelings of calmness and equanimity, and their output of catecholamines fell. The second night they watched Stanley Kubrick's *Paths of Glory* and reported feeling intense excitement and anger. Adrenalin output shot upward. The third night they viewed *Charley's Aunt*, and roared with laughter at the comedy. Despite the pleasant feelings and the absence of any scenes of aggression or violence, their catecholamines rose significantly again. The fourth night they saw *The Devil's Mask*, a thriller during which they actually screamed with fright. Not unexpectedly, catecholamine output soared. In short, emotional response, almost without regard for its character, is accompanied by (or, indeed, reflects) adrenal activity.

Similar findings have been demonstrated again and again in the case of men and women—not to speak of rats, dogs, deer and other experimental animals—involved in "real" as distinct from "vicarious" experiences. Sailors in underwater demolition training, men stationed in lonely outposts in Antarctica, astronauts, factory workers, executives have all shown similar chemical responsiveness to change in the external environment.

The implications of this have hardly begun to register, yet there is increasing evidence that repeated stimulation of the adaptive reaction can be seriously damaging, that excessive activation of the endocrine system leads to irreversible "wear and tear." Thus, we are warned by Dr. René Dubos, author of *Man Adapting*, that such changeful circumstances as "competitive situations, operation within a crowded environment, change in a very profound manner the secretion of hormones. One can type-read that in the blood or the urine. Just a mere contact with the complex human situation almost automatically brings this about, this stimulation of the whole endocrine system."

What of it?

"There is," Dubos declares, "absolutely no question that one can overshoot the stimulation of the endocrine system and that this has physiological consequences that last throughout the whole lifetime of the organs."

Years ago, Dr. Hans Selye, a pioneer investigator of the body's adaptive responses, reported that "animals in which intense and prolonged stress is produced by any means suffer from sexual derangements . . . Clinical studies have confirmed the fact that people exposed to stress react very much like experimental animals in all these respects. In women the monthly cycles become irregular or stop altogether, and during

lactation milk secretion may become insufficient for
the baby. In men both the sexual urge and sperm-cell
formation are diminished."

Since then population experts and ecologists have
compiled impressive evidence that heavily stressed
populations of rats, deer—and people—show lower fertility levels than less stressed control groups. Crowding, for example, a condition that involves a constant
high level of interpersonal interaction and compels
the individual to make extremely frequent adaptive
reactions has been shown, at least in animals, to enlarge the adrenals and cause a noticeable drop in
fertility.

The repeated firing of the OR and the adaptive reaction, by overloading the neural and endocrine systems, is linked to other diseases and physical problems
as well. Rapid change in the environment makes
repeated calls on the energy supply of the body. This
leads to a speedup of fat metabolism. In turn, this
creates grave difficulties for certain diabetics. Even
the common cold has been shown to be affected by
the rate of change in the environment. In studies
reported by Dr. Hinkle it was found that the frequency
of colds in a sample of New York working women
correlated with "changes in the mood and pattern of
activity of the woman, in response to changing relationships to the people around her and the events that
she encountered."

In short, if we understand the chain of biological
events touched off by our efforts to adapt to change
and novelty, we can begin to understand why health
and change seem to be inextricably linked to one
another. The findings of Holmes, Rahe, Arthur and
others now engaged in life change research are entirely compatible with on-going research in endocrinology and experimental psychology. It is quite clearly
impossible to accelerate the rate of change in society,
or to raise the novelty ratio in society, without triggering significant changes in the body chemistry of
the population. By stepping up the pace of scientific,

technological and social change, we are tampering with the chemistry and biological stability of the human race.

This, one must immediately add, is not necessarily bad. "There are worse things than illness," Dr. Holmes wryly reminds us. "No one can live without experiencing some degree of stress all the time," Dr. Selye has written. To eliminate ORs and adaptive reactions would be to eliminate all change, including growth, self-development, maturation. It presupposes complete stasis. Change is not merely necessary to life; it *is* life. By the same token, life is adaptation.

There are, however, limits on adaptability. When we alter our life style, when we make and break relationships with things, places or people, when we move restlessly through the organizational geography of society, when we learn new information and ideas, we adapt; we live. Yet there are finite boundaries; we are not infinitely resilient. Each orientation response, each adaptive reaction exacts a price, wearing down the body's machinery bit by minute bit, until perceptible tissue damage results.

Thus man remains in the end what he started as in the beginning: a biosystem with a limited capacity for change. When this capacity is overwhelmed, the consequence is future shock.

Chapter 16

FUTURE SHOCK:
THE PSYCHOLOGICAL
DIMENSION

If future shock were a matter of physical illness alone,
it might be easier to prevent and to treat. But future
shock attacks the psyche as well. Just as the body
cracks under the strain of environmental overstimulation, the "mind" and its decision processes behave
erratically when overloaded. By indiscriminately racing the engines of change, we may be undermining
not merely the health of those least able to adapt, but
their very ability to act rationally on their own behalf.

The striking signs of confusional breakdown we see
around us—the spreading use of drugs, the rise of
mysticism, the recurrent outbreaks of vandalism and
undirected violence, the politics of nihilism and nostalgia, the sick apathy of millions—can all be understood
better by recognizing their relationship to future
shock. These forms of social irrationality may well
reflect the deterioration of individual decision-making
under conditions of environmental overstimulation.

Psychophysiologists studying the impact of change
on various organisms have shown that successful adaptation can occur only when the level of stimulation—
the amount of change and novelty in the environment
—is neither too low nor too high. "The central nervous
system of a higher animal," says Professor D. E. Berlyne of the University of Toronto, "is designed to cope

with environments that produce a certain rate of . . . stimulation . . . It will naturally not perform at its best in an environment that overstresses or overloads it." He makes the same point about environments that understimulate it. Indeed, experiments with deer, dogs, mice and men all point unequivocally to the existence of what might be called an "adaptive range" below which and above which the individual's ability to cope simply falls apart.

Future shock is the response to overstimulation. It occurs when the individual is forced to operate above his adaptive range. Considerable research has been devoted to studying the impact of inadequate change and novelty on human performance. Studies of men in isolated Antarctic outposts, experiments in sensory deprivation, investigations into on-the-job performance in factories, all show a falling off of mental and physical abilities in response to understimulation. We have less direct data on the impact of overstimulation, but such evidence as does exist is dramatic and unsettling.

THE OVERSTIMULATED INDIVIDUAL

Soldiers in battle often find themselves trapped in environments that are rapidly changing, unfamiliar, and unpredictable. The soldier is torn this way and that. Shells burst on every side. Bullets whiz past erratically. Flares light the sky. Shouts, groans and explosions fill his ears. Circumstances change from instant to instant. To survive in such overstimulating environments, the soldier is driven to operate in the upper reaches of his adaptive range. Sometimes, he is pushed beyond his limits.

During World War II a bearded Chindit soldier, fighting with General Wingate's forces behind the Japanese lines in Burma, actually fell asleep while a storm of machine gun bullets splattered around him. Subsequent investigation revealed that this soldier was not merely reacting to physical fatigue or lack of sleep, but surrendering to a sense of overpowering apathy.

Death-inviting lassitude was so common, in fact, among guerrilla troops who had penetrated behind enemy lines that British military physicians gave it a name. They termed it Long Range Penetration Strain. A soldier who suffered from it became, in their words, "incapable of doing the simplest thing for himself and seemed to have the mind of a child." This deadly lethargy, moreover, was not confined to guerrilla troops. One year after the Chindit incident, similar symptoms cropped up en masse among the allied troops who invaded Normandy, and British researchers, after studying 5000 American and English combat casualties, concluded that this strange apathy was merely the final stage in a complex process of psychological collapse.

Mental deterioration often began with fatigue. This was followed by confusion and nervous irritability. The man became hypersensitive to the slightest stimuli around him. He would "hit the dirt" at the least provocation. He showed signs of bewilderment. He seemed unable to distinguish the sound of enemy fire from other, less threatening sounds. He became tense, anxious, and heatedly irascible. His comrades never knew when he would flail out in anger, even violence, in response to minor inconvenience.

Then the final stage of emotional exhaustion set in. The soldier seemed to lose the very will to live. He gave up the struggle to save himself, to guide himself rationally through the battle. He became, in the words of R. L. Swank, who headed the British investigation, "dull and listless . . . mentally and physically retarded, preoccupied." Even his face became dull and apathetic. The fight to adapt had ended in defeat. The stage of total withdrawal was reached.

That men behave irrationally, acting against their own clear interest, when thrown into conditions of high change and novelty is also borne out by studies of human behavior in times of fire, flood, earthquake and other crises. Even the most stable and "normal" people, unhurt physically, can be hurled into anti-adaptive states. Often reduced to total confusion and mindlessness, they seem incapable of the most elementary rational decision-making.

Thus in a study of the responses to tornadoes in Texas, H. E. Moore writes that "the first reaction . . . may be one of dazed bewilderment, sometimes one of disbelief, or at least of refusal to accept the fact. This, it seems to us, is the essential explanation of the behavior of persons and groups in Waco when it was devastated in 1953 . . . On the personal level, it explains why a girl climbed into a music store through a broken display window, calmly purchased a record, and walked out again, even though the plate glass front of the building had blown out and articles were flying through the air inside the building."

A study of a tornado in Udall, Kansas, quotes a housewife as saying: "After it was over, my husband and I just got up and jumped out the window and ran. I don't know where we were running to but . . . I didn't care. I just wanted to run." The classic disaster photograph shows a mother holding a dead or wounded baby in her arms, her face blank and numb as though she could no longer comprehend the reality around her. Sometimes she sits rocking gently on her porch with a doll, instead of a baby, in her arms.

In disaster, therefore, exactly as in certain combat situations, individuals can be psychologically overwhelmed. Once again the source may be traced to a high level of environmental stimulation. The disaster victim finds himself suddenly caught in a situation in which familiar objects and relationships are transformed. Where once his house stood, there may be nothing more than smoking rubble. He may encounter a cabin floating on the flood tide or a rowboat sailing through the air. The environment is filled with change and novelty. And once again the response is marked by confusion, anxiety, irritability and withdrawal into apathy.

Culture shock, the profound disorientation suffered by the traveler who has plunged without adequate preparation into an alien culture, provides a third example of adaptive breakdown. Here we find none of the obvious elements of war or disaster. The scene may be totally peaceful and riskless. Yet the situation demands repeated adaptation to novel conditions. Culture shock, according to psychologist Sven Lundstedt, is a "form of personality maladjustment which is a reaction to a temporarily unsuccessful attempt to adjust to new surroundings and people."

The culture shocked person, like the soldier and disaster victim, is forced to grapple with unfamiliar and unpredictable events, relationships and objects. His habitual ways of accomplishing things—even simple tasks like placing a telephone call—are no longer appropriate. The strange society may itself be changing only very slowly, yet for him it is all new. Signs, sounds and other psychological cues rush past him before he can grasp their meaning. The entire experience takes on a surrealistic air. Every word, every action is shot through with uncertainty.

In this setting, fatigue arrives more quickly than usual. Along with it, the cross-cultural traveler often experiences what Lundstedt describes as "a subjective feeling of loss, and a sense of isolation and loneliness."

The unpredictability arising from novelty undermines his sense of reality. Thus he longs, as Professor Lundstedt puts it, "for an environment in which the gratification of important psychological and physical needs is predictable and less uncertain." He becomes "anxious, confused and often appears apathetic." In fact, Lundstedt concludes, "culture shock can be viewed as a response to stress by emotional and intellectual withdrawal."

It is hard to read these (and many other) accounts of behavior breakdown under a variety of stresses without becoming acutely aware of their similarities. While there are differences, to be sure, between a

soldier in combat, a disaster victim, and a culturally
dislocated traveler, all three face rapid change, high
novelty, or both. All three are required to adapt rapidly and repeatedly to unpredictable stimuli. And there
are striking parallels in the way all three respond to
this overstimulation.

First, we find the same evidences of confusion,
disorientation, or distortion of reality. Second, there
are the same signs of fatigue, anxiety, tenseness, or
extreme irritability. Third, in all cases there appears
to be a point of no return—a point at which apathy
and emotional withdrawal set in.

In short, the available evidence strongly suggests
that overstimulation may lead to bizarre and anti-
adaptive behavior.

BOMBARDMENT OF THE SENSES

We still know too little about this phenomenon to explain authoritatively why overstimulation seems to
produce maladaptive behavior. Yet we pick up important clues if we recognize that overstimulation can
occur on at least three different levels: the sensory,
the cognitive and the decisional.*

The easiest to understand is the sensory level.
Experiments in sensory deprivation, during which
volunteers are cut off from normal stimulation of their
senses, have shown that the absence of novel sensory
stimuli can lead to bewilderment and impaired mental
functioning. By the same token, the input of too much
disorganized, patternless or chaotic sensory stimuli
can have similar effects. It is for this reason that prac-
titioners of political or religious brainwashing make
use not only of sensory deprivation (solitary confine-

---

* The line between each of these is not completely clear,
even to psychologists, but if we simply, in commonsense fashion, equate the sensory level with perceiving, the cognitive
with thinking, and the decisional with deciding, we will not go
too far astray.

ment, for example) but of sensory bombardment involving flashing lights, rapidly shifting patterns of color, chaotic sound effects—the whole arsenal of psychedelic kaleidoscopy.

The religious fervor and bizarre behavior of certain hippie cultists may arise not merely from drug abuse, but from group experimentation with both sensory deprivation and bombardment. The chanting of monotonous mantras, the attempt to focus the individual's attention on interior, bodily sensation to the exclusion of outside stimuli, are efforts to induce the weird and sometimes hallucinatory effects of understimulation.

At the other end of the scale, we note the glazed stares and numb, expressionless faces of youthful dancers at the great rock music auditoriums where light shows, split-screen movies, high decibel screams, shouts and moans, grotesque costumes and writhing, painted bodies create a sensory environment characterized by high input and extreme unpredictability and novelty.

An organism's ability to cope with sensory input is dependent upon its physiological structure. The nature of its sense organs and the speed with which impulses flow through its neural system set biological bounds on the quantity of sensory data it can accept. If we examine the speed of signal transmission within various organisms, we find that the lower the evolutionary level, the slower the movement. Thus, for example, in a sea urchin egg, lacking a nervous system as such, a signal moves along a membrane at a rate of about a centimeter an hour. Clearly, at such a rate, the organism can respond to only a very limited part of its environment. By the time we move up the ladder to a jellyfish, which already has a primitive nervous system, the signal travels 36,000 times faster: ten centimeters per second. In a worm, the rate leaps to 100 cps. Among insects and crustaceans, neural pulses race along at 1000 cps. Among anthropoids the rate reaches 10,000 cps. Crude as these figures no doubt

are, they help explain why man is unquestionably
among the most adaptable of creatures.

Yet even in man, with a neural transmission rate of
about 30,000 cps, the boundaries of the system are
imposing. (Electrical signals in a computer, by contrast, travel billions of times faster.) The limitations
of the sense organs and nervous system mean that
many environmental events occur at rates too fast for
us to follow, and we are reduced to sampling experience at best. When the signals reaching us are regular and repetitive, this sampling process can yield a
fairly good mental representation of reality. But when
it is highly disorganized, when it is novel and unpredictable, the accuracy of our imagery is necessarily
reduced. Our image of reality is distorted. This may
explain why, when we experience sensory overstimulation, we suffer confusion, a blurring of the line between illusion and reality.

INFORMATION OVERLOAD

If overstimulation at the sensory level increases the
distortion with which we perceive reality, cognitive
overstimulation interferes with our ability to "think."
While some human responses to novelty are involuntary, others are preceded by conscious thought, and
this depends upon our ability to absorb, manipulate,
evaluate and retain information.

Rational behavior, in particular, depends upon a
ceaseless flow of data from the environment. It depends upon the power of the individual to predict,
with at least fair success, the outcome of his own
actions. To do this, he must be able to predict how
the environment will respond to his acts. Sanity, itself,
thus hinges on man's ability to predict his immediate,
personal future on the basis of information fed him
by the environment.

When the individual is plunged into a fast and
irregularly changing situation, or a novelty-loaded

context, however, his predictive accuracy plummets. He can no longer make the reasonably correct assessments on which rational behavior is dependent.

To compensate for this, to bring his accuracy up to the normal level again, he must scoop up and process far more information than before. And he must do this at extremely high rates of speed. In short, the more rapidly changing and novel the environment, the more information the individual needs to process in order to make effective, rational decisions.

Yet just as there are limits on how much sensory input we can accept, there are in-built constraints on our ability to process information. In the words of psychologist George A. Miller of Rockefeller University, there are "severe limitations on the amount of information that we are able to receive, process, and remember." By classifying information, by abstracting and "coding" it in various ways, we manage to stretch these limits, yet ample evidence demonstrates that our capabilities are finite.

To discover these outer limits, psychologists and communications theorists have set about testing what they call the "channel capacity" of the human organism. For the purpose of these experiments, they regard man as a "channel." Information enters from the outside. It is processed. It exits in the form of actions based on decisions. The speed and accuracy of human information processing can be measured by comparing the speed of information input with the speed and accuracy of output.

Information has been defined technically and measured in terms of units called "bits."* By now, experiments have established rates for the processing involved in a wide variety of tasks from reading, typing, and playing the piano to manipulating dials or doing mental arithmetic. And while researchers

---

* A bit is the amount of information needed to make a decision between two equally likely alternatives. The number of bits needed increases by one as the number of such alternatives doubles.

differ as to the exact figures, they strongly agree on two basic principles: first, that man has limited capacity; and second, that overloading the system leads to serious breakdown of performance.

Imagine, for example, an assembly line worker in a factory making children's blocks. His job is to press a button each time a red block passes in front of him on the conveyor belt. So long as the belt moves at a reasonable speed, he will have little difficulty. His performance will approach 100 percent accuracy. We know that if the pace is too slow, his mind will wander, and his performance will deteriorate. We also know that if the belt moves too fast, he will falter, miss, grow confused and uncoordinated. He is likely to become tense and irritable. He may even take a swat at the machine out of pure frustration. Ultimately, he will give up trying to keep pace.

Here the information demands are simple, but picture a more complex task. Now the blocks streaming down the line are of many different colors. His instructions are to press the button only when a certain color pattern appears—a yellow block, say, followed by two reds and a green. In this task, he must take in and process far more information before he can decide whether or not to hit the button. All other things being equal, he will have even greater difficulty keeping up as the pace of the line accelerates.

In a still more demanding task, we not only force the worker to process a lot of data before deciding *whether* to hit the button, but we then force him to decide *which* of several buttons to press. We can also vary the number of times each button must be pressed. Now his instructions might read: For color pattern yellow-red-red-green, hit button number two once; for pattern green-blue-yellow-green, hit button number six three times; and so forth. Such tasks require the worker to process a large amount of data in order to carry out his task. Speeding up the conveyor now will destroy his accuracy even more rapidly.

Experiments like these have been built up to dismaying degrees of complexity. Tests have involved flashing lights, musical tones, letters, symbols, spoken words, and a wide array of other stimuli. And subjects, asked to drum fingertips, speak phrases, solve puzzles, and perform an assortment of other tasks, have been reduced to blithering ineptitude.

The results unequivocally show that no matter what the task, there is a speed above which it cannot be performed—and not simply because of inadequate muscular dexterity. The top speed is often imposed by mental rather than muscular limitations. These experiments also reveal that the greater the number of alternative courses of action open to the subject, the longer it takes him to reach a decision and carry it out.

Clearly, these findings can help us understand certain forms of psychological upset. Managers plagued by demands for rapid, incessant and complex decisions; pupils deluged with facts and hit with repeated tests; housewives confronted with squalling children, jangling telephones, broken washing machines, the wail of rock and roll from the teenager's living room and the whine of the television set in the parlor—may well find their ability to think and act clearly impaired by the waves of information crashing into their senses. It is more than possible that some of the symptoms noted among battle-stressed soldiers, disaster victims, and culture shocked travelers are related to this kind of information overload.

One of the men who has pioneered in information studies, Dr. James G. Miller, director of the Mental Health Research Institute at the University of Michigan, states flatly that "Glutting a person with more information than he can process may . . . lead to disturbance." He suggests, in fact, that information overload may be related to various forms of mental illness.

One of the striking features of schizophrenia, for example, is "incorrect associative response." Ideas and words that ought to be linked in the subject's mind are not, and vice versa. The schizophrenic tends to think in arbitrary or highly personalized categories. Confronted with a set of blocks of various kinds—triangles, cubes, cones, etc.—the normal person is likely to categorize them in terms of geometric shape. The schizophrenic asked to classify them is just as likely to say "They are all soldiers" or "They all make me feel sad."

In the volume *Disorders of Communication*, Miller describes experiments using word association tests to compare normals and schizophrenics. Normal subjects were divided into two groups, and asked to associate various words with other words or concepts. One group worked at its own pace. The other worked under time pressure—i.e., under conditions of rapid information input. The time-pressed subjects came up with responses more like those of schizophrenics than of self-paced normals.

Similar experiments conducted by psychologists G. Usdansky and L. J. Chapman made possible a more refined analysis of the types of errors made by subjects working under forced-pace, high information-input rates. They, too, concluded that increasing the speed of response brought out a pattern of errors among normals that is peculiarly characteristic of schizophrenics.

"One might speculate," Miller suggests, ". . . that schizophrenia (by some as-yet-unknown process, perhaps a metabolic fault which increases neural 'noise') lowers the capacities of channels involved in cognitive information processing. Schizophrenics consequently . . . have difficulties in coping with information inputs at standard rates like the difficulties experienced by normals at rapid rates. As a result, schizophrenics make errors at standard rates like those made by normals under fast, forced-input rates."

In short, Miller argues, the breakdown of human performance under heavy information loads may be related to psychopathology in ways we have not yet begun to explore. Yet, even without understanding its potential impact, we are accelerating the generalized rate of change in society. We are forcing people to adapt to a new life pace, to confront novel situations and master them in ever shorter intervals. We are forcing them to choose among fast-multiplying options. We are, in other words, forcing them to process information at a far more rapid pace than was necessary in slowly-evolving societies. There can be little doubt that we are subjecting at least some of them to cognitive overstimulation. What consequences this may have for mental health in the techno-societies has yet to be determined.

DECISION STRESS

Whether we are submitting masses of men to information overload or not, we are affecting their behavior negatively by imposing on them still a third form of overstimulation—decision stress. Many individuals trapped in dull or slowly changing environments yearn to break out into new jobs or roles that require them to make faster and more complex decisions. But among the people of the future, the problem is reversed. "Decisions, decisions . . ." they mutter as they race anxiously from task to task. The reason they feel harried and upset is that transience, novelty and diversity pose contradictory demands and thus place them in an excruciating double bind.

The accelerative thrust and its psychological counterpart, transience, force us to quicken the tempo of private and public decision-making. New needs, novel emergencies and crises demand rapid response.

Yet the very newness of the circumstances brings about a revolutionary change in the nature of the decisions they are called upon to make. The rapid injection of novelty into the environment upsets the delicate balance of "programmed" and "non-programmed" decisions in our organizations and our private lives.

A programmed decision is one that is routine, repetitive and easy to make. The commuter stands at the edge of the platform as the 8:05 rattles to a stop. He climbs aboard, as he has done every day for months or years. Having long ago decided that the 8:05 is the most convenient run on the schedule, the actual decision to board the train is programmed. It seems more like a reflex than a decision at all. The immediate criteria on which the decision is based are relatively simple and clear-cut, and because all the circumstances are familiar, he scarcely has to think about it. He is not required to process very much information. In this sense, programmed decisions are low in psychic cost.

Contrast this with the kind of decisions that same commuter thinks about on his way to the city. Should he take the new job Corporation X has just offered him? Should he buy a new house? Should he have an affair with his secretary? How can he get the Management Committee to accept his proposals about the new ad campaign? Such questions demand non-routine answers. They force him to make one-time or first-time decisions that will establish new habits and behavioral procedures. Many factors must be studied and weighed. A vast amount of information must be processed. These decisions are non-programmed. They are high in psychic cost.

For each of us, life is a blend of the two. If this blend is too high in programmed decisions, we are not challenged; we find life boring and stultifying. We search for ways, even unconsciously, to introduce novelty into our lives, thereby altering the decision "mix." But if this mix is too high in non-programmed decisions, if we are hit by so many novel situations that programming becomes impossible, life becomes painfully disorganized, exhausting and anxiety-filled. Pushed to its extreme, the end-point is psychosis.

"Rational behavior . . . ," writes organization theorist Bertram M. Gross, "always includes an intricate combination of routinization and creativity. Routine is essential . . . [because it] frees creative energies for dealing with the more baffling array of new problems for which routinization is an irrational approach."

When we are unable to program much of our lives, we suffer. "There is no more miserable person," wrote William James, "than one ... for whom the lighting of every cigar, the drinking of every cup ... the beginning of every bit of work, are subjects of deliberation." For unless we can extensively program our behavior, we waste tremendous amounts of information-processing capacity on trivia.

This is why we form habits. Watch a committee break for lunch and then return to the same room: almost invariably its members seek out the same seats they occupied earlier. Some anthropologists drag in the theory of "territoriality" to explain this behavior —the notion that man is forever trying to carve out for himself a sacrosanct "turf." A simpler explanation lies in the fact that programming conserves information-processing capacity. Choosing the same seat spares us the need to survey and evaluate other possibilities.

In a familiar context, we are able to handle many of our life problems with low-cost programmed decisions. Change and novelty boost the psychic price of decision-making. When we move to a new neighborhood, for example, we are forced to alter old relationships and establish new routines or habits. This cannot be done without first discarding thousands of formerly programmed decisions and making a whole series of costly new first-time, non-programmed decisions. In effect, we are asked to re-program ourselves.

Precisely the same is true of the unprepared visitor to an alien culture, and it is equally true of the man who, still in his own society, is rocketed into the future without advance warning. The arrival of the future in the form of novelty and change makes all his painfully pieced-together behavioral routines obsolete. He suddenly discovers to his horror that these old routines, rather than solving his problems, merely intensify them. New and as yet unprogrammable decisions are demanded. In short, novelty disturbs the decision mix, tipping the balance toward the most difficult, most costly form of decision-making.

It is true that some people can tolerate more novelty than others. The optimum mix is different for each of us. Yet the number and type of decisions demanded of us are not under our autonomous control. It is the society that basically determines the mix of decisions we must make and the pace at which we must make them. Today there is a hidden conflict in our lives between the pressures of acceleration and those of novelty. One forces us to make faster decisions while the other compels us to make the hardest, most time-consuming type of decisions.

The anxiety generated by this head-on collision is sharply intensified by expanding diversity. Incontrovertible evidence shows that increasing the number of choices open to an individual also increases the amount of information he needs to process if he is to deal with them. Laboratory tests on men and animals alike prove that the more the choices, the slower the reaction time.

It is the frontal collision of these three incompatible demands that is now producing a decision-making crisis in the techno-societies. Taken together these pressures justify the term "decisional overstimulation," and they help explain why masses of men in these societies already feel themselves harried, futile, incapable of working out their private futures. The conviction that the rat-race is too tough, that things are out of control, is the inevitable consequence of these clashing forces. For the uncontrolled acceleration of scientific, technological and social change subverts the power of the individual to make sensible, competent decisions about his own destiny.

VICTIMS OF FUTURE SHOCK

When we combine the effects of decisional stress with sensory and cognitive overload, we produce several common forms of individual maladaptation. For example, one widespread response to high-speed change ① is outright denial. The Denier's strategy is to "block out" unwelcome reality. When the demand for decisions reaches crescendo, he flatly refuses to take in new information. Like the disaster victim whose face registers total disbelief, The Denier, too, cannot accept the evidence of his senses. Thus he concludes that things really are the same, and that all evidences of change are merely superficial. He finds comfort in such clichés as "young people were always rebellious" or "there's nothing new on the face of the earth," or "the more things change, the more they stay the same."

An unknowing victim of future shock, The Denier sets himself up for personal catastrophe. His strategy for coping increases the likelihood that when he finally is forced to adapt, his encounter with change will come in the form of a single massive life crisis, rather than a sequence of manageable problems.

② A second strategy of the future shock victim is specialism. The Specialist doesn't block out *all* novel ideas or information. Instead, he energetically attempts to keep pace with change—but only in a specific narrow sector of life. Thus we witness the spectacle of the physician or financier who makes use of all the latest innovations in his profession, but remains rigidly closed to any suggestion for social, political, or economic innovation. The more universities undergo paroxysms of protest, the more ghettos go up in flames, the less he wants to know about them, and the more closely he narrows the slit through which he sees the world.

Superficially, he copes well. But he, too, is running the odds against himself. He may awake one morning to find his specialty obsolete or else transformed beyond recognition by events exploding outside his field of vision.

③ A third common response to future shock is obsessive reversion to previously successful adaptive routines that are now irrelevant and inappropriate. The

Reversionist sticks to his previously programmed decisions and habits with dogmatic desperation. The more change threatens from without, the more meticulously he repeats past modes of action. His social outlook is regressive. Shocked by the arrival of the future, he offers hysterical support for the not-so-status quo, or he demands, in one masked form or another, a return to the glories of yesteryear.

The Barry Goldwaters and George Wallaces of the world appeal to his quivering gut through the politics of nostalgia. Police maintained order in the past; hence, to maintain order, we need only supply more police. Authoritarian treatment of children worked in the past; hence, the troubles of the present spring from permissiveness. The middle-aged, right-wing reversionist yearns for the simple, ordered society of the small town—the slow-paced social environment in which his old routines were appropriate. Instead of adapting to the new, he continues automatically to apply the old solutions, growing more and more divorced from reality as he does so.

If the older reversionist dreams of reinstating a small-town past, the youthful, left-wing reversionist dreams of reviving an even older social system. This accounts for some of the fascination with rural communes, the bucolic romanticism that fills the posters and poetry of the hippie and post-hippie subcultures, the deification of Ché Guevara (identified with mountains and jungles, not with urban or post-urban environments), the exaggerated veneration of pre-technological societies and the exaggerated contempt for science and technology. For all their fiery demands for change, at least some sectors of the left share with the Wallacites and Goldwaterites a secret passion for the past.

Just as their Indian headbands, their Edwardian capes, their Deerslayer boots and gold-rimmed glasses mimic various eras of the past, so, too, their ideas. Turn-of-the-century terrorism and quaint Black Flag anarchy are suddenly back in vogue. The Rousseauian cult of the noble savage flourishes anew. Antique Marxist ideas, applicable at best to yesterday's industrialism, are hauled out as knee-jerk answers for the problems of tomorrow's super-industrialism. Reversionism masquerades as revolution.

Finally, we have the Super-Simplifier. With old heroes and institutions toppling, with strikes, riots, and demonstrations stabbing at his consciousness, he seeks a single neat equation that will explain all the complex novelties threatening to engulf him. Grasping erratically at this idea or that, he becomes a temporary true believer.

This helps account for the rampant intellectual faddism that already threatens to outpace the rate of turnover in fashion. McLuhan? Prophet of the electric age? Levi-Strauss? Wow! Marcuse? Now I see it all! The Maharishi of Whatchmacallit? Fantastic! Astrology? Insight of the ages!

The Super-Simplifier, groping desperately, invests every idea he comes across with universal relevance —often to the embarrassment of its author. Alas, no idea, not even mine or thine, is omni-insightful. But for the Super-Simplifier nothing less than total relevance suffices. Maximization of profits explains America. The Communist conspiracy explains race riots. Participatory democracy is the answer. Permissiveness (or Dr. Spock) are the root of all evil.

This search for a unitary solution at the intellectual level has its parallels in action. Thus the bewildered, anxious student, pressured by parents, uncertain of his draft status, nagged at by an educational system whose obsolescence is more strikingly revealed every day, forced to decide on a career, a set of values, and a worthwhile life style, searches wildly for a way to simplify his existence. By turning on to LSD, Methedrine or heroin, he performs an illegal act that has, at least, the virtue of consolidating his miseries. He trades a host of painful and seemingly insoluble troubles for one big problem, thus radically, if temporarily, simplifying existence.

The teen-age girl who cannot cope with the daily mounting tangle of stresses may choose another dramatic act of super-simplification: pregnancy. Like drug abuse, pregnancy may vastly complicate her life later, but it immediately plunges all her other problems into relative insignificance.

Violence, too, offers a "simple" way out of burgeoning complexity of choice and general overstimulation. For the older generation and the political establishment, police truncheons and military bayonets loom as attractive remedies, a way to end dissent once and for all. Black extremists and white vigilantes both employ violence to narrow their choices and clarify their lives. For those who lack an intelligent, comprehensive program, who cannot cope with the novelties and complexities of blinding change, terrorism substitutes for thought. Terrorism may not topple regimes, but it removes doubts.

Most of us can quickly spot these patterns of behavior in others—even in ourselves—without, at the same time, understanding their causes. Yet information scientists will instantly recognize denial, specialization, reversion and super-simplification as classical techniques for coping with overload.

All of them dangerously evade the rich complexity of reality. They generate distorted images of reality. The more the individual denies, the more he specializes at the expense of wider interests, the more mechanically he reverts to past habits and policies, the more desperately he super-simplifies, the more inept his responses to the novelty and choices flooding into his life. The more he relies on these strategies, the more his behavior exhibits wild and erratic swings and general instability.

Every information scientist recognizes that some of these strategies may, indeed, be necessary in overload situations. Yet, unless the individual begins with a clear grasp of relevant reality, and unless he begins with cleanly defined values and priorities, his reliance on such techniques will only deepen his adaptive difficulties.

These preconditions, however, are increasingly difficult to meet. Thus the future shock victim who does employ these strategies experiences a deepening sense of confusion and uncertainty. Caught in the turbulent flow of change, called upon to make significant, rapid-fire life decisions, he feels not simply intellectual bewilderment, but disorientation at the level of personal values. As the pace of change quickens, this confusion is tinged with self-doubt, anxiety and fear. He grows tense, tires easily. He may fall ill. As the pressures relentlessly mount, tension shades into irritability, anger, and sometimes, senseless violence. Little events trigger enormous responses; large events bring inadequate responses.

Pavlov many years ago referred to this phenomenon as the "paradoxical phase" in the breakdown of the dogs on whom he conducted his conditioning experiments. Subsequent research has shown that humans, too, pass through this stage under the impact of over-stimulation, and it may explain why riots sometimes occur even in the absence of serious provocation, why, as though for no reason, thousands of teenagers at a resort will suddenly go on the rampage, smashing windows, heaving rocks and bottles, wrecking cars. It may explain why pointless vandalism is a problem in all of the techno-societies, to the degree that an editorialist in the *Japan Times* reports in cracked, but passionate English: "We have never before seen anything like the extensive scope that these psychopathic acts are indulged in today."

And finally, the confusion and uncertainty wrought by transience, novelty and diversity may explain the profound apathy that de-socializes millions, old and young alike. This is not the studied, temporary withdrawal of the sensible person who needs to unwind or slow down before coping anew with his problems. It is total surrender before the strain of decision-making in conditions of uncertainty and overchoice.

Affluence makes it possible, for the first time in history, for large numbers of people to make their withdrawal a full-time proposition. The family man who retreats into his evening with the help of a few martinis and allows televised fantasy to narcotize him, at least works during the day, performing a social function upon which others are dependent. His is a part-time withdrawal. But for some (not all) hippie dropouts, for many of the surfers and lotus-eaters, withdrawal is full-time and total. A check from an indulgent parent may be the only remaining link with the larger society.

On the beach at Matala, a tiny sun-drenched village in Crete, are forty or fifty caves occupied by runaway American troglodytes, young men and women who, for the most part, have given up any further effort to cope with the exploding high-speed complexities of life. Here decisions are few and time plentiful. Here the choices are narrowed. No problem of overstimulation. No need to comprehend or even to feel. A reporter visiting them in 1968 brought them news of the assassination of Robert F. Kennedy. Their response: silence. "No shock, no rage, no tears. Is this the new phenomenon? Running away from America *and* running away from emotion? I understand uninvolvement, disenchantment, even noncommitment. But where has all the feeling gone?"

The reporter might understand where all the feeling has gone if he understood the impact of overstimulation, the apathy of the Chindit guerrilla, the blank face of the disaster victim, the intellectual and emotional withdrawal of the culture shock victim. For these young people, and millions of others—the confused, the violent, and the apathetic—already evince the symptoms of future shock. They are its earliest victims.

THE FUTURE-SHOCKED SOCIETY

It is impossible to produce future shock in large numbers of individuals without affecting the rationality of the society as a whole. Today, according to Daniel P. Moynihan, the chief White House advisor on urban affairs, the United States "exhibits the qualities of an individual going through a nervous breakdown." For the cumulative impact of sensory, cognitive or decisional overstimulation, not to mention the physical effects of neural or endocrine overload, creates sickness in our midst.

This sickness is increasingly mirrored in our culture, our philosophy, our attitude toward reality. It is no accident that so many ordinary people refer to the world as a "madhouse" or that the theme of insanity has recently become a staple in literature, art, drama and film. Peter Weiss in his play *Marat/Sade* portrays a turbulent world as seen through the eyes of the inmates of the Charenton asylum. In movies like *Morgan*, life within a mental institution is depicted as superior to that in the outside world. In *Blow-Up*, the climax comes when the hero joins in a tennis game in which players hit a non-existent ball back and forth over the net. It is his symbolic acceptance of the unreal and irrational—recognition that he can no longer distinguish between illusion and reality. Millions of viewers identified with the hero in that moment.

The assertion that the world has "gone crazy," the graffiti slogan that "reality is a crutch," the interest in hallucinogenic drugs, the enthusiasm for astrology and the occult, the search for truth in sensation, ecstasy and "peak experience," the swing toward extreme subjectivism, the attacks on science, the snowballing belief that reason has failed man, reflect the everyday experience of masses of ordinary people who find they can no longer cope rationally with change.

Millions sense the pathology that pervades the air, but fail to understand its roots. These roots lie not in this or that political doctrine, still less in some mystical core of despair or isolation presumed to inhere in the "human condition." Nor do they lie in science, technology, or legitimate demands for social change. They are traceable, instead, to the uncontrolled, non-selective nature of our lunge into the future. They lie in our failure to direct, consciously and imaginatively, the advance toward super-industrialism.

Thus, despite its extraordinary achievements in art, science, intellectual, moral and political life, the United States is a nation in which tens of thousands of young people flee reality by opting for drug-induced lassitude; a nation in which millions of their parents retreat into video-induced stupor or alcoholic haze; a nation in which legions of elderly folk vegetate and die in loneliness; in which the flight from family and occupational responsibility has become an exodus; in which masses tame their raging anxieties with Miltown, or Librium, or Equanil, or a score of other tranquilizers and psychic pacifiers. Such a nation, whether it knows it or not, is suffering from future shock.

"I'm not going back to America," says Ronald Bierl, a young expatriate in Turkey. "If you can establish your own sanity, you don't have to worry about other people's sanity. And so many Americans are going stone insane." Multitudes share this unflattering view of American reality. Lest Europeans or Japanese or Russians rest smugly on their presumed sanity, however, it is well to ask whether similar symptoms are not already present in their midst as well. Are Americans unique in this respect, or are they simply suffering the initial brunt of an assault on the psyche that soon will stagger other nations as well?

Social rationality presupposes individual rationality, and this, in turn, depends not only on certain biological equipment, but on continuity, order and regularity in the environment. It is premised on some correlation between the pace and complexity of change and man's decisional capacities. By blindly stepping up the rate of change, the level of novelty, and the extent of choice, we are thoughtlessly tampering with these environmental preconditions of rationality. We are condemning countless millions to future shock.

Part Six:

STRATEGIES FOR SURVIVAL

Chapter 17

COPING WITH TOMORROW

In the blue vastness of the South Pacific just north of New Guinea lies the island of Manus, where, as every first-year anthropology student knows, a stone age population emerged into the twentieth century within a single generation. Margaret Mead, in *New Lives for Old*, tells the story of this seeming miracle of cultural adaptation and argues that it is far more difficult for a primitive people to accept a few fragmentary crumbs of Western technological culture than it is for them to adopt a whole new way of life at once.

"Each human culture, like each language, is a whole," she writes, and if "individuals or groups of people have to change . . . it is most important that they should change from one whole pattern to another."

There is sense in this, for it is clear that tensions arise from incongruities between cultural elements. To introduce cities without sewage, anti-malarial medicines without birth control, is to tear a culture apart, and to subject its members to excruciating, often insoluble problems.

Yet this is only part of the story, for there are definite limits to the amount of newness that any individual or group can absorb in a short span of time, regardless of how well integrated the whole may be. Nobody, Manus or Muscovite, can be pushed above his adaptive range without suffering disturbance and disorientation. Moreover, it is dangerous to generalize from the experience of this small South Sea population.

The success story of the Manus, told and retold like a modern folk tale, is often cited as evidence that we, in the high-technology countries, will also be able to leap to a new stage of development without undue hardship. Yet our situation, as we speed into the super-industrial era, is radically different from that of the islanders.

We are not in a position, as they were, to import wholesale an integrated, well-formed culture, matured and tested in another part of the world. We must invent super-industrialism, not import it. During the next thirty or forty years we must anticipate not a single wave of change, but a series of terrible heaves and shudders. The parts of the new society, rather than being carefully fitted, one to the other, will be strikingly incongruous filled with missing linkages and glaring contradictions. There is no "whole pattern" for us to adopt.

More important, the transience level has risen so high, the pace is now so forced, that a historically unprecedented situation has been thrust upon us. We are not asked, as the Manus were, to adapt to a new culture, but to a blinding succession of new temporary cultures. This is why we may be approaching the upper limits of the adaptive range. No previous generation has ever faced this test.

It is only now, therefore, in our lifetime, and only in the techno-societies as yet, that the potential for mass future shock has crystallized.

To say this, however, is to court grave misunderstanding. First, any author who calls attention to a social problem runs the risk of deepening the already profound pessimism that envelops the techno-societies. Self-indulgent despair is a highly salable literary commodity today. Yet despair is not merely a refuge for irresponsibility; it is unjustified. Most of the problems besieging us, including future shock, stem not from implacable natural forces but from man-made processes that are at least potentially subject to our control.

Second, there is danger that those who treasure the status quo may seize upon the concept of future shock as an excuse to argue for a moratorium on change. Not only would any such attempt to suppress change fail, triggering even bigger, bloodier and more unmanageable changes than any we have seen, it would be moral lunacy as well. By any set of human standards, certain radical social changes are already desperately overdue. The answer to future shock is not non-change, but a different kind of change.

The only way to maintain any semblance of equilibrium during the super-industrial revolution will be to meet invention with invention—to design new personal and social change-regulators. Thus we need neither blind acceptance nor blind resistance, but an array of creative strategies for shaping, deflecting, accelerating or decelerating change selectively. The individual needs new principles for pacing and planning his life along with a dramatically new kind of education. He may also need specific new technological aids to increase his adaptivity. The society, meanwhile, needs new institutions and organizational forms, new buffers and balance wheels.

All this implies still further change, to be sure—but of a type designed from the beginning to harness the accelerative thrust, to steer it and pace it. This will not be easy to do. Moving swiftly into uncharted social territory, we have no time-tried techniques, no blueprints. We must, therefore, experiment with a wide range of change-regulating measures, inventing and discarding them as we go along. It is in this tentative spirit that the following tactics and strategies are suggested—not as sure-fire panaceas, but as examples of new approaches that need to be tested

and evaluated. Some are personal, others technological and social. For the struggle to channel change
must take place at all these levels simultaneously.

Given a clearer grasp of the problems and more
intelligent control of certain key processes, we can
turn crisis into opportunity, helping people not merely
to survive, but to crest the waves of change, to grow,
and to gain a new sense of mastery over their own
destinies.

DIRECT COPING

We can begin our battle to prevent future shock at
the most personal level. It is clear, whether we know
it or not, that much of our daily behavior is, in fact,
an attempt to ward off future shock. We employ a
variety of tactics to lower the levels of stimulation
when they threaten to drive us above our adaptive
range. For the most part, however, these techniques
are employed unconsciously. We can increase their
effectiveness by raising them to consciousness.

We can, for example, introvert periodically to examine our own bodily and psychological reactions
to change, briefly tuning out the external environment to evaluate our inner environment. This is not
a matter of wallowing in subjectivity, but of coolly appraising our own performance. In the words of Hans
Selye, whose work on stress opened new frontiers in
biology and psychiatry, the individual can "consciously look for signs of being keyed up too much."

Heart palpitations, tremors, insomnia or unex-
plained fatigue may well signal overstimulation, just
as confusion, unusual irritability, profound lassitude
and a panicky sense that things are slipping out of
control are psychological indications. By observing
ourselves, looking back over the changes in our recent past, we can determine whether we are operating comfortably within our adaptive range or press-

ing its outer limits. We can, in short, consciously assess our own life pace.

Having done this, we can also begin consciously to influence it—speeding it up or slowing it down—first with respect to small things, the micro-environment, and then in terms of the larger, structural patterns of experience. We can learn how by scrutinizing our own unpremeditated responses to overstimulation.

We employ a de-stimulating tactic, for example, when we storm into the teen-ager's bedroom and turn off a stereo unit that has been battering our eardrums with unwanted and interruptive sounds. We virtually sigh with relief when the noise level drops. We act to reduce sensory bombardment in other ways, too—when we pull down the blinds to darken a room, or search for silence on a deserted strip of beach. We may flip on an air conditioner not so much to lower the temperature as to mask novel and unpredictable street sounds with a steady, predictable drone.

We close doors, wear sunglasses, avoid smelly places and shy away from touching strange surfaces when we want to decrease novel sensory input. Similarly, when we choose a familiar route home from the office, instead of turning a fresh corner, we opt for sensory non-novelty. In short, we employ "sensory shielding"—a thousand subtle behavioral tricks to "turn off" sensory stimuli when they approach our upper adaptive limit.

We use similar tactics to control the level of cognitive stimulation. Even the best of students periodically gazes out the window, blocking out the teacher, shutting off the flow of new data from that source. Even voracious readers sometimes go through periods when they cannot bear to pick up a book or magazine.

Why, during a gregarious evening at a friend's house, does one person in the group refuse to learn a new card game while others urge her on? Many factors play a part: the self-esteem of the individual,

the fear of seeming foolish, and so on. But one overlooked factor affecting willingness to learn may well
be the general level of cognitive stimulation in the
individual's life at the time. "Don't bother me with
new facts!" is a phrase usually uttered in jest. But
the joke often disguises a real wish to avoid being
pressed too hard by new data.

This accounts in part for our specific choices of
entertainment—of leisure-time reading, movies or television programs. Sometimes we seek a high novelty
ratio, a rich flow of information. At other moments
we actively resist cognitive stimulation and reach for
"light" entertainment. The typical detective yarn, for
example, provides a trace of unpredictability—who-
dunnit?—within a carefully structured ritual framework, a set of non-novel, hence easily predictable
relationships. In this way, we employ entertainment
as a device to raise or lower stimulation, adjusting
our intake rates so as not to overload our capacities.

By making more conscious use of such tactics, we
can "fine-tune" our micro-environment. We can also
cut down on unwanted stimulation by acting to
lighten our cognitive burdens. "Trying to remember
too many things is certainly one of the major sources
of psychologic stress," writes Selye. "I make a conscious effort to forget immediately all that is unimportant and to jot down data of possible value . . .
This technique can help anyone to accomplish the
greatest simplicity compatible with the degree of
complexity of his intellectual life."

We also act to regulate the flow of decisioning. We
postpone decisions or delegate them to others when
we are suffering from decision overload. Sometimes
we "freeze up" decisionally. I have seen a woman
sociologist, just returned from a crowded, highly
stimulating professional conference, sit down in a
restaurant and absolutely refuse to make any decisions whatever about her meal. "What would you like?"
her husband asked. "You decide for me," she replied.
When pressed to choose between specific alternatives,

she still explicitly refused, insisting angrily that she lacked the "energy" to make the decision.

Through such methods we attempt, as best we can, to regulate the flow of sensory, cognitive and decisional stimulation, perhaps also attempting in some complicated and as yet unknown way to balance them with one another. But we have stronger ways of coping with the threat of overstimulation. These involve attempts to control the rates of transience, novelty and diversity in our milieu.

PERSONAL STABILITY ZONES

The rate of turnover in our lives, for example, can be influenced by conscious decisions. We can, for example, cut down on change and stimulation by consciously maintaining longer-term relationships with the various elements of our physical environment. Thus, we can refuse to purchase throw-away products. We can hang onto the old jacket for another season; we can stoutly refuse to follow the latest fashion trend; we can resist when the salesman tells us it's time to trade in our automobile. In this way, we reduce the need to make and break ties with the physical objects around us.

We can use the same tactic with respect to people and the other dimensions of experience. There are times when even the most gregarious person feels anti-social and refuses invitations to parties or other events that call for social interaction. We consciously disconnect. In the same way, we can minimize travel. We can resist pointless reorganizations in our company, church, fraternal or community groups. In making important decisions, we can consciously weigh the hidden costs of change against the benefits.

None of this is to suggest that change can or should be stopped. Nothing is less sensible than the advice of the Duke of Cambridge who is said to have harumphed: "Any change, at any time, for any reason is to be deplored." The theory of the adaptive range suggests that, despite its physical costs, some level of change is as vital to health as too much change is damaging.

Some people, for reasons still not clear, are pitched at a much higher level of stimulus hunger than others. They seem to crave change even when others are reeling from it. A new house, a new car, another trip, another crisis on the job, more house guests, visits, financial adventures and misadventures—they seem to accept all these and more without apparent ill effect.

Yet close analysis of such people often reveals the existence of what might be called "stability zones" in their lives—certain enduring relationships that are carefully maintained despite all kinds of other changes.

One man I know has run through a series of love affairs, a divorce and remarriage—all within a very short span of time. He thrives on change, enjoys travel, new foods, new ideas, new movies, plays and books. He has a high intellect and a low "boring point," is impatient with tradition and restlessly eager for novelty. Ostensibly, he is a walking exemplar of change.

When we look more closely, however, we find that he has stayed on the same job for ten years. He drives a battered, seven-year-old automobile. His clothes are several years out of style. His closest friends are long-time professional associates and even a few old college buddies.

Another case involves a man who has changed jobs at a mind-staggering rate, has moved his family thirteen times in eighteen years, travels extensively, rents cars, uses throw-away products, prides himself on leading the neighborhood in trying out new gadgets, and generally lives in a restless whirl of transience, newness and diversity. Once more, however, a second look reveals significant stability zones in his life: a good, tightly woven relationship with his wife of nineteen years; continuing ties with his parents; old college friends interspersed with the new acquaintances.

A different form of stability zone is the habit pattern that goes with the person wherever he travels, no matter what other changes alter his life. A professor who has moved seven times in ten years, who travels constantly in the United States, South America, Europe and Africa, who has changed jobs repeatedly, pursues the same daily regimen wherever he is. He reads between eight and nine in the morning, takes forty-five minutes for exercise at lunch time, and then catches a half-hour cat-nap before plunging into work that keeps him busy until 10:00 P.M.

The problem is not, therefore, to suppress change, which cannot be done, but to manage it. If we opt for rapid change in certain sectors of life, we can consciously attempt to build stability zones elsewhere. A divorce, perhaps, should not be too closely followed by a job transfer. Since the birth of a child alters all the human ties within a family, it ought not, perhaps, be followed too closely by a relocation which causes tremendous turnover in human ties outside the family. The recent widow should not, perhaps, rush to sell her house.

To design workable stability zones, however, to alter the larger patterns of life, we need far more potent tools. We need, first of all, a radically new orientation toward the future.

Ultimately, to manage change we must anticipate it. However, the notion that one's personal future can be, to some extent, anticipated, flies in the face of persistent folk prejudice. Most people, deep down, believe that the future is a blank. Yet the truth is that we *can* assign probabilities to some of the changes that lie in store for us, especially certain large structural changes, and there are ways to use this knowledge in designing personal stability zones.

We can, for example, predict with certainty that

unless death intervenes, we shall grow older; that our children, our relatives and friends will also grow older; and that after a certain point our health will begin to deteriorate. Obvious as this may seem, we can, as a result of this simple statement, infer a great deal about our lives one, five or ten years hence, and about the amount of change we will have to absorb in the interim.

Few individuals or families plan ahead systematically. When they do, it is usually in terms of a budget. Yet we can forecast and influence our expenditure of time and emotion as well as money. Thus it is possible to gain revealing glimpses of one's own future, and to estimate the gross level of change lying ahead, by periodically preparing what might be called a Time and Emotion Forecast. This is an attempt to assess the percentage of time and emotional energy invested in various important aspects of life —and to see how this might change over the years.

One can, for example, list in a column those sectors of life that seem most important to us: Health, Occupation, Leisure, Marital Relations, Parental Relations, Filial Relations, etc. It is then possible to jot down next to each item a "guesstimate" of the amount of time we presently allocate to that sector. By way of illustration: given a nine-to-five job, a half-hour commute, and the usual vacations and holidays, a man employing this method would find that he devotes approximately 25 percent of his time to work. Although it is, of course, much more difficult, he can also make a subjective assessment of the percentage of his emotional energy invested in the job. If he is bored and secure, he may invest very little—there being no necessary correlation between time devoted and emotion invested.

If he performs this exercise for each of the important sectors of his life, forcing himself to write in a percentage even when it is no more than an extremely crude estimate, and toting up the figures to make sure they never exceed 100 percent, he will be rewarded with some surprising insights. For the way he distributes his time and emotional energies is a direct clue to his value system and his personality.

The payoff for engaging in this process really begins, however, when he projects forward, asking himself honestly and in detail how his job, or his marriage, or his relationship with his children or his parents is likely to develop within the years ahead.

If, for example, he is a forty-year-old middle manager with two teen-age sons, two surviving parents or in-laws, and an incipient duodenal ulcer, he can assume that within half a decade his boys will be off to college or living away on their own. Time devoted to parental concerns will probably decline. Similarly, he can anticipate some decline in the emotional energies demanded by his parental role. On the other hand, as his own parents and in-laws grow older, his filial responsibility will probably loom larger. If they are sick, he may have to devote large amounts of time and emotion to their care. If they are statistically likely to die within the period under study, he needs to face this fact. It tells him that he can expect a major change in his commitments. His own health, in the meantime, will not be getting any better. In the same way, he can hazard some guesses about his job—his chances for promotion, the possibility of reorganization, relocation, retraining, etc.

All this is difficult, and it does not yield "knowledge of the future." Rather, it helps him make explicit some of his assumptions about the future. As he moves forward, filling in the forecast for the present year, the next year, the fifth or tenth year, patterns of change will begin to emerge. He will see that in certain years there are bigger shifts and redistributions to be expected than in others. Some years are choppier, more change-filled than others. And he can then, on the strength of these systematic assumptions, decide how to handle major decisions in the present.

Should the family move next year—or will there be

enough turmoil and change without that? Should he quit his job? Buy a new car? Take a costly vacation? Put his elderly father-in-law in a nursing home? Have an affair? Can he afford to rock his marriage or change his profession? Should he attempt to maintain certain levels of commitment unchanged?

These techniques are extremely crude tools for personal planning. Perhaps the psychologists and social psychologists can design sharper instruments, more sensitive to differences in probability, more refined and insight-yielding. Yet, if we search for clues rather than certainties, even these primitive devices can help us moderate or channel the flow of change in our lives. For, by helping us identify the zones of rapid change, they also help us identify—or invent—stability zones, patterns of relative constancy in the overwhelming flux. They improve the odds in the personal struggle to manage change.

Nor is this a purely negative process—a struggle to suppress or limit change. The issue for any individual attempting to cope with rapid change is how to maintain himself within the adaptive range, and, beyond that, how to find the exquisite optimum point at which he lives at peak effectiveness. Dr. John L. Fuller, a senior scientist at the Jackson Laboratory, a bio-medical research center in Bar Harbor, Maine, has conducted experiments in the impact of experiential deprivation and overload. "Some people," he says, "achieve a certain sense of serenity, even in the midst of turmoil, not because they are immune to emotion, but because they have found ways to get just the 'right' amount of change in their lives." The search for that optimum may be what much of the "pursuit of happiness" is about.

Trapped, temporarily, with the limited nervous and endocrine systems given us by evolution, we must work out new tactics to help us regulate the stimulation to which we subject ourselves.

SITUATIONAL GROUPING

The trouble is that such personal tactics become less
effective with every passing day. As the rate of change
climbs, it becomes harder for individuals to create
the personal stability zones they need. The costs of
non-change escalate.

We may stay in the old house—only to see the neighborhood transformed. We may keep the old car—
only to see repair bills mount beyond reach. We
may refuse to transfer to a new location—only to lose
our job as a result. For while there are steps we can
take to reduce the impact of change in our personal
lives, the real problem lies outside ourselves.

To create an environment in which change enlivens
and enriches the individual, but does not overwhelm
him, we must employ not merely personal tactics but
social strategies. If we are to carry people through
the accelerative period, we must begin now to build
"future shock absorbers" into the very fabric of super-
industrial society. And this requires a fresh way of
thinking about change and non-change in our lives.
It even requires a different way of classifying people.

Today we tend to categorize individuals not according to the changes they happen to be undergoing
at the moment, but according to their status or position between changes. We consider a union man as
someone who has joined a union and not yet quit.
Our designation refers not to joining or quitting, but
to the "non-change" that happens in between. Welfare
recipient, college student, Methodist, executive—all
refer to the person's condition between changes, as it
were.

There is, however, a radically different way to view
people. For example, "one who is moving to a new
residence" is a classification into which more than
100,000 Americans fit on any given day, yet they are
seldom thought of as a group. The classification "one

who is changing his job" or "one who is joining a church," or "one who is getting a divorce" are all based on temporary, transitional conditions, rather than on the more enduring conditions between transitions.

This sudden shift of focus, from thinking about what people "are" to thinking about what they are "becoming," suggests a whole array of new approaches to adaptation.

One of the most imaginative and simplest of these comes from Dr. Herbert Gerjuoy, a psychologist on the staff of the Human Resources Research Organization. He terms it "situational grouping," and like most good ideas, it sounds obvious once it is described. Yet it has never been systematically exploited. Situational grouping may well become one of the key social services of the future.

Dr. Gerjuoy argues that we should provide temporary organizations—"situational groups"—for people who happen to be passing through similar life transitions at the same time. Such situational groups should be established, Gerjuoy contends, "for families caught in the upheaval of relocation, for men and women about to be divorced, for people about to lose a parent or a spouse, for those about to gain a child, for men preparing to switch to a new occupation, for families that have just moved into a community, for those about to marry off their last child, for those facing imminent retirement—for anyone, in other words, who faces an important life change.

"Membership in the group would, of course, be temporary—just long enough to help the person with the transitional difficulties. Some groups might meet for a few months, others might not do more than hold a single meeting."

By bringing together people who are sharing, or are about to share, a common adaptive experience, he argues, we help equip them to cope with it. "A man required to adapt to a new life situation loses some of his bases for self-esteem. He begins to doubt his own abilities. If we bring him together with others who are moving through the same experience, people he can identify with and respect, we strengthen him. The members of the group come to share, even if briefly, some sense of identity. They see their problems more objectively. They trade useful ideas and insights. Most important, they suggest future alternatives for one another."

This emphasis on the future, says Gerjuoy, is critical. Unlike some group therapy sessions, the meetings of situational groups should not be devoted to hashing over the past, or to griping about it, or to soul-searching self-revelation, but to discussing personal objectives, and to planning practical strategies for future use in the new life situation. Members might watch movies of other similar groups wrestling with the same kinds of problems. They might hear from others who are more advanced in the transition than they are. In short, they are given the opportunity to pool their personal experiences and ideas before the moment of change is upon them.

In essence, there is nothing novel about this approach. Even now certain organizations are based on situational principles. A group of Peace Corps volunteers preparing for an overseas mission is, in effect, just such a situational grouping, as are pre- and postnatal classes. Many American towns have a "Newcomer's Club" that invites new residents to casserole dinners or other socials, permitting them to mix with other recent arrivals and compare problems and plans. Perhaps there ought to be an "Outmovers Club" as well. What is new is the suggestion that we systematically honeycomb the society with such "coping classrooms."

CRISIS COUNSELING

Not all help for the individual can, or necessarily should come from groups. In many cases, what the change-pressed person needs most is one-to-one counseling during the crisis of adaptation. In psychiatric jargon a "crisis" is any significant transition. It is roughly synonymous with "major life change."

Today persons in transitional crisis turn to a variety of experts—doctors, marriage counselors, psychiatrists, vocational specialists and others—for individualized advice. Yet for many kinds of crisis there are no appropriate experts. Who helps the family or individual faced with the need to move to a new city for the third time in five years? Who is available to counsel a leader who is up- or down-graded by a reorganization of his or her club or community organization? Who is there to help the secretary just bounced back to the typing pool?

People like these are not sick. They neither need nor should receive psychiatric attention, yet there is, by and large, no counseling machinery available to them.

Not only are there many kinds of present-day life transitions for which no counseling help is provided, but the invasion of novelty will slam individuals up against wholly new kinds of personal crises in the future. And as the society races toward heterogeneity, the variety of problems will increase. In slowly changing societies the types of crises faced by individuals are more uniform and the sources of specialized advice more easily identifiable. The crisis-caught person went to his priest, his witch doctor or his local chief. Today personalized counseling services in the high technology countries have become so specialized that we have developed, in effect, second-layer advice-givers who do nothing but counsel the individual about where to seek advice.

These referral services interpose additional red tape and delay between the individual and the assistance he needs. By the time help reaches him, he may already have made the crucial decision—and done so badly. So long as we assume that advice is something that must come from evermore specialized professionals, we can anticipate ever greater difficulty. Moreover, so long as we base specialties on what people "are" instead of what they are "becoming" we miss many of the real adaptive problems altogether. Conventional social service systems will never be able to keep up.

The answer is a counterpart to the situational grouping system—a counseling set-up that not only draws on full-time professional advice givers, but on multitudes of lay experts as well. We must recognize that what makes a person an expert in one type of crisis is not necessarily formal education, but the very experience of having undergone a similar crisis himself.

To help tide millions of people over the difficult transitions they are likely to face, we shall be forced to "deputize" large numbers of non-professional people in the community—businessmen, students, teachers, workers, and others—to serve as "crisis counselors." Tomorrow's crisis counselors will be experts not in such conventional disciplines as psychology or health, but in specific transitions such as relocation, job promotion, divorce, or subcult-hopping. Armed with their own recent experience, working on a volunteer basis or for minimal pay, they will set aside some small part of their time for listening to other lay people talk out their problems, apprehensions and plans. In return, they will have access to others for similar assistance in the course of their own adaptive development.

Once again, there is nothing new about people seeking advice from one another. What is new is our ability, through the use of computerized systems, to assemble situational groups swiftly, to match up individuals with counselors, and to do both with considerable respect for privacy and anonymity.

. We can already see evidence of a move in this direction in the spread of "listening" and "caring" services. In Davenport, Iowa, lonely people can dial a telephone number and be connected with a "listener"—one of a rotating staff of volunteers who man the telephone twenty-four hours a day. The program, initiated by a local commission on the aging, is similar to, but not the same as, the Care-Ring service in New York. Care-Ring charges its subscribers a fee, in return for which they receive two check-in calls each day at designated times. Subscribers provide the service with the names of their doctor, a neighbor, their building superintendent, and a close relative. In the event they fail to respond to a call, the service tries again half an hour later. If they still do not respond, the doctor is notified and a nurse dispatched to the scene. Care-Ring services are now being franchised in other cities. In both these services we see forerunners of the crisis-counseling system of the future.

Under that system, the giving and getting of advice becomes not a "social service" in the usual bureaucratic, impersonal sense, but a highly personalized process that not only helps individuals crest the currents of change in their own lives, but helps cement the entire society together in a kind of "love network"—an integrative system based on the principle of "I need you as much as you need me." Situational grouping and person-to-person crisis counseling are likely to become a significant part of everyone's life as we all move together into the uncertainties of the future.

HALF-WAY HOUSES

A "future shock absorber" of a quite different type is the "half-way house" idea already employed by progressive prison authorities to ease the convict's way back into normal life. According to criminologist Daniel Glaser, the distinctive feature of the correctional institutions of the future will be the idea of "gradual release."

Instead of taking a man out of the under-stimulating, tightly regimented life of the prison and plunging him violently and without preparation into open society, he is moved first to an intermediate institution which permits him to work in the community by day, while continuing to return to the institution at night. Gradually, restrictions are lifted until he is fully adjusted to the outside world. The same principle has been explored by various mental institutions.

Similarly it has been suggested that the problems of rural populations suddenly shifted to urban centers might be sharply reduced if something like this half-way house principle were employed to ease their entry into the new way of life. What cities need, according to this theory, are reception facilities where newcomers live for a time under conditions halfway between those of the rural society they are leaving behind and the urban society they are seeking to penetrate. If instead of treating city-bound migrants with contempt and leaving them to find their own way, they were first acclimatized, they would adapt far more successfully.

A similar idea is filtering through the specialists who concern themselves with "squatter housing" in major cities in the technologically underdeveloped world. Outside Khartoum in the Sudan, thousands of former nomads have created a concentric ring of settlements. Those furthest from the city live in tents, much like the ones they occupied before migration. The next-closer group lives in mud-walled huts with tent roofs. Those still closer to the city occupy huts with mud walls and tin roofs.

When police set out to tear down the tents, urban planner Constantinos Doxiadis recommended that they not only *not* destroy them, but that certain municipal services be provided to their inhabitants. Instead of seeing these concentric rings in wholly negative terms, he suggested, they might be viewed as a tremendous teaching machine through which individuals and families move, becoming urbanized step by step.

The application of this principle, however, need not

be limited to the poor, the insane or the criminal.
The basic idea of providing change in controlled,
graduated stages, rather than abrupt transitions, is
crucial to any society that wishes to cope with rapid
social or technological upheaval. The veteran, for
example, could be released from service more gradually. The student from a rural community could
spend a few weeks at a college in a medium-size
city before entering the large urban university. The
long-term hospital patient might be encouraged to go
home on a trial basis, once or twice, before being discharged.

We are already experimenting with these strategies, but others are possible. Retirement, for example,
should not be the abrupt, all-or-nothing, ego-crush-
ing change that it now is for most men. There is no
reason why it cannot be gradualized. Military induc-
tion, which typically separates a young man from
his family in a sudden and almost violent fashion,
could be done by stages. Legal separation, which is
supposed to serve as a kind of half-way house on the
way to divorce, could be made less legally complicated and psychologically costly. Trial marriage could
be encouraged, instead of denigrated. In short,
wherever a change of status is contemplated, the possibility of gradualizing it should be considered.

ENCLAVES OF THE PAST

No society racing through the turbulence of the next
several decades will be able to do without specialized
centers in which the rate of change is artificially de-
pressed. To phrase it differently, we shall need enclaves of the past—communities in which turnover,
novelty and choice are deliberately limited.

These may be communities in which history is
partially frozen, like the Amish villages of Pennsylvania, or places in which the past is artfully simulated,
like Williamsburg, Virginia or Mystic, Connecticut.

Unlike Williamsburg or Mystic, however, through which visitors stream at a steady and rapid clip, tomorrow's enclaves of the past must be places where people faced with future shock can escape the pressures of overstimulation for weeks, months, even years, if they choose.

In such slow-paced communities, individuals who need or want a more relaxed, less stimulating existence should be able to find it. The communities must be consciously encapsulated, selectively cut off from the surrounding society. Vehicular access should be limited to avoid traffic. Newspapers should be weeklies instead of dailies. If permitted at all, radio and television should be broadcast only for a few hours a day, instead of round the clock. Only special emergency services—health, for example—should be maintained at the maximum efficiency permitted by advanced technology.

Such communities not only should not be derided, they should be subsidized by the larger society as a form of mental and social insurance. In times of extremely rapid change, it is possible for the larger society to make some irreversible, catastrophic error. Imagine, for instance, the widespread diffusion of a food additive that accidentally turns out to have thalidomide-like effects. One can conceive of accidents capable of sterilizing or even killing whole populations.

By proliferating enclaves of the past, living museums as it were, we increase the chances that someone will be there to pick up the pieces in case of massive calamity. Such communities might also serve as experiential teaching machines. Thus children from the outside world might spend a few months in a simulated feudal village, living and actually working as children did centuries ago. Teenagers might be required to spend some time living in a typical early industrial community and to actually work in its mill or factory. Such living education would give them a historical perspective no book could ever provide.

In these communities, the men and women who want a slower life might actually make a career out of "being" Shakespeare or Ben Franklin or Napoleon—not merely acting out their parts on stage, but living, eating, sleeping, as they did. The career of "historical simulant" would attract a great many naturally talented actors.

In short, every society will need sub-societies whose members are committed to staying away from the latest fads. We may even want to pay people *not* to use the latest goods, not to enjoy the most automated and sophisticated conveniences.

ENCLAVES OF THE FUTURE

By the same token, just as we make it possible for some people to live at the slower pace of the past, we must also make it possible for individuals to experience aspects of their future in advance. Thus, we shall also have to create enclaves of the future.

In a limited sense, we are already doing this. Astronauts, pilots and other specialists are often trained by placing them in carefully assembled simulations of the environments they will occupy at some date in the future when they actually participate in a mission. By duplicating the interior of a cockpit or a capsule, we allow them to become accustomed, by degrees, to their future environment. Police and espionage agents, as well as commandos and other military specialists, are pre-trained by watching movies of the people they will have to deal with, the factories they are supposed to infiltrate, the terrain they will have to cover. In this way they are prepared to cope with a variety of future contingencies.

There is no reason why the same principle cannot be extended. Before dispatching a worker to a new location, he and his family ought to be shown detailed movies of the neighborhood they will live in, the school their children will attend, the stores in which they will shop, perhaps even of the teachers, shopkeepers, and neighbors they will meet. By pre-adapting them in this way, we can lower their anxieties about the unknown and prepare them, in advance, to cope with many of the problems they are likely to encounter.

Tomorrow, as the technology of experiential simulation advances, we shall be able to go much further. The pre-adapting individual will be able not merely to see and hear, but to touch, taste and smell the environment he is about to enter. He will be able to interact vicariously with the people in his future, and to undergo carefully contrived experiences designed to improve his coping abilities.

The "psych-corps" of the future will find a fertile market in the design and operation of such pre-adaptive facilities. Whole families may go to "work-learn-and-play" enclaves which will, in effect, constitute museums of the future, preparing them to cope with their own personal tomorrows.

GLOBAL SPACE PAGEANTS

"Mesmerized as we are by the very idea of change," writes John Gardner in *Self-Renewal*, "we must guard against the notion that continuity is a negligible—if not reprehensible—factor in human history. It is a vitally important ingredient in the life of individuals, organizations and societies."

In the light of theory of the adaptive range, it becomes clear that an insistence on continuity in our experience is not necessarily "reactionary," just as the demand for abrupt or discontinuous change is not necessarily "progressive." In stagnant societies, there is a deep psychological need for novelty and stimulation. In an accelerative society, the need may well be for the preservation of certain continuities.

In the past, ritual provided an important change-buffer. Anthropologists tell us that certain repeated ceremonial forms—rituals surrounding birth, death, puberty, marriage and so on—helped individuals in primitive societies to re-establish equilibrium after some major adaptive event had taken place.

"There is no evidence," writes S. T. Kimball, "that a secularized urban world has lessened the need for ritualized expression . . ." Carleton Coon declares that "Whole societies, whatever their sizes and degrees of complexity, need controls to ensure the maintenance of equilibrium, and control comes in several forms. One is ritual." He points out that ritual survives today in the public appearances of heads of state, in religion, in business.

These, however, represent the merest tip of the ritual iceberg. In Western societies, for example, the sending of Christmas cards is an annual ritual that not only represents continuity in its own right, but which helps individuals prolong their all-too-temporary friendships or acquaintanceships. The celebration of birthdays, holidays or anniversaries are additional examples. The fast-burgeoning greeting-card industry—2,248,000,000 Christmas cards are sold annually in the United States alone—is an economic monument to the society's continuing need for some semblance of ritual.

Repetitive behavior, whatever else its functions, helps give meaning to non-repetitive events, by providing the backdrop against which novelty is silhouetted. Sociologists James Bossard and Eleanor Boll, after examining one hundred published autobiographies, found seventy-three in which the writers described procedures which were "unequivocally classifiable as family rituals." These rituals, arising from "some simple or random bits of family interaction, started to set, because they were successful or satisfying to members, and through repetition they 'jelled' into very definite forms."

As the pace of change accelerates, many of these rituals are broken down or denatured. Yet we struggle to maintain them. One non-religious family periodically offers a secular grace at the dinner table, to honor such benefactors of mankind as Johann Sebastian Bach or Martin Luther King. Husbands and wives speak of "our song" and periodically revisit "the place we first met." In the future, we can anticipate greater variety in the kinds of rituals adhered to in family life.

As we accelerate and introduce arhythmic patterns into the pace of change, we need to mark off certain regularities for preservation, exactly the way we now mark off certain forests, historical monuments, or bird sanctuaries for protection. We may even need to manufacture ritual.

No longer at the mercy of the elements as we once were, no longer condemned to darkness at night or frost in the morning, no longer positioned in an unchanging physical environment, we are helped to orient ourselves in space and time by social, as distinct from natural, regularities.

In the United States, the arrival of spring is marked for most urban dwellers not by a sudden greenness —there is little green in Manhattan—but by the opening of the baseball season. The first ball is thrown by the President or some other dignitary, and thereafter millions of citizens follow, day by day, the unfolding of a mass ritual. Similarly, the end of summer is marked as much by the World Series as by any natural symbol.

Even those who ignore sports cannot help but be aware of these large and pleasantly predictable events. Radio and television carry baseball into every home. Newspapers are filled with sports news. Images of baseball form a backdrop, a kind of musical obbligato that enters our awareness. Whatever happens to the stock market, or to world politics, or to family life, the American League and the National League run through their expected motions. Outcomes of individual games vary. The standings of the teams go up and down. But the drama plays itself out within a set of reassuringly rigid and durable rules.

The opening of Congress every January; the appearance of new car models in the fall; seasonal variations in fashion; the April 15 deadline for filing income tax; the arrival of Christmas; the New Year's Eve party; the fixed national holidays. All these punctuate our time predictably, supplying a background of temporal regularity that is necessary (though hardly sufficient) for mental health.

The pressure of change, however, is to "unhitch" these from the calendar, to loosen and irregularize them. Often there are economic benefits for doing so. But there may also be hidden costs through the loss of stable temporal points of reference that today still lend some pattern and continuity to everyday life. Instead of eliminating these wholesale, we may wish to retain some, and, indeed, to introduce certain regularities where they do not exist. (Boxing championship matches are held at irregular, unpredictable times. Perhaps these highly ritualistic events should be held at fixed intervals as the Olympic games are.)

As leisure increases, we have the opportunity to introduce additional stability points and rituals into the society, such as new holidays, pageants and games. Such mechanisms could not only provide a backdrop of continuity in everyday life, but serve to integrate societies, and cushion them somewhat against the fragmenting impact of super-industrialism. We might, for example, create holidays to honor Galileo or Mozart, Einstein or Cézanne. We might create a global pageantry based on man's conquest of outer space.

Even now the succession of space launchings and capsule retrievals is beginning to take on a kind of ritual dramatic pattern. Millions stand transfixed as the countdown begins and the mission works itself out. For at least a fleeting instant, they share a realization of the oneness of humanity and its potential competence in the face of the universe.

By regularizing such events and by greatly adding to the pageantry that surrounds them, we can weave them into the ritual framework of the new society and use them as sanity-preserving points of temporal reference. Certainly, July 20, the day Astronaut Armstrong took "one small step for man, one giant leap for mankind," ought to be made into an annual global celebration of the unity of man.

In this way, by making use of new materials, as well as already existing rituals, by introducing change, wherever possible, in the form of predictable, rather than erratic chains of events, we can help provide elements of continuity even in the midst of social upheaval.

The cultural transformation of the Manus Islanders was simple compared with the one we face. We shall survive it only if we move beyond personal tactics to social strategies—providing new support services for the change-harassed individual, building continuity and change-buffers into the emergent civilization of tomorrow.

All this is aimed at minimizing the human damage wrought by rapid change. But there is another way of attacking the problem, too. This is to expand man's adaptive capacities—the central task of education during the Super-industrial Revolution.

Chapter 18

EDUCATION IN
THE FUTURE TENSE

In the quickening race to put men and machines on the planets, tremendous resources are devoted to making possible a "soft landing." Every sub-system of the landing craft is exquisitely designed to withstand the shock of arrival. Armies of engineers, geologists, physicists, metallurgists and other specialists concentrate years of work on the problem of landing impact. Failure of any sub-system to function after touch-down could destroy human lives, not to mention billions of dollars worth of apparatus and tens of thousands of man-years of labor.

Today one billion human beings, the total population of the technology-rich nations, are speeding toward a rendezvous with super-industrialism. Must we experience mass future shock? Or can we, too, achieve a "soft landing?" We are rapidly accelerating our approach. The craggy outlines of the new society are emerging from the mists of tomorrow. Yet even as we speed closer, evidence mounts that one of our most critical sub-systems—education—is dangerously malfunctioning.

What passes for education today, even in our "best" schools and colleges, is a hopeless anachronism. Parents look to education to fit their children for life in the future. Teachers warn that lack of an education will cripple a child's chances in the world of tomorrow. Government ministries, churches, the mass media —all exhort young people to stay in school, insisting that now, as never before, one's future is almost wholly dependent upon education.

Yet for all this rhetoric about the future, our schools face backward toward a dying system, rather than forward to the emerging new society. Their vast energies are applied to cranking out Industrial Men— people tooled for survival in a system that will be dead before they are.

To help avert future shock, we must create a super-industrial education system. And to do this, we must search for our objectives and methods in the future, rather than the past.

THE INDUSTRIAL ERA SCHOOL

Every society has its own characteristic attitude toward past, present and future. This time-bias, formed in response to the rate of change, is one of the least noticed, yet most powerful determinants of social behavior, and it is clearly reflected in the way the society prepares its young for adulthood.

In stagnant societies, the past crept forward into the present and repeated itself in the future. In such a society, the most sensible way to prepare a child was to arm him with the skills of the past—for these were precisely the same skills he would need in the future. "With the ancient is wisdom," the Bible admonished.

Thus father handed down to son all sorts of practical techniques along with a clearly defined, highly traditional set of values. Knowledge was transmitted not by specialists concentrated in schools, but through the family, religious institutions, and apprenticeships. Learner and teacher were dispersed throughout the entire community. The key to the system, however, was its absolute devotion to yesterday. The curriculum of the past was the past.

· The mechanical age smashed all this, for industrialism required a new kind of man. It demanded skills that neither family nor church could, by themselves, provide. It forced an upheaval in the value system. Above all, it required that man develop a new sense of time.

Mass education was the ingenious machine constructed by industrialism to produce the kind of adults it needed. The problem was inordinately complex. How to pre-adapt children for a new world—a world of repetitive indoor toil, smoke, noise, machines, crowded living conditions, collective discipline, a world in which time was to be regulated not by the cycle of sun and moon, but by the factory whistle and the clock.

The solution was an educational system that, in its very structure, simulated this new world. This system did not emerge instantly. Even today it retains throwback elements from pre-industrial society. Yet the whole idea of assembling masses of students (raw material) to be processed by teachers (workers) in a centrally located school (factory) was a stroke of industrial genius. The whole administrative hierarchy of education, as it grew up, followed the model of industrial bureaucracy. The very organization of knowledge into permanent disciplines was grounded on industrial assumptions. Children marched from place to place and sat in assigned stations. Bells rang to announce changes of time.

The inner life of the school thus became an anticipatory mirror, a perfect introduction to industrial society. The most criticized features of education today—the regimentation, lack of individualization, the rigid systems of seating, grouping, grading and marking, the authoritarian role of the teacher—are precisely those that made mass public education so effective an instrument of adaptation for its place and time.

Young people passing through this educati
machine emerged into an adult society whose structure of jobs, roles and institutions resembled that of
the school itself. The schoolchild did not simply
learn facts that he could use later on; he lived, as
well as learned, a way of life modeled after the one
he would lead in the future.

The schools, for example, subtly instilled the new
time-bias made necessary by industrialism. Faced
with conditions that had never before existed, men
had to devote increasing energy to understanding the
present. Thus the focus of education itself began to
shift, ever so slowly, away from the past and toward
the present.

The historic struggle waged by John Dewey and
his followers to introduce "progressive" measures into
American education was, in part, a desperate effort
to alter the old time-bias. Dewey battled against the
past-orientation of traditional education, trying to
refocus education on the here-and-now. "The way out
of scholastic systems that make the past an end in
itself," he declared, "is to make acquaintance with
the past a *means* of understanding the present."

Nevertheless, decades later traditionalists like
Jacques Maritain and neo-Aristotelians like Robert
Hutchins still lashed out against anyone who attempted to shift the balance in favor of the present. Hutchins, former president of the University of Chicago
and now head of the Center for the Study of Democratic Institutions, accused educators who wanted
their students to learn about modern society of being
members of a "cult of immediacy." The progressives
were accused of a dastardly crime: "presentism."

Echoes of this conflict over the time-bias persist
even now, in the writings, for example, of Jacques
Barzun, who insists that "It is . . . absurd to try educating . . . 'for' a present day that defies definition."
Thus our education systems had not yet fully adapted themselves to the industrial age when the need for
a new revolution—the super-industrial revolution—

burst upon them. And just as the progressives of yesterday were accused of "presentism," it is likely that
the education reformers of tomorrow will be accused
of "futurism." For we shall find that a truly super-
industrial education is only possible if we once more
shift our time-bias forward.

THE NEW EDUCATIONAL REVOLUTION

In the technological systems of tomorrow—fast, fluid
and self-regulating—machines will deal with the flow
of physical materials; men with the flow of information and insight. Machines will increasingly perform
the routine tasks; men the intellectual and creative
tasks. Machines and men both, instead of being concentrated in gigantic factories and factory cities, will
be scattered across the globe, linked together by
amazingly sensitive, near-instantaneous communications. Human work will move out of the factory and
mass office into the community and the home.

Machines will be synchronized, as some already
are, to the billionth of a second; men will be de-syn-
chronized. The factory whistle will vanish. Even the
clock, "the key machine of the modern industrial
age," as Lewis Mumford called it a generation ago,
will lose some of its power over human, as distinct
from purely technological, affairs. Simultaneously,
the organizations needed to control technology will
shift from bureaucracy to Ad-hocracy, from permanence to transience, and from a concern with the
present to a focus on the future.

In such a world, the most valued attributes of the
industrial era become handicaps. The technology of
tomorrow requires not millions of lightly lettered
men, ready to work in unison at endlessly repetitious
jobs, it requires not men who take orders in unblink-
ing fashion, aware that the price of bread is mechanical submission to authority, but men who can make
critical judgments, who can weave their way through

novel environments, who are quick to sp
lationships in the rapidly changing reality
men who, in C. P. Snow's compelling
the future in their bones."

Finally, unless we capture control of the accelerative
thrust—and there are few signs yet that we will—
tomorrow's individual will have to cope with even
more hectic change than we do today. For education
the lesson is clear: its prime objective must be to
increase the individual's "cope-ability"—the speed and
economy with which he can adapt to continual change.
And the faster the rate of change, the more attention
must be devoted to discerning the pattern of future
events.

It is no longer sufficient for Johnny to understand
the past. It is not even enough for him to understand
the present, for the here-and-now environment will
soon vanish. Johnny must learn to anticipate the directions and rate of change. He must, to put it technically,
learn to make repeated, probabilistic, increasingly
long-range assumptions about the future. And so must
Johnny's teachers.

To create a super-industrial education, therefore,
we shall first need to generate successive, alternative
images of the future—assumptions about the kinds of
jobs, professions, and vocations that may be needed
twenty to fifty years in the future; assumptions about
the kind of family forms and human relationships that
will prevail; the kinds of ethical and moral problems
that will arise; the kind of technology that will surround us and the organizational structures with which
we must mesh.

It is only by generating such assumptions, defining,
debating, systematizing and continually updating
them, that we can deduce the nature of the cognitive
and affective skills that the people of tomorrow will
need to survive the accelerative thrust.

In the United States there are now two federally
funded "education policy research centers"—one at
Syracuse University, another at Stanford Research In-

...itute—charged with scanning the horizon with these purposes in mind. In Paris, the Organization for Economic Cooperation and Development has recently created a division with similar responsibilities. A handful of people in the student movement have also begun to turn attention to the future. Yet these efforts are pitifully thin compared with the difficulty of shifting the time-bias of education. What is needed is nothing less than a future-responsive mass movement.

We must create a "Council of the Future" in every school and community: Teams of men and women devoted to probing the future in the interests of the present. By projecting "assumed futures," by defining coherent educational responses to them, by opening these alternatives to active public debate, such councils—similar in some ways to the "prognostic cells" advocated by Robert Jungk of the Technische Hochschule in Berlin—could have a powerful impact on education.

Since no group holds a monopoly of insight into tomorrow, these councils must be democratic. Specialists are vitally needed in them. But Councils of the Future will not succeed if they are captured by professional educators, planners, or any unrepresentative elite. Thus students must be involved from the very start—and not merely as co-opted rubber stamps for adult notions. Young people must help lead, if not, in fact, initiate, these councils so that "assumed futures" can be formulated and debated by those who will presumably invent and inhabit the future.

The council of the future movement offers a way out of the impasse in our schools and colleges. Trapped in an educational system intent on turning them into living anachronisms, today's students have every right to rebel. Yet attempts by student radicals to base a social program on a pastiche of nineteenth-century Marxism and early twentieth-century Freudianism have revealed them to be as resolutely chained to the past and present as their elders. The creation of future-oriented, future-shaping task forces in education could revolutionize the revolution of the young.

For those educators who recognize the bankruptcy of the present system, but remain uncertain about next steps, the council movement could provide purpose as well as power, through alliance with, rather than hostility toward, youth. And by attracting community and parental participation—businessmen, trade unionists, scientists, and others—the movement could build broad political support for the super-industrial revolution in education.

It would be a mistake to assume that the present-day educational system is unchanging. On the contrary, it is undergoing rapid change. But much of this change is no more than an attempt to refine the existent machinery, making it ever more efficient in pursuit of obsolete goals. The rest is a kind of Brownian motion, self-canceling, incoherent, directionless. What has been lacking is a consistent direction and a logical starting point.

The council movement could supply both. The direction is super-industrialism. The starting point: the future.

THE ORGANIZATIONAL ATTACK

Such a movement will have to pursue three objectives —to transform the organizational structure of our educational system, to revolutionize its curriculum, and to encourage a more future-focused orientation. It must begin by asking root questions about the status quo.

We have noted, for example, that the basic organization of the present school system parallels that of the factory. For generations, we have simply assumed that the proper place for education to occur is in a school. Yet if the new education is to simulate the society of tomorrow, should it take place in school at all?

As levels of education rise, more and more parents

are intellectually equipped to assume some responsibilities now delegated to the schools. Near Santa Monica, California, where the RAND Corporation has its headquarters, in the research belt around Cambridge, Massachusetts, or in such science cities as Oak Ridge, Los Alamos or Huntsville, many parents are clearly more capable of teaching certain subjects to their children than are the teachers in the local schools. With the move toward knowledge-based industry and the increase of leisure, we can anticipate a small but significant tendency for highly educated parents to pull their children at least partway out of the public education system, offering them home instruction instead.

This trend will be sharply encouraged by improvements in computer-assisted education, electronic video recording, holography and other technical fields. Parents and students might sign short-term "learning contracts" with the nearby school, committing them to teach-learn certain courses or course modules. Students might continue going to school for social and athletic activities or for subjects they cannot learn on their own or under the tutelage of parents or family friends. Pressures in this direction will mount as the schools grow more anachronistic, and the courts will find themselves deluged with cases attacking the present obsolete compulsory attendance laws. We may witness, in short, a limited dialectical swing back toward education in the home.

At Stanford, learning theorist Frederick J. McDonald has proposed a "mobile education" that takes the student out of the classroom not merely to observe but to participate in significant community activity.

In New York's Bedford-Stuyvesant District, a sprawling tension-ridden black slum, a planned experimental college would disperse its facilities throughout the stores, offices, and homes of a forty-five-block area, making it difficult to tell where the college ends and the community begins. Students would be taught skills by adults in the community as well as by regular faculty. Curricula would be shaped by students and community groups as well as professional educators. The former United States Commissioner of Education, Harold Howe, II, has also suggested the reverse: bringing the community into the school so that local stores, beauty parlors, printing shops, be given free space in the schools in return for free lessons by the adults who run them. This plan, designed for urban ghetto schools, could be given more bite through a different conception of the nature of the enterprises invited into the school: computer service bureaus, for example, architectural offices, perhaps even medical laboratories, broadcasting stations and advertising agencies.

Elsewhere, discussion centers on the design of secondary and higher education programs that make use of "mentors" drawn from the adult population. Such mentors would not only transmit skills, but would show how the abstractions of the textbook are applied in life. Accountants, doctors, engineers, businessmen, carpenters, builders and planners might all become part of an "outside faculty" in another dialectical swing, this time toward a new kind of apprenticeship.

Many similar changes are in the wind. They point, however tentatively, to a long overdue breakdown of the factory-model school.

This dispersal in geographical and social space must be accompanied by dispersal in time. The rapid obsolescence of knowledge and the extension of life span make it clear that the skills learned in youth are unlikely to remain relevant by the time old age arrives. Super-industrial education must therefore make provision for life-long education on a plug-in/plug-out basis.

If learning is to be stretched over a lifetime, there is reduced justification for forcing kids to attend school full time. For many young people, part-time schooling and part-time work at low-skill, paid and unpaid community service tasks will prove more satisfying and educational.

Such innovations imply enormous changes in instructional techniques as well. Today lectures still dominate the classroom. This method symbolizes the old top-down, hierarchical structure of industry. While still useful for limited purposes, lectures must inevitably give way to a whole battery of teaching techniques, ranging from role playing and gaming to computer-mediated seminars and the immersion of students in what we might call "contrived experiences." Experiential programming methods, drawn from recreation, entertainment and industry, developed by the psych-corps of tomorrow, will supplant the familiar, frequently brain-draining lecture. Learning may be maximized through the use of controlled nutrition or drugs to raise IQ, to accelerate reading, or to enhance awareness. Such changes and the technologies underlying them will facilitate basic change in the organizational pattern.

The present administrative structures of education, based on industrial bureaucracy, will simply not be able to cope with the complexities and rate of change inherent in the system just described. They will be forced to move toward ad-hocratic forms of organization merely to retain some semblance of control. More important, however, are the organizational implications for the classroom itself.

Industrial Man was machine-tooled by the schools to occupy a comparatively permanent slot in the social and economic order. Super-industrial education must prepare people to function in temporary organizations —the Ad-hocracies of tomorrow.

Today children who enter school quickly find themselves part of a standard and basically unvarying organizational structure: a teacher-led class. One adult and a certain number of subordinate young people, usually seated in fixed rows facing front, is the standardized basic unit of the industrial-era school. As they move, grade by grade, to the higher levels, they remain in this same fixed organizational frame. They gain no experience with other forms of organization, or with the problems of shifting from one organizational form to another. They get no training for role versatility.

Nothing is more clearly anti-adaptive. Schools of the future, if they wish to facilitate adaptation later in life, will have to experiment with far more varied arrangements. Classes with several teachers and a single student; classes with several teachers and a group of students; students organized into temporary task forces and project teams; students shifting from group work to individual or independent work and back—all these and their permutations will need to be employed to give the student some advance taste of the experience he will face later on when he begins to move through the impermanent organizational geography of super-industrialism.

Organizational goals for the Councils of the Future thus become clear: dispersal, decentralization, interpenetration with the community, ad-hocratic administration, a break-up of the rigid system of scheduling and grouping. When these objectives are accomplished, any organizational resemblance between education and the industrial-era factory will be purely coincidental.

YESTERDAY'S CURRICULUM TODAY

As for curriculum, the Councils of the Future, instead of assuming that every subject taught today is taught for a reason, should begin from the reverse premise: nothing should be included in a required curriculum unless it can be strongly justified in terms of the future. If this means scrapping a substantial part of the formal curriculum, so be it.

This is not intended as an "anti-cultural" statement or a plea for total destruction of the past. Nor does it suggest that we can ignore such basics as reading, writing and math. What it does mean is that tens of millions of children today are forced by law to spend precious hours of their lives grinding away at material whose future utility is highly questionable. (Nobody even claims it has much present utility.) Should they spend as much time as they do learning French, or Spanish or German? Are the hours spent on English maximally useful? Should all children be required to study algebra? Might they not benefit more from studying probability? Logic? Computer programming? Philosophy? Aesthetics? Mass communications?

Anyone who thinks the present curriculum makes sense is invited to explain to an intelligent fourteen-year-old why algebra or French or any other subject is essential for him. Adult answers are almost always evasive. The reason is simple: the present curriculum is a mindless holdover from the past.

Why, for example, must teaching be organized around such fixed disciplines as English, economics, mathematics or biology? Why not around stages of the human life cycle: a course on birth, childhood, adolescence, marriage, career, retirement, death. Or around contemporary social problems? Or around significant technologies of the past and future? Or around countless other imaginable alternatives?

The present curriculum and its division into air-tight compartments is not based on any well thought out conception of contemporary human needs. Still less is it based on any grasp of the future, any understanding of what skills Johnny will require to live in the hurricane's eye of change. It is based on inertia—and a bloody clash of academic guilds, each bent on aggrandizing its budget, pay scales and status.

This obsolete curriculum, furthermore, imposes standardization on the elementary and secondary schools. Youngsters are given little choice in determining what they wish to learn. Variations from school to school are minimal. The curriculum is nailed into place by the rigid entrance requirements of the colleges, which, in turn, reflect the vocational and social requirements of a vanishing society.

In fighting to update education, the prognostic cells

of the revolution must set themselves up as curriculum review boards. Attempts by the present educational leadership to revise the physics curriculum, or improve the methods for teaching English or math are piecemeal at best. While it may be important to preserve aspects of the present curriculum and to introduce changes gradually, we need more than haphazard attempts to modernize. We need a systematic approach to the whole problem.

These revolutionary review groups must not, however, set out to design a single all-purpose, permanent new curriculum. Instead, they must invent sets of temporary curricula—along with procedures for evaluation and renovation as time goes by. There must be a systematic way to make curricular changes without necessarily triggering bloody intramural conflict each time.

A fight must also be waged to alter the balance between standardization and variety in the curriculum. Diversity carried to its extreme could produce a non-society in which the lack of common frames of reference would make communication between people even more difficult than it is today. Yet the dangers of social fragmentation cannot be met by maintaining a highly homogeneous education system while the rest of the society races toward heterogeneity.

One way to resolve the conflict between the need for variety and the need for common reference points is to distinguish in education between "data," as it were, and "skills."

A DIVERSITY OF DATA

Society is differentiating. What is more, we shall never, no matter how refined our predictive tools become, be able to forecast the exact sequence of future states of the society. In this situation, it makes eminent good sense to hedge our educational bets. Just as genetic diversity favors the survival of species, educational diversity increases the odds for the survival of societies.

Instead of a standardized elementary and secondary school curriculum in which all students are essentially exposed to the same data base—the same history, math, biology, literature, grammar, foreign languages, etc.— the futurist movement in education must attempt to create widely diversified data offerings. Children should be permitted far greater choice than at present; they should be encouraged to taste a wide variety of short-term courses (perhaps two or three weeks in length) before making longer-term commitments. Each school should provide scores of optional subjects, all based on identifiable assumptions about future needs.

The range of subject matter should be broad enough so that apart from dealing with the "known" (i.e., highly probable) elements of the super-industrial future, some provision would be made for dealing with the unknown, the unexpected, the possible. We might do this by designing "contingency curricula"—educational programs aimed at training people to handle problems that not only do not exist now, but which may, in fact, never materialize. We need, for example, a wide range of specialists to cope with potentially calamitous, though perhaps unlikely, contingencies: back-contamination of the earth from the planets or stars, the need to communicate with extra-terrestrial life, monstrosities produced by genetic experimentation, etc.

Even now we should be training cadres of young people for life in submarine communities. Part of the next generation may well find itself living under the oceans. We should be taking groups of students out in submarines, teaching them to dive, introducing them to underwater housing materials, power requirements, the perils and promises involved in a human invasion of the oceans. And we should be doing this not merely with graduate students, but with children drawn from elementary schools, even the nurseries.

Simultaneously, other young people should be introduced to the wonders of outer space, living with or near the astronauts, learning about planetary environments, becoming as familiar with space technology as most teen-agers today are with that of the family car. Still others should be encouraged, not discouraged, from experimenting with communal and other family forms of the future. Such experimentation, under responsible supervision and constructively channeled, should be seen as part of an appropriate education, not as an interruption or negation of the learning process.

The principle of diversity will dictate fewer required courses, increasing choice among esoteric specialties. By moving in this direction and creating contingency curricula, the society can bank a wide range of skills, including some it may never have to use, but which it must have at its instant command in the event our highest probability assumptions about the future turn out to be mistaken.

The result of such a policy will be to produce far more individualized human beings, more differences among people, more varied ideas, political and social sub-systems, and more color.

A SYSTEM OF SKILLS

Unfortunately, this necessary diversification of data offerings will deepen the problems of overchoice in our lives. Any program of diversification must therefore be accompanied by strong efforts to create common reference points among people through a unifying system of skills. While all students *should not* study the same course, imbibe the same facts, or store the same sets of data, all students *should* be grounded in certain common skills needed for human communication and social integration.

If we assume a continuing rise in transience, novelty and diversity, the nature of some of these behavioral skills becomes clear. A powerful case can be made, for example, that the people who must live in super-industrial societies will need new skills in three crucial areas: learning, relating and choosing.

Learning. Given further acceleration, we can conclude that knowledge will grow increasingly perishable. Today's "fact" becomes tomorrow's "misinformation." This is no argument against learning facts or data—far from it. But a society in which the individual constantly changes his job, his place of residence, his social ties and so forth, places an enormous premium on learning efficiency. Tomorrow's schools must therefore teach not merely data, but ways to manipulate it. Students must learn how to discard old ideas, how and when to replace them. They must, in short, learn how to learn.

Early computers consisted of a "memory" or bank of data plus a "program" or set of instructions that told the machine how to manipulate the data. Large late-generation computer systems not only store greater masses of data, but multiple programs, so that the operator can apply a variety of programs to the same data base. Such systems also require a "master program" that, in effect, tells the machine which program to apply and when. The multiplication of programs and addition of a master program vastly increased the power of the computer.

A similar strategy can be used to enhance human adaptability. By instructing students how to learn, unlearn and relearn, a powerful new dimension can be added to education.

Psychologist Herbert Gerjuoy of the Human Resources Research Organization phrases it simply: "The new education must teach the individual how to classify and reclassify information, how to evaluate its veracity, how to change categories when necessary, how to move from the concrete to the abstract and back, how to look at problems from a new direction—how to teach himself. Tomorrow's illiterate will not be the man who can't read; he will be the man who has not learned how to learn."

Relating. We can also anticipate increasing difficulty in making and maintaining rewarding human ties, if life pace continues its acceleration.

Listening intently to what young people are saying makes it clear that the once-simple business of forging real friendships has already assumed new complexity for them. When students complain, for instance, that "people can't communicate," they are not simply referring to crossing the generational divide, but to problems they have among themselves as well. "New people in the last four days are all the ones that I remember," writes Rod McKuen, a songwriter and poet currently popular among the youth.

Once the transience factor is recognized as a cause of alienation, some of the superficially puzzling behavior of young people becomes comprehensible. Many of them, for example, regard sex as a quick way to "get to know someone." Instead of viewing sexual intercourse as something that follows a long process of relationship-building, they see it, rightly or not, as a shortcut to deeper human understanding.

The same wish to accelerate friendship helps explain their fascination with such psychological techniques as "sensitivity training," "T-grouping," "micro-labs," so-called "touchie-feelie" or non-verbal games, and the whole group dynamics phenomenon in general. Their enthusiasm for communal living, too, expresses the underlying sense of loneliness and inability to "open up" with others.

All these activities throw participants into intimate psychological contact without lengthy preparation, often without advance acquaintanceship. In many cases, the relationships are short-lived by design, the purpose of the game being to intensify affective relationships despite the temporariness of the situation.

By speeding the turnover of people in our lives, we allow less time for trust to develop, less time for friendships to ripen. Thus we witness a search for ways to cut through the polite "public" behavior directly to the sharing of intimacy.

One may doubt the effectiveness of these experimental techniques for breaking down suspicion and reserve, but until the rate of human turnover is substantially slowed, education must help people to accept the absence of deep friendships, to accept loneliness and mistrust—or it must find new ways to accelerate friendship formation. Whether by more imaginative grouping of students, or by organizing new kinds of work-teams, or through variations of the techniques discussed above, education will have to teach us to relate.

Choosing. If we also assume that the shift toward super-industrialism will multiply the kinds and complexities of decisions facing the individual, it becomes apparent that education must address the issue of overchoice directly.

Adaptation involves the making of successive choices. Presented with numerous alternatives, an individual chooses the one most compatible with his values. As overchoice deepens, the person who lacks a clear grasp of his own values (whatever these may be) is progressively crippled. Yet the more crucial the question of values becomes, the less willing our present schools are to grapple with it. It is no wonder that millions of young people trace erratic pathways into the future, ricocheting this way and that like unguided missiles.

In pre-industrial societies, where values are relatively stable, there is little question about the right of the older generation to impose its values on the young. Education concerns itself as much with the inculcation of moral values as with the transmission of skills. Even during early industrialism, Herbert Spencer maintained that "Education has for its object the formation of character," which, freely translated, means the seduction or terrorization of the young into the value systems of the old.

As the shock waves of the industrial revolution rattled the ancient architecture of values and new conditions demanded new values, educators backed off.

As a reaction against clerical education, teaching facts and "letting the student make up his own mind" came to be regarded as a progressive virtue. Cultural relativism and an appearance of scientific neutrality displaced the insistence on traditional values. Education clung to the rhetoric of character formation, but educators fled from the very idea of value inculcation, deluding themselves into believing that they were not in the value business at all.

Today it embarrasses many teachers to be reminded that all sorts of values are transmitted to students, if not by their textbooks then by the informal curriculum—seating arrangements, the school bell, age segregation, social class distinctions, the authority of the teacher, the very fact that students are in a school instead of the community itself. All such arrangements send unspoken messages to the student, shaping his attitudes and outlook. Yet the formal curriculum continues to be presented as though it were value-free. Ideas, events, and phenomena are stripped of all value implications, disembodied from moral reality.

Worse yet, students are seldom encouraged to analyze their own values and those of their teachers and peers. Millions pass through the education system without once having been forced to search out the contradictions in their own value systems, to probe their own life goals deeply, or even to discuss these matters candidly with adults and peers. Students hurry from class to class. Teachers and professors are harried and grow increasingly remote. Even the "bull session"—informal, extra-curricular discussions about sex, politics or religion that help participants identify and clarify their values—grow less frequent and less intimate as transience rises.

Nothing could be better calculated to produce people uncertain of their goals, people incapable of effective decision-making under conditions of overchoice. Super-industrial educators must not attempt to impose a rigid set of values on the student; but they must systematically organize formal and informal activities that help the student define, explicate and test his values, whatever they are. Our schools will continue to turn out industrial men until we teach young people the skills necessary to identify and clarify, if not reconcile, conflicts in their own value systems.

The curriculum of tomorrow must thus include not only an extremely wide range of data-oriented courses, but a strong emphasis on future-relevant behavioral skills. It must combine variety of factual content with universal training in what might be termed "life know-how." It must find ways to do both at the same time, transmitting one in circumstances or environments that produce the other.

In this way, by making definite assumptions about the future and designing organizational and curricular objectives based on them, the Councils of the Future can begin to shape a truly super-industrial education system. One final critical step remains, however. For it is not enough to refocus the *system* on the future. We must shift the time-bias of the *individual* as well.

THE STRATEGY OF FUTURENESS

Three hundred and fifty years after his death, scientists are still finding evidence to support Cervantes' succinct insight into adaptational psychology: "Forewarned fore-armed." Self-evident as it may seem, in most situations we can help individuals adapt better if we simply provide them with advance information about what lies ahead.

Studies of the reactions of astronauts, displaced families, and industrial workers almost uniformly point to this conclusion. "Anticipatory information," writes psychologist Hugh Bowen, "allows . . . a dramatic change in performance." Whether the problem is that of driving a car down a crowded street, piloting a plane, solving intellectual puzzles, playing a cello or dealing with interpersonal difficulties, performance improves when the individual knows what to expect next.

The mental processing of advance data about any subject presumably cuts down on the amount of processing and the reaction time during the actual period of adaptation. It was Freud, I believe, who said: "Thought is action in rehearsal."

Even more important than any specific bits of advance information, however, is the habit of anticipation. This conditioned ability to look ahead plays a key role in adaptation. Indeed, one of the hidden clues to successful coping may well lie in the individual's sense of the future. The people among us who keep up with change, who manage to adapt well, seem to have a richer, better developed sense of what lies ahead than those who cope poorly. Anticipating the future has become a habit with them. The chess player who anticipates the moves of his opponent, the executive who thinks in long range terms, the student who takes a quick glance at the table of contents before starting to read page one, all seem to fare better.

People vary widely in the amount of thought they devote to the future, as distinct from past and present. Some invest far more resources than others in projecting themselves forward—imagining, analyzing and evaluating future possibilities and probabilities. They also vary in how *far* they tend to project. Some habitually think in terms of the "deep future." Others penetrate only into the "shallow future."

We have, therefore, at least two dimensions of "futureness"—how much and how far. There is evidence that among normal teenagers maturation is accompanied by what sociologist Stephen L. Klineberg of Princeton describes as "an increasing concern with distant future events." This suggests that people of different ages characteristically devote different amounts of attention to the future. Their "time horizons" may also differ. But age is not the only influence on our futureness. Cultural conditioning affects it, and one of the most important cultural influences of all is the rate of change in the environment.

This is why the individual's sense of the future plays so critical a part in his ability to cope. The faster the pace of life, the more rapidly the present environment slips away from us, the more rapidly do future potentialities turn into present reality. As the environment churns faster, we are not only pressured to devote more mental resources to thinking about the future, but to extend our time horizon—to probe further and further ahead. The driver dawdling along an expressway at twenty miles per hour can successfully negotiate a turn into an exit lane, even if the sign indicating the cut-off is very close to the exit. The faster he drives, however, the further back the sign must be placed to give him the time needed to read and react. In quite the same way, the generalized acceleration of life compels us to lengthen our time horizon or risk being overtaken and overwhelmed by events. The faster the environment changes, the more the need for futureness.

Some individuals, of course, project themselves so far into the future for such long periods that their anticipations become escapist fantasies. Far more common, however, are those individuals whose anticipations are so thin and short-range that they are continually surprised and flustered by change.

The adaptive individual appears to be able to project himself forward just the "right" distance in time, to examine and evaluate alternative courses of action open to him before the need for final decision, and to make tentative decisions beforehand.

Studies by social scientists like Lloyd Warner in the United States and Elliott Jaques in Britain, for example, have shown how important this time element is in management decision-making. The man on the assembly line is given work that requires him to concern himself only with events close to him in time. The men who rise in management are expected, with each successive promotion, to concern themselves with events further in the future.

Sociologist Benjamin D. Singer of the University of Western Ontario, whose field is social psychiatry, has gone further. According to Singer, the future plays an enormous, largely unappreciated part in present behavior. He argues, for instance, that "the 'self' of the child is in part feedback from what it is toward what it is becoming." The target toward which the child is moving is his "future focused role image"—a conception of what he or she wishes to be like at various points in the future.

This "future focused role image," Singer writes, "tends . . . to organize and give meaning to the pattern of life he is expected to take. Where, however, there is only a hazily defined or functionally non-existent future role, then the meaning which is attached to behavior valued by the larger society does not exist; schoolwork becomes meaningless, as do the rules of middle-class society and of parental discipline."

Put more simply, Singer asserts that each individual carries in his mind not merely a picture of himself at present, a self-image, but a set of pictures of himself as he wishes to be in the future. "This person of the future provides a focus for the child; it is a magnet toward which he is drawn; the framework for the present, one might say, is created by the future."

One would think that education, concerned with the development of the individual and the enhancement of adaptability, would do all in its power to help children develop the appropriate time-bias, the suitable degree of futureness. Nothing could be more dangerously false.

Consider, for example, the contrast between the way schools today treat space and time. Every pupil, in virtually every school, is carefully helped to position himself in space. He is required to study geography. Maps, charts and globes all help pinpoint his spatial location. Not only do we locate him with respect to his city, region, or country, we even try to explain the spatial relationship of the earth to the rest of the solar system and, indeed, to the universe.

When it comes to locating the child in time, however, we play a cruel and disabling trick on him. He is steeped, to the extent possible, in his nation's past and that of the world. He studies ancient Greece and Rome, the rise of feudalism, the French Revolution, and so forth. He is introduced to Bible stories and patriotic legends. He is peppered with endless accounts of wars, revolutions and upheavals, each one dutifully tagged with its appropriate date in the past.

At some point he is even introduced to "current events." He may be asked to bring in newspaper clippings, and a really enterprising teacher may go so far as to ask him to watch the evening news on television. He is offered, in short, a thin sliver of the present.

And then time stops. The school is silent about tomorrow. "Not only do our history courses terminate with the year they are taught," wrote Professor Ossip Flechtheim a generation ago, "but the same situation exists in the study of government and economics, psychology and biology." Time comes racing to an abrupt halt. The student is focused backward instead of forward. The future, banned as it were from the classroom, is banned from his consciousness as well. It is as though there were no future.

This violent distortion of his time sense shows up in a revealing experiment conducted by psychologist John Condry, Professor in the Department of Human Development, Cornell University. In separate studies at Cornell and UCLA, Condry gave groups of students the opening paragraph of a story. This paragraph described a fictional "Professor Hoffman," his wife and their adopted Korean daughter. The daughter is found crying, her clothes torn, a group of other children staring at her. The students were asked to complete the story.

What the subjects did not know is that they had previously been divided into two groups. In the case of one group, the opening paragraph was set in the past. The characters "heard," "saw" or "ran." The students were asked to "Tell what Mr. and Mrs. Hoffman did and what was said by the children." For the second group, the paragraph was set entirely in the future tense. They were asked to "Tell what Mr. and Mrs. Hoffman will do and what will be said by the children." Apart from this shift of tense, both paragraphs and instructions were identical.

The results of the experiment were sharply etched. One group wrote comparatively rich and interesting story-endings, peopling their accounts with many characters, creatively introducing new situations and dialogue. The other produced extremely sketchy endings, thin, unreal and forced. The past was richly conceived; the future empty. "It is," Professor Condry commented, "as if we find it easier to talk about the past than the future."

If our children are to adapt more successfully to rapid change, this distortion of time must be ended. We must sensitize them to the possibilities and probabilities of tomorrow. We must enhance their sense of the future.

Society has many built-in time spanners that help to link the present generation with the past. Our sense of the past is developed by contact with the older generation, by our knowledge of history, by the accumulated heritage of art, music, literature, and science passed down to us through the years. It is enhanced by immediate contact with the objects that surround us, each of which has a point of origin in the past, each of which provides us with a trace of identification with the past.

No such time spanners enhance our sense of the future. We have no objects, no friends, no relatives, no works of art, no music or literature, that originate in the future. We have, as it were, no heritage of the future.

Despite this, there are ways to send the human mind arching forward as well as backward. We need to begin by creating a stronger future-consciousness on the part of the public, and not just by means of Buck Rogers comic strips, films like *Barbarella,* or articles about the marvels of space travel or medical research. These make a contribution, but what is needed is a concentrated focus on the social and personal implications of the future, not merely on its technological characteristics.

If the contemporary individual is going to have to cope with the equivalent of millennia of change within the compressed span of a single lifetime, he must carry within his skull reasonably accurate (even if gross) images of the future.

Medieval men possessed an image of the afterlife, complete with vivid mental pictures of heaven and hell. We need now to propagate dynamic, non-supernatural images of what temporal life will be like, what it will sound and smell and taste and feel like in the fast-onrushing future.

To create such images and thereby soften the impact of future shock, we must begin by making speculation about the future respectable. Instead of deriding the "crystal-ball gazer," we need to encourage people, from childhood on, to speculate freely, even fancifully, not merely about what next week holds in store for them but about what the next generation holds in store for the entire human race. We offer our children courses in history; why not also courses in "Future," courses in which the possibilities and probabilities of the future are systematically explored, exactly as we now explore the social system of the Romans or the rise of the feudal manor?

Robert Jungk, one of Europe's leading futurist-philosophers, has said: "Nowadays almost exclusive stress is laid on learning what has happened and has been done. Tomorrow . . . at least one third of all lectures and exercises ought to be concerned with scientific, technical, artistic and philosophical work in progress, anticipated crises and possible future answers to these challenges."

We do not have a literature *of* the future for use in these courses, but we do have literature *about* the future, consisting not only of the great utopias but also of contemporary science fiction. Science fiction is held in low regard as a branch of literature, and perhaps it deserves this critical contempt. But if we view it as a kind of sociology of the future, rather than as literature, science fiction has immense value as a mind-stretching force for the creation of the habit of anticipation. Our children should be studying Arthur C. Clarke, William Tenn, Robert Heinlein, Ray Bradbury and Robert Sheckley, not because these writers can tell them about rocket ships and time machines but, more important, because they can lead young minds through an imaginative exploration of the jungle of political, social, psychological, and ethical issues that will confront these children as adults. Science fiction should be required reading for Future I.

But students should not only read. Various games have been designed to educate young people and adults about future possibilities and probabilities. *Future*, a game distributed by Kaiser Aluminum and Chemical Corporation on the occasion of its twentieth anniversary, introduces players to various technological and social alternatives of the future, and forces them to choose among them. It reveals how technological and social events are linked to one another, encourages the player to think in probabilistic terms, and, with various modifications, can help clarify the role of values in decision-making. At Cornell, Professor José Villegas of the Department of Design and Environmental Analysis, has, with the aid of a group of students, created a number of games having to do with housing and community action in the future. Another game developed under his direction is devoted to elucidating the ways in which technology and values will interact in the world of tomorrow.

With younger children, other exercises are possible. To sharpen the individual's future-focused role image, students can be asked to write their own "future

autobiographies" in which they picture themselves
five, ten or twenty years in the future. By submitting
these to class discussion, by comparing different assumptions in them, contradictions in the child's own
projections can be identified and examined. At a time
when the self is being broken into successive selves,
this technique can be used to provide continuity for
the individual. If children at fifteen, for example, are
given the future autobiographies they themselves
wrote at age twelve, they can see how maturation has
altered their own images of the future. They can be
helped to understand how their values, talents, skills,
and knowledge have shaped their own possibilities.

Students, asked to imagine themselves several years
hence, might be reminded that their brothers, parents,
and friends will also be older, and asked to imagine
the "important others" in their lives as *they* will be.

Such exercises, linked with the study of probability
and simple methods of prediction that can be used in
one's personal life, can delineate and modify each
individual's conception of the future, both personal
and social. They can create a new individual time-
bias, a new sensitivity to tomorrow that will prove
helpful in coping with the exigencies of the present.

Among highly adaptive individuals, men and wom-
en who are truly alive in, and responsive to, their
times, there is a virtual nostalgia for the future. Not
an uncritical acceptance of all the potential horrors of
tomorrow, not a blind belief in change for its own
sake, but an overpowering curiosity, a drive to *know*
what will happen next.

This drive does strange and wonderful things. One
winter night I witnessed a poignant quiver run through
a seminar room when a white-haired man explained
to a group of strangers what had brought him there
to attend my class on the Sociology of the Future.
The group included corporate long-range planners,
staff from major foundations, publishers and research
centers. Each participant spieled off his reason for
attending. Finally, it was the turn of the little man in

the corner. He spoke in cracked, but eloquent English:

"My name is Charles Stein. I am a needle worker all my life. I am seventy-seven years old, and I want to get what I didn't get in my youth. I want to *know* about the future. I want to die an educated man!"

The abrupt silence that greeted this simple affirmation still rings in the ears of those present. Before this eloquence, all the armor of graduate degrees, corporate titles and prestigious rank fell. I hope Mr. Stein is still alive, enjoying his future, and teaching others, as he did us that night.

When millions share this passion about the future we shall have a society far better equipped to meet the impact of change. To create such curiosity and awareness is a cardinal task of education. To create an education that will create this curiosity is the third, and perhaps central, mission of the super-industrial revolution in the schools.

Education must shift into the future tense.

Chapter 19

TAMING TECHNOLOGY

Future shock—the disease of change—can be prevented. But it will take drastic social, even political action. No matter how individuals try to pace their lives, no matter what psychic crutches we offer them, no matter how we alter education, the society as a whole will still be caught on a runaway treadmill until we capture control of the accelerative thrust itself.

The high velocity of change can be traced to many factors. Population growth, urbanization, the shifting proportions of young and old—all play their part. Yet technological advance is clearly a critical node in the network of causes; indeed, it may be the node that activates the entire net. One powerful strategy in the battle to prevent mass future shock, therefore, involves the conscious regulation of technological advance.

We cannot and must not turn off the switch of technological progress. Only romantic fools babble about returning to a "state of nature." A state of nature is one in which infants shrivel and die for lack of elementary medical care, in which malnutrition stultifies the brain, in which, as Hobbes reminded us, the typical life is "poor, nasty, brutish, and short." To turn our back on technology would be not only stupid but immoral.

Given that a majority of men still figuratively live in the twelfth century, who are we even to contemplate throwing away the key to economic advance? Those who prate anti-technological nonsense in the name of some vague "human values" need to be asked "which humans?" To deliberately turn back the clock would be to condemn billions to enforced and permanent misery at precisely the moment in history when their liberation is becoming possible. We clearly need not less but more technology.

At the same time, it is undeniably true that we frequently apply new technology stupidly and selfishly. In our haste to milk technology for immediate economic advantage, we have turned our environment into a physical and social tinderbox.

The speed-up of diffusion, the self-reinforcing character of technological advance, by which each forward step facilitates not one but many additional further steps, the intimate link-up between technology and social arrangements—all these create a form of psychological pollution, a seemingly unstoppable acceleration of the pace of life.

This psychic pollution is matched by the industrial vomit that fills our skies and seas. Pesticides and herbicides filter into our foods. Twisted automobile carcasses, aluminum cans, non-returnable glass bottles and synthetic plastics form immense kitchen middens in our midst as more and more of our detritus resists decay. We do not even begin to know what to do with our radioactive wastes—whether to pump them into the earth, shoot them into outer space, or pour them into the oceans.

Our technological powers increase, but the side effects and potential hazards also escalate. We risk thermopollution of the oceans themselves, overheating them, destroying immeasurable quantities of marine life, perhaps even melting the polar icecaps. On land we concentrate such large masses of population in such small urban-technological islands, that we threaten to use up the air's oxygen faster than it can be

replaced, conjuring up the possibility of new Saharas
where the cities are now. Through such disruptions
of the natural ecology, we may literally, in the words
of biologist Barry Commoner, be "destroying this
planet as a suitable place for human habitation."

TECHNOLOGICAL BACKLASH

As the effects of irresponsibly applied technology become more grimly evident, a political backlash mounts.
An offshore drilling accident that pollutes 800 square
miles of the Pacific triggers a shock wave of indigna-
tion all over the United States. A multi-millionaire
industrialist in Nevada, Howard Hughes, prepares a
lawsuit to prevent the Atomic Energy Commission
from continuing its underground nuclear tests. In
Seattle, the Boeing Company fights growing public
clamor against its plans to build a supersonic jet
transport. In Washington, public sentiment forces a
reassessment of missile policy. At MIT, Wisconsin,
Cornell, and other universities, scientists lay down
test tubes and slide rules during a "research moratorium" called to discuss the social implications of
their work. Students organize "environmental teach-
ins" and the President lectures the nation about the
ecological menace. Additional evidences of deep concern over our technological course are turning up in
Britain, France and other nations.

We see here the first glimmers of an international
revolt that will rock parliaments and congresses in the
decades ahead. This protest against the ravages of
irresponsibly used technology could crystallize in
pathological form—as a future-phobic fascism with
scientists substituting for Jews in the concentration
camps. Sick societies need scapegoats. As the pressures
of change impinge more heavily on the individual and
the prevalence of future shock increases, this nightmarish outcome gains plausibility. It is significant

that a slogan scrawled on a wall by striking students in Paris called for "death to the technocrats!"

The incipient worldwide movement for control of technology, however, must not be permitted to fall into the hands of irresponsible technophobes, nihilists and Rousseauian romantics. For the power of the technological drive is too great to be stopped by Luddite paroxysms. Worse yet, reckless attempts to halt technology will produce results quite as destructive as reckless attempts to advance it.

Caught between these twin perils, we desperately need a movement for responsible technology. We need a broad political grouping rationally committed to further scientific research and technological advance—but on a selective basis only. Instead of wasting its energies in denunciations of The Machine or in negativistic criticism of the space program, it should formulate a set of positive technological goals for the future.

Such a set of goals, if comprehensive and well worked out, could bring order to a field now in total shambles. By 1980, according to Aurelio Peccei, the Italian economist and industrialist, combined research and development expenditures in the United States and Europe will run to $73 billion per year. This level of expense adds up to three-quarters of a trillion dollars per decade. With such large sums at stake, one would think that governments would plan their technological development carefully, relating it to broad social goals, and insisting on strict accountability. Nothing could be more mistaken.

"No one—not even the most brilliant scientist alive today—really knows where science is taking us," says Ralph Lapp, himself a scientist-turned-writer. "We are aboard a train which is gathering speed, racing down a track on which there are an unknown number of switches leading to unknown destinations. No single scientist is in the engine cab and there may be demons at the switch. Most of society is in the caboose looking backward."

It is hardly reassuring to learn that when the Organization for Economic Cooperation and Development issued its massive report on science in the United States, one of its authors, a former premier of Belgium, confessed: "We came to the conclusion that we were looking for something . . . which was not there: a science policy." The committee could have looked even harder, and with still less success, for anything resembling a conscious technological policy.

Radicals frequently accuse the "ruling class" or the "establishment" or simply "they" of controlling society in ways inimical to the welfare of the masses. Such accusations may have occasional point. Yet today we face an even more dangerous reality: many social ills are less the consequence of oppressive control than of oppressive lack of control. The horrifying truth is that, so far as much technology is concerned, no one is in charge.

SELECTING CULTURAL STYLES

So long as an industrializing nation is poor, it tends to welcome without argument any technical innovation that promises to improve economic output or material welfare. This is, in fact, a tacit technological policy, and it can make for extremely rapid economic growth. It is, however, a brutally unsophisticated policy, and as a result all kinds of new machines and processes are spewed into the society without regard for their secondary or long-range effects.

Once the society begins its take-off for super-industrialism, this "anything goes" policy becomes wholly and hazardously inadequate. Apart from the increased power and scope of technology, the options multiply as well. Advanced technology helps create overchoice with respect to available goods, cultural products, services, subcults and life styles. At the same time overchoice comes to characterize technology itself.

Increasingly diverse innovations are arrayed before

the society and the problems of selection grow more and more acute. The old simple policy, by which choices were made according to short-run economic advantage, proves dangerous, confusing, destabilizing.

Today we need far more sophisticated criteria for choosing among technologies. We need such policy criteria not only to stave off avoidable disasters, but to help us discover tomorrow's opportunities. Faced for the first time with technological overchoice, the society must now select its machines, processes, techniques and systems in groups and clusters, instead of one at a time. It must choose the way an individual chooses his life style. It must make super-decisions about its future.

Furthermore, just as an individual can exercise conscious choice among alternative life styles, a society today can consciously choose among alternative cultural styles. This is a new fact in history. In the past, culture emerged without premeditation. Today, for the first time, we can raise the process to awareness. By the application of conscious technological policy—along with other measures—we can contour the culture of tomorrow.

In their book, *The Year 2000*, Herman Kahn and Anthony Wiener list one hundred technical innovations "very likely in the last third of the twentieth century." These range from multiple applications of the laser to new materials, new power sources, new airborne and submarine vehicles, three-dimensional photography, and "human hibernation" for medical purposes. Similar lists are to be found elsewhere as well. In transportation, in communications, in every conceivable field and some that are almost inconceivable, we face an inundation of innovation. In consequence, the complexities of choice are staggering.

This is well illustrated by new inventions or discoveries that bear directly on the issue of man's

adaptability. A case in point is the so-called OLIVER*
that some computer experts are striving to develop to
help us deal with decision overload. In its simplest
form, OLIVER would merely be a personal computer
programmed to provide the individual with information and to make minor decisions for him. At this level,
it could store information about his friends' preferences for Manhattans or martinis, data about traffic
routes, the weather, stock prices, etc. The device could
be set to remind him of his wife's birthday—or to
order flowers automatically. It could renew his magazine subscriptions, pay the rent on time, order razor
blades and the like.

As computerized information systems ramify, moreover, it would tap into a worldwide pool of data
stored in libraries, corporate files, hospitals, retail
stores, banks, government agencies and universities.
OLIVER would thus become a kind of universal
question-answerer for him.

However, some computer scientists see much beyond this. It is theoretically possible to construct an
OLIVER that would analyze the content of its owner's
words, scrutinize his choices, deduce his value system,
update its own program to reflect changes in his
values, and ultimately handle larger and larger decisions for him.

Thus OLIVER would know how its owner would,
in all likelihood, react to various suggestions made at
a committee meeting. (Meetings could take place
among groups of OLIVERs representing their respec-
tive owners, without the owners themselves being
present. Indeed, some "computer-mediated" conferences of this type have already been held by the
experimenters.)

OLIVER would know, for example, whether its
owner would vote for candidate X, whether he would

---

* On-Line Interactive Vicarious Expediter and Responder.
The acronym was chosen to honor Oliver Selfridge, originator
of the concept.

contribute to charity Y, whether he would accept a dinner invitation from Z. In the words of one OLIVER enthusiast, a computer-trained psychologist: "If you are an impolite boor, OLIVER will know and act accordingly. If you are a marital cheater, OLIVER will know and help. For OLIVER will be nothing less than your mechanical alter ego." Pushed to the extremes of science fiction, one can even imagine pin-size OLIVERs implanted in baby brains, and used, in combination with cloning, to create living—not just mechanical—alter egos.

Another technological advance that could enlarge the adaptive range of the individual pertains to human IQ. Widely reported experiments in the United States, Sweden and elsewhere, strongly suggest that we may, within the foreseeable future, be able to augment man's intelligence and informational handling abilities. Research in biochemistry and nutrition indicate that protein, RNA and other manipulable properties are, in some still obscure way, correlated with memory and learning. A large-scale effort to crack the intelligence barrier could pay off in fantastic improvement of man's adaptability.

It may be that the historic moment is right for such amplifications of humanness, for a leap to a new super-human organism. But what are the consequences and alternatives? Do we want a world peopled with OLIVERs? When? Under what terms and conditions? Who should have access to them? Who should not? Should biochemical treatments be used to raise mental defectives to the level of normals, should they be used to raise the average, or should we concentrate on trying to breed super-geniuses?

In quite different fields, similar complex choices abound. Should we throw our resources behind a crash effort to achieve low-cost nuclear energy? Or should a comparable effort be mounted to determine the biochemical basis of aggression? Should we spend billions of dollars on a supersonic jet transport—or should these funds be deployed in the development of arti-

ficial hearts? Should we tinker with the human gene?
Or should we, as some quite seriously propose, flood
the interior of Brazil to create an inland ocean the size
of East and West Germany combined? We will soon,
no doubt, be able to put super-LSD or an anti-aggression additive or some Huxleyian soma into our breakfast foods. We will soon be able to settle colonists on
the planets and plant pleasure probes in the skulls of
our newborn infants. But should we? Who is to decide? By what human criteria should such decisions
be taken?

It is clear that a society which opts for OLIVER,
nuclear energy, supersonic transports, macroengineer-
ing on a continental scale, along with LSD and
pleasure probes, will develop a culture dramatically
different from the one that chooses, instead, to raise
intelligence, diffuse anti-aggression drugs and provide
low-cost artificial hearts.

Sharp differences would quickly emerge between
the society that presses technological advance selectively, and that which blindly snatches at the first
opportunity that comes along. Even sharper differences would develop between the society in which
the pace of technological advance is moderated and
guided to prevent future shock, and that in which
masses of ordinary people are incapacitated for rational decision-making. In one, political democracy
and broad-scale participation are feasible; in the other
powerful pressures lead toward political rule by a tiny
techno-managerial elite. Our choice of technologies,
in short, will decisively shape the cultural styles of
the future.

This is why technological questions can no longer
be answered in technological terms alone. They are
political questions. Indeed, they affect us more deeply
than most of the superficial political issues that occupy
us today. This is why we cannot continue to make
technological decisions in the old way. We cannot
permit them to be made haphazardly, independently
of one another. We cannot permit them to be dictated

by short-run economic considerations alone. We cannot permit them to be made in a policy vacuum. And we cannot casually delegate responsibility for such decisions to businessmen, scientists, engineers or administrators who are unaware of the profound consequences of their own actions.

TRANSISTORS AND SEX

To capture control of technology, and through it gain some influence over the accelerative thrust in general, we must, therefore, begin to submit new technology to a set of demanding tests before we unleash it in our midst. We must ask a whole series of unaccustomed questions about any innovation before giving it a clean bill of sale.

First, bitter experience should have taught us by now to look far more carefully at the potential physical side effects of any new technology. Whether we are proposing a new form of power, a new material, or a new industrial chemical, we must attempt to determine how it will alter the delicate ecological balance upon which we depend for survival. Moreover, we must anticipate its indirect effects over great distances in both time and space. Industrial waste dumped into a river can turn up hundreds, even thousands of miles away in the ocean. DDT may not show its effects until years after its use. So much has been written about this that it seems hardly necessary to belabor the point further.

Second, and much more complex, we must question the long-term impact of a technical innovation on the social, cultural and psychological environment. The automobile is widely believed to have changed the shape of our cities, shifted home ownership and retail trade patterns, altered sexual customs and loosened family ties. In the Middle East, the rapid spread of transistor radios is credited with having contributed to the resurgence of Arab nationalism. The birth control pill, the computer, the space effort, as well as the invention and diffusion of such "soft" technologies as systems analysis, all have carried significant social changes in their wake.

We can no longer afford to let such secondary social and cultural effects just "happen." We must attempt to anticipate them in advance, estimating, to the degree possible, their nature, strength and timing. Where these effects are likely to be seriously damaging, we must also be prepared to block the new technology. It is as simple as that. Technology cannot be permitted to rampage through the society.

It is quite true that we can never know all the effects of any action, technological or otherwise. But it is not true that we are helpless. It is, for example, sometimes possible to test new technology in limited areas, among limited groups, studying its secondary impacts before releasing it for diffusion. We could, if we were imaginative, devise living experiments, even volunteer communities, to help guide our technological decisions. Just as we may wish to create enclaves of the past where the rate of change is artificially slowed, or enclaves of the future in which individuals can pre-sample future environments, we may also wish to set aside, even subsidize, special high-novelty communities in which advanced drugs, power sources, vehicles, cosmetics, appliances and other innovations are experimentally used and investigated.

A corporation today will routinely field test a product to make sure it performs its primary function. The same company will market test the product to ascertain whether it will sell. But, with rare exception, no one post-checks the consumer or the community to determine what the human side effects have been. Survival in the future may depend on our learning to do so.

Even when life-testing proves unfeasible, it is still possible for us systematically to anticipate the distant effects of various technologies. Behavioral scientists are rapidly developing new tools, from mathematical modeling and simulation to so-called Delphi analyses, that permit us to make more informed judgments about the consequences of our actions. We are piecing together the conceptual hardware needed for the social evaluation of technology; we need but to make use of it.

Third, an even more difficult and pointed question: Apart from actual changes in the social structure, how will a proposed new technology affect the value system of the society? We know little about value structures and how they change, but there is reason to believe that they, too, are heavily impacted by technology. Elsewhere I have proposed that we develop a new profession of "value impact forecasters"—men and women trained to use the most advanced behavioral science techniques to appraise the value implications of proposed technology.

At the University of Pittsburgh in 1967 a group of distinguished economists, scientists, architects, planners, writers, and philosophers engaged in a day-long simulation intended to advance the art of value forecasting. At Harvard, the Program on Technology and Society has undertaken work relevant to this field. At Cornell and at the Institute for the Study of Science in Human Affairs at Columbia, an attempt is being made to build a model of the relationship between technology and values, and to design a game useful in analyzing the impact of one on the other. All these initiatives, while still extremely primitive, give promise of helping us assess new technology more sensitively than ever before.

Fourth and finally, we must pose a question that until now has almost never been investigated, and which is, nevertheless, absolutely crucial if we are to prevent widespread future shock. For each major technological innovation we must ask: What are its accelerative implications?

The problems of adaptation already far transcend the difficulties of coping with this or that invention or technique. Our problem is no longer the innovation, but the chain of innovations, not the supersonic transport, or the breeder reactor, or the ground effect machine, but entire inter-linked sequences of such innovations and the novelty they send flooding into the society.

Does a proposed innovation help us control the rate and direction of subsequent advance? Or does it tend to accelerate a host of processes over which we have no control? How does it affect the level of transience, the novelty ratio, and the diversity of choice? Until we systematically probe these questions, our attempts to harness technology to social ends—and to gain control of the accelerative thrust in general—will prove feeble and futile.

Here, then, is a pressing intellectual agenda for the social and physical sciences. We have taught ourselves to create and combine the most powerful of technologies. We have not taken pains to learn about their consequences. Today these consequences threaten to destroy us. We must learn, and learn fast.

A TECHNOLOGY OMBUDSMAN

The challenge, however, is not solely intellectual; it is political as well. In addition to designing new research tools—new ways to understand our environment —we must also design creative new political institutions for guaranteeing that these questions are, in fact, investigated; and for promoting or discouraging (perhaps even banning) certain proposed technologies. We need, in effect, a machinery for screening machines.

A key political task of the next decade will be to create this machinery. We must stop being afraid to exert systematic social control over technology. Responsibility for doing so must be shared by public agencies and the corporations and laboratories in which technological innovations are hatched.

Any suggestion for control over technology immediately raises scientific eyebrows. The specter of ham-handed governmental interference is invoked. Yet controls over technology need not imply limitations on the freedom to conduct research. What is at issue is not discovery but diffusion, not invention but application. Ironically, as sociologist Amitai Etzioni points out, "many liberals who have fully accepted Keynesian economic controls take a laissez-faire view of technology. Theirs are the arguments once used to defend laissez-faire economics: that any attempt to control technology would stifle innovation and initiative."

Warnings about overcontrol ought not be lightly ignored. Yet the consequences of lack of control may be far worse. In point of fact, science and technology are never free in any absolute sense. Inventions and the rate at which they are applied are both influenced by the values and institutions of the society that gives rise to them. Every society, in effect, does pre-screen technical innovations before putting them to wide-spread use.

The haphazard way in which this is done today, however, and the criteria on which selection is based, need to be changed. In the West, the basic criterion for filtering out certain technical innovations and ap-plying others remains economic profitability. In com-munist countries, the ultimate tests have to do with whether the innovation will contribute to overall eco-nomic growth and national power. In the former, decisions are private and pluralistically decentralized. In the latter, they are public and tightly centralized.

Both systems are now obsolete—incapable of dealing with the complexity of super-industrial society. Both tend to ignore all but the most immediate and obvious consequences of technology. Yet, increasingly, it is these non-immediate and non-obvious impacts that must concern us. "Society must so organize itself that a proportion of the very ablest and most imaginative of scientists are continually concerned with trying to foresee the long-term effects of new technology," writes O. M. Solandt, chairman of the Science Council of Canada. "Our present method of depending on the alertness of individuals to foresee danger and to form pressure groups that try to correct mistakes will not do for the future."

One step in the right direction would be to create a technological ombudsman—a public agency charged with receiving, investigating, and acting on complaints having to do with the irresponsible application of technology.

Who should be responsible for correcting the adverse effects of technology? The rapid diffusion of detergents used in home washing machines and dishwashers intensified water purification problems all over the United States. The decisions to launch detergents on the society were privately taken, but the side effects have resulted in costs borne by the taxpayer and (in the form of lower water quality) by the consumer at large.

The costs of air pollution are similarly borne by taxpayer and community even though, as is often the case, the sources of pollution are traceable to individual companies, industries or government installations. Perhaps it is sensible for de-pollution costs to be borne by the public as a form of social overhead, rather than by specific industries. There are many ways to allocate the cost. But whichever way we choose, it is absolutely vital that the lines of responsibility are made clear. Too often no agency, group or institution has clear responsibility.

A technology ombudsman could serve as an official sounding board for complaints. By calling press attention to companies or government agencies that have applied new technology irresponsibly or without adequate forethought, such an agency could exert pressure for more intelligent use of new technology. Armed with the power to initiate damage suits where necessary, it could become a significant deterrent to technological irresponsibility.

THE ENVIRONMENTAL SCREEN

But simply investigating and apportioning responsibility after the fact is hardly sufficient. We must create an environmental screen to protect ourselves against dangerous intrusions as well as a system of public incentives to encourage technology that is both safe and socially desirable. This means governmental and private machinery for reviewing major technological advances *before* they are launched upon the public.

Corporations might be expected to set up their own "consequence analysis staffs" to study the potential effects of the innovations they sponsor. They might, in some cases, be required not merely to test new technology in pilot areas but to make a public report about its impact before being permitted to spread the innovation through the society at large. Much responsibility should be delegated to industry itself. The less centralized the controls the better. If self-policing works, it is preferable to external, political controls.

Where self-regulation fails, however, as it often does, public intervention may well be necessary, and we should not evade the responsibility. In the United States, Congressman Emilio Q. Daddario, chairman of the House Subcommittee on Science, Research and Development, has proposed the establishment of a Technology Assessment Board within the federal government. Studies by the National Academy of Sciences, the National Academy of Engineering, the Legislative Reference Service of the Library of Congress, and by the science and technology program of the George Washington University are all aimed at defining the appropriate nature of such an agency. We may wish to debate its form; its need is beyond dispute.

The society might also set certain general principles for technological advance. Where the introduction of an innovation entails undue risk, for example, it might require that funds be set aside by the responsible agency for correction of adverse effects should they materialize. We might also create a "technological insurance pool" to which innovation-diffusing agencies might pay premiums.

Certain large-scale ecological interventions might be delayed or prohibited altogether—perhaps in line with the principle that if an incursion on nature is too big and sudden for its effects to be monitored and possibly corrected, it should not take place. For example, it has been suggested that the Aswan Dam, far from helping Egyptian agriculture, might someday lead to salinization of the land on both banks of the Nile. This could prove disastrous. But such a process would not occur overnight. Presumably, therefore, it can be monitored and prevented. By contrast, the plan to flood the entire interior of Brazil is fraught with such instant and imponderable ecological effects that it should not be permitted at all until adequate monitoring can be done and emergency corrective measures are available.

At the level of social consequences, a new technology might be submitted for clearance to panels of behavioral scientists—psychologists, sociologists, economists, political scientists—who would determine, to the best of their ability, the probable strength of its social impact at different points in time. Where an innovation appears likely to entail seriously disruptive consequences, or to generate unrestrained accelerative pressures, these facts need to be weighed in a social cost-benefit accounting procedure. In the case of some high-impact innovations, the technological appraisal agency might be empowered to seek restraining legislation, or to obtain an injunction forcing delay until full public discussion and study is completed. In other cases, such innovations might still be released for diffusion—provided ample steps were taken in advance to offset their negative consequences. In this way, the society would not need to wait for disaster before dealing with its technology-induced problems.

By considering not merely specific technologies,

but their relationship to one another, the time lapse between them, the proposed speed of diffusion, and similar factors, we might eventually gain some control over the pace of change as well as its direction.

Needless to say, these proposals are themselves fraught with explosive social consequences, and need careful assessment. There may be far better ways to achieve the desired ends. But the time is late. We simply can no longer afford to hurtle blindfolded toward super-industrialism. The politics of technology control will trigger bitter conflict in the days to come. But conflict or no, technology must be tamed, if the accelerative thrust is to be brought under control. And the accelerative thrust must be brought under control, if future shock is to be prevented.

Chapter 20

THE STRATEGY
OF SOCIAL FUTURISM

Can one live in a society that is out of control? That
is the question posed for us by the concept of future
shock. For that is the situation we find ourselves in.
If it were technology alone that had broken loose, our
problems would be serious enough. The deadly fact is,
however, that many other social processes have also
begun to run free, oscillating wildly, resisting our best
efforts to guide them.

Urbanization, ethnic conflict, migration, population,
crime—a thousand examples spring to mind of fields
in which our efforts to shape change seem increasingly
inept and futile. Some of these are strongly related to
the breakaway of technology; others partially independent of it. The uneven, rocketing rates of change,
the shifts and jerks in direction, compel us to ask
whether the techno-societies, even comparatively small
ones like Sweden and Belgium, have grown too complex, too fast to manage?

How can we prevent mass future shock, selectively
adjusting the tempos of change, raising or lowering
levels of stimulation, when governments—including
those with the best intentions—seem unable even to
point change in the right direction?

Thus a leading American urbanologist writes with
unconcealed disgust: "At a cost of more than three

billion dollars, the Urban Renewal Agency has succeeded in materially reducing the supply of low cost housing in American cities." Similar debacles could be cited in a dozen fields. Why do welfare programs today often cripple rather than help their clients? Why do college students, supposedly a pampered elite, riot and rebel? Why do expressways add to traffic congestion rather than reduce it? In short, why do so many well-intentioned liberal programs turn rancid so rapidly, producing side effects that cancel out their central effects? No wonder Raymond Fletcher, a frustrated Member of Parliament in Britain, recently complained: "Society's gone random!"

If random means a literal absence of pattern, he is, of course, overstating the case. But if random means that the outcomes of social policy have become erratic and hard to predict, he is right on target. Here, then, is the political meaning of future shock. For just as individual future shock results from an inability to keep pace with the rate of change, governments, too, suffer from a kind of collective future shock—a breakdown of their decisional processes.

With chilling clarity, Sir Geoffrey Vickers, the eminent British social scientist, has identified the issue: "The rate of change increases at an accelerating speed, without a corresponding acceleration in the rate at which further responses can be made; and this brings us nearer the threshold beyond which control is lost."

THE DEATH OF TECHNOCRACY

What we are witnessing is the beginning of the final breakup of industrialism and, with it, the collapse of technocratic planning. By technocratic planning, I do not mean only the centralized national planning that has, until recently, characterized the USSR, but also the less formal, more dispersed attempts at systematic change management that occur in all the high technology nations, regardless of their political persuasion.

Michael Harrington, the socialist critic, arguing that we have rejected planning, has termed ours the "accidental century." Yet, as Galbraith demonstrates, even within the context of a capitalist economy, the great corporations go to enormous lengths to rationalize production and distribution, to plan their future as best they can. Governments, too, are deep into the planning business. The Keynesian manipulation of post-war economies may be inadequate, but it is not a matter of accident. In France, *Le Plan* has become a regular feature of national life. In Sweden, Italy, Germany and Japan, governments actively intervene in the economic sector to protect certain industries, to capitalize others, and to accelerate growth. In the United States and Britain, even local governments come equipped with what are at least *called* planning departments.

Why, therefore, despite all these efforts, should the system be spinning out of control? The problem is not simply that we plan too little; we also plan too poorly. Part of the trouble can be traced to the very premises implicit in our planning.

First, technocratic planning, itself a product of industrialism, reflects the values of that fast-vanishing era. In both its capitalist and communist variants, industrialism was a system focused on the maximization of material welfare. Thus, for the technocrat, in Detroit as well as Kiev, economic advance is the primary aim; technology the primary tool. The fact that in one case the advance redounds to private advantage and in the other, theoretically, to the public good, does not alter the core assumptions common to both. Technocratic planning is *econocentric*.

Second, technocratic planning reflects the time-bias of industrialism. Struggling to free itself from the stifling past-orientation of previous societies, industrialism focused heavily on the present. This meant, in practice, that its planning dealt with futures near at hand. The idea of a five-year plan struck the world as insanely futuristic when it was first put forward by the Soviets in the 1920's. Even today, except in the most advanced organizations on both sides of the ideological curtain, one- or two-year forecasts are regarded as "long-range planning." A handful of corporations and government agencies, as we shall see, have begun to concern themselves with horizons ten, twenty, even fifty years in the future. The majority, however, remain blindly biased toward next Monday. Technocratic planning is *short-range*.

Third, reflecting the bureaucratic organization of industrialism, technocratic planning was premised on hierarchy. The world was divided into manager and worker, planner and plannee, with decisions made by one for the other. This system, adequate while change unfolds at an industrial tempo, breaks down as the pace reaches super-industrial speeds. The increasingly unstable environment demands more and more nonprogrammed decisions down below; the need for instant feedback blurs the distinction between line and staff; and hierarchy totters. Planners are too remote, too ignorant of local conditions, too slow in responding to change. As suspicion spreads that top-down controls are unworkable, plannees begin clamoring for the right to participate in the decision-making. Planners, however, resist. For like the bureaucratic system it mirrors, technocratic planning is essentially *undemocratic*.

The forces sweeping us toward super-industrialism can no longer be channeled by these bankrupt industrial-era methods. For a time they may continue to work in backward, slowly moving industries or communities. But their misapplication in advanced industries, in universities, in cites—wherever change is swift —cannot but intensify the instability, leading to wilder and wilder swings and lurches. Moreover, as the evidences of failure pile up, dangerous political, cultural and psychological currents are set loose.

One response to the loss of control, for example, is a revulsion against intelligence. Science first gave man a sense of mastery over his environment, and hence over the future. By making the future seem malleable, instead of immutable, it shattered the opiate religions that preached passivity and mysticism. Today, mounting evidence that society is out of control breeds disillusionment with science. In consequence, we witness a garish revival of mysticism. Suddenly astrology is the rage. Zen, yoga, seances, and witchcraft become popular pastimes. Cults form around the search for Dionysian experience, for non-verbal and supposedly nonlinear communication. We are told it is more important to "feel" than to "think," as though there were a contradiction between the two. Existentialist oracles join Catholic mystics, Jungian psychoanalysts, and Hindu gurus in exalting the mystical and emotional against the scientific and rational.

This reversion to pre-scientific attitudes is accompanied, not surprisingly, by a tremendous wave of nostalgia in the society. Antique furniture, posters from a bygone era, games based on the remembrance of yesterday's trivia, the revival of Art Nouveau, the spread of Edwardian styles, the rediscovery of such faded pop-cult celebrities as Humphrey Bogart or W. C. Fields, all mirror a psychological lust for the simpler, less turbulent past. Powerful fad machines spring into action to capitalize on this hunger. The nostalgia business becomes a booming industry.

The failure of technocratic planning and the consequent sense of lost control also feeds the philosophy of "now-ness." Songs and advertisements hail the appearance of the "now generation," and learned psychiatrists, discoursing on the presumed dangers of repression, warn us not to defer our gratifications. Acting out and a search for immediate payoff are encouraged. "We're more oriented to the present," says a teen-age girl to a reporter after the mammoth Woodstock rock music festival. "It's like do what you want to do now. . . . If you stay anywhere very long you get into a planning thing. . . . So you just move on." Spontaneity, the personal equivalent of social planlessness, is elevated into a cardinal psychological virtue.

All this has its political analog in the emergence of a strange coalition of right wingers and New Leftists in support of what can only be termed a "hang loose" approach to the future. Thus we hear increasing calls for anti-planning or non-planning, sometimes euphemized as "organic growth." Among some radicals, this takes on an anarchist coloration. Not only is it regarded as unnecessary or unwise to make long-range plans for the future of the institution or society they wish to overturn, it is sometimes even regarded as poor taste to plan the next hour and a half of a meeting. Planlessness is glorified.

Arguing that planning imposes values on the future, the anti-planners overlook the fact that non-planning does so, too—often with far worse consequence. Angered by the narrow, econocentric character of technocratic planning, they condemn systems analysis, cost benefit accounting, and similar methods, ignoring the fact that, used differently, these very tools might be converted into powerful techniques for humanizing the future.

When critics charge that technocratic planning is anti-human, in the sense that it neglects social, cultural and psychological values in its headlong rush to maximize economic gain, they are usually right. When they charge that it is shortsighted and undemocratic, they are usually right. When they charge it is inept, they are usually right.

But when they plunge backward into irrationality, anti-scientific attitudes, a kind of sick nostalgia, and an exaltation of now-ness, they are not only wrong, but dangerous. Just as, in the main, their alternatives to industrialism call for a return to pre-industrial institutions, their alternative to technocracy is not post-, but pre-technocracy.

Nothing could be more dangerously maladaptive. Whatever the theoretical arguments may be, brute forces are loose in the world. Whether we wish to prevent future shock or control population, to check pollution or defuse the arms race, we cannot permit decisions of earth-jolting importance to be taken heedlessly, witlessly, planlessly. To hang loose is to commit collective suicide.

We need not a reversion to the irrationalisms of the past, not a passive acceptance of change, not despair or nihilism. We need, instead, a strong new strategy. For reasons that will become clear, I term this strategy "social futurism." I am convinced that, armed with this strategy, we can arrive at a new level of competence in the management of change. We can invent a form of planning more humane, more far-sighted, and more democratic than any so far in use. In short, we can transcend technocracy.

THE HUMANIZATION OF THE PLANNER

Technocrats suffer from econo-think. Except during war and dire emergency, they start from the premise that even non-economic problems can be solved with economic remedies.

Social futurism challenges this root assumption of both Marxist and Keynesian managers. In its historical time and place, industrial society's single-minded pursuit of material progress served the human race well. As we hurtle toward super-industrialism, however, a new ethos emerges in which other goals begin to gain parity with, and even supplant those of economic welfare. In personal terms, self-fulfillment, social responsibility, aesthetic achievement, hedonistic individualism, and an array of other goals vie with and often overshadow the raw drive for material success. Affluence serves as a base from which men begin to strive for varied post-economic ends.

At the same time, in societies arrowing toward super-industrialism, economic variables—wages, balance of payments, productivity—grow increasingly sensitive to changes in the non-economic environment. Economic problems are plentiful, but a whole range of issues that are only secondarily economic break into prominence. Racism, the battle between the generations, crime, cultural autonomy, violence— all these have economic dimensions; yet none can be effectively treated by econocentric measures alone.

The move from manufacturing to service production, the psychologization of both goods and services, and ultimately the shift toward experiential production all tie the economic sector much more tightly to non-economic forces. Consumer preferences turn over in accordance with rapid life style changes, so that the coming and going of subcults is mirrored in economic turmoil. Super-industrial production requires workers skilled in symbol manipulation, so that what goes on in their heads becomes much more important than in the past, and much more dependent upon cultural factors.

There is even evidence that the financial system is becoming more responsive to social and psychological pressures. It is only in an affluent society on its way to super-industrialism that one witnesses the invention of new investment vehicles, such as mutual funds, that are consciously motivated or constrained by non-economic considerations. The Vanderbilt Mutual Fund and the Provident Fund refuse to invest in liquor or tobacco shares. The giant Mates Fund spurns the stock of any company engaged in munitions production, while the tiny Vantage 10/90 Fund invests part of its assets in industries working to alleviate food and population problems in developing nations. There are funds that invest only, or primarily, in racially integrated housing. The Ford Foundation and the Presbyterian Church both invest part of their sizeable portfolios in companies selected not for economic payout alone, but for their potential contribution to solving urban problems. Such developments, still small in number, accurately signal the direction of change.

In the meantime, major American corporations

with fixed investments in urban centers, are being
sucked, often despite themselves, into the roaring vor-
tex of social change. Hundreds of companies are now
involved in providing jobs for hard-core unemployed,
in organizing literacy and job-training programs, and
in scores of other unfamiliar activities. So important
have these new involvements grown that the largest
corporation in the world, the American Telephone
and Telegraph Company, recently set up a Department of Environmental Affairs. A pioneering venture,
this agency has been assigned a range of tasks that
include worrying about air and water pollution, improving the aesthetic appearance of the company's
trucks and equipment, and fostering experimental pre-
school learning programs in urban ghettos. None of
this necessarily implies that big companies are growing altruistic; it merely underscores the increasing intimacy of the links between the economic sector and
powerful cultural, psychological and social forces.

While these forces batter at our doors, however,
most technocratic planners and managers behave as
though nothing had happened. They continue to act
as though the economic sector were hermetically
sealed off from social and psychocultural influences.
Indeed, econocentric premises are buried so deeply
and held so widely in both the capitalist and communist nations, that they distort the very information
systems essential for the management of change.

For example, all modern nations maintain elaborate machinery for measuring economic performance.
We know virtually day by day the directions of
change with respect to productivity, prices, investment, and similar factors. Through a set of "economic
indicators" we gauge the overall health of the economy, the speed at which it is changing, and the overall directions of change. Without these measures, our
control of the economy would be far less effective.

By contrast, we have no such measures, no set of
comparable "social indicators" to tell us whether the
society, as distinct from the economy, is also healthy.

We have no measures of the "quality of life." We have no systematic indices to tell us whether men are more or less alienated from one another; whether education is more effective; whether art, music and literature are flourishing; whether civility, generosity or kindness are increasing. "Gross National Product is our Holy Grail," writes Stewart Udall, former United States Secretary of the Interior, ". . . but we have no environmental index, no census statistics to measure whether the country is more livable from year to year."

On the surface, this would seem a purely technical matter—something for statisticians to debate. Yet it has the most serious political significance, for lacking such measures it becomes difficult to connect up national or local policies with appropriate long-term social goals. The absence of such indices perpetuates vulgar technocracy.

Little known to the public, a polite, but increasingly bitter battle over this issue has begun in Washington. Technocratic planners and economists see in the social indicators idea a threat to their entrenched position at the ear of the political policy maker. In contrast, the need for social indicators has been eloquently argued by such prominent social scientists as Bertram M. Gross of Wayne State University, Eleanor Sheldon and Wilbert Moore of the Russell Sage Foundation, Daniel Bell and Raymond Bauer of Harvard. We are witnessing, says Gross, a "widespread rebellion against what has been called the 'economic philistinism' of the United States government's present statistical establishment."

This revolt has attracted vigorous support from a small group of politicians and government officials who recognize our desperate need for a post-technocratic social intelligence system. These include Daniel P. Moynihan, a key White House adviser; Senators Walter Mondale of Minnesota and Fred Harris of Oklahoma; and several former Cabinet officers. In the near future, we can expect the same revolt to break out in other world capitals as well, once again drawing a line between technocrats and post-techno-crats.

The danger of future shock, itself, however, points to the need for new social measures not yet even mentioned in the fast-burgeoning literature on social indicators. We urgently need, for example, techniques for measuring the level of transience in different communities, different population groups, and in individual experience. It is possible, in principle, to design a "transience index" that could disclose the rate at which we are making and breaking relation-ships with the things, places, people, organizations and informational structures that comprise our en-vironment.

Such an index would reveal, among other things, the fantastic differences in the experiences of different groups in the society—the static and tedious quality of life for very large numbers of people, the frenetic turnover in the lives of others. Government policies that attempt to deal with both kinds of people in the same way are doomed to meet angry resistance from one or the other—or both.

Similarly, we need indices of novelty in the environ-ment. How often do communities, organizations or individuals have to cope with first-time situations? How many of the articles in the home of the average working-class family are actually "new" in function or appearance; how many are traditional? What level of novelty—in terms of things, people or any other significant dimension—is required for stimulation without over-stimulation? How much more novelty can children absorb than their parents—if it is true that they can absorb more? In what way is aging re-lated to lower novelty tolerances, and how do such differences correlate with the political and intergen-erational conflict now tearing the techno-societies apart? By studying and measuring the invasion of newness, we can begin, perhaps, to control the influx of change into our social structures and personal lives.

And what about choice and overchoice? Can we construct measures of the degree of significant choice in human lives? Can any government that pretends to be democratic not concern itself with such an issue? For all the rhetoric about freedom of choice, no government agency in the world can claim to have made any attempt to measure it. The assumption simply is that more income or affluence means more choice and that more choice, in turn, means freedom. Is it not time to examine these basic assumptions of our political systems? Post-technocratic planning must deal with precisely such issues, if we are to prevent future shock and build a humane super-industrial society.

A sensitive system of indicators geared to measuring the achievement of social and cultural goals, and integrated with economic indicators, is part of the technical equipment that any society needs before it can successfully reach the next stage of eco-technological development. It is an absolute precondition for post-technocratic planning and change management.

This humanization of planning, moreover, must be reflected in our political structures as well. To connect the super-industrial social intelligence system with the decisional centers of society, we must institutionalize a concern for the quality of life. Thus Bertram Gross and others in the social indicators movement have proposed the creation of a Council of Social Advisers to the President. Such a Council, as they see it, would be modeled after the already existing Council of Economic Advisers and would perform parallel functions in the social field. The new agency would monitor key social indicators precisely the way the CEA keeps its eye on economic indices, and interpret changes to the President. It would issue an annual report on the quality of life, clearly spelling out our social progress (or lack of it) in terms of specified

goals. This report would thus supplement and balance
the annual economic report prepared by the CEA. By
providing reliable, useful data about our social condition, the Council of Social Advisers would begin
to influence planning generally, making it more sensitive to social costs and benefits, less coldly technocratic and econocentric.*

The establishment of such councils, not merely at
the federal level but at state and municipal levels
as well, would not solve all our problems; it would
not eliminate conflict; it would not guarantee that
social indicators are exploited properly. In brief, it
would not eliminate politics from political life. But it
would lend recognition—and political force—to the
idea that the aims of progress reach beyond economics. The designation of agencies to watch over the
indicators of change in the quality of life would carry
us a long way toward that humanization of the planner which is the essential first stage of the strategy of
social futurism.

TIME HORIZONS

Technocrats suffer from myopia. Their instinct is to
think about immediate returns, immediate consequences. They are premature members of the now
generation.

If a region needs electricity, they reach for a power
plant. The fact that such a plant might sharply alter
labor patterns, that within a decade it might throw
men out of work, force large-scale retraining of workers, and swell the social welfare costs of a nearby city
—such considerations are too remote in time to concern them. The fact that the plant could trigger

---

* Proponents differ as to whether the Council of Social Advisers ought to be organizationally independent or become a
part of a larger Council of Economic *and* Social Advisers. All
sides agree, however, on the need for integrating economic and
social intelligence.

devastating ecological consequences a generation later simply does not register in their time frame.

In a world of accelerant change, next year is nearer to us than next month was in a more leisurely era. This radically altered fact of life must be internalized by decision-makers in industry, government and elsewhere. Their time horizons must be extended.

To plan for a more distant future does not mean to tie oneself to dogmatic programs. Plans can be tentative, fluid, subject to continual revision. Yet flexibility need not mean shortsightedness. To transcend technocracy, our social time horizons must reach decades, even generations, into the future. This requires more than a lengthening of our formal plans. It means an infusion of the entire society, from top to bottom, with a new socially aware future-consciousness.

One of the healthiest phenomena of recent years has been the sudden proliferation of organizations devoted to the study of the future. This recent development is, in itself, a homeostatic response of the society to the speed-up of change. Within a few years we have seen the creation of future-oriented think tanks like the Institute for the Future; the formation of academic study groups like the Commission on the Year 2000 and the Harvard Program on Technology and Society; the appearance of futurist journals in England, France, Italy, Germany and the United States; the spread of university courses in forecasting and related subjects; the convocation of international futurist meetings in Oslo, Berlin and Kyoto; the coalescence of groups like Futuribles, Europe 2000, Mankind 2000, the World Future Society.

Futurist centers are to be found in West Berlin, in Prague, in London, in Moscow, Rome and Washington, in Caracas, even in the remote jungles of Brazil at Belém and Belo Horizonte. Unlike conventional technocratic planners whose horizons usually extend no further than a few years into tomorrow, these groups concern themselves with change fifteen, twenty-five, even fifty years in the future.

Every society faces not merely a succession of *probable* futures, but an array of *possible* futures, and a conflict over *preferable* futures. The management of change is the effort to convert certain possibles into probables, in pursuit of agreed-on preferables. Determining the probable calls for a science of futurism. Delineating the possible calls for an art of futurism. Defining the preferable calls for a politics of futurism.

The worldwide futurist movement today does not yet differentiate clearly among these functions. Its heavy emphasis is on the assessment of probabilities. Thus in many of these centers, economists, sociologists, mathematicians, biologists, physicists, operations researchers and others invent and apply methods for forecasting future probabilities. At what date could aquaculture feed half the world's population? What are the odds that electric cars will supplant gas-driven automobiles in the next fifteen years? How likely is a Sino-Soviet détente by 1980? What changes are most probable in leisure patterns, urban government, race relations?

Stressing the interconnectedness of disparate events and trends, scientific futurists are also devoting increasing attention to the social consequences of technology. The Institute for the Future is, among other things, investigating the probable social and cultural effects of advanced communications technology. The group at Harvard is concerned with social problems likely to arise from bio-medical advances. Futurists in Brazil examine the probable outcomes of various economic development policies.

The rationale for studying probable futures is compelling. It is impossible for an individual to live through a single working day without making thousands of assumptions about the probable future. The commuter who calls to say, "I'll be home at six" bases his prediction on assumptions about the probability that the train will run on time. When mother sends Johnny to school, she tacitly assumes the school will be there when he arrives. Just as a pilot cannot steer a ship without projecting its course, we cannot steer our personal lives without continually making such assumptions, consciously or otherwise.

Societies, too, construct an architecture of premises about tomorrow. Decision-makers in industry, government, politics, and other sectors of society could not function without them. In periods of turbulent change, however, these socially-shaped images of the probable future become less accurate. The breakdown of control in society today is directly linked to our inadequate images of probable futures.

Of course, no one can "know" the future in any absolute sense. We can only systematize and deepen our assumptions and attempt to assign probabilities to them. Even this is difficult. Attempts to forecast the future inevitably alter it. Similarly, once a forecast is disseminated, the act of dissemination (as distinct from investigation) also produces a perturbation. Forecasts tend to become self-fulfilling or self-defeating. As the time horizon is extended into the more distant future, we are forced to rely on informed hunch and guesswork. Moreover, certain unique events—assassinations, for example—are, for all intents and purposes, unpredictable at present (although we can forecast classes of such events).

Despite all this, it is time to erase, once and for all, the popular myth that the future is "unknowable." The difficulties ought to chasten and challenge, not paralyze. William F. Ogburn, one of the world's great students of social change, once wrote: "We should admit into our thinking the idea of approximations, that is, that there are varying degrees of accuracy and inaccuracy of estimate." A rough idea of what lies ahead is better than none, he went on, and for many purposes extreme accuracy is wholly unnecessary.

We are not, therefore, as helpless in dealing with future probabilities as most people assume. The British social scientist Donald G. MacRae correctly asserts that "modern sociologists can in fact make a large number of comparatively short term and limited predictions with a good deal of assurance." Apart from the standard methods of social science, however, we are experimenting with potentially powerful new tools for probing the future. These range from complex ways of extrapolating existing trends, to the construction of highly intricate models, games and simulations, the preparation of detailed speculative scenarios, the systematic study of history for relevant analogies, morphological research, relevance analysis, contextual mapping and the like. In a comprehensive investigation of technological forecasting, Dr. Erich Jantsch, formerly a consultant to the OECD and a research associate at MIT, has identified scores of distinct new techniques either in use or in the experimental stage.

The Institute for the Future in Middletown, Connecticut, a prototype of the futurist think tank, is a leader in the design of new forecasting tools. One of these is Delphi—a method largely developed by Dr. Olaf Helmer, the mathematician-philosopher who is one of the founders of the IFF. Delphi attempts to deal with very distant futures by making systematic use of the "intuitive" guesstimates of large numbers of experts. The work on Delphi has led to a further innovation which has special importance in the attempt to prevent future shock by regulating the pace of change. Pioneered by Theodore J. Gordon of the IFF, and called Cross Impact Matrix Analysis, it traces the effect of one innovation on another, making possible, for the first time, anticipatory analysis of complex chains of social, technological and other occurrences—and the rates at which they are likely to occur.

We are, in short, witnessing a perfectly extraordinary thrust toward more scientific appraisal of future probabilities, a ferment likely, in itself, to have a powerful impact on the future. It would be foolish to oversell the ability of science, as yet, to forecast complex events accurately. Yet the danger today is not that we will overestimate our ability; the real danger is that we will under-utilize it. For even when our still-primitive attempts at scientific forecasting turn out to be grossly in error, the very effort helps us identify key variables in change, it helps clarify goals, and it forces more careful evaluation of policy alternatives. In these ways, if no others, probing the future pays off in the present.

Anticipating *probable* futures, however, is only part of what needs doing if we are to shift the planner's time horizon and infuse the entire society with a greater sense of tomorrow. For we must also vastly widen our conception of possible futures. To the rigorous discipline of science, we must add the flaming imagination of art.

Today as never before we need a multiplicity of visions, dreams and prophecies—images of potential tomorrows. Before we can rationally decide which alternative pathways to choose, which cultural styles to pursue, we must first ascertain which are possible. Conjecture, speculation and the visionary view thus become as coldly practical a necessity as feet-on-the-floor "realism" was in an earlier time.

This is why some of the world's biggest and most tough-minded corporations, once the living embodiment of presentism, today hire intuitive futurists, science fiction writers and visionaries as consultants. A gigantic European chemical company employs a futurist who combines a scientific background with training as a theologian. An American communications empire engages a future-minded social critic. A glass manufacturer searches for a science fiction writer to imagine the possible corporate forms of the future. Companies turn to these "blue-skyers" and "wild birds" not for scientific forecasts of probabilities, but for mind-stretching speculation about possibilities.

Corporations must not remain the only agencies with access to such services. Local government, schools, voluntary associations and others also need to examine their potential futures imaginatively. One way to help them do so would be to establish in each community "imaginetic centers" devoted to technically assisted brainstorming. These would be places where people noted for creative imagination, rather than technical expertise, are brought together to examine present crises, to anticipate future crises, and to speculate freely, even playfully, about possible futures.

What, for example, are the possible futures of urban transportation? Traffic is a problem involving space. How might the city of tomorrow cope with the movement of men and objects through space? To speculate about this question, an imaginetic center might enlist artists, sculptors, dancers, furniture designers, parking lot attendants, and a variety of other people who, in one way or another, manipulate space imaginatively. Such people, assembled under the right circumstances, would inevitably come up with ideas of which the technocratic city planners, the highway engineers and transit authorities have never dreamed.

Musicians, people who live near airports, jack-hammer men and subway conductors might well imagine new ways to organize, mask or suppress noise. Groups of young people might be invited to ransack their minds for previously unexamined approaches to urban sanitation, crowding, ethnic conflict, care of the aged, or a thousand other present and future problems.

In any such effort, the overwhelming majority of ideas put forward will, of course, be absurd, funny or technically impossible. Yet the essence of creativity is a willingness to play the fool, to toy with the absurd, only later submitting the stream of ideas to harsh critical judgment. The application of the imagination to the future thus requires an environment in which it is safe to err, in which novel juxtapositions of ideas can be freely expressed before being critically sifted. We need sanctuaries for social imagination.

While all sorts of creative people ought to participate in conjecture about possible futures, they should have immediate access—in person or via telecommunications—to technical specialists, from acoustical engineers to zoologists, who could indicate when a suggestion is technically impossible (bearing in mind that even impossibility is often temporary).

Scientific expertise, however, might also play a generative, rather than merely a damping role in the imaginetic process. Skilled specialists can construct models to help imagineers examine all possible permutations of a given set of relationships. Such models are representations of real life conditions. In the words of Christoph Bertram of the Institute for Strategic Studies in London, their purpose is "not so much to predict the future, but, by examining alternative futures, to show the choices open."

An appropriate model, for example, could help a group of imagineers visualize the impact on a city if its educational expenditures were to fluctuate—how this would affect, let us say, the transport system, the theaters, the occupational structure and health of the community. Conversely, it could show how changes in these other factors might affect education.

The rushing stream of wild, unorthodox, eccentric or merely colorful ideas generated in these sanctuaries of social imagination must, after they have been expressed, be subjected to merciless screening. Only a tiny fraction of them will survive this filtering process. These few, however, could be of the utmost importance in calling attention to new possibilities that might otherwise escape notice. As we move from poverty toward affluence, politics changes from what mathematicians call a zero sum game into a non-zero sum game. In the first, if one player wins another must lose. In the second, all players can win. Finding non-zero sum solutions to our social problems requires all the imagination we can muster. A system for generating imaginative policy ideas could help us take maximum advantage of the non-zero opportunities ahead.

While imaginetic centers concentrate on partial images of tomorrow, defining possible futures for a single industry, an organization, a city or its subsystems, however, we also need sweeping, visionary ideas about the society as a whole. Multiplying our images of possible futures is important; but these images need to be organized, crystallized into structured form. In the past, utopian literature did this for us. It played a practical, crucial role in ordering men's dreams about alternative futures. Today we suffer for lack of utopian ideas around which to organize competing images of possible futures.

Most traditional utopias picture simple and static societies—i.e., societies that have nothing in common with super-industrialism. B. F. Skinner's *Walden Two*, the model for several existing experimental communes, depicts a pre-industrial way of life—small, close to the earth, built on farming and handcraft. Even those two brilliant anti-utopias, *Brave New World* and *1984*, now seem oversimple. Both describe societies based on high technology and low complexity: the machines are sophisticated but the social and cultural relationships are fixed and deliberately simplified.

Today we need powerful new utopian and anti-utopian concepts that look forward to super-industrialism, rather than backward to simpler societies. These concepts, however, can no longer be produced in the old way. First, no book, by itself, is adequate to describe a super-industrial future in emotionally compelling terms. Each conception of a super-industrial utopia or anti-utopia needs to be embodied in many forms—films, plays, novels and works of art—rather than a single work of fiction. Second, it may now be too difficult for any individual writer, no matter how gifted, to describe a convincingly complex future. We need, therefore, a revolution in the production of utopias: collaborative utopianism. We need to construct "utopia factories."

One way might be to assemble a small group of top social scientists—an economist, a sociologist, an anthropologist, and so on—asking them to work together, even live together, long enough to hammer out among themselves a set of well-defined values on which they believe a truly super-industrial utopian society might be based.

Each member of the team might then attempt to describe in nonfiction form a sector of an imagined society built on these values. What would its family structure be like? Its economy, laws, religion, sexual practices, youth culture, music, art, its sense of time, its degree of differentiation, its psychological problems? By working together and ironing out inconsistencies, where possible, a comprehensive and adequately complex picture might be drawn of a seamless, temporary form of super-industrialism.

At this point, with the completion of detailed analysis, the project would move to the fiction stage. Novelists, film-makers, science fiction writers and others, working closely with psychologists, could prepare creative works about the lives of individual characters in the imagined society.

Meanwhile, other groups could be at work on counter-utopias. While Utopia A might stress materialist, success-oriented values, Utopia B might base itself on sensual, hedonistic values, C on the primacy of aesthetic values, D on individualism, E on collectivism, and so forth. Ultimately, a stream of books, plays, films and television programs would flow from this collaboration between art, social science and futurism, thereby educating large numbers of people about the costs and benefits of the various proposed utopias.

Finally, if social imagination is in short supply, we are even more lacking in people willing to subject utopian ideas to systematic test. More and more young people, in their dissatisfaction with industrialism, are experimenting with their own lives, forming utopian communities, trying new social arrangements, from group marriage to living-learning communes. Today, as in the past, the weight of established society comes down hard on the visionary who attempts to practice, as well as merely preach. Rather than ostracizing utopians, we should take advantage of their willingness to experiment, encouraging them with money and tolerance, if not respect.

Most of today's "intentional communities" or utopian colonies, however, reveal a powerful preference for the past. These may be of value to the individuals in them, but the society as a whole would be better served by utopian experiments based on super- rather than pre-industrial forms. Instead of a communal farm, why not a computer software company whose program writers live and work communally? Why not an education technology company whose members pool their money and merge their families? Instead of raising radishes or crafting sandals, why not an oceanographic research installation organized along utopian lines? Why not a group medical practice that takes advantage of the latest medical technology but whose members accept modest pay and pool their profits to run a completely new-style medical school? Why not recruit living groups to try out the proposals of the utopia factories?

In short, we can use utopianism as a tool rather than an escape, if we base our experiments on the technology and society of tomorrow rather than that of the past. And once done, why not the most rigorous, scientific analysis of the results? The findings could be priceless, were they to save us from mistakes or lead us toward more workable organizational forms for industry, education, family life or politics.

Such imaginative explorations of possible futures would deepen and enrich our scientific study of probable futures. They would lay a basis for the radical forward extension of the society's time horizon.

They would help us apply social imagination to the future of futurism itself.

Indeed, with these as a background, we must consciously begin to multiply the scientific future-sensing organs of society. Scientific futurist institutes must be spotted like nodes in a loose network throughout the entire governmental structure in the techno-societies, so that in every department, local or national, some staff devotes itself systematically to scanning the probable long-term future in its assigned field. Futurists should be attached to every political party, university, corporation, professional association, trade union and student organization.

We need to train thousands of young people in the perspectives and techniques of scientific futurism, inviting them to share in the exciting venture of mapping probable futures. We also need national agencies to provide technical assistance to local communities in creating their own futurist groups. And we need a similar center, perhaps jointly funded by American and European foundations, to help incipient futurist centers in Asia, Africa, and Latin America.

We are in a race between rising levels of uncertainty produced by the acceleration of change, and the need for reasonably accurate images of what at any instant is the most probable future. The generation of reliable images of the most probable future thus becomes a matter of the highest national, indeed, international urgency.

As the globe is itself dotted with future-sensors, we might consider creating a great international institute, a world futures data bank. Such an institute, staffed with top caliber men and women from all the sciences and social sciences, would take as its purpose the collection and systematic integration of predictive reports generated by scholars and imaginative thinkers in all the intellectual disciplines all over the world.

Of course, those working in such an institute would know that they could never create a single, static diagram of the future. Instead, the product of their effort would be a constantly changing geography of the future, a continually re-created overarching image based on the best predictive work available. The men and women engaged in this work would know that nothing is certain; they would know that they must work with inadequate data; they would appreciate the difficulties inherent in exploring the uncharted territories of tomorrow. But man already knows more about the future than he has ever tried to formulate and integrate in any systematic and scientific way. Attempts to bring this knowledge together would constitute one of the crowning intellectual efforts in history—and one of the most worthwhile.

Only when decision-makers are armed with better forecasts of future events, when by successive approximation we increase the accuracy of forecast, will our attempts to manage change improve perceptibly. For reasonably accurate assumptions about the future are a precondition for understanding the potential consequences of our own actions. And without such understanding, the management of change is impossible.

If the humanization of the planner is the first stage in the strategy of social futurism, therefore, the forward extension of our time horizon is the second. To transcend technocracy, we need not only to reach beyond our economic philistinism, but to open our minds to more distant futures, both probable and possible.

ANTICIPATORY DEMOCRACY

In the end, however, social futurism must cut even deeper. For technocrats suffer from more than econothink and myopia; they suffer, too, from the virus of elitism. To capture control of change, we shall, therefore, require a final, even more radical breakaway from technocratic tradition: we shall need a revolution in the very way we formulate our social goals.

Rising novelty renders irrelevant the traditional goals of our chief institutions—state, church, corporation, army and university. Acceleration produces a faster turnover of goals, a greater transience of purpose. Diversity or fragmentation leads to a relentless multiplication of goals. Caught in this churning, goal-cluttered environment, we stagger, future shocked, from crisis to crisis, pursuing a welter of conflicting and self-cancelling purposes.

Nowhere is this more starkly evident than in our pathetic attempts to govern our cities. New Yorkers, within a short span, have suffered a nightmarish succession of near disasters: a water shortage, a subway strike, racial violence in the schools, a student insurrection at Columbia University, a garbage strike, a housing shortage, a fuel oil strike, a breakdown of telephone service, a teacher walkout, a power blackout, to name just a few. In its City Hall, as in a thousand city halls all over the high-technology nations, technocrats dash, firebucket in fist, from one conflagration to another without the least semblance of a coherent plan or policy for the urban future.

This is not to say no one is planning. On the contrary; in this seething social brew, technocratic plans, sub-plans and counter-plans pour forth. They call for new highways, new roads, new power plants, new schools. They promise better hospitals, housing, mental health centers, welfare programs. But the plans cancel, contradict and reinforce one another by accident. Few are logically related to one another, and none to any overall image of the preferred city of the future. No vision—utopian or otherwise—energizes our efforts. No rationally integrated goals bring order to the chaos. And at the national and international levels, the absence of coherent policy is equally marked and doubly dangerous.

It is not simply that we do not know which goals to pursue, as a city or as a nation. The trouble lies

deeper. For accelerating change has made obsolete
the methods by which we arrive at social goals. The
technocrats do not yet understand this, and, reacting to the goals crisis in knee-jerk fashion, they reach
for the tried and true methods of the past.

Thus, intermittently, a change-dazed government
will try to define its goals publicly. Instinctively, it
establishes a commission. In 1960 President Eisenhower pressed into service, among others, a general,
a judge, a couple of industrialists, a few college presidents, and a labor leader to "develop a broad outline
of coordinated national policies and programs" and to
"set up a series of goals in various areas of national
activity." In due course, a red-white-and-blue paperback appeared with the commission's report, *Goals for
Americans*. Neither the commission nor its goals had
the slightest impact on the public or on policy. The
juggernaut of change continued to roll through America untouched, as it were, by managerial intelligence.

A far more significant effort to tidy up governmental priorities was initiated by President Johnson,
with his attempt to apply PPBS (Planning-Program-
ming-Budgeting-System) throughout the federal establishment. PPBS is a method for tying programs
much more closely and rationally to organizational
goals. Thus, for example, by applying it, the Department of Health, Education and Welfare can assess
the costs and benefits of alternative programs to accomplish specified goals. But who specifies these larger, more important goals? The introduction of PPBS
and the systems approach is a major governmental
achievement. It is of paramount importance in managing large organizational efforts. But it leaves entirely untouched the profoundly political question of
how the overall goals of a government or a society are
to be chosen in the first place.

President Nixon, still snarled in the goals crisis,
tried a third tack. "It is time," he declared, "we addressed ourselves, consciously and systematically, to
the question of what kind of a nation we want to be

. . ." He thereupon put his finger on the quintessential question. But once more the method chosen for answering it proved to be inadequate. "I have today ordered the establishment, within the White House, of a National Goals Research Staff," the President announced. "This will be a small, highly technical staff, made up of experts in the collection . . . and processing of data relating to social needs, and in the projection of social trends."

Such a staff, located within shouting distance of the Presidency, could be extremely useful in compiling goal proposals, in reconciling (at least on paper) conflicts between agencies, in suggesting new priorities. Staffed with excellent social scientists and futurists, it could earn its keep if it did nothing but force high officials to question their primary goals.

Yet even this step, like the two before it, bears the unmistakable imprint of the technocratic mentality. For it, too, evades the politically charged core of the issue. How are preferable futures to be defined? And by whom? Who is to set goals for the future?

Behind all such efforts runs the notion that national (and, by extension, local) goals for the future of society ought to be formulated at the top. This technocratic premise perfectly mirrors the old bureaucratic forms of organization in which line and staff were separated, in which rigid, undemocratic hierarchies distinguished leader from led, manager from managed, planner from plannee.

Yet the real, as distinct from the glibly verbalized, goals of any society on the path to super-industrialism are already too complex, too transient and too dependent for their achievement upon the willing participation of the governed, to be perceived and defined so easily. We cannot hope to harness the runaway forces of change by assembling a kaffee klatsch of elders to set goals for us or by turning the task over to a "highly technical staff." A revolutionary new approach to goal-setting is needed.

Nor is this approach likely to come from those who

play-act at revolution. One radical group, seeing all problems as a manifestation of the "maximization of profits" displays, in all innocence, an econocentricism as narrow as that of the technocrats. Another hopes to plunge us willy-nilly back into the pre-industrial past. Still another sees revolution exclusively in subjective and psychological terms. None of these groups is capable of advancing us toward post-technocratic forms of change management.

By calling attention to the growing ineptitudes of the technocrats and by explicitly challenging not merely the means, but the very goals of industrial society, today's young radicals do us all a great service. But they no more know how to cope with the goals crisis than the technocrats they scorn. Exactly like Messrs. Eisenhower, Johnson and Nixon, they have been noticeably unable to present any positive image of a future worth fighting for.

Thus Todd Gitlin, a young American radical and former president of the Students for a Democratic Society, notes that while "an orientation toward the future has been the hallmark of every revolutionary —and, for that matter, liberal—movement of the last century and a half," the New Left suffers from "a disbelief in the future." After citing all the ostensible reasons why it has so far not put forward a coherent vision of the future, he succinctly confesses: "We find ourselves incapable of formulating the future."

Other New Left theorists fuzz over the problem, urging their followers to incorporate the future in the present by, in effect, living the life styles of tomorrow today. So far, this has led to a pathetic charade—"free societies," cooperatives, pre-industrial communes, few of which have anything to do with the future, and most of which reveal, instead, only a passionate penchant for the past.

The irony is compounded when we consider that some (though hardly all) of today's young radicals also share with the technocrats a streak of virulent elitism. While decrying bureaucracy and demanding "participatory democracy" they, themselves, frequently attempt to manipulate the very groups of workers, blacks or students on whose behalf they demand participation.

The working masses in the high-technology societies are totally indifferent to calls for a political revolution aimed at exchanging one form of property ownership for another. For most people, the rise in affluence has meant a better, not a worse, existence, and they look upon their much despised "suburban middle class lives" as fulfillment rather than deprivation.

Faced with this stubborn reality, undemocratic elements in the New Left leap to the Marcusian conclusion that the masses are too bourgeoisified, too corrupted and addled by Madison Avenue to know what is good for them. And so, a revolutionary elite must establish a more humane and democratic future even if it means stuffing it down the throats of those who are too stupid to know their own interests. In short, the goals of society have to be set by an elite. Technocrat and anti-technocrat often turn out to be elitist brothers under the skin.

Yet systems of goal formulation based on elitist premises are simply no longer "efficient." In the struggle to capture control of the forces of change, they are increasingly counter-productive. For under superindustrialism, democracy becomes not a political luxury, but a primal necessity.

Democratic political forms arose in the West not because a few geniuses willed them into being or because man showed an "unquenchable instinct for freedom." They arose because the historical pressure toward social differentiation and toward faster paced systems demanded sensitive social feedback. In complex, differentiated societies, vast amounts of information must flow at ever faster speeds between the formal organizations and subcultures that make up the whole, and between the layers and sub-structures within these.

Political democracy, by incorporating larger and larger numbers in social decision-making, facilitates feedback. And it is precisely this feedback that is essential to control. To assume control over accelerant change, we shall need still more advanced—and more democratic—feedback mechanisms.

The technocrat, however, still thinking in top-down terms, frequently makes plans without arranging for adequate and instantaneous feedback from the field, so that he seldom knows how well his plans are working. When he does arrange for feedback, what he usually asks for and gets is heavily economic, inadequately social, psychological or cultural. Worse yet, he makes these plans without sufficiently taking into account the fast-changing needs and wishes of those whose participation is needed to make them a success. He assumes the right to set social goals by himself or he accepts them blindly from some higher authority.

He fails to recognize that the faster pace of change demands—and creates—a new kind of information system in society: a loop, rather than a ladder. Information must pulse through this loop at accelerating speeds, with the output of one group becoming the input for many others, so that no group, however politically potent it may seem, can independently set goals for the whole.

As the number of social components multiplies, and change jolts and destabilizes the entire system, the power of subgroups to wreak havoc on the whole is tremendously amplified. There is, in the words of W. Ross Ashby, a brilliant cyberneticist, a mathematically provable law to the effect that "when a whole system is composed of a number of subsystems, the one that tends to dominate is the one that is *least* stable."

Another way of stating this is that, as the number of social components grows and change makes the whole system less stable, it becomes less and less possible to ignore the demands of political minorities

—hippies, blacks, lower-middle-class Wallacites, school teachers, or the proverbial little old ladies in tennis shoes. In a slower-moving, industrial context, America could turn its back on the needs of its black minority; in the new, fast-paced cybernetic society, this minority can, by sabotage, strike, or a thousand other means, disrupt the entire system. As interdependency grows, smaller and smaller groups within society achieve greater and greater power for critical disruption. Moreover, as the rate of change speeds up, the length of time in which they can be ignored shrinks to near nothingness. Hence: "Freedom now!"

This suggests that the best way to deal with angry or recalcitrant minorities is to open the system further, bringing them into it as full partners, permitting them to participate in social goal-setting, rather than attempting to ostracize or isolate them. A Red China locked out of the United Nations and the larger international community, is far more likely to destabilize the world than one laced into the system. Young people forced into prolonged adolescence and deprived of the right to partake in social decision-making will grow more and more unstable until they threaten the overall system. In short, in politics, in industry, in education, goals set without the participation of those affected will be increasingly hard to execute. The continuation of top-down technocratic goal-setting procedures will lead to greater and greater social instability, less and less control over the forces of change; an ever greater danger of cataclysmic, man-destroying upheaval.

To master change, we shall therefore need both a clarification of important long-range social goals *and* a democratization of the way in which we arrive at them. And this means nothing less than the next political revolution in the techno-societies—a breathtaking affirmation of popular democracy.

The time has come for a dramatic reassessment of the directions of change, a reassessment made not by the politicians or the sociologists or the clergy or the elitist revolutionaries, not by technicians or college presidents, but by the people themselves. We need, quite literally, to "go to the people" with a question that is almost never asked of them: "What kind of a world do you want ten, twenty, or thirty years from now?" We need to initiate, in short, a continuing plebiscite on the future.

The moment is right for the formation in each of the high-technology nations of a movement for total self-review, a public self-examination aimed at broadening and defining in social, as well as merely economic, terms, the goals of "progress." On the edge of a new millennium, on the brink of a new stage of human development, we are racing blindly into the future. But where do we *want* to go?

What would happen if we actually tried to answer this question?

Imagine the historic drama, the power and evolutionary impact, if each of the high-technology nations literally set aside the next five years as a period of intense national self-appraisal; if at the end of five years it were to come forward with its own tentative agenda for the future, a program embracing not merely economic targets but, equally important, broad sets of social goals—if each nation, in effect, stated to the world what it wished to accomplish for its people and mankind in general during the remaining quarter century of the millennium.

Let us convene in each nation, in each city, in each neighborhood, democratic constituent assemblies charged with social stock-taking, charged with defining and assigning priorities to specific social goals for the remainder of the century.

Such "social future assemblies" might represent not merely geographical localities, but social units—industry, labor, the churches, the intellectual community, the arts, women, ethnic and religious groups, students, with organized representation for the unorganized as well. There are no sure-fire techniques for guaranteeing equal representation for all, or for eliciting the wishes of the poor, the inarticulate or the isolated. Yet once we recognize the need to include them, we shall find the ways. Indeed, the problem of participating in the definition of the future is not merely a problem of the poor, the inarticulate and the isolated. Highly paid executives, wealthy professionals, extremely articulate intellectuals and students—all at one time or another feel cut off from the power to influence the directions and pace of change. Wiring them into the system, making them a part of the guidance machinery of the society, is the most critical political task of the coming generation. Imagine the effect if at one level or another a place were provided where all those who will live in the future might voice their wishes about it. Imagine, in short, a massive, global exercise in anticipatory democracy.

Social future assemblies need not—and, given the rate of transience—cannot be anchored, permanent institutions. Instead, they might take the form of ad hoc groupings, perhaps called into being at regular intervals with different representatives participating each time. Today citizens are expected to serve on juries when needed. They give a few days or a few weeks of their time for this service, recognizing that the jury system is one of the guarantees of democracy, that, even though service may be inconvenient, someone must do the job. Social future assemblies could be organized along similar lines, with a constant stream of new participants brought together for short periods to serve as society's "consultants on the future."

Such grass roots organisms for expressing the will of large numbers of hitherto unconsulted people could become, in effect, the town halls of the future, in which millions help shape their own distant destinies.

To some, this appeal for a form of neo-populism will no doubt seem naive. Yet nothing is more naive than the notion that we can continue politically to run the society the way we do at present. To some, it will appear impractical. Yet nothing is more impractical than the attempt to impose a humane future from above. What was naive under industrialism may be realistic under super-industrialism; what was practical may be absurd.

The encouraging fact is that we now have the potential for achieving tremendous breakthroughs in democratic decision-making if we make imaginative use of the new technologies, both "hard" and "soft," that bear on the problem. Thus, advanced tele-communications mean that participants in a social future assembly need not literally meet in a single room, but might simply be hooked into a communications net that straddles the globe. A meeting of scientists to discuss research goals for the future, or goals for environmental quality, could draw participants from many countries at once. An assembly of steelworkers, unionists and executives, convened to discuss goals for automation and for the improvement of work, itself, could link up participants from many mills, offices and warehouses, no matter how scattered or remote.

A meeting of the cultural community in New York or Paris—artists and gallery-goers, writers and readers, dramatists and audiences—to discuss appropriate long-range goals for the cultural development of the city could be shown, through the use of video recordings and other techniques, actual samples of the kinds of artistic production under discussion, architectural designs for new facilities, samples of new artistic media made available by technological advance, etc. What kind of cultural life should a great city of the future enjoy? What resources would be needed to realize a given set of goals?

All social future assemblies, in order to answer such questions, could and should be backed with technical staff to provide data on the social and economic costs of various goals, and to show the costs and benefits of proposed trade-offs, so that participants would be in a position to make reasonably informed choices, as it were, among alternative futures.

In this way, each assembly might arrive, in the end, not merely in vaguely expressed, disjointed hopes, but at coherent statements of priorities for tomorrow—posed in terms that could be compared with the goal statements of other groups.

Nor need these social future assemblies be glorified "talkfests." We are fast developing games and simulation exercises whose chief beauty is that they help players clarify their own values. At the University of Illinois, in Project Plato, Charles Osgood is experimenting with computers and teaching machines that would involve large sectors of the public in planning imaginary, preferable futures through gaming.

At Cornell University, José Villegas, a professor in the Department of Design and Environmental Analysis, has begun constructing with the aid of black and white students, a variety of "ghetto games" which reveal to the players the consequences of various proposed courses of action and thus help them clarify goals. *Ghetto 1984* showed what would happen if the recommendations made by the Kerner riot commission—the U. S. National Advisory Commission on Civil Disorder—were actually to be adopted. It showed how the sequence in which these recommendations were enacted would affect their ultimate impact on the ghetto. It helped players, both black and white, to identify their shared goals as well as their unresolved conflicts. In games like *Peru 2000* and *Squatter City 2000*, players design communities for the future.

In *Lower East Side*, a game Villegas hopes actually to play in the Manhattan community that bears that name, players would not be students, but real-life residents of the community—poverty workers, middle-class whites, Puerto Rican small businessmen or youth, unemployed blacks, police, landlords and city officials.

In the spring of 1969, 50,000 high school students in Boston, in Philadelphia and in Syracuse, New York, participated in a televised game involving a simulated

war in the Congo in 1975. While televised teams
simulated the cabinets of Russia, Red China, and the
United States, and struggled with the problems of
diplomacy and policy planning, students and teachers
watched, discussed, and offered advice via telephone
to the central players.

Similar games, involving not tens, but hundreds of
thousands, even millions of people, could be devised
to help us formulate goals for the future. While televised players act out the role of high government
officials attempting to deal with a crisis—an ecological
disaster, for example—meetings of trade unions,
women's clubs, church groups, student organizations
and other constituencies might be held at which large
numbers could view the program, reach collective
judgments about the choices to be made, and forward those judgments to the primary players. Special
switchboards and computers could pick up the advice
or tabulate the yes-no votes and pass them on to the
"decision-makers." Vast numbers of people could also
participate from their own homes, thus opening the
process to unorganized, otherwise non-participating
millions. By imaginatively constructing such games, it
becomes not only possible but practical to elicit
futural goals from previously unconsulted masses.

Such techniques, still primitive today, will become
fantastically more sophisticated in the years immediately ahead, providing us with a systematic way to
collect and reconcile conflicting images of the preferable future, even from people unskilled in academic
debate or parliamentary procedure.

It would be pollyanna-like to expect such town
halls of the future to be tidy or harmonious affairs,
or that they would be organized in the same way
everywhere. In some places, social future assemblies
might be called into being by community organizations, planning councils or government agencies. Elsewhere, they might be sponsored by trade unions,
youth groups, or individual, future-oriented political
leaders. In other places, churches, foundations or

voluntary organizations might initiate the call. And in still other places, they might arise not from a formal convention call, but as a spontaneous response to crisis.

It would similarly be a mistake to think of the goals drawn up by these assemblies as constituting permanent, Platonic ideals, floating somewhere in a metaphysical never-never land. Rather, they must be seen as temporary direction-indicators, broad objectives good for a limited time only, and intended as advisory to the elected political representatives of the community or nation.

Nevertheless, such future-oriented, future-forming events could have enormous political impact. Indeed, they could turn out to be the salvation of the entire system of representative politics—a system now in dire crisis.

The mass of voters today are so far removed from contact with their elected representatives, the issues dealt with are so technical, that even well educated middle-class citizens feel hopelessly excluded from the goal-setting process. Because of the generalized acceleration of life, so much happens so fast between elections, that the politician grows increasingly less accountable to "the folks back home." What's more, these folks back home keep changing. In theory, the voter unhappy with the performance of his representative can vote against him the next time around. In practice, millions find even this impossible. Mass mobility removes them from the district, sometimes disenfranchising them altogether. Newcomers flood into the district. More and more, the politician finds himself addressing new faces. He may never be called to account for his performance—or for promises made to the last set of constituents.

Still more damaging to democracy is the time-bias of politics. The politician's time horizon usually extends no further than the next election. Congresses, diets, parliaments, city councils—legislative bodies in general—lack the time, the resources, or the organizational forms needed to think seriously about the long-term future. As for the citizen, the last thing he is ever consulted about are the larger, more distant, goals of his community, state or nation.

The voter may be polled about specific issues, never about the general shape of the preferable future. Indeed, nowhere in politics is there an institution through which an ordinary man can express his ideas about what the distant future ought to look, feel or taste like. He is never asked to think about this, and on the rare occasions when he does, there is no organized way for him to feed his ideas into the arena of politics. Cut off from the future, he becomes a political eunuch.

We are, for these and other reasons, rushing toward a fateful breakdown of the entire system of political representation. If legislatures are to survive at all, they will need new links with their constituencies, new ties with tomorrow. Social future assemblies could provide the means for reconnecting the legislator with his mass base, the present with the future.

Conducted at frequent and regular intervals, such assemblies could provide a more sensitive measure of popular will than any now available to us. The very act of calling such assemblies would attract into the flow of political life millions who now ignore it. By confronting men and women with the future, by asking them to think deeply about their own private destinies as well as our accelerating public trajectories, it would pose profound ethical issues.

Simply putting such questions to people would, by itself, prove liberating. The very process of social assessment would brace and cleanse a population weary to death of technical discussions of how to get someplace it is not sure it wants to go. Social future assemblies would help clarify the differences that increasingly divide us in our fast-fragmenting societies; they would, conversely, identify common social needs —potential grounds for temporary unities. In this way, they would bring various polities together in a fresh framework out of which new political mechanisms would inevitably spring.

Most important of all, however, social future assemblies would help shift the culture toward a more super-industrial time-bias. By focusing public attention for once on long-range goals rather than immediate programs alone, by asking people to choose a preferable future from among a range of alternative futures, these assemblies could dramatize the possibilities for humanizing the future—possibilities that all too many have already given up as lost. In so doing, social future assemblies could unleash powerful constructive forces—the forces of conscious evolution.

By now the accelerative thrust triggered by man has become the key to the entire evolutionary process on the planet. The rate and direction of the evolution of other species, their very survival, depends upon decisions made by man. Yet there is nothing inherent in the evolutionary process to guarantee man's own survival.

Throughout the past, as successive stages of social evolution unfolded, man's awareness followed rather than preceded the event. Because change was slow, he could adapt unconsciously, "organically." Today unconscious adaptation is no longer adequate. Faced with the power to alter the gene, to create new species, to populate the planets or depopulate the earth, man must now assume conscious control of evolution itself. Avoiding future shock as he rides the waves of change, he must master evolution, shaping tomorrow to human need. Instead of rising in revolt against it, he must, from this historic moment on, anticipate and design the future.

This, then, is the ultimate objective of social futurism, not merely the transcendence of technocracy and the substitution of more humane, more far-sighted, more democratic planning, but the subjection of the process of evolution itself to conscious human guidance. For this is the supreme instant, the turning

point in history at which man either vanquishes the
processes of change or vanishes, at which, from being
the unconscious puppet of evolution he becomes
either its victim or its master.

A challenge of such proportions demands of us a
dramatically new, a more deeply rational response
toward change. This book has had change as its
protagonist—first as potential villain and then, it
would seem, as potential hero. In calling for the
moderation and regulation of change, it has called for
additional revolutionary changes. This is less paradoxical than it appears. Change is essential to man,
as essential now in our 800th lifetime as it was in
our first. Change is life itself. But change rampant,
change unguided and unrestrained, accelerated
change overwhelming not only man's physical defenses but his decisional processes—such change is the
enemy of life.

Our first and most pressing need, therefore, before
we can begin to gently guide our evolutionary destiny, before we can build a humane future, is to halt
the runaway acceleration that is subjecting multitudes
to the threat of future shock while, at the very same
moment, intensifying all the problems they must deal
with—war, ecological incursions, racism, the obscene
contrast between rich and poor, the revolt of the
young, and the rise of a potentially deadly mass ir-
rationalism.

There is no facile way to treat this wild growth, this
cancer in history. There is no magic medicine, either,
for curing the unprecedented disease it bears in its
rushing wake: future shock. I have suggested pallia-
tives for the change-pressed individual and more
radically curative procedures for the society—new
social services, a future-facing education system, new
ways to regulate technology, and a strategy for capturing control of change. Other ways must also be
found. Yet the basic thrust of this book is diagnosis.
For diagnosis precedes cure, and we cannot begin

to help ourselves until we become sensitively conscious of the problem.

These pages will have served their purpose if, in some measure, they help create the consciousness needed for man to undertake the control of change, the guidance of his evolution. For, by making imaginative use of change to channel change, we cannot only spare ourselves the trauma of future shock, we can reach out and humanize distant tomorrows.

ACKNOWLEDGMENTS

Among the more hallowed clichés of our time are the notions that an author's life is a lonely one, that his ideas spring from some mystical inner source, and that he writes under the spell of inspiration. Most professional writers know better. However well these descriptions may apply to other authors and other books, they do not apply to this one. *Future Shock* is a product of gregarious, face-to-face and mind-to-mind contact with hundreds of people, so many, in fact, in so many different universities, research institutes and offices, that it would be impossible for me to list them all.

Apart from my own, the single most important influence on the book has been that of my wife, Heidi, who has been not the proverbial "patient spouse who kept the children out of the authorial den," but, rather, an active intellectual partner in the enterprise, arguing through point after point, forcing me to clarify and integrate the concepts on which the book is based. As in the past, she also served as resident editor, reading or listening to each chapter, suggesting cuts, additions, and fresh insights. It is, in large measure, her book as well as mine.

Several friends also read all or part of the manuscript in advance, offering valuable comments. Dr.

Donald F. Klein, director of psychiatric research, Hillside Hospital, New York, Dr. Herbert Gerjuoy, a psychologist, Dr. Benjamin Singer, a sociologist, and Harold Lee Strudler, Esq., were each kind enough to help me in this way. I must also thank Miss Bonnie Brower who served as research assistant during the early stages of the project, and cheerfully helped me filter the masses of material that mounted depressingly at times on my desk.

A special note of gratitude is owed to Professor Ellis L. Phillips of the Columbia University School of Law and to the Ellis L. Phillips Foundation for displaying superhuman patience, allowing me, again and again, to defer important commitments to the Foundation while completing this book.

NOTES

Bracketed [ ] *numbers indicate items listed in the accompanying* Bibliography. *Thus, in the* Notes [1] *will stand for the first item in the* Bibliography, Design for a Brain *by W. Ross Ashby.*

CHAPTER ONE

PAGE

12 The Thomson comparison appears in [175], p. 1.

13 Bagrit is quoted from *The New York Times*, March 17, 1965.

13 The Diebold item is from [57], p. 48.

13 Read's statement is found in his essay, "New Realms of Art" in [302], p. 77.

13 The Marek quote is from [165], pp. 20–21. A remarkable little book.

13 Boulding on post-civilization: [134], p. 7.

13 Boulding's reference to Julius Caesar is from "The Prospects of Economic Abundance," his lecture at the Nobel Conference, Gustavus Adolphus College, 1966.

14 Figures on US agricultural output are from "Malthus, Marx and the North American Breadbasket" by Orville Freeman in *Foreign Affairs*, July, 1967, p. 587.

15 There is, as yet, no widely accepted or wholly satisfactory term to describe the new stage of social development toward which we seem to be racing. Daniel Bell, the sociologist, coined the term "post-industrial" to signify a society in which the economy is largely based on service, the professional and technical classes dominate, theoretical knowledge is central, intellectual technology—systems analysis, model building, and the like—is highly developed, and technology is, at least potentially, capable of self-sustaining growth. The term has been criticized for suggesting that the society to come will no longer be technologically based—an implication that Bell specifically and carefully avoids.

PAGE

Kenneth Boulding's favorite term, "post-civilization," is employed to contrast the future society with "civilization"—the era of settled communities, agriculture, and war. The difficulty with "post-civilization" is its hint that what will follow will somehow be barbaric. Boulding rejects this mis-connotation as vigorously as Bell does his. Zbigniew Brzezinski's choice is the "technotronic society," by which he means one based heavily on advanced communications and electronics. The objection to this is that, in its heavy emphasis on technology, and, in fact, on a special form of technology, it does little to characterize the social aspects of the society.

Then, of course, there is McLuhan's "global village" and "electric age"—once again an attempt to describe the future in terms of one or two rather narrow dimensions: communications and togetherness. A variety of other terms are possible, too: transindustrial, post-economic, etc. My own choice, after all is said and done, is "super-industrial society." It, too, suffers from serious shortcomings. It is intended to mean a complex, fast-paced society dependent upon extremely advanced technology and a post-materialist value system.

15 Fourastié is quoted in [272], p. 28.
15 U Thant's statement is quoted in [217], p. 184.

CHAPTER TWO

19 The progeria case is reported in the Toronto *Daily Star*, March 8, 1967.
22 Huxley on the tempo of change is from [267], pp. viii–ix.
23 Data on growth of cities are from *Ekistics*, July, 1965, Table 4, p. 48.
23 Estimate of the rate of urbanization is from *World Health*, December, 1964, p. 4.
24 French productivity data from [283], p. 64.
26 Early transportation speeds are estimated in "Biggest Challenge: Getting Wisdom" by Peter Goldmark in *Printer's Ink*, May 29, 1964, p. 280. See also: [137], p. 61 and [151], p. 5 .
27 For material on the delay between invention and application, see [291], pp. 47–48.
27 The reference to Appert is drawn from "Radiation Preservation of Food" by S. A. Goldblith, *Science Journal*, January, 1966, p. 41.

PAGE

28 The Lynn study is reported briefly in "Our Accelerating Technological Change" by Frank Lynn, *Management Review*, March, 1967, pp. 67–70. See also: [64], pp.3–4.

28 Young's work is found in "Product Growth Cycles—A Key to Growth Planning" by Robert B. Young, Menlo Park, Calif.: Stanford Research Institute. Undated.

30 Data on book production are drawn from [206], p. 21, [200], p. 74, and [207], article on Incunabuli.

31 The rate of discovery of new elements is given in [146], Document I, p. 21.

34 Erikson's statement appears in [105], p. 197.

CHAPTER THREE

38 Data on the brain drain is from "Motivation Underlying the Brain Drain" [131], pp. 438, 447.

39 The passage of time as experienced by different age groups is discussed in "Subjective Time" by John Cohen in [342], p. 262.

40 Author's interviews with F. M. Esfandiary.

41 For further discussion of cultural differences in attitudes toward time, see "White People's Time, Colored People's Time" by Jules Henry in *Trans-action*, March-April, 1965, pp. 31–34.

42 On man's biological rhythms, see "The Physiological Control of Judgments of Duration: Evidence for a Chemical Clock" by Hudson Hoagland in [339].
The notion of "durational expectancy" is supported by research on the eating habits of the obese. Psychologist Stanley Schachter has shown, by making imaginative use of clocks that run at half the normal speed, that hunger is partly conditioned by one's perception of time. See: "Obesity and Eating" by Stanley Schachter in *Science*, August 23, 1968, pp. 751–756.

45 Albee and Clurman quotes are from the latter's essay on the former, *The New York Times*, November 13, 1966.

CHAPTER FOUR

51 The Barbie story is told in "Marketing Briefs," *Business Week*, March 11, 1967, p. 188.

55 Age of dwellings is discussed in "Homes of the Future" by E. F. Carter in [136], vol. 2, p. 35.

PAGE

55 Michael Wood has caught the spirit of transcience in his article, "America the Unreal" in *New Society,* April 14, 1966.

55 Auchincloss is quoted from *The New York Times,* March 17, 1966.

56 Buckminster Fuller's remark is from [146], Document 3, pp. 61–62.

58 Data on portable classrooms are drawn from *The Schoolhouse in the City,* a report of the Educational Facilities Laboratories, Inc. Not to be confused with [115].

60 For a description of the "thinkbelt" idea, see "Potteries Thinkbelt" by Cedric Price, *New Society,* June 2, 1966, p. 14.

62 The development of clip-on architecture is described by Reyner Banham in *Design Quarterly 63.* Minneapolis: Walker Art Center, 1965.

63 Data on the rental business are partially based on: Correspondence with C. A. Siegfried, Jr., Executive Secretary, American Rental Association. "You Name It—We Rent It" by Harland Manchester, *Reader's Digest,* July, 1966, p. 114.

66 *Svensk Damtidning,* November 2, 1965.

67 Rentalism has many unnoticed implications. A continuing swing toward rentalism could profoundly alter the balance of power between producer and consumer in many industries. The rise of vast rental organizations on a national and even international scale places a powerful new force between the producer and the ultimate consumer. Hertz and Avis, for example, operate such large fleets of autos and purchase on so large a scale, that they can win price, design, and service concessions from the manufacturers that no individual car buyer could hope to obtain. The same is true in any industry. Thus the formation of large rental organizations, by concentrating purchasing power, creates countervailing force in the precise Galbraithian sense of the term. This fact has not been overlooked by the American automotive manufacturers, at least one of which, Ford, has looked into the possibility of heading off this development by going directly into the rental business itself.

Even if manufacturers go into the rental business themselves, rentalism compels them to make revolutionary changes in organization and outlook. Whereas the ordinary producer need not concern himself too greatly with what happens to his product after it is sold, those who rent equipment are responsible for servicing it. This puts extreme pressure on them to improve the reliability of the product. In turn, this may require a radical reorientation of management thinking, right down to the design level.

Not long ago I interviewed the chief engineer of one of the largest corporations in the United States—a company which, like some computer manufacturers, rents its equipment directly to the user. I asked whether this had any implications for his engineering staff. His reply dramatically revealed the contrast between design for sale and design for rental:

> The first thing you have to do is change the attitude of the people you're hiring . . . A lot of engineers we hire from other industries come in here and are happy when they can save two cents for us by redesigning some part. We have to explain that cutting a corner like that could cost us a service call, and a service call costs us from $20 to $30 . . . It's a rough proposition to get people educated for high quality and reliability in the product after they've been trained in other ways. It boils down to this: we don't ship our headaches. Our headaches may go out the shipping door, but as long as we are responsible for servicing them, they remain our headaches.

The economics of rentalism could raise the quality of products and relieve consumers of the increasingly exasperating problems of service and repair.

But the implications of rentalism go even further, for they tend to speed up the already highly accelerated pace of technological change. The company that sells a product disposes of it once and for all. The company that rents a product may get that product back. Rental arrangements are short term. This mean that, if a technologically advanced model appears on the market, a renter can, with little difficulty, unburden himself of the old model and switch to the new. This raises for some manufacturers the specter of receiving thousands of their products back all at once—a terrifying prospect that compels them to pour a high percentage of their revenues into research and development in a frantic, never-ending effort to stay ahead of the pack. It is no accident that IBM, which rents its computers, or Xerox Corporation, which rents its copying machines, are both so deeply committed to R&D. As Joseph Wilson, president of Xerox, has put it: "We, not our customers, must assume the risk of obsolescence."

Rentalism also holds deep and as yet little known implications for the financial structure of any economy. It conjures up, for one thing, the image of a completely propertyless society. Whether this image is realistic or not, rentalism alters the flow of capital in the society. The manufacturer or rental organization advances capital for use by the consumer. This permits consumers to shift capital out of what economists term "real and personal property" and into securities. Indeed, if one imagines an entire society built on rentalism, in which vast rental organizations have become the pivots of power and profit, the best investment of all might turn out to be shares in the rental organizations.

70 Turner is quoted from [67], p. 41.

70 On brand switching and share of market see [67], p. 54.

71 The turnover of top brands is discussed in "Advertising, Competition, and the Anti-Trust Laws" by Henry Schachtre in 26 *American Bar Association Anti-Trust Section*, p. 161.

71 Diebold's comments are in [57], pp. 19–20.

71 On rates of attrition among consumer products, see *The New York Times*, June 9, 1967; also *Time*, October 24, 1969, p. 92.

72 Theobald is quoted from [63], p. 29.

CHAPTER FIVE

75 The Fuller estimates are from [146], Document 3, pp. 28–29.

77 Transport problems of the developing nations are examined in "Immobility: Barrier to Development" by Wilfred Owen in [243], p. 30.

78 Drucker is quoted from [140], p. 92.

78 The nomadic city dweller is discussed in "Are We a Nation of Cities?" by Daniel Elazar, *Public Interest*, Summer, 1966, p. 53.

78 The figure on Americans who move is drawn from *Population Characteristics*, Series P–20, # 188. US Department of Commerce, August 14, 1969.

79 French data from "A Cohort Analysis of Geographical

PAGE

and Occupational Mobility" by Guy Pourcher in *Population*, March-April, 1966.

See also: Supplement to Chapter Five, "Les Moyens de Regulation de la Politique de l'Emploi" by Thérèse Join-Lambert and François Lagrange in *Revue Française du Travail*, January-March, 1966, pp. 305–307.

81　Intra-US brain drain is examined in "An Exploratory Study of the Structure and Dynamics of the R&D Industry" by Albert Shapero, Richard P. Howell, and James R. Tombaugh. Menlo Park, California: Stanford Research Institute, June, 1964.

82　Whyte is quoted from [197], p. 269.

82　Jacobson story from *Wall Street Journal*, April 26, 1966.

A more recent study of executive mobility has found that a middle manager can anticipate being moved once every two to five years. One executive reported moving 19 times in 25 years. Eighty percent of the companies surveyed were increasing the rate of transfer. See paper by William F. Glueck in the *Journal of Management Studies*, Vol. 6, #2 or summary in *New Society*, July 17, 1969, p. 98.

84　Dichter's remark is from [76], p. 266.

85　Hitch-hikers: see "Traveling Girls" by Ellen Goyder, *New Society*, January 20, 1966, p. 5.

86　Touraine is quoted from *Acceptance and Resistance*, [49], p. 95.

86　Clark is cited in [249], p. 26.

88　The emotional response of the mover is the subject of "Grieving for a Lost Home" by Marc Fried in [241], p. 151, 160.

88　Interview with Monique Viot.

88　Clifton Fadiman's account appears in his essay, "Mining-Camp Megalopolis" in *Holiday*, October, 1965, p. 8.

88　For the Crestwood Heights study, see [236], p. 360.

88–89　Tyhurst's statement is from his paper "The Role of Transition States—Including Disasters—in Mental Illness" in [33], p. 154.

92　Dyckman's comment is found in "The Changing Uses of the City" in [173], p. 154.

93　The demise of geography has, of course, important implications for the future of the city. According to Melvin M. Webber, Professor of City Planning at Berkeley, "A new kind of large-scale urban society is emerging that is increasingly independent of the city . . . Because societies in the past had been

PAGE

spatially and locally structured, and because urban societies used to be exclusively city-based, we seem still to assume that territoriality is a necessary attribute of social systems." This, he argues, leads us to wholly misunderstand such urban problems as drug addiction, race riots, mental illness, poverty, etc. See his provocative essay, "The Post-City Age" in *Daedalus*, Fall, 1968, pp. 1091–1110.

93 Average residence duration is taken from "New Urban Structures" by David Lewis in [131], p. 313.

CHAPTER SIX

96 References to Weber, Simmel and Wirth are from [239], pp. 70–71.

98 Cox on limited involvements: [217], pp. 41–46.

102 On the number of people who preceded us, see "How Many People Have Lived on Earth?" by Nathan Keyfitz in *Demography*, 1966, vol 3, #2, p. 581.

104 Integrator concept and Gutman quote from "Population Mobility in the American Middle Class" by Robert Gutman in [241], pp. 175–182.

106 *Crestwood Heights* material is from [236], p. 365.

107 Barth quote from [216], pp. 13–14.

109 *Fortune* survey in [84], pp. 136–155.

110 I am indebted to Marvin Adelson, formerly Principal Scientist, System Development Corp., for the idea of occupational trajectories.

110 The quote from Rice is from "An Examination of the Boundaries of Part-Institutions" by A. K. Rice in *Human Relations*, vol. 4, #4, 1951, p. 400.

112 Job turnover among scientists and engineers discussed in "An Exploratory Study of the Structure and Dynamics of the R&D Industry" by Albert Shapero, Richard P. Howell, and James R. Tombaugh. Menlo Park, California: Stanford Research Institute, 1966, p. 117.

112 Westinghouse data from "Creativity: A Major Business Challenge" by Thomas J. Watson, Jr., *Columbia Journal of World Business*, Fall, 1965, p. 32.

112 British advertising turnover rates from "The Rat Race" by W. W. Daniel in *New Society*, April 14, 1966, p. 7.

112 Leavitt quoted from "Are Managers Becoming Obsolete?" by Harold F. Leavitt in *Carnegie Tech Quarterly*, November, 1963.

113 Company officials' quotes from "The Churning Market

PAGE

for Executives," by Seymour Freedgood in *Fortune*,
September, 1965, pp. 152, 236. See also: [84], p. 71.

113   S.R.I. quote is from [183], p. 148.

116   Class differences in mobility are discussed in "The
Human Measure," by Leonard Duhl in [51], p. 138
and in "Urban Design and Mental Health," by
Leonard Duhl in *AIA Journal*, March, 1961, p. 48.

117   Lipset and Bendix [242], p. 249.

117   Warner quoted from [350], p. 51 and [96], p. 62.

120   Florence estimate is drawn from "The Pattern of Cities
to Come," *New Society*, March 10, 1966, p. 6.

120   Gurevitch study and Milgram data can be found in
"The Small-World Problem," by Stanley Milgram
in *Psychology Today*, May, 1967, pp. 61–67.

120   The Nebraska study is detailed in "The Primary Relations of Middle-Class Couples," by Nicholas Bab-
chuk and Alan P. Bates in [122], p. 126.

121   Pupil turnover: "The Schoolhouse in the City," a report by the Educational Facilities Laboratories, Inc.,
1966, p. 8. Not to be confused with [115].

121   Whyte quote in [197], p. 383.

122   Moore study mentioned in *American Education*, April,
1967.

Poignant note on transcience from bulletin board of
communal farm, U.S.A., Summer, 1969. Quoted in
*Difficult But Possible Supplement to Whole Earth
Catalog*, September, 1969, p. 23.

"I hope that this week is the Farm's lowest point for
the summer, because if it gets any lower I don't have
a decent place to live . . . I think of this as my (at
least) temporary home. And I like my home to be
clear of broken glass and papers, my tools and supplies put away, I like to keep track of my guests,
take care of my animals . . . But this farm is far
from that . . .

"Our average farmer (Asshole) says to himself: 'I'm
here visiting (for a day, a week, a month or a year)
and I'm not really a part of this farm, just a guest,
so I can't do anything really effective about the
Farm's condition . . .' I believe the key to the problem is: STABILITY LEADS TO A FEELING OF
COMMUNITY.

"We have very little sense of community here . . .
This is social decay: where the natural forces of
the family (helping, loving, working together) are
driven out by selfishness . . . I believe that the

decay, the pigs-at-the-trough feeling, is caused by the INSTABILITY.

"When a stable group of ten lives together for weeks, natural forces work *for* community feeling. When the Farm is more than 20% tourists, when the family feeling is broken every day or two by departures and arrivals, I see no hope."

CHAPTER SEVEN

126   For Weber, see Chapter Eight in [256].

129   Zakon cited in "Finding Buyers for the Bad Buys," *Business Week*, September 13, 1969, pp. 49–51.

129   Organizational change is discussed in "Reorganizing for Results" by D. Ronald Daniel in *Harvard Business Review*, November-December, 1966, p. 96; also in "Patterns of Organization Change" by Larry E. Greiner in *Harvard Business Review*, May-June, 1967, pp. 119–120.

131   Gardner quoted from [39], p. 26.

134   On scientific task forces and the rise of "non-routine" industries, see "The Usefulness of Scientists" by Howard Reiss and Jack Balderston in *International Science and Technology*, May, 1966, p. 44; and a profile of George Kozmetsky in "How a Businessman Ramrods a B-School" in *Business Week*, May 24, 1969, p. 84.

135   Schon is quoted from [179], vol. 1, p. 106.

137   "The Decline of Hierarchy in Industrial Organizations" is discussed by William H. Read in *Business Horizons*, Fall, 1965, pp. 71–75.

142   For quotes from Warren Bennis on this page and in the remainder of Chapter Seven, see his articles: "Beyond Bureaucracy" in *Transaction*, July-August, 1965, pp. 31–35; and "Changing Organizations" in the *Journal of Applied Behavioral Science*, vol. 2, #3, p. 261. For more detailed treatment see [252].

146   Guzzardi is from [84], p. 71.

146   Gardner is quoted from [39], p. 83.

148   Pareto is quoted in [19], p. 231.

CHAPTER EIGHT

153–54   Not only are British prime ministers moving in and out of office faster since the days of Lloyd George, but the rate of turnover among other cabinet ministers has risen, too. According to political scientist Anthony King of the University of Essex, "Britain

PAGE

now has one of the most rapid rates of turnover in high ministerial office of any major country in the Western world—or the Eastern for that matter. The rate is considerably higher than in Britain before 1939 or 1914." See "Britain's Ministerial Turnover," *New Society*, August 18, 1966, p. 257.

154   Fishwick's quote is from "Is American History A Happening?" by Marshall Fishwick in *Saturday Review*, May 13, 1967, p. 20.

154   Klapp is cited from [228], pp. 251, 261.

156   Childe quoted from [203], pp. 108–109.

159   For information on childrearing, see [102], pp. 168–169.

159   The spread of Freudianism is discussed in [190], pp. 94–95.

161   Mr. Cornberg's quote can be found in "Libraries" by Alvin Toffler in *Bricks and Mortarboards*, A Report from Educational Facilities Laboratories, Inc., on College Planning and Building, p. 93.

166   For exposure to advertising messages see [65], pp. 5–6.

168   On the conference of composers and computer specialists, see *The New York Times*, November 14, 1966.

169   The acceleration of music is also commented on by David Riesman in [192], p. 178. Professional composers and musicians I have asked generally confirm the belief that, note for note, we are playing faster today. (We are also, for whatever *that* means, playing classical music at higher pitches.)

169   Quotes from Flexner are taken from an interview with the author.

171   The article on Sontag and "camp" appeared in *Time*, December 11, 1964, p. 75.

173   Hauser reference is from [208], vol. 4, p. 167.

174   The turnover of art schools is noted in "Stop Wasting Time" by Robert Hughes in *New Society*, February 2, 1967, pp. 170–171.

174   McHale's comments are from his essay "The Plastic Parthenon" (draft version) from *Lineastruttura*, June, 1966; and from his "The Expendable Ikon" in *Architectural Design*, February/March, 1959. See also [164].

177   Rate of conceptual turnover in science is drawn from [200], p. 163.

179   Comments on the costs of relearning are from "The Changing Nature of Human Nature" by Harold D. Lasswell in the *American Journal of Psychoanalysis*, vol. XXVI, #2, p. 164.

CHAPTER NINE

PAGE

188   On ocean mining and Spiess, see *The New York Times*, July 17, 1966; "Lure of a Lost World" in the *Kaiser Aluminum News*, #2, 1966; and "The Feedback between Technology and Values" by T. J. Gordon in [131], pp. 167–169. See also: "Aquaculture" by John Bardach, *Science*, September 13, 1968, pp. 1098–1106. Data on world fishing industry will be found in [130], p. 43.

191   Dr. Walter Orr Roberts is quoted from his essay "Science—the Wellspring of Our Discontent" in *Space Digest*, June, 1967, p. 78.

192   Statement by the American Meteorological Society is from "Forecast: Weatherman in the Sky" in *Time*, July 29, 1966, p. 18. See also: "Weather Modification" by Gordon J. F. MacDonald in *Science Journal*, January, 1968, p. 39.

193   For Capek, see [271].

193   Use of fish and dolphins is described in various issues of the *Bulletin of the Centre d'Etude des Consequences Generales des Grandes Techniques Nouvelles*. See especially #32, June, 1965; #33, August-September, 1965; and #35, January, 1966.

193   For data on communication between man and dolphin, see [294] and subsequent works by Lilly.

194   Thomson on animals: [175], p. 125.

194   Clarke's quote is from [137], p. 24.

149   Delgado's famed experiment is summarized in popular form in *Science Digest*, August, 1965, p. 38. See his book: [275].

195   Johnson is quoted from his paper, "Horizons of Industrial Microbiology" in *Impact*, vol. XVII, #3. For an excellent non-technical introduction to microbiology, see also: "Living Chemical Factories" by Robert K. Finn and Victor H. Edwards in *Engineering*, a Cornell University quarterly, Winter, 1968, vol. 2.

195   Tiselius quoted from his interview with the author.

196   Fourastié is cited from [78], p. 17.

197   Information on cloning is drawn from "Experimental Genetics and Human Evolution" by Joshua Lederberg, a mimeographed paper, Department of Genetics, Stanford University School of Medicine, and from author's interview with Lederberg.

200   The work of Hafez and Petrucci is reported in "On the Frontiers of Medicine," *Life*, September 10, 1965,

PAGE

in "The Dead Body and the Living Brain" by
Oriana Fallaci in *Look*, November 28, 1967, p. 99.

215   Editor on the telephone and press coverage of Wright
Brothers are described in [162], p. 11.

215   Newcomb quote is from [137], p. 2.

216   The infeasibility of the automobile is cited in [97],
p. 177.

216   The millionth Ford: see [270], p. 151.

216   Rutherford is discussed in [306], p. 34.

CHAPTER TEN

222   Demby quotes from interviews with the author.

222   British Overseas Airways Corporation venture in experientialism is described in *The New York Times*,
September 13 and 16, 1969.

229   "Hon" is described in the *Scandinavian Times*, August-
September, 1966. The author visited the Moderna
Museet during the summer of 1966 and "experi-
enced" the show himself.

229   Cerebrum: the author donned the diaphanous robes
on opening night. Cerebrum is described in the
Village Voice, November 7, 1968, pp. 10–11.

231   The case of the topless prize is reported in *Sweden
Now*, April, 1968, p. 6.

234   Stanford Research Institute quote is drawn from "A
Social and Cultural Framework for 1975" by Ely
M. Brandes and Arnold Mitchell in [183], p. 172.

235   For data on earlier maturation of children, see [166],
pp. 39–40.

CHAPTER ELEVEN

238   Lundberg is quoted from [163], p. 295.

238   Wolf's remarks are from an interview with the author.

239   On leisure as a family-cement, see [183], p. 7.

239   Greenberg is quoted from an interview with the author.

240   Weitzen's comments are from his article, "The Programmed Child," in *Mademoiselle*, January, 1966,
pp. 70–71.

240   The "multi-mouse" experiments are reported in *The
New York Times*, May 30, 1968.

242   Margaret Mead on childlessness: from her paper "The
Life Cycle and its Variations: The Division of Roles"
in [132], p. 872.

245   For the novels of Skinner and Rimmer, see [125],
[126], and [328].

PAGE

246 The work of the Ecumenical Institute is described in *The New York Times*, November 9, 1968.

248 The British Sexual Offenses Act became law on July 27, 1967.

250 Nelson Foote is cited in "The American Family Today" by Reuben Hill in [109], pp. 93–94.

252 The black civil rights worker is quoted from ". . . Because He was Black and I was White" by Elizabeth Sutherland in *Mademoiselle*, April, 1967, p. 244.

253 The Swedish article is from *Svensk Damtidning*, November 9, 1965. It is Part 4 of a five-part series entitled "Woman '85."

253 Keil and Lazure are both quoted in "Trial by Marriage," *Time*, April 14, 1967, p. 112.

258 Neugarten is quoted from her unpublished paper, "The Changing Age-Status System." On early childbearing, see also: [121], p. 68 and [118], p. 33.

CHAPTER TWELVE

263 The Ellul quotes can be found in [186], pp. 77, 80, and 93.

264 On Toynbee, see specifically: "Why I Dislike Western Civilization" by Arnold Toynbee in *The New York Times Magazine*, May 10, 1964.

265 For the Kenneth Schwartz quote, see his "Fragmentation of the Mass Market" in *Dun's Review*, July, 1962. See also: "More Sense About Market Segmentation" by William H. Reynolds in *Harvard Business Review*, September–October, 1965.

266 Saunders is cited in "Putting a New Face on the Office," *Business Week*, September 13, 1969, p. 152.

266 Yavitz is quoted from his article, "The Anomie of the 'Paper Factory' Worker." Hare's remarks are from his paper, "The Horse that Can Save More than a Kingdom." Both appear in the *Columbia Journal of World Business*, vol. VII, #3, pp. 32, 59

268 The Mustang quote is found in "Anti-technology" by Reyner Banham in *New Society*, May 4, 1967, p. 645; see also "Selling the Golden Calf" by Jeremy Bugler in *New Society*, October 17, 1968, p. 556.

269 McLuhan: from "The Future of Education" by Marshall McLuhan and George B. Leonard, *Look*, February 21, 1967, p. 23.

270 Data on literary diversity are from [206], p. 83.

271 McHale is quoted from his paper, "Education for

Real" in the *World Academy of Art and Science
Newsletter*, Transnational Forum, June, 1966, p. 3.

273 On tendencies toward differentiation in education, see
"Decentralizing Urban School Systems" by Mario
Fantini and Richard Magat; "The Community-Cen-
tered School" by Preston Wilcox; and "Alternatives
to Urban Public Schools" by Kenneth Clark, all in
[115].

277 London movies are discussed in "The Smaller the
Better," *Economist*, January 11, 1969, p. 66.

On diversity of film fare, an advertisement placed
in *The New York Times* of August 10, 1969, by
Walter Reade, Jr., a leading film exhibitor, is worth
quoting:

> The movie-goers of this country are not as ho-
> mogeneous or as sophisticated as you might think
> . . . It isn't widely known but many films are de-
> signed and produced exclusively for specific re-
> gions of the country, and with specific audiences
> in mind.
> Two years ago there was a Don Knotts comedy
> called *The Ghost and Mr. Chicken*, a low-budget
> Hollywood film that earned a phenomenal $2.5
> million—outside of New York. Who saw it? The
> Middle West and the South, in the 'grass roots'
> areas, which also like films about stock car racing,
> and with country music themes. Another Holly-
> wood studio has been very successful with a
> series of 'beach party' and motorcycle films. These
> surface only briefly in New York but are a staple
> of suburban drive-in theaters and their predomi-
> nantly under-25 audiences.
> The West Coast is offered dozens of Japanese
> films, because of its large Oriental population,
> while New York sees only one or two a year . . .
> What are we to make of the failure of *Isadora* in
> Los Angeles, and its success here? What of *The
> Shameless Old Lady*—successful here *and* Los
> Angeles, not so elsewhere?

277 An interesting experiment in providing radio services
for small, homogeneous audiences has taken place
in Buffalo, New York, where station WBFO-FM has
set up a storefront studio in the black ghetto. There,
people from the neighborhood, itself, produce six
hours of programming aimed at informing their
neighbors about job opportunities, health measures,
black history and culture.

PAGE

278 Trends in the magazine industry are discussed in *The New York Times*, April 17, 1966, April 27, 1969; *The Wall Street Journal*, August 18, 1964; and in "Aiming at the Hip" in *Time*, June 2, 1967. See also: "Fat Days for the 'How-To' Publishers," *Business Week*, July 30, 1966; and "City Magazines are the Talk of the Town," *Business Week*, February 18, 1967.

279 On underground press, see "Admen Groove on Underground," in *Business Week*, April 12, 1969.

280 Moosmann is quoted from interview with the author.

282 For Naughton, see "Goodbye to Gutenberg" in *Newsweek*, January 24, 1966; Japanese developments are reported in *The Times* (London), December 12, 1969.

CHAPTER THIRTEEN

288 On surfers, see Nadeau [231], p. 144 and "Is J. J. Really King of the Surf" by Jordan Bonfante in *Life*, June 10, 1966, p. 81.

289 For a colorful account of life among the sky-divers, see "Death-Defying Sports of the Sixties" by Mario Puzo in *Cavalier*, December, 1965, p. 19.

289 Data on the decline of the society's overall commitment to work are to be found in [74], pp. 13–14.

290 Pynchon: [235].

290 Sheckley's story is found in [237].

291 Age segregation is discussed in "The Youth Ghetto" by John Lofland in the *Journal of Higher Education*, March, 1968, pp. 126–139.

292 James W. Carey's remarks are from his paper, "Harold Adams Innis and Marshall McLuhan," given at the Association for Education in Journalism Convention, Iowa City, Iowa, August 28-September 3, 1966.

293 Post-marital tribalism is examined in "The World of the Formerly Married" by Morton M. Hunt in *McCall's*, August, 1966.

295 The best short account of the origins and early development of the hippie movement is found in "A Social History of the Hippies" by Warren Hinckle in *Ramparts*, March, 1967, p. 5. See also: [223], pp. 63–68.

295 On distinctions among hippie-like subcults, see "Tell It Like It Really Is . . ." by David Andrew Seeley, *Center Diary*, May-June, 1967.

296 The death of the hippie movement is reported in

PAGE

     "Love is Dead" by Earl Shorris in *The New York Times Magazine*, October 29, 1967, p. 27.

297 For an early description of the skinhead phenomenon, see "Hippies vs. Skinheads," *Newsweek*, October 6, 1969, p. 90.

297 Material on street gangs: [240]; [114], p. 20; and "Violence" by James Q. Wilson in [179], vol. 4, p. 7.

299 Gardner on conformity is from [39], pp. 62–63.

299 Material on the Temne people is from "Independence and Conformity in Subsistence-Level Societies" by J. W. Berry in the *Journal of Personality and Social Psychology*, December, 1967, p. 417.

CHAPTER FOURTEEN

304 The loss of consensus is discussed in "Anything Goes: Taboos in Twilight" by Paul D. Zimmerman in *Newsweek*, November 13, 1967, p. 74.

305 Gruen reports his work in "Composition and Some Correlates of the American Core Culture" in *Psychological Reports*, vol. 18, pp. 483–486. Material is drawn from this source and from an interview.

305 The life style of the English gentleman is examined in [215], p. 138.

308 Klapp is quoted from [228], pp. 37–38.

308 On the West Side Intellectual subcult, see [234].

308 For the role of life style models, see "The New Heroes" by John Speicher in *Cheetah*, November, 1967, pp. 27–28.

309 Ginsberg's letter is from "In the beginning, Leary turned on Ginsberg and saw that it was good . . ." by Timothy Leary in *Esquire*, July, 1968, p. 87.

314 On the pressure of overchoice: The adoption of a style also relates to the conquest of unpredictability in the society. As the level of novelty around us rises, we become more uncertain of the behavior of other individuals, leading to a withdrawal of commitment, a fear of self-revelation or deep feelings. When young people don outlandish costumes, thrift-store gowns and kooky hats, they touch off a subtle fear among the "straights" in society because they announce, by their clothing, that their behavior is likely to be unpredictable. The strength of their attachment to their own subculture, at the same time, derives from the fact that within the group, unpredictability is reduced. They can make better predictions about the behavior of their peers and subcult colleagues than about the outside world.

Adoption of a life style and the affiliation with a subcult can be seen as efforts to lower the level of novelty or unpredictability in the microenvironment.

321   Mannheim is quoted from [189], p. 46.

321   The Gross quote is from "The State of the Nation: Social Systems Accounting" by Bertram M. Gross in [313], p. 198.

CHAPTER FIFTEEN

327   The "human ecology" approach to medicine is discussed in "The Doctor, His Patient, and the Environment" by Lawrence E. Hinkle, Jr., in *The American Journal of Public Health*, January, 1964, p. 11.

328   Material on life changes research is based partially on interviews with Dr. Thomas H. Holmes of the University of Washington School of Medicine; and Dr. Ransom J. Arthur and E. K. Eric Gunderson of the U.S. Navy Medical Neuropsychiatric Research Unit, San Diego.

See the following papers in the *Journal of Psychosomatic Research*:

"A Longitudinal Study of Life-Change and Illness Patterns" by Richard H. Rahe, Joseph D. McKean, Jr., and Ransom J. Arthur. vol. 10, 1967, pp. 355–366.

"The Social Readjustment Rating Scale" by Thomas H. Holmes and Richard H. Rahe. vol. 11, 1967, pp. 213–218.

"Magnitude Estimations of Social Readjustments" by Minoru Masuda and Thomas H. Holmes. vol. 11, 1967, pp. 219–225.

"The Social Readjustment Rating Scale: A Cross-Cultural Study of Japanese and Americans" by Minoru Masuda and Thomas H. Holmes. vol. 11, 1967, pp. 227–237.

"Quantitative Study of Recall of Life Events" by Robert L. Casey, Minoru Masuda, and Thomas H. Holmes. vol. 11, 1967, pp. 239–247.

"Seriousness of Illness Rating Scale" by Allen R. Wyler, Minoru Masuda and Thomas H. Holmes. vol. 11, 1968, pp. 363–374.

and:

"Social and Environmental Factors in Illness Behavior" by E. K. Eric Gunderson, Richard H. Rahe, and Ransom J. Arthur. Paper presented to the Annual Meetings of the Western Psychological Association, San Diego, California, March, 1968.

"Life Crisis and Disease Onset—I. Qualitative and Quantitative Definition of the Life Crisis and its Association with Health Change; II. A Prospective Study of Life Crises and Health Changes," by Richard H. Rahe and Thomas H. Holmes. (Mimeo) Department of Psychiatry, University of Washington School of Medicine, Seattle, Washington.

The general pattern discovered in these studies is supported by the findings of George Brown and J. L. T. Birley of the Social Psychiatry Unit, Maudsley Hospital, London. Brown and Birley studied cases of schizophrenic relapse and correlated them with life change histories. See: *Journal of Health and Social Behavior*, vol. 9, ¶3 (1968), p. 263.

333 The death rate of spouses is studied in "The Mortality of Widowers" by Michael Young, Bernard Benjamin and Chris Wallis, in *Lancet*, August 31, 1963, pp. 454–456.

334 For a brief but comprehensive treatment of the orientation response, see [21].

Also:

"Neurophysiological Contributions to the Subject of Human Communication" by Mary A. B. Brazier in [7], p. 63.

"Neuronal Models and the Orienting Reflex" by E. N. Sokolov in Brazier, M. A. B. (ed.), *The Central Nervous System and Behavior*, New York: J. Macy, 1960, pp. 187–276.

"Higher Nervous Functions: The Orienting Reflex" by E. N. Sokolov, *Annual Review of Physiology*, 1963, vol. 3, pp. 545–580.

"Neuronal Model of the Stimulus: I. The Formation of a Neuronal Model by Repeated Representation of the Stimulus," by E. N. Sokolov in *Rep. Acad. Pedagog. Sc.*, USSR (1959), pp. 93–96 (in Russian).

335 Lubin is quoted from an interview with the author.

338 No discussion of the adaptive reaction and stress can overlook Dr. Hans Selye whose work laid the basis

for much of the research conducted in recent years. His book [26] has become a classic.

A brief section on ACTH and its relation to stress appears in [10], p. 306. See also [12], pp. 330–334.

339 Levi's work is discussed in [20]; in "Life Stress and Urinary Excretion of Adrenaline and Noradrenaline" by Lennart Levi in [24]; and in "Conditions of Work and Their Influence on Psychological and Endocrine Stress Reactions" by J. Froberg, C. Karlsson, L. Levi, L. Lidberg and K. Seeman, Report #8, The Laboratory for Clinical Stress Research, Karolinska Sjukhuset, Stockholm, October, 1969.

340 Dubos is quoted from his speech at the Nobel Conference, Gustavus Adolphus College, 1966, entitled "Adaptation to the Environment and Man's Future."

340 Selye is quoted from [26], p. 176.

341 Data on the effects of crowding will be found in [343]. See also "Population Density and Social Pathology" by John B. Calhoun in [241]; and *The New York Times*, December 28, 1966.

341 Hinkle's studies are reported in his paper, "Studies of Human Ecology in Relation to Health and Behavior," *BioScience*, August, 1965, pp. 517–520.

342 Selye: [26], p. vii.

CHAPTER SIXTEEN

343 The limits of the nervous system are discussed in "Curiosity and Exploration," by D. E. Berlyne, *Science*, July 1, 1966, p. 26.

See also a highly significant paper by Bruce L. Welch entitled "Psychophysiological Response to the Mean Level of Environmental Stimulation: A Theory of Environmental Integration." It appears in [32]. Welch posits a general level of stimulation which he terms the MLES (Mean Level of Environmental Stimulation) and shows how fluctuations in this level can produce distinct physiological and behavioral changes in men and animals.

The effects of understimulation are examined in "Adaptation of Small Groups to Extreme Environments," by E. K. Eric Gunderson and Paul D. Nelson, *Aerospace Medicine*, December, 1963, p. 1114.

Also:

"Biographical Predictors of Performance in an Extreme Environment," by E. K. Eric Gunderson and

PAGE

Paul D. Nelson in the *Journal of Psychology*, 1965, #61, pp. 59–67.

"Emotional Health in Extreme and Normal Environments," by E. K. Eric Gunderson. Paper presented at the International Congress on Occupational Health, Vienna, September 19–24, 1966.

"Performance Evaluations of Antarctic Volunteers," by E. K. Eric Gunderson, Report #64–19, US Navy Medical Neuropsychiatric Research Unit, San Diego, Calif.

344 The case of the Chindit soldier is described in the *Daily Telegraph*, (London) August 30, 1966.

345 The Normandy research is reported in "Combat Neurosis. Development of Combat Exhaustion" by R. L. Swank and E. Marchand in the *Archives of Neurology and Psychiatry*, LV, 236; 1946. An earlier report is to be found in "Chronic Symptomatology of Combat Neurosis" by R. L. Swank and B. Cohen in *War Medicine*, VIII, 143; 1945.

345 Swank is quoted in [25], pp. 38–39.

346 The Waco disaster is described in [23], p. 311.

346 The Udall case is covered in [16]. For a more general study of disaster behavior, see [54].

347 On culture shock: see "Personality Determinants and Assessment," by Sven Lundstedt, *Journal of Social Issues*, July, 1963, p. 3.

348 Sensory deprivation experiments are described in "Sensory and Perceptual Deprivation" by Thomas L. Myers in [32].

Also:

"Effects of Experiential Deprivation Upon Behavior in Animals," by John L. Fuller, paper presented at Third World Congress of Psychiatry, Montreal, 1961. A shorter version will be found in [31].

"Emotional Symptoms in Extremely Isolated Groups," by E. K. Eric Gunderson, *Archives of General Psychiatry*, October, 1963, pp. 362–368.

"Summary of Research in Sensory Deprivation and Social Isolation," by Howard H. McFann, *NATO Symposium on Defense Psychology*, August, 1961.

350 Neural transmission rates are given in "Biological Models and Empirical Histories of the Growth of Organizations" by Mason Haire in [37], p. 375 and in [279], p. 107.

350 A lucid introduction to information theory is found in "Coping with Administrators' Information Over-

PAGE

load" by James G. Miller, Mental Health Research
Institute, University of Michigan. Paper delivered at
the First Institute on Medical School Administration,
Association of American Medical Colleges in Atlanta,
Georgia, October, 1963.

351   Limitations on information processing capacity in humans are discussed in [22], pp. 41–42.

352   The breakdown of worker performance is described
in [6], pp. 47–53.

Also:

"Automation: Some underlying Psychological Processes," by E. D. Poulton, *Transactions* (Journal of
the Association of Industrial Medical Officers) 15
(3) 96–99, 1965.

The mental rather than muscular limitations are
noted in "Components of Skilled Performance" by
Michael I. Posner, *Science,* June 24, 1966, pp. 1712–
1718.

353   Information glut is discussed in "A Theoretical Review
of Individual and Group Psychological Reactions to
Stress" by James G. Miller in Grosser *et al.,* [14],
p. 14.

353   The possible relationship of overload to mental illness
is examined in *Disorders of Communication,* vol.
XLII, Research Publications, Association for Research in Nervous and Mental Disease, 1964, pp.
98–99.

Also: "Schizophrenic-like Responses in Normal Subjects Under Time Pressure" by G. Usdansky and
L. J. Chapman, *Journal of Abnormal and Social Psychology, 60,* pp. 143–146, 1960.

356   The Gross quote is from his paper, "The State of the
Nation: Social Systems Accounting" in [313], p. 250.

358   Reaction time is discussed in "Information Processing
in the Nervous System" by D. E. Broadbent, *Science,*
October 22, 1965, p. 460.

358   For an insightful discussion of the modes of organizational response to overload conditions, see "Information Input Overload: Features of Growth in Com-
munications-Oriented Institutions" by Richard L.
Meier in [41], pp. 233–273.

Also:

"Some Sociological Aspects of Message Load" by
Lindsey Churchill, in [41], pp. 274–284.

The strategies of denial, specialization, reversion and super-simplification are analogues of some familiar organizational responses discussed in these papers.

363 For "paradoxical phase" see [25], pp. 30–32, 44.

363 Violence as a response to stress is discussed in "Violence and Man's Struggle to Adapt," by Marshall F. Gilula and David N. Daniels, *Science*, April 25, 1969, p. 404.

363 *Japan Times*, July 3, 1966.

364 The story of the Crete cop-outs is told in "Crete: A Stop in the New Odyssey," by Thomas Thompson, *Life*, July 19, 1968, p. 23.

365 The nervous breakdown analogy is from "Has This Country Gone Mad?" by Daniel P. Moynihan, *Saturday Evening Post*, May 4, 1968, p. 13.

366 The Bierl quote is from the Thompson story in *Life*, July 19, 1968, p. 28.

A Note on Understimulation:

The emphasis in this chapter has been on the problems of overstimulation. What is striking to anyone who reads through the scientific literature is the similarity of human response to both high *and* low stimulation. Apparently, when men are pushed either above or below the adaptive range, they exhibit some of the same symptoms of distress. Thus psychologists have recently completed extensive studies of the men who live in the seven US outposts in Antarctica. The most inhospitable environment inhabited by man, Antarctica subjects these men to enforced monotony and understimulation. The Amundsen-Scott station at the South Pole is literally isolated from the rest of the world, except for sporadic radio communications, for ten months of the year. Temperatures plummet to as low as −100° (F) and the winds that sweep across the ice sometimes reach velocities of 100 mph. In all these outposts small groups of men are compelled to live indoors, in extremely close quarters, for protracted periods. Life inside these stations is probably as "changeless" as in any social environment in which modern men find themselves.

According to E. K. Eric Gunderson and Paul D. Nelson, in the studies noted above, "Under conditions of restricted stimulation and activity for prolonged periods, participants reported an increase in the incidence and severity of emotional and somatic symptoms, particularly on items reflecting sleep

disturbances, depression, irritability, and anxiety."
The men felt leaden and fatigued. Some suffered
loneliness and depression. Many exhibited extremely
short tempers, flaring easily into anger.

The chronicles of polar explorers confirm the picture
of psychological distress. There are repeated references to "polar ennui" and frequent symptoms of
withdrawal and deadly apathy. Admiral Byrd, for
example, after five months of total isolation at a
remote weather station, suffered a behavior breakdown whose effects lasted for months afterward. In
his diary, Byrd wrote: "Mornings it's a tough job
to drive myself out of the sleeping bag. I feel as
if I had been drugged. But I tell myself, over and
over again, that if I give in—if I let this stupor
claim me—I may never awake . . . Why bother? . . .
Why not let things drift? . . . That is the direction
of everlasting peace. So why resist?" (Byrd, R. E.,
Alone, New York: Putnam, 1938.)

Significantly, one of the worst punishments known
to man is solitary confinement—a situation in which
the individual is not only cut off from the stimulation
of social interaction, but deprived of change and
novelty of any kind. For this reason, it is employed
by interrogators and psychologists to "soften up"
prisoners whom they wish to brainwash.

It was, in fact, the successful brainwashing of captured American troops by the Red Chinese and
North Koreans during the Korean conflict that
spurred research into "sensory deprivation."

The psychologist D. O. Hebb, a pioneer in this field,
found that monotonous sensory stimulation produces
confusion—a disruption of the ability to think clearly.
His associates, Heron, Scott, Bexton and Doane,
confirmed that stimuli-deprived subjects had difficulty concentrating. The volunteers reported anxiety,
somatic complaints, occasional hallucinations, and
difficulty in judging the passage of time.

Myers, a US Navy researcher, summarized a decade
of sensory deprivation research: "Most subjects find
sensory isolation difficult to endure, are tempted to
withdrawal, and have little appetite to repeat the
experience. . . . Subjects have unusual and compelling reactions. They experience severe tedium,
restlessness, anxiety, difficulty in mental concentra-

tion, blurring of the boundaries of sleeping and wak-
ing activities and of reality . . . Performance on
intellectual tasks tends to decline . . ." In a word,
according to Myers, "Sensory deprivation apparently increases the desire for informative stimulation,
though not necessarily the desire for relatively redundant and meaningless stimulation." ("Sensory
and Perceptual Deprivation" by Thomas I. Myers
in [32]).

Moving out of the laboratory, we find that certain
employees in advanced automated plants frequently
exhibit similar symptoms of understimulation. These
workers are compelled to spend many hours alone in
control booths scanning a variety of dials and screens
for signs of equipment breakdown. But while there
are many signals for them to monitor, the signals
are, by and large, repetitive and predictable. Only
rarely is there an "abnormal" or novel signal. When
novelty is too low, the worker's alertness fades and
he increasingly misses or fails to report abnormalities. Boredom sets in, and his very self-confidence
evaporates. He begins to doubt his own ability to
distinguish between normal and abnormal signals.
(See [6]).

There is convincing evidence, moreover, that when
deprived of the necessary stimulation we will take
action to create it. Like the laboratory monkey who
pushes a lever hundreds of times per hour for no
reward other than the opportunity to look out a
window, man exhibits a deep-seated hunger for
novelty when his environment becomes too changeless. He attempts to alter his surroundings, to create
change, thereby bringing the level of stimulation
back into the "adaptive range." .

So strong is man's need to stay within the adaptive
range that internal mechanisms sometimes take over
when the external environment fails to provide the
needed excitement. Recent scientific research suggests that dreaming is a way of boosting the level
of arousal of the brain and body at a time when
they are largely cut off from needed external stimuli.
Something analogous to dreaming seems to occur
even in unborn babies. Indeed, the "rapid eye
movements" associated with dreaming occur more
frequently in young children than in adults, and
even more frequently in the foetus.

This suggests that within the womb, the least ex-
ternally stimulating environment of all, internal stimulation keeps the brain, the neutral network and
the endocrine systems in action. Later, as the baby
develops into an adult, as levels of external stimulation rise, and as the individual develops greater
control over his external environment, dreaming and
rapid eye movements tend to fall off in frequency.

To sum up: when the level of environmental stimulation or change falls below a certain point, the
individual is forced below his adaptive range, he
suffers distinct distress and takes action to increase
the level of stimulation. When the level of environmental stimulation forces him above his adaptive
range, he exhibits many of the same symptoms—
anxiety, confusion, irritability, and eventual apathy.
In this situation, as we see in Chapter 17, the individual strives to reduce stimulation. In short, all of
us, from before the instant of birth to our very
deathbed, wage a continuing, sometimes desperate,
sometimes quite creative struggle to keep the level
of stimulation from pushing us above or below our
adaptive range.

CHAPTER SEVENTEEN

371   The Manus story is told in [44], p. 415.
374   Selye references are from [26], pp. 265, 269.
382   Fuller is quoted from interview with the author.
383   The 100,000 figure is extrapolated from *Population
      Characteristics*, U.S. Department of Commerce,
      August 14, 1969, Series P-20, #188, p. 161.
384   Situational grouping material was developed in inter-
      views with Gerjuoy.
387   For a discussion of crisis intervention, see "Crisis: A
      Review of Theory, Practice and Research" by Allen
      Darbonne in *International Journal of Psychiatry*,
      November, 1968, p. 372.
388   The reference to half-way houses in the penal field is
      from "Correctional Institutions in a Great Society"
      by Daniel Glaser in *Excerpta Criminologica*, 3 (2/3)
      –3–6, 1965.
388   An analogous proposal for adapting slum dwellers to
      new housing has been made by Margaret Mead.
      See *Chicago Sun-Times*, November 2, 1966.
389   Khartoum: based on author's interview with Doxiadis.
393   Gardner on continuity is from [39], p. 6.
394   Kimball is quoted from his introduction to [50], p. xvii.

PAGE

394   Coon's remark is from his paper, "Growth and Development of Social Groups" in [177], p. 124.

394   Data on Christmas cards are based on *Preliminary 1967 Census of Manufactures*. Industry Series—Greeting card publishers. MC-67 (P-27C-1) US Department of Commerce.

394   Family ritual is examined in [5], p. 32.

CHAPTER EIGHTEEN

401   Dewey and Hutchins are quoted in [112], the dedication and p. 70.

401   The Barzun reference is from [101], p. 125.

402   The significance of the clock is explored in "The Monastery and the Clock" by Lewis Mumford in [293], p. 61. See also the excellent paper entitled "Time, Work-Discipline, and Industrial Capitalism" by E. P. Thompson in *Past and Present*, December, 1967, pp. 56–97.

403   Snow is quoted from [306], p. 12.

406   For a description of McDonald's proposal see "Beyond the Schoolhouse" by Frederick J. McDonald in [115], p. 230.

406   On the proposed school in Bedford-Stuyvesant, see: "A College in the City: An Alternative" report issued by Educational Facilities Laboratories, Inc., March, 1969.

407   Howe's suggestions are in his paper, "This City as Teacher" in [115], p. 22.

414   Gerjuoy's comments are from an interview with the author.

415   McKuen is quoted [230], p. 60.

418   For Bowen quote, see [6], p. 52.

419   The development of future perspectives is examined in "Changes in Outlook on the Future Between Childhood and Adolescence" by Stephen L. Klineberg in the *Journal of Personality and Social Psychology*, vol. 7, #2, 1967, p. 192.

420   For Warner on time, see [350], pp. 54–55; Jaques is cited in [260], pp. 231–233. See also "A Note on Time-span and Economic Theory" by J. M. M. Hill in *Human Relations*, vol. XI, #4, p. 373.

421   The future as an organizing principle is studied in "The Future-Focused Role Image," an unpublished paper by Benjamin D. Singer, Department of Sociology, University of Western Ontario.

422   The comment on the lack of future perspective in the curriculum is from "Teaching the Future" by Ossip

PAGE

K. Flechtheim in *The Futurist*, February, 1968, p. 7.

422   Description of the Condry experiment is based on an interview with the experimenter and/or test materials. Publication planned by Professor Condry. See also: "Time and Social Class" by Lawrence L. Le Shan in [339].

424   The quote from Jungk is from his paper, "Technological Forecasting as a Tool of Social Strategy" in *Analysen und Prognosen*, January, 1969, p. 12.

425–26   For a fascinating account of experiments with future autobiographies of mental patients, see [345].

CHAPTER NINETEEN

429   Material on effects of technology is partially drawn from [332]. See also: "Man's Deteriorating Environment" by Julian Huxley and Max Nicholson in *The Times* (London), October 7, 1969.

430   Commoner quote is from "Attitudes Toward the Environment: A Nearly Fatal Solution." Paper presented at the Annual Meeting of the American Association for the Advancement of Science, Dallas, Texas, December, 1968.
See also: *The New York Times*, December 29, 1968.

430   For additional material on technological impacts, see [329] and *The New York Times* for March 31, April 15, and April 27, 1969.

430   The research moratorium is described in *The New York Times*, March 5, 1969.

430   Evidences of British concern are found in "Britain: Scientists Form New Group to Promote Social Responsibility" by D. S. Greenberg, *Science*, May 23, 1969, p. 931. For a report on international efforts, see "Of Muck and Men," *Economist*, December 20, 1969, p. 15.

430   Attitudes of the youth movement toward technocracy are discussed in "Altering the Direction of Technology" by Robert Jungk in *Student World*, #3, 1968. Geneva: World Student Christian Federation, p. 224.

431   Research and development figures are from [169], p. 24.

431   Lapp is quoted from [290], p. 29.

432   Lack of science policy is charged in OECD report [335]; see also *The New York Times*, January 13, 1968.

433   Technological likelihoods are discussed in [159], pp. 51–52.

PAGE

434 OLIVER's potentials are explored in "Computer as a Communications Device" by J. C. R. Licklider and Robert W. Taylor in *Science and Technology*, April, 1968, p. 31.

435 For discussions of the supersonic transport, see "The SST and the Government: Critics Shout into a Vacuum," *Science*, September 8, 1967, and "Sonic Booms from Supersonic Transport" by Karl D. Kryter, *Science*, January 24, 1969.

436 The proposal for an artificial ocean in Brazil is described in "A Wild Plan for South America's Wilds" by Tom Alexander in *Fortune*, December, 1967, p. 148.

439 On forecasting value change, see "Value Impact Forecaster—A Profession of the Future" by Alvin Toffler in [131].

440-41 Scientists' resistance to regulation is commented on in "Change and Adaptation" by Amitai Etzioni in *Science*, December, 1966, p. 1533.

441 The case for the regulation of technology is argued in "The Control of Technology" by O. M. Solandt in *Science*, August 1, 1969. See also a thoughtful discussion of policy problems in science and technology in [333] and a short statement by the leading Congressional advocate of technological assessment in [314].

443 For detailed theoretical and historical studies of the problems of technological assessment, see the papers of Mayo, [323], [324], and [325]. See also: "Early Experiences with the Hazards of Medical Use of X-rays: 1896–1906" by Barbara Spencer Marx. Staff Discussion Paper 205. Program of Policy Studies in Science and Technology. Washington: George Washington University.
On the need for technological policy, see [290], p. 220.

CHAPTER TWENTY

446-47 Urbanologist Scott Greer is quoted from "Urban Environment: General" by Daniel P. Moynihan in [313], p. 497.

447 Author's interview with Raymond Fletcher.

447 Vickers is quoted from "Ecology, Planning and the American Dream" by Sir Geoffrey Vickers in [241], p. 374–395.

448 For Harrington's argument see [318].

448 Galbraith's position is elaborated in [82].

PAGE

450   The Woodstock participant is quoted from *The New York Times*, August 25, 1969.

453   Information on the funds is from "Playboy's Guide to Mutual Funds" by Michael Laurence in *Playboy*, June, 1969, p. 152. The non-economic interests of mutual funds are discussed in "The Funds of the Future: 2000 A.D." by Alvin Toffler, Channing Balanced Fund Annual Report, New York, 1969, p. 6.

453   Ford's "program related investment" program is described in "New Options in the Philanthropic Process," Ford Foundation Statement of policy, New York: Ford Foundation, 1968. See also: "New Agency Lends First Million to Aid Ghetto Businesses" by Vic Jameson in *Presbyterian Life*, reprint dated 1968; and mimeographed "PEDCO Guidelines for Loan Approval" issued by Presbyterian Economic Development Corp.

455   Udall is cited in "The Idea of a Social Report" by Daniel Bell in the *Public Interest*, Spring, 1969, p. 81.

455   Gross' quote is from his Preface to [313], p. ix.

455   The social indicators movement is one of the most significant forces in the social and behavioral sciences today. Yet, the literature is still small enough to be manageable. Five basic works are: [313], [317], [327], [330], [337].

461   Ogburn is cited from a longer discussion of prediction in [47], p. 304.

461   MacRae's remark is from his chapter, "The Crisis of Sociology" in [298].

462   For a valuable, though already dated listing and evaluation of forecasting methodologies, see [157].

       Delphi is described in [155].

       A short, useful introduction to Cross Impact work appears as "Initial Experiments with the Cross Impact Matrix Method of Forecasting" by T. J. Gordon and H. Hayward in *Futures*, December, 1968, pp. 100–116.

465   Christoph Bertram is quoted from his paper, "Models of Western Europe in the 1970's—the Alternative Choices" in *Futures*, December, 1968, p. 143.

472   For the report of President Eisenhower's goals commission, see [331]. The quotation is from p. xi.

472–73 Nixon: from *Statement by the President on the Establishment of a National Goals Research Staff*, White

PAGE

      House Press Release, July 13, 1969.

474 "The Politics and Vision of the New Left" by Todd Gitlin, *Radical Education Project*, San Francisco. (mimeo) pp. 2, 5.

476 "The Application of Cybernetics to Psychiatry" by W. Ross Ashby in [48], p. 376; see also [1].

481 Osgood's Project PLATO is noted in "Report of Developments since the Conference of Overseas Sponsors held in London in November, 1965," Mankind 2000, London: Preparatory International Secretariat, August, 1966, p. 2; a further report appears in "Involving the Public in Futures" in *Futures*, September, 1968, p. 69.

481–82 The televised games are mentioned in *Education Daily*, April 25, 1969.

BIBLIOGRAPHY

Since articles, scientific and scholarly papers, and specialized reports are fully described in the accompanying Notes, this listing is limited to books and to a small number of monographs and proceedings. I have grouped the entries under a few headings. These are not intended to indicate the main subject matter of the work, but the context in which I found it of interest.

ADAPTATION/Individual

[1]   Ashby, W. Ross, *Design for a Brain.* (London: Chapman and Hall, 1952.)

[2]   Beer, Stafford, *Cybernetics and Management.* (New York: John Wiley, 1964.)

[3]   Berlyne, D. E., *Conflict, Arousal and Curiosity.* (New York: McGraw-Hill, 1960.)

[4]   Bettelheim, Bruno, *The Informed Heart.* (Glencoe, Ill.: The Free Press, 1960.)

[5]   Bossard, James H. S., and Boll, Eleanor S., *Ritual in Family Living.* (Philadelphia: University of Pennsylvania Press, 1950.)

[6]   Bowen, Hugh M., *Rational Design.* Reprint of seven articles from *Industrial Design,* February-August, 1964. (Distributed by Dunlap and Associates, Darien, Conn.)

[7]   Dance, Frank E. X., (ed.), *Human Communication Theory.* (New York: Holt, Rinehart and Winston, 1967.)

[8]   Dubos, René, *Man Adapting.* (New Haven: Yale University Press, 1965.)

[9]   Dunlop, John T., *Automation and Technological Change.* (Englewood Cliffs, N.J.: Prentice-Hall, 1962.)

[10] Ganong, William F., *Review of Medical Physiology.* (Los Altos, California: Lange Medical Publications, 1967.)

[11] Glass, David C., (ed.), *Environmental Influences.* (New York: Rockefeller University Press and Russell Sage Foundation, 1968.)

[12] Goreman, Aubrey, and Bern, Howard A., *A Textbook of Comparative Endocrinology.* (New York: John Wiley, 1962.)

[13] Grinker, Roy R., and Spiegel, John P., *Men Under Stress*. (New York: McGraw-Hill, 1945.)

[14] Grosser, George M., Wechsler, Henry, and Greenblatt, Milton, (eds.), *The Threat of Impending Disaster*. (Cambridge, Mass.: The MIT Press, 1964.)

[15] Gurin, Gerald, Veroff, Joseph, and Feld, Sheila, *Americans View Their Mental Health*. (New York: Basic Books, 1960.)

[16] Hamilton, R. V., Taylor, R. M., and Rice, G. E., Jr., *A Social Psychological Interpretation of the Udall, Kansas, Tornado*. (Washington: National Academy of Sciences-National Research Council, 1955.)

[17] Hollingshead, August B., and Redlich, Frederick C., *Social Class and Mental Illness*. (New York: John Wiley, 1964.)

[18] James, William, *The Principles of Psychology*. (New York: Dover, 1958.) (2 vols.)

[19] Lee, Alfred McClung, *Multi-Valent Man*. (New York: George Braziller, 1966.)

[20] Levi, Lennart, *Stress*. (New York: Liveright, 1967.)

[21] Lynn, R., *Attention, Arousal and the Orientation Reaction*. (Oxford: Pergamon, 1966.)

[22] Miller, George A., *The Psychology of Communication*. (New York: Basic Books, 1967.)

[23] Moore, H. E., *Tornadoes Over Texas*. (Austin, Texas: University of Texas Press, 1958.)

[24] Raab, Wilhelm, *Prevention of Ischemic Heart Disease: Principles and Practice*. (Springfield, Ill.: Chas. C. Thomas, 1966.)

[25] Sargant, William, *Battle for the Mind*. (London: Pan Books, 1963.)

[26] Selye, Hans, *The Stress of Life*. (New York: McGraw-Hill, 1956.)

[27] Skinner, B. F., *Science and Human Behavior*. (New York: The Free Press, 1953.)

[28] Vernon, Jack, *Inside the Black Room*. (New York: Clarkson N. Potter, 1963.)

[29] Vickers, Sir Geoffrey, *The Art of Judgment*. (New York: Basic Books, 1965.)

[30] Wooldridge, Dean E., *The Machinery of the Brain*. (New York: McGraw-Hill, 1963.)

[31] ———, *Proceedings of the Third World Congress of Psychiatry*. (Toronto: Toronto University Press, 1964.)

[32] ———, *Symposium on Medical Aspects of Stress in the Military Climate*. (Washington: Walter Reed Army Institute of Research, Walter Reed Army Medical Center, 1964.)

[33] ———, *Symposium on Preventive and Social Psychiatry*. (Washington: Walter Reed Army Institute of Research, Walter Reed Medical Center, 1957.)

ADAPTATION/Social

[34] Bloch, Herbert A., *Disorganization*. (New York: Alfred
      A. Knopf, 1952.)
[35] Demerath, N. J., and Peterson, Richard A., (eds.),
      System, Change and Conflict. (New York: The Free
      Press, 1967.)
[36] De Vries, Egbert, *Man in Rapid Social Change*. (New
      York: Doubleday, 1961.)
[37] Etzioni, Amitai and Eva, (eds.), *Social Change*. (New
      York: Basic Books, 1964.)
[38] Frank, Lawrence K., *Society as the Patient*. (New Bruns-
      wick, N.J.: Rutgers University Press, 1948.)
[39] Gardner, John, *Self-Renewal*. (Evanston, Ill.: Harper,
      1963.)
[40] Lerner, Daniel, *The Passing of Traditional Society*.
      (New York: The Free Press, 1958.)
[41] Massarik, Fred, and Ratoosh, Philburn, (eds.), *Mathe-
      matical Explorations in Behavioral Science*. (Home-
      wood, Ill.: Richard D. Irwin and Dorsey Press, 1965.
[42] Mead, Margaret, *Continuities in Cultural Evolution*.
      (New Haven: Yale University Press, 1964.)
[43] Mead, Margaret, (ed.), *Cultural Patterns and Techni-
      cal Change*. (New York: New American Library,
      1955.)
[44] Mead, Margaret, *New Lives for Old*. (New York: New
      American Library, 1956.)
[45] Meier, Richard L., *Developmental Planning*. (New York:
      McGraw-Hill, 1965.)
[46] Moore, Wilbert E., *Social Change*. (Englewood Cliffs,
      N.J.: Prentice-Hall, 1964.)
[47] Ogburn, William F., *On Culture and Social Change:
      Selected Papers*. (Chicago: University of Chicago
      Press, 1964.)
[48] Smith, Alfred G., (ed.), *Communications and Culture*.
      (New York: Holt, Rinehart and Winston, 1966.)
[49] Touraine, Alain, Durand, Claude, Pecaut, Daniel, and
      Willener, Alfred, *Workers' Attitudes to Technical
      Change*. (Paris: Organization for Economic Cooper-
      ation and Development, 1965.) (Summary version
      entitled *Acceptance and Resistance*.)
[50] Van Gennep, Arnold, *The Rites of Passage*. (Chicago:
      University of Chicago Press, 1960.)
[51] Wingo, Lowdon, Jr., (ed.), *Cities and Space*. (Balti-
      more: Johns Hopkins Press, 1963.)
[52] ———, *Africa: Social Change and Mental Health*. (Lon-
      don: World Federation for Mental Health, 1959.)
[53] ———, *Mental Health Aspects of Urbanization*. (Lon-
      don: World Federation for Mental Health, 1957.)
[54] ———, *Training Requirements for Postattack Adaptive
      Behavior*. (Report for US Office of Civil Defense,

prepared by Dunlap and Associates, Darien, Conn., December, 1965.)

[55] ——, *Urban America and the Planning of Mental Health Services.* (Philadelphia: Group for the Advancement of Psychiatry, vol. V, Symposium No. 10, November, 1964.)

AUTOMATION

[56] Bagrit, Leon, *The Age of Automation.* (New York: New American Library, 1965.)

[57] Diebold, John, *Beyond Automation.* (New York: McGraw-Hill, 1964.)

[58] Friedmann, Georges, *Industrial Society.* (Glencoe, Ill.: The Free Press, 1955.)

[59] Greenberger, Martin, (ed.), *Computers and the World of the Future.* (Cambridge, Mass.: The MIT Press, 1962.)

[60] Henderson, Mary Stephens-Caldwell, *Managerial Innovations of John Diebold.* (Washington: The LeBaron Foundation, 1965.)

[61] Michael, Donald N., *Cybernation: The Silent Conquest.* (Santa Barbara, Calif.: Center for the Study of Democratic Institutions, 1962.)

[62] Simon, Herbert A., *The Shape of Automation for Men and Management.* (New York: Harper & Row, 1965.)

[63] Theobald, Robert, *The Challenge of Abundance.* (New York: New American Library, 1961.)

[64] ——, *Technology and the American Economy.* (Report of the Commission on Technology, Automation and Economic Progress, Vol. 1, February, 1966.)

BUSINESS/ECONOMICS/CONSUMER PATTERNS

[65] Adams, Charles F., *Common Sense in Advertising.* (New York: McGraw-Hill, 1965.)

[66] Anshen, Melvin, and Bach, George Leland, (eds.), *Management and Corporations, 1985.* (New York: McGraw-Hill, 1960.)

[67] Backman, Julius, *Advertising and Competition.* (New York: New York University Press, 1967.)

[68] Baird, Mary K., *International Consumer Expenditure Patterns* (Report No. 196). (Menlo Park, Calif.: Stanford Research Institute, December, 1963.)

[69] Barish, Norman, and Verhulst, Michel, *Management Sciences in the Emerging Countries.* (Oxford: England-Alden Press, 1965.)

[70] Berle, Adolf A., Jr., *Power without Property.* (New York: Harcourt, Brace & World, 1959.)

[71] Best, Katherine, and Hillyer, Katherine, *Las Vegas: Playtown, USA.* (New York: David McKay, 1955.)

[72] Bogart, Ernest L., and Kemmerer, Donald L., *Economic History of the American People.* (New York: Longmans, Green, 1946.)

[73] Borges, Jorge Luis, *Labyrinths.* (New York: New Directions, 1964.)

[74] Boyd, Robert D., (ed.), *Changing Concepts of Productive Living.* (Madison, Wis.: University Extension, University of Wisconsin, 1957.)

[75] Brightbill, Charles K., *The Challenge of Leisure.* (Englewood Cliffs, N.J.: Prentice-Hall, 1960.)

[76] Dichter, Ernest, *Handbook of Consumer Motivations.* (New York: McGraw-Hill, 1964.)

[77] Fabricant, Solomon, *Basic Facts on Productivity Change.* (New York: National Bureau of Economic Research [Occasional Paper 63], 1959.)

[78] Fourastié, Jean, *Les 40,000 Heures.* (Paris: Editions Laffont, 1965.)

[79] Fuchs, Victor R., *The Growing Importance of the Service Industries.* (New York: National Bureau of Economic Research [Occasional Paper 96], 1965.)

[80] Galbraith, John Kenneth, *The Affluent Society.* (Boston: Houghton-Mifflin, 1958.)

[81] Galbraith, John Kenneth, *The Liberal Hour.* (New York: New American Library, 1960.)

[82] Galbraith, John Kenneth, *The New Industrial State.* (Boston: Houghton-Mifflin, 1967.)

[83] Gordon, Theodore J., *A Study of Potential Changes in Employee Benefits.* (Middletown, Conn.: Institute for the Future, April, 1969.) (3 vols).

[84] Guzzardi, Walter, Jr., *The Young Executives.* (New York: New American Library, 1966.)

[85] Johnson, Arno H., Jones, Gilbert E., and Lucas, Darrell B., *The American Market of the Future.* (New York: New York University Press, 1966.)

[86] Katona, George, *The Mass Consumption Society.* (New York: McGraw-Hill, 1964.)

[87] Larrabee, Eric, and Meyersohn, Rolf, (eds.), *Mass Leisure.* (Glencoe, Ill.: The Free Press, 1958.)

[88] Miller, Herman P., *Rich Man Poor Man.* (New York: Thomas Y. Crowell, 1964.)

[89] Packard, Vance. *The Hidden Persuaders.* (New York: David McKay, 1965.)

[90] Packard, Vance, *The Pyramid Climbers.* (New York: McGraw-Hill, 1962.)

[91] Packard, Vance, *The Waste Makers.* (New York: Pocket Books, 1964.)

[92] Scarff, Harold, *Multifamily Housing* (Report No. 151). (Menlo Park, Calif.: Stanford Research Institute, November, 1962.)

[93] Servan-Schreiber, J.-J., *The American Challenge.* (New York: Avon, 1967.)

[94] Tawney, R. H., *Religion and the Rise of Capitalism.* (New York: New American Library, 1948.)

[95] Uris, Auren, *The Executive Job Market.* (New York: McGraw-Hill, 1965.)

[96] Warner, W. Lloyd, and Abegglen, James, *Big Business Leaders in America.* (New York: Atheneum, 1963.)

[97] ———, *How American Buying Habits Change.* (Washington: US Department of Labor, 1959.)

[98] ———, *Markets of the Sixties* by the Editors of Fortune. (New York: Harper & Row, 1960.)

EDUCATION/YOUTH

[99] Asbell, Bernard, *The New Improved American.* (New York: McGraw-Hill, 1965.)

[100] Ashby, Eric, *Technology and the Academics.* (New York: St. Martin's Press, 1963.)

[101] Barzun, Jacques, *The American University.* (New York: Harper & Row, 1968.)

[102] Brim, Orville G., Jr., *Education for Child Rearing.* (New York: The Free Press, 1965.)

[103] De Grazia, Alfred, and Sohn, David, (eds.), *Revolution in Teaching.* (New York: Bantam Books, 1964.)

[104] Dewey, John, *Democracy and Education.* (New York: The Free Press, 1966.)

[105] Erikson, Erik H., (ed.), *The Challenge of Youth.* (Garden City, New York: Anchor Books, 1963.)

[106] Erikson, Erik H., *Childhood and Society.* (New York: W. W. Norton, 1963.)

[107] Evans, Luther H., and Arnstein, George, (eds.), *Automation and the Challenge to Education.* (Washington: National Education Association, 1962.)

[108] Friedenberg, Edgar Z., *The Vanishing Adolescent.* (New York: Dell Publishing, 1959.)

[109] Ginzberg, Eli, (ed.), *The Nation's Children.* (New York: Columbia University Press, 1960.) (3 vols.)

[110] Hamblett, Charles, and Deverson, Jane, *Generation X.* (Greenwich, Conn.: Fawcett Publications, 1964.)

[111] Hirsch, Werner Z., (ed.), *Inventing Education for the Future.* (San Francisco: Chandler, 1967.)

[112] Hook, Sidney, *Education for Modern Man.* (New York: Dial Press, 1946.)

[113] Newson, John and Elizabeth, *Patterns of Infant Care in an Urban Community.* (Baltimore: Penguin Books, 1965.)

[114] Salisbury, Harrison E., *The Shook-Up Generation.* (Greenwich, Conn.: Fawcett World Library, 1958.)

[115] Toffler, Alvin, (ed.), *The Schoolhouse in the City.* (New York: Praeger, 1968.)

[116] Weerlee, Duco van, *Wat De Provo's Willen.* (Amsterdam: Unitgeverij De Bezige Bij, 1966.)

FAMILY/SEX

[117] Bell, Norman W., and Vogel, Ezra F., (eds.), *A Modern Introduction to the Family.* (Glencoe, Ill.: The Free Press, 1960.)

[118] Farber, Seymour, Mustacchi, Piero, and Wilson, Roger H. L., (eds.), *Man and Civilization.* (New York: McGraw-Hill, 1965.)

[119] Friedan, Betty, *The Feminine Mystique.* (New York: W. W. Norton, 1963.)

[120] Galdston, Iago, (ed.), *The Family in Contemporary Society.* (New York: International Universities Press, 1958.)

[121] Goode, William J., (ed.), *The Family.* (Englewood Cliffs, N. J.: Prentice-Hall, 1964.)

[122] Goode, William J., *Readings on the Family and Society.* (Englewood Cliffs, N. J.: Prentice-Hall, 1964.)

[123] Hunt, Morton M., *Her Infinite Variety.* (New York: Harper & Row, 1962.)

[124] Ogburn, W. F., and Nimkoff, M. F., *Technology and the Changing Family.* (Cambridge, Mass.: Houghton Mifflin Co., 1955.)

[125] Rimmer, Robert, *The Harrad Experiment.* (New York: Bantam Books, 1967.)

[126] Rimmer, Robert, *Proposition 31.* (New York: New American Library, 1968.)

[127] Schur, Edwin M., (ed.), *The Family and the Sexual Revolution.* (Bloomington, Ind.: Indiana University Press, 1964.)

FUTURE STUDIES

[128] Adelson, Marvin, *The Technology of Forecasting and the Forecasting of Technology* (Report SP 3151-000-01). (Santa Monica, Calif.: System Development Corporation, April, 1968.)

[129] Adelson, Marvin, *Toward a Future for Planning* (Report SP-2022). (Santa Monica, Calif.: System Development Corporation, June 1966.)

[130] Baade, Fritz, *The Race to the Year 2000.* (New York: Doubleday, 1962.)

[131] Baior, Kurt, and Rescher, Nicholas, *Values and the Future.* (New York: The Free Press, 1969.)

[132] Bell, Daniel, (ed.), *Toward the Year 2000.* (Boston: Houghton Mifflin, 1968.) (Book version of special issue of *Daedalus*, Summer, 1967, based on work of Commission on the Year 2000.)

[133] Bohler, Eugene, *El Futuro, Problema del Hombre Moderno.* (Madrid: Alianza Editorial, 1967.)

[134] Boulding, Kenneth, *The Meaning of the 20th Century.* (New York: Harper & Row, 1964.)

[135] Brown, Harrison, *The Challenge of Man's Future.* (New York: Viking, 1954).

[136] Calder, Nigel, (ed.), *The World in 1984.* (Baltimore: Penguin Books, 1965.) (2 vols.)

[137] Clarke, Arthur C., *Profiles of the Future.* (New York: Bantam Books, 1958.)

[138] De Jouvenel, Bertrand, *Futuribles.* (Santa Monica, Calif.: The RAND Corporation, January, 1965.)

[139] De Jouvenel, Bertrand, *The Art of Conjecture.* (New York: Basic Books, 1967.)

[140] Drucker, Peter F., *America's Next Twenty Years.* (New York: Harper & Row, 1955.)

[141] Drucker, Peter F., *The Age of Discontinuity.* (New York: Harper & Row, 1968.)

[142] Duffus, R. L., *Tomorrow's News.* (New York: W. W. Norton, 1967.)

[143] Ernst, Morris L., *Utopia 1976.* (New York: Rinehart, 1955.)

[144] Ewald, William R., Jr., (ed.), *Environment For Man.* (Bloomington, Ind.: Indiana University Press, 1967.)

[145] Franklin, H. Bruce, *Future Perfect.* (New York: Oxford University Press, 1966.)

[146] Fuller, R. Buckminster, and McHale, John, *World Design Science Decade, 1965–1975; Phase I Documents 1–4.* (Carbondale, Ill.: World Resources Inventory, Southern Illinois University, 1963.)

[147] Gabor, Dennis, *Inventing the Future.* (New York: Alfred A. Knopf, 1969.)

[148] Gibson, Tony, *Breaking in the Future.* (London: Hodder and Stoughton, 1965.)

[149] Gordon, Theodore J., *The Future.* (New York: St. Martin's Press, 1965.)

[150] Gordon, Theodore J., and Helmer, Olaf, *Report on a Long-Range Forecasting Study.* (Santa Monica, Calif.: The RAND Corporation, September, 1964.)

[151] Gross, Bertram M., *Space-Time and Post-Industrial Society.* (Syracuse, N. Y.: Maxwell Graduate School, Syracuse University. Comparative Administration Group Occasional Paper, May, 1966.)

[152] Gumucio, Mariano B., *Los Días Que Vendrán.* (Caracas: Monte Avila Editores, 1968.)

[153] Heilbroner, Robert, *The Future as History.* (New York: Grove Press, 1959.)

[154] Helmer, Olaf, Gordon, Theodore J., Enzer, Selwyn, De Brigard, Raul, and Rochbert, Richard, *Development of Long-Range Forecasting Methods for Connecticut.* (Middletown, Conn.: Institute for the Future, September, 1969.)

[155] Helmer, Olaf, *Social Technology.* (New York: Basic Books, 1966.)

[156]   Helton, Roy, *Sold Out to the Future*. (New York: Har-
        per & Row, 1935.)
[157]   Jantsch, Erich, *Technological Forecasting in Perspective*.
        (Paris: Organization for Economic Cooperation and
        Development, October, 1966.)
[158]   Jungk, Robert, *Tomorrow is Already Here*. (New York:
        Simon and Schuster, 1954.)
[159]   Kahn, Herman and Wiener, Anthony J., *The Year 2000*.
        (New York: Macmillan, 1967.)
[160]   Kostelanetz, Richard, (ed.), *Beyond Left and Right*.
        (New York: William Morrow, 1968.)
[161]   Lewinsohn, Richard, *Science, Prophecy and Prediction*.
        (Greenwich, Conn.: Fawcett, 1962.)
[162]   Low, A. M., *What's the World Coming To?* (New York:
        J. B. Lippincott, 1951.)
[163]   Lundberg, Ferdinand, *The Coming World Transforma-
        tion*. (Garden City, N. Y.: Doubleday, 1963.)
[164]   McHale, John, *The Future of the Future*. (New York:
        George Braziller, 1969.)
[165]   Marek, Kurt W., *Yestermorrow*. (New York: Alfred A.
        Knopf, 1961.)
[166]   Medawar, P. B., *The Future of Man*. (New York: New
        American Library, 1959.)
[167]   Michael, Donald N., *The Unprepared Society*. (New
        York: Basic Books, 1968.)
[168]   Pauwels, Louis, and Bergier, Jacques, *The Morning of
        the Magicians*. (New York: Stein and Day, 1963.)
[169]   Peccei, Aurelio, *The Chasm Ahead*. (London: Macmil-
        lan, 1969.)
[170]   Platt, John Rader, *The Step to Man*. (New York: John
        Wiley, 1966.)
[171]   Polak, Fred L., *The Image of the Future*. (New York:
        Oceana Publications, 1961.) (2 vols.)
[172]   Ritner, Peter, *The Society of Space*. (New York: Mac-
        millan, 1961.)
[173]   Rodwin, Lloyd, (ed.), *The Future Metropolis*. (New
        York: George Braziller, 1961.)
[174]   Shinn, Roger L., *Tangled World*. (New York: Charles
        Scribner's Sons, 1965.)
[175]   Thomson, George, *The Foreseeable Future*. (New York:
        Viking, 1960.)
[176]   Vickers, Geoffrey, *Value Systems and Social Process*.
        (New York: Basic Books, 1968.)
[177]   Wolstenholme, Gordon, (ed.), *Man and his Future*.
        (London: J. and A. Churchill, 1963.)
[178]   Zwicky, Fritz, *Discovery, Invention, Research*. (Toronto:
        Macmillan, 1969.)
[179]   ———, *Commission on the Year 2000*. Working Papers.
        (Cambridge, Mass.: American Academy of Arts and
        Sciences, 1965-1967.) (5 vols.) Private circulation.

[180] ———, *El Futuro Immediato*, (Barcelona: Plaza and Janes, 1969.)

[181] ———, *Prospect for America: The Rockefeller Panel Reports*. (Garden City, N. Y.: Doubleday, 1961.)

[182] ———, *Prospective Changes in Society by 1980*. (Denver: Designing Education for the Future, July, 1966.)

[183] ———, *The World of 1975*. (Menlo Park, Calif.: Stanford Research Institute, 1964.)

Also consulted:

[184] *Analyse et Prévision* (Paris). A monthly.
Analysen und Prognosen (Berlin). A bi-monthly.
Futures (Surrey, England). A quarterly.
Futuribili (Rome). A quarterly.
Prospeccion Siglo XXI (Caracas). Irregular.
Prospective (Paris). Irregular.
The Futurist (Washington). A bi-monthly.

INDIVIDUALISM

[185] Brooks, John, *The One and The Many*. (New York: Harper & Row, 1962.)

[186] Ellul, Jacques, *The Technological Society*. (New York: Vintage Books, 1967.)

[187] Kardiner, Abram, *The Individual and His Society*. (New York: Columbia University Press, 1939.)

[188] Kluckhohn, Clyde, *Mirror For Man*. (Greenwich, Conn.: Fawcett, 1965.)

[189] Mannheim, Karl, *Systematic Sociology*. (New York: Grove Press, 1957.)

[190] Menaker, Esther and William, *Ego in Evolution*. (New York: Grove Press, 1965.)

[191] Odajnyk, Walter, *Marxism and Existentialism*. (Garden City, N. Y.: Anchor Books, 1965.)

[192] Riesman, David, *Abundance for What? and Other Essays*. (Garden City, N. Y.: Doubleday, 1964.)

[193] Riesman, David, with Glazer, Nathan and Denney, Reuel, *The Lonely Crowd*. (Garden City, N. Y.: Anchor Books, 1950.)

[194] Riesman, David, *Selected Essays from Individualism Reconsidered*. (New York: Doubleday, 1954.)

[195] Sayles, Leonard R., *Individualism and Big Business*. (New York: McGraw-Hill, 1963.)

[196] Tenn, William, *The Human Angle*. (New York: Ballantine, 1968.)

[197] Whyte, William H., *The Organization Man*. (New York: Simon and Schuster, 1956.)

INFORMATION/KNOWLEDGE

[198] Barraclough, Geoffrey, *An Introduction to Contemporary History*. (New York: Basic Books, 1964.)

[199] Barrett, William, *Irrational Man*. (Garden City, N. Y.: Doubleday Anchor, 1962.)

[200] Bell, Daniel, *The Reforming of General Education*. (New York: Columbia University Press, 1966.)

[201] Boulding, Kenneth, *The Image*. (Ann Arbor, Mich.: University of Michigan Press, 1956.)

[202] Bram, Joseph, *Language and Society*. (Garden City, N. Y.: Doubleday, 1955.)

[203] Childe, V. Gordon, *Society and Knowledge*. (New York: Harper & Row, 1956.)

[204] De Chardin, Teilhard, *The Phenomenon of Man*. (New York: Harper & Row, 1959.)

[205] De Fleur, Melvin L., and Larsen, Otto, *The Flow of Information*. (New York: Harper & Row, 1958.)

[206] Escarpit, Robert, *The Book Revolution*. (London: UNESCO and George, G. Harrap, 1966.)

[207] Glaister, G. A., *Encyclopedia of the Book*. (Cleveland: World Publishing, 1960.)

[208] Hauser, Arnold, *The Social History of Art*. (New York: Vintage Books, 1958.) (4 vols.)

[209] Knight, Arthur, *The Liveliest Art*. (New York: New American Library, 1959.)

[210] Kuhn, Thomas S., *The Structure of Scientific Revolutions*. (Chicago: University of Chicago Press, 1962.)

[211] Machlup, Fritz, *The Production and Distribution of Knowledge in the United States*. (Princeton, N. J.: Princeton University Press, 1962.)

[212] Robinson, John A. T., *Honest to God*. (London: SCM Press Ltd., 1963.)

LIFE STYLES/SUBCULTURES/INTERPERSONAL RELATIONS

[213] Amory, Cleveland, *Who Killed Society?* (New York: Harper & Row, 1960.)

[214] Baltzell, E. Digby, *The Protestant Establishment*. (New York: Random House, 1964.)

[215] Barber, Bernard, *Social Stratification*. (New York: Harcourt, Brace & World, 1957.)

[216] Barth, John, *The Floating Opera*. (New York: Avon Books, 1956.)

[217] Cox, Harvey, *The Secular City*. (New York: Macmillan, 1965.)

[218] Dahrendorf, Ralf, *Class and Class Conflict in Industrial Society*. (Stanford, Calif.: Stanford University Press, 1966.)

[219] Fishwick, Marshall, *The Hero, American Style*. (New York: David McKay, 1969.)

[220] Glazer, Nathan, and Moynihan, Daniel, *Beyond The Melting Pot*. (Cambridge, Mass.: The MIT Press, 1963.)

[221] Goffman, Erving, *Behavior in Public Places*. (New York: The Free Press, 1963.)

[222] Goffman, Erving, *Interaction Ritual*. (Garden City, N. Y.: Doubleday, 1967.)

[223] Goodman, Paul, *Growing Up Absurd*. (New York: Vintage Books, 1960.)

[224] Greer, Scott, *The Emerging City*. (New York: The Free Press, 1965.)

[225] Hausknecht, Murray, *The Joiners*. (New York: Bedminster Press, 1962.)

[226] Hyman, Herbert H., and Singer, Eleanor, (eds.), *Readings in Reference Group Theory and Research*. (New York: The Free Press, 1968.)

[227] Josephson, Eric and Mary, (eds.), *Man Alone*. (New York: Dell Publishing, 1962.)

[228] Klapp, Orrin E., *Symbolic Leaders*. (Chicago: Aldine, 1964.)

[229] McClelland, David C., *The Achieving Society*. (New York: The Free Press, 1961.)

[230] McKuen, Rod, *Stanyan Street and Other Sorrows*. (New York: Random House, 1963.)

[231] Nadeau, Remi, *California: The New Society*. (New York: David McKay Co., 1963.)

[232] Newcomb, Theodore M., and Wilson, Everett K., (eds.), *College Peer Groups*. (Chicago: Aldine, 1966.)

[233] Packard, Vance, *The Status Seekers*. (New York: David McKay, 1959.)

[234] Podhoretz, Norman, *Making It*. (New York: Random House, 1967.)

[235] Pynchon, Thomas, *The Crying of Lot 49*. (Philadelphia: J. B. Lippincott, 1966.)

[236] Seeley, John R., Sim, R. Alexander, and Loosley, Elizabeth W., *Crestwood Heights*. (New York: John Wiley, 1963.)

[237] Sheckley, Robert, *Untouched By Human Hands*. (New York: Ballantine Books, 1954.)

[238] Sherif, Muzafer, and Carolyn W., *Reference Groups*. (New York: Harper & Row, 1964.)

[239] Wirth, Louis, *On Cities and Social Life*. (Chicago: The University of Chicago Press, 1964.)

[240] Yablonsky, Lewis, *The Violent Gang*. (Baltimore: Penguin Books, 1966.)

MOBILITY

[241] Duhl, Leonard J., (ed.), *The Urban Condition*, (New York: Basic Books, 1963.)

[242] Lipset, Seymour M., and Bendix, Reinhard, *Social Mobility in Industrial Society*. (Berkeley, Calif.: University of California Press, 1964.)

[243] Morton, Herbert C., (ed.), *Brookings Papers on Public Policy*. (Washington: Brookings Institution, 1965.)

[244] Neymark, Ejnar, *Selectiv Rörlighet*. (Stockholm: Personaladministrativa Radet, 1961.)

[245] Österberg, Gunnar R., *An Empirical Study of Labour Reallocation Gains in Sweden Between 1950 and 1960*. (Stockholm: Industriens Utredningsinstitut, 1965.)

[246] Rundblad, Bengt G., *Arbetskraftens Rörlighet*. (Stockholm: Almqvist and Wiksells, 1964.)

[247] Weil, Simone, *The Need for Roots*. (Boston: Beacon Press, 1952.)

[248] Woodward, Eliot G., and Kaufman, Joan, *International Travel* (Report No. 193). (Menlo Park, Calif.: Stanford Research Institute, December, 1963.)

[249] ———, *International Joint Seminar on Geographical and Occupational Mobility of Manpower, (Final Report*. (Paris: Organization for Economic Cooperation and Development, 1964.)

[250] ———, *Joint International Seminar on Geographical and Occupational Mobility of Manpower; Supplement to the Final Report*. Castelfusano, Nov. 19–22, 1963. (Paris: Organization for Economic Cooperation and Development, 1964.)

[251] ———, *L'Evolution de l'emploi dans les Etats membres (1954–1958)*. (Brussels: Communaute Economique Europeene Commission, March, 1961.)

ORGANIZATION THEORY

[252] Bennis, Warren G., *Changing Organizations*. (New York: McGraw-Hill, 1966.)

[253] Blau, Peter M., *Bureaucracy in Modern Society*. (New York: Random House, 1956.)

[254] Blau, Peter M., and Scott, W. Richard, *Formal Organizations*. (San Francisco: Chandler, 1962.)

[255] Boulding, Kenneth, *The Organizational Revolution*. (New York: Harper & Row, 1953.)

[256] Gerth, H. H., and Mills, C. Wright, (eds.), *From Max Weber: Essays in Sociology*. (New York: Oxford University Press, 1958.)

[257] Gross, Bertram M., *The Managing of Organizations*. (New York: The Free Press, 1964.) (2 vols.)

[258] Kafka, Franz, *The Trial*. (New York: Alfred A. Knopf, 1945.)

[259] Likert, Rensis, *The Human Organization*. (New York: McGraw-Hill, 1967.)

[260] Rice, A. K., *The Enterprise and Its Environment*. (London: Tavistock Publications, 1963.)

PERMANENCE/CHANGE

[261] Donham, W. B., *Business Adrift.* (New York: Whittlesey House/McGraw-Hill, 1931.) (Introduction by Alfred North Whitehead.)
[262] Dunham, Barrows, *Giant in Chains.* (Boston: Little, Brown, 1953.)
[263] Gellner, Ernest, *Thought and Change.* (Chicago: University of Chicago Press, 1965.)
[264] Huxley, Julian, *Essays of a Humanist.* (New York: Harper & Row, 1964.)
[265] Huxley, Julian, *Man in the Modern World.* (New York: New American Library, 1959.)
[266] Huxley, Julian, *New Bottles for New Wine.* (New York: Harper & Row, 1957.)
[267] Huxley, Julian, *On Living in a Revolution.* (New York: Harper & Row, 1942.)
[268] Schon, Donald A., *Technology and Change.* (New York: Dell, 1967.)
[269] Van Gennep, Arnold, *The Rites of Passage.* (Chicago: The University of Chicago Press, 1960.)

SCIENCE/TECHNOLOGY

[270] Burlingame, Roger, *Machines that Built America.* (New York: New American Library, 1955.)
[271] Capek, Karel, *War with the Newts.* (New York: Bantam Books, 1964.)
[272] Cipolla, Carlo M., *The Economic History of World Population.* (Baltimore: Penguin Books, 1962.)
[273] Clarke, Arthur C., *The Challenge of the Spaceship.* (New York: Ballantine, 1961.)
[274] Clarke, Arthur C., (ed.), *Time Probe.* (New York: Dell, 1967.)
[275] Delgado, José M. R. *Physical Control of the Mind.* (New York: Harper & Row, 1969.)
[276] De Solla Price, Derek J., *Little Science, Big Science.* (New York: Columbia University Press, 1963.)
[277] De Solla Price, Derek J., *Science Since Babylon.* (New Haven: Yale University Press, 1961.)
[278] Dole, Stephen, *Habitable Planets for Man.* (Santa Monica, Calif.: The RAND Corp., March, 1964.)
[279] Ettinger, Robert C. W., *The Prospect of Immortality.* (New York: Doubleday, 1964.)
[280] Farrington, Benjamin, *Head and Hand in Ancient Greece.* (London: Watts and Co., 1947.)
[281] Fidell, Oscar, (ed.), *Ideas in Science.* (New York: Washington Square Press, 1966.)
[282] Forbes, R. J., and Dijksterhuis, E. J., *A History of Science and Technology.* (Baltimore: Penguin Books, 1963.) (2 vols.)

[283] Fourastié, Jean, *Idées Majeures.* (Paris: Editions Gonthier, 1966.)

[284] Fourastié, Jean, *Les Conditions de l'Esprit Scientifique.* (Paris: Editions Gallimard, 1966.)

[285] Gilman, William, *Science: U.S.A.* (New York: Viking, 1965.)

[286] Gordon, Theodore J., and Shef, Arthur L., *National Programs and the Progress of Technological Societies.* (Huntington Beach, Calif.: McDonnell Douglas Corporation, March, 1968.)

[287] Hanrahan, James S., and Bushnell, David, *Space Biology.* (New York: Science Editions, 1961.)

[288] Hulten, K. G. Pontus, *The Machine.* (New York: Museum of Modern Art, 1968.)

[289] Jewkes, John, Sawers, David, and Stillerman, Richard, *The Sources of Invention.* (New York: St. Martin's Press, 1958.)

[290] Lapp, Ralph E., *The New Priesthood.* (New York: Harper & Row, 1961.)

[291] Lesher, Richard, and Howick, George, *Background, Guidelines, and Recommendations for use in Assessing Effective Means of Channeling New Technologies in Promising Directions.* (Washington: National Commission on Technology, Automation and Economic Progress, November, 1965.)

[292] Levy, Lillian, (ed.), *Space: Its Impact on Man and Society.* (New York: W. W. Norton, 1965.)

[293] Lewis, Arthur O., Jr., (ed.), *Of Men and Machines.* (New York: E. P. Dutton, 1963.)

[294] Lilly, John C, *Man and Dolphin.* (New York: Pyramid, 1962.)

[295] London, Perry, *Behavior Control.* (New York: Harper & Row, 1969.)

[296] McLuhan, Marshall, *Understanding Media.* (New York: McGraw-Hill, 1965.)

[297] Newman, James R., (ed.), *What is Science?* (New York: Washington Square Press, 1961.)

[298] Plumb, J. H., (ed.), *Crisis in the Humanities.* (Baltimore: Penguin Books, 1964.)

[299] Rapport, Samuel, and Wright, Helen, *Science: Method and Meaning.* (New York: Washington Square Press, 1964.)

[300] Reichenbach, Hans, *The Rise of Scientific Philosophy.* (Los Angeles: University of California Press, 1951.)

[301] Schmeck, Harold, Jr., *The Semi-Artificial Man.* (New York: Walker, 1965.)

[302] Schnapper, M. B., (ed.), *New Frontiers of Knowledge.* (Washington: Public Affairs Press, 1957.)

[303] Schramm, Wilbur, (ed.), *Mass Communications.* (Urbana, Ill.: University of Illinois Press, 1960.)

[304] Shannon, C. E., and McCarthy, J., (eds.), *Automata*

Studies. (Princeton, N. J.: Princeton University Press, 1956.)

[305] Snow, C. P., *Science and Government.* (Cambridge, Mass.: Harvard University Press, 1961.)

[306] Snow, C. P., *The Two Cultures and The Scientific Revolution.* (New York: Cambridge University Press, 1959.)

[307] Stover, Carl F., *The Government of Science.* (Santa Barbara, Calif.: The Center for the Study of Democratic Institutions, 1962.)

[308] Strachey, John, *The Strangled Cry.* (New York: William Sloane Associates, 1962.)

[309] Sullivan, Walter, *We Are Not Alone.* (New York: McGraw-Hill, 1964.)

[310] Vercors, *You Shall Know Them.* (New York: Popular Library, 1953.)

[311] Wiener, Norbert, *The Human Use of Human Beings.* (Garden City, N. Y.: Anchor Books, 1954.)

[312] ———, *Implications of Biomedical Technology,* (Cambridge, Mass.: Harvard University Program on Technology and Society, Research Review No. 1.)

SOCIAL INDICATORS/PLANNING/TECHNOLOGICAL ASSESSMENT

[313] Bauer, Raymond A., (ed.), *Social Indicators.* (Cambridge, Mass.: The MIT Press, 1966.)

[314] Daddario, Emilio Q., *Technology Assessment.* Statement by the chairman of the Subcommittee on Science, Research and Development of the Committee on Science and Astronautics, U.S. House of Representatives. Ninetieth Congress. First Session. (Washington: Government Printing Office, 1968.)

[315] Elsner, Henry, Jr., *The Technocrats.* (Syracuse, N. Y.: Syracuse University Press, 1967.)

[316] Gross, Bertram M., *A Great Society?* (New York: Basic Books, 1968.)

[317] Gross, Bertram M., (ed.), *Social Intelligence for America's Future.* (Boston: Allyn and Bacon, 1969.)

[318] Harrington, Michael, *The Accidental Century.* (New York: Macmillan, 1965.)

[319] Huxley, Aldous, *Brave New World.* (New York: Bantam Books, 1958.)

[320] Kahn, Alfred J., *Studies in Social Policy and Planning.* (New York: Russell Sage Foundation, 1969.)

[321] Kahn, Alfred J., *Theory and Practice of Social Planning.* (New York: Russell Sage Foundation, 1969.)

[322] Lyons, Gene M., *The Uneasy Partnership.* (New York: Russell Sage Foundation, 1969.)

[323] Mayo, Louis H., *Comments on Senate Resolution 78.* (Washington: George Washington University, March 4, 1969.)

[324] Mayo, Louis H., *The Technology Assessment Function.* Part I. Internal Reference Document 25. (Washington: George Washington University, July, 1968.)

[325] Mayo, Louis H., and Rao, P. L., *The Technological Assessment Function.* Part II. Internal Reference Document 25. (Washington: George Washington University, July, 1968.)

[326] Orwell, George, *1984.* (New York: New American Library, 1949.)

[327] Sheldon, Eleanor and Moore, Wilbert, *Indicators of Social Change.* (New York: Russell Sage Foundation, 1968.)

[328] Skinner, B. F., *Walden II.* (New York: Macmillan, 1962.)

[329] ———, *Establish a Select Senate Committee on Technology and the Human Environment,* Hearings on Senate Resolution 68 before the Subcommittee on Intergovernmental Relations of the Committee on Government Operations, US Senate. (Washington: Government Printing Office, March and April, 1967.)

[330] ———, *Full Opportunity and Social Accounting Act (Seminar).* Hearings before the Subcommittee on Government Research, Committee on Government Operations, US Senate. Ninetieth Congress. First Session. S. 843, Parts 1–3. (Washington: Government Printing Office, 1967.)

[331] ———, *Goals for Americans.* Report of the President's Commission on National Goals. (Englewood Cliffs, N. J.: Prentice-Hall, 1964.)

[332] ———, *Inquiries, Legislation, Policy Studies Re: Science and Technology.* 2nd Progress Report. Subcommittee on Science, Research and Development of the Committee on Science and Astronautics, US House of Representatives. Eighty-ninth Congress. Second Session. (Washington: Government Printing Office, 1966.)

[333] ———, *Policy Issues in Science and Technology.* Third progress report. Subcommittee on Science, Research and Development of the Committee on Science and Astronautics, US House of Representatives. Ninetieth Congress. Second Session. (Washington: Government Printing Office, 1968.)

[334] ———, *Préparation du Vᵉ Plan: Rapport sur les Principales Options.* (Paris: *Journal Officiel de la République Française,* 1964.)

[335] ———, *Review of National Science Policy—United States.* (Paris: Organization for Economic Cooperation and Development, 1968.)

[336] ———, *Technology Assessment Seminar.* Proceedings before the Subcommittee on Science, Research and Development of the Committee on Science and Astro-

nautics, US House of Representatives. (Washington: Government Printing Office, September, 1967.)

[337] ———, *Toward A Social Report.* (Washington: US Department of Health, Education and Welfare, January, 1969.)

TIME

[338] Abé, Kobo, *The Woman in the Dunes.* (New York: Berkley, 1964.)

[339] Beardslee, David C., and Wertheimer, Michael, (eds.), *Readings in Perception.* (Princeton, N.J.: Van Nostrand, 1958.)

[340] Cohen, John, (ed.), *Readings in Psychology.* (London: Allen and Unwin, 1964.)

[341] De Grazia, Sebastian, *Of Time, Work and Leisure.* (New York: Twentieth Century Fund, 1962.)

[342] Fraser, J. T., (ed.), *The Voices of Time.* (New York: George Braziller, 1966.)

[343] Hall, Edward T., *The Hidden Dimension.* (New York: Doubleday, 1966.)

[344] Hall, Edward T., *The Silent Language.* (New York: Doubleday, 1959.)

[345] Israeli, Nathan, *Abnormal Personality and Time.* (New York: Science Press Printing Company, 1936.)

[346] Mac Iver, R. M., *The Challenge of The Passing Years.* (New York: Pocket Books, 1962.)

[347] Poulet, Georges, *Studies in Human Time.* (Baltimore: Johns Hopkins Press, 1956.)

[348] Priestley, J. B., *Man and Time.* (New York: Dell, 1964.)

[349] Wallis, Robert, *Time: Fourth Dimension of the Mind.* (New York: Harcourt, Brace & World, 1966.)

[350] Warner, W. Lloyd, *The Corporation in the Emergent American Society.* (New York: Harper & Row, 1962.)

GENERAL

[351] Berelson, Bernard, and Steiner, Gary A., *Human Behavior.* (New York: Harcourt, Brace & World, 1964.)

[352] Chapple, Eliot Dismore, and Coon, Carleton Stevens, *Principles of Anthropology,* (New York: Henry Holt, 1942.)

[353] Deutsch, Morton and Krauss, Robert M., *Theories in Social Psychology.* (New York: Basic Books, 1965.)

[354] Hartley, Eugene, Maccoby, Eleanor, and Newcomb, Theodore, (eds.), *Readings in Social Psychology.* (New York: Holt, Rinehart and Winston, 1947.)

[355] Lindzey, Gardiner, (ed.), *Handbook of Social Psychology.* (Cambridge, Mass.: Addison-Wesley, 1954.)

[356] Natanson, Maurice, (ed.), *Philosophy of the Social Sciences.* (New York: Random House, 1963.)

[357] Newcomb, Theodore, Turner, Ralph H., and Converse, Philip E., *Social Psychology*. (New York: Holt, Rinehart, and Winston, 1965.)

[358] Wattenberg, Ben J. with Scammon, Richard M., *This U.S.A.* (New York: Doubleday, 1965.)

[359] ———, *The American Workers' Fact Book*. (Washington: United States Department of Labor, 1956.)

INDEX

ABOUT THE AUTHOR

A world-renowned scholar and futurist, Alvin Toffler is the author of highly influential works read in over 50 countries, where he is among the best known of contemporary American authors. *Future Shock*, which deals with the acceleration of change, won the prestigious Prix du Meilleur Livre Etranger in France, drew comment from the White House, and added a phrase to the English language. *The Third Wave*, which describes the emerging society, has drawn the attention of many world leaders, from Mikhail Gorbachev to successive Japanese prime ministers. After first being banned, it became a "Bible" of intellectuals in China and the second bestselling book after the speeches of Deng Xiaoping.

Mr. Toffler works closely with his wife, Heidi Toffler, who is his collaborator and intellectual partner. Their analyses of today's changing world, presented in these works, as well as in such books as *The Adaptive Corporation*, *Previews & Premises*, and *The Eco-Spasm Report*, are closely read by top managers. They are studied in many universities around the world, in courses ranging from economics and business to sociology, literature, and philosophy.

Formerly a Washington correspondent and later on the staff of *Fortune* magazine, Mr. Toffler subsequently served as a Visiting Scholar at the Russell Sage Foundation, a Visiting Professor at Cornell University, and a member of the faculty of the New School for Social Research. He is a member of the International Institute for Strategic Studies.

Because of his wide-ranging work, he has been named a Fellow of the American Association for the Advance of Science, was awarded the McKinsey Foundation Book Award for "distinguished contributions to management literature," and was honored by the French government, which has named him an Officier de l'Ordre des Arts et des Lettres. Heidi Toffler holds an honorary doctorate in law and the Medal of the President of the Italian Republic for her work as a futurist and intellectual.